THE IMPOSSIBLE STATE

THE IMPOSSIBLE STATE

Islam, Politics, and Modernity's Moral Predicament

Wael B. Hallaq

Columbia University Press
New York

Columbia University Press
Publishers Since 1893
New York Chichester, West Sussex
cup.columbia.edu

Paperback edition, 2014

Library of Congress Cataloging-in-Publication Data

Hallaq, Wael B., 1955–
The impossible state : islam, politics, and modernity's moral
predicament / Wael B. Hallaq.
p. cm.
Includes bibliographical references and index.
ISBN 978-0-231-16256-2 (cloth : alk. paper)—ISBN 978-0-231-16257-9
(pbk. : alk. paper)—ISBN 978-0-231-53086-6 (e-book)
1. Islam and state. 2. Islam and politics. I. Title.
BP173.6.H29 2013
297.2′72—dc23
2012014567

∞
Columbia University Press books are printed on permanent and durable acid-free paper.
This book is printed on paper with recycled content.
Printed in the United States of America

c 10 9 8 7 6 5 4 3 2
p 10 9 8 7 6 5 4 3 2 1

COVER DESIGN: Martin Hinze

Contents

Preface and Acknowledgments

Although the greater part of this book was written during 2011, it has been in the making for at least a decade. It formed part of the preparation necessary to write my *Sharīʿa: Theory, Practice, Transformations*, published by Cambridge University Press in 2009. The plan and structure of *Sharīʿa* did not allow for a full, or at least fuller, statement about the modern state and the reasons for and meanings of its incompatibility with the Sharīʿa. The present book may therefore be regarded as a continuation of and expansion upon *Sharīʿa*'s interest in the state, in *both empirical substance and theoretical direction*. In terms of substance, it is clear that much more needed to be said about the modern state in the 2009 book that could not be included in an already very long work. In terms of direction—by which I mean teasing out the wider theoretical implications of the empirical narrative of so-called Islamic law and its governance—*Sharīʿa* was largely silent. The present work attempts to fill this gap and in the process engage the Western disciplines of political science, moral philosophy, and law.

In thinking about the themes of this book, I have benefited from the intellectual companionship of a number of individuals. My graduate students and former colleagues at McGill University have for years afforded me the luxury of engagement in first-rate conversations about the modern state and much else. At Columbia, my department's fortnightly colloquium and other extensive conversations with colleagues have continued this engagement, providing me with much insight that resulted in sharpening the text. I am grateful to Talal Asad's and Sudipta Kaviraj's always fruitful intellectual companionship; to Akeel Bilgrami and Kaoukab Chebaro for insightful remarks they made on the second part of chapter 5; to Mahmood Mamdani's observations on chapter 3; to Abed Awad's useful critique of the entire manuscript, but most especially of chapter 3, which benefited greatly from his comments; and last but certainly not least to Muhammad Qasim Zaman, for reading and perspicaciously and constructively commenting on the entire text.

I am also grateful to my gifted and efficient research assistants: Maura Donovan, Shawn Higgins, Aelfie Starr Tuff, and Elizabeth Rghebi. Stephen Millier of McGill continues to make what I write appear more elegant. To all these individuals and to others I may have neglected to mention, I record here my profound gratitude.

Introduction

The argument of this book is fairly simple: The "Islamic state," judged by any standard definition of what the modern state represents,[1] is both an impossibility and a contradiction in terms.

Until the early nineteenth century, and for twelve centuries before then, the moral law of Islam, the Sharīʿa, had successfully negotiated customary law and local customary practices and had emerged as the supreme moral and legal force regulating both society and government. This "law" was paradigmatic, having been accepted as a central system of high and general norms by societies and the dynastic powers that ruled over them. It was a moral law that created and maintained a "well-ordered society," to borrow John Rawls's effective expression.[2] However, beginning in the nineteenth century, and at the hands of colonialist Europe, the socioeconomic and political system regulated by the Sharīʿa was structurally dismantled, which is to say that the Sharīʿa itself was eviscerated, reduced to providing no more than the raw materials for the legislation of personal status by the modern state.[3] Even in this relatively limited sphere, the Sharīʿa lost its autonomy and social agency in favor of the modern state; Sharīʿa was henceforth needed only to the limited extent that deriving certain provisions from it—provisions that were reworked and *re-created* according to modern expediency—legitimized the state's legislative ventures.

For the great majority of Muslims today, the Sharīʿa undoubtedly remains a source of religious and moral authority. Whereas some "Islamic" regimes have adopted the policy of distilling from the Sharīʿa—while flagrantly disregarding both its procedural laws and communal context—such punishments as dismemberment and stoning,[4] the average Muslim individual continues to find in the Sharīʿa a spiritual resource, a connection with God, and a way to discipline the inner self—what we discuss later under the rubric of technologies of the self.[5] To say that the overwhelming majority of modern Muslims wish for the Sharīʿa to return in one form or another is to state what anyone with even a cursory knowledge of world affairs would readily acknowledge. The question of *why* they entertain this wish will be answered in good part in the following chapters, although this is not an intended objective of this book.

Yet, as located in the modern condition, this wish entails an aporia. Muslims today, including their leading intellectuals, have come to take the modern state for granted, accepting it as a natural reality. They often assume it not only to have existed throughout the long course of their history but also to have been sanctioned by no less an authority than the Qurʾān itself.[6] Even nationalism, an unprecedented phenomenon and one uniquely constitutive of the modern state, is said to have been "launched into the world by the Islamic Holy Constitution" similarly drafted in Medina fourteen centuries ago.[7] Early Islamic societies are also viewed as having developed the concepts of citizenship, democracy, and suffrage.[8] Unlike some globalization theorists and political scientists who call into question the future durability of the state, modern Islamist thinkers and scholars[9] take the modern state for granted and, in effect, as a timeless phenomenon,[10] this being partly a reflection of a present reality in which they must confront what seems to them to be an indestructible and powerful machine on a daily basis.

Modern Muslims are therefore faced with the challenge of reconciling two facts: first, the ontological fact of the state and its undeniably powerful presence, and, second, the deontological fact of the necessity to bring about a form of Sharīʿa governance. This challenge is further complicated by the recognition that the state in Muslim countries has not done much to rehabilitate any acceptable form of genuine Sharīʿa governance. The constitutional battles of the Islamists in Egypt and Pakistan, the failures of the Iranian Revolution as an Islamic political and legal project, and other similar disappointments amply testify to this proposition.[11] Yet the state remains the favored template of the Islamists and the ulama (so-called Muslim clergymen).[12] In a recent and highly representative statement, the powerful Muslim Brothers argue that the modern nation-state

> does not stand in contradiction with the implementation of Islamic Sharīʿa, because Islam is the highest authority in Muslim lands, *or so it should be.* With its mechanisms, regulations, laws, and systems, the modern state—if it contains no contradiction to the founding and indubitable principles of Islam—does not preclude the possibility of being *developed* . . . [so that] we can benefit from it in achieving for ourselves progress and advancement.[13]

Note that "developed" here should be taken to mean "adapted to our needs and purposes," as the text makes clear later. Any attempt by the nation-state to quarantine religion or undermine commitment to the supreme authority of Islam will no doubt "be rejected by any Muslim." Thus, the state is expected to promote Islamic values, including general public interest, the rule of law, freedom and equal opportunity for all citizens, and to "deepen the conception of citizenship. . . . In our understanding of what Islam means, these are [the tasks] that the modern state should accomplish." A subtitle in the document sums it up: "There is no Contradiction between the Nation-State and Islamic Sharīʿa."[14]

But surely there is. The argument of this book, as we have already intimated, is that *any* conception of a modern Islamic state is *inherently self-contradictory*.[15] We must remember that Muslims today constitute nearly one-fifth of the world's population and that inasmuch as they live *in* modernity, they also *live* the modern project. They are as much a part of this project as anyone else. It is the argument of this book that the inherent self-contradictions entailed by a modern Islamic state are primarily grounded in modernity's moral predicament. The political and the economic, however integral to this self-contradiction, remain derivative of this moral predicament, which is to say that resolving these contradictions as moral issues would by definition resolve the political and economic problems. To state the matter even more explicitly, the inherent contradictions of any conception of a modern Muslim state—by virtue of the formidable vertical effect and horizontal power of the modern state—capture not only the entire spectrum of what has been described as the "crisis of modern Islam" but also implicate the moral dimensions of the modern project in our world from beginning to end. This book, therefore, is an essay in moral thought even more so than it is a commentary on politics or law.

In order to elaborate our argument, we must first arrive at descriptions of what we shall call "paradigmatic Islamic governance" and the "paradigmatic modern state," these being the preoccupation of chapters 1 and 2, respectively. However, chapter 1 also delineates the conception of "paradigm" as we use it here, a conception central to our overall argument. And since this argument will fly in the face of many modernist assumptions about law, politics, morality, and the meaning of the good life, we must also address the ideology inhabiting—nay, dominating—our thinking about modernity and the achievements of the modern project. We must therefore call into question the latent and not so latent conceptual assumptions undergirding modern discourse, namely, the rhetorical and substantive discourse of the modern theory of progress. On the other hand, while recognizing synchronic changes and diachronic variants in the makeup of the modern state, chapter 2 attempts to identify what we will call form-properties that, for our purposes, represent the essential qualities of this state.

Interdependent in their constitution and effects, these form-properties will be disentangled for analytical purposes. The ideas of sovereign will and the rule of law will be examined in chapter 3 in terms of the doctrine and practice of separation of powers, an examination that serves two purposes. First, it will allow us to set forth the constitutional frameworks and structures of both the modern state and Islamic governance, since these are the larger contexts in which law, the legal system, government, and politics are deemed to operate. In other words, this will serve to outline the constitutional backgrounds and boundaries of the two systems. The second and simultaneous purpose, on the other hand, will be to highlight the constitutional differences between these two systems of governance, differences that will permit a further exploration, in chapter 4, of the meaning of law and its relationship to morality. This largely philosophical account, underscoring the qualitative differences between the legal conception of the modern state and that of Islamic governance, will turn political in the second part of the chapter. Here, the legal-moral differentials identified in the first part will be augmented by political differentials that will reveal yet another sphere of incompatibility.

Chapter 5 narrows the focus of chapter 4, moving from the macro- to the microlevels, from systems of thought and of politics to the realms of self and subjectivity. Chapter 5 argues that the modern nation-state and Islamic governance tend to produce (by their very nature and by virtue of the technologies of the self that both inherently possess) two different fields of subjectivity formation. Again, the subjects produced by these paradigmatic fields stand at great variance with each other, engendering two different types of moral, political, epistemic, and psychosocial conceptions of the world. These profound differences between the subjects of the modern nation-state and those of Islamic governance merely represent the microcosmic manifestations of the macrocosmic differences that are material, structural, constitutional, and, just as importantly, philosophical and conceptual.

In chapter 6 we concede, for the sake of argument, that against all odds and despite staggering impediments, a form of Islamic governance comes into existence. We then argue that modern forms of globalization and the position of the state in the ever increasing intensity of these forms are sufficient to render any brand of Islamic governance either impossible or, if possible, incapable of survival in the long run. However, the aggregate implications of this and earlier arguments in the foregoing chapters are clear: all things considered, Islamic governance is unsustainable, given the conditions prevailing in the modern world.

Capitalizing on the concept of paradigm and central domain, we move in the final chapter to the interrogation of modern moral dilemmas, pointing to their structural conceptual foundations as constituting the root of the moral predicaments that modernity, in all its Eastern and Western forms, has been encountering. We insist that if the impossibility of Islamic governance in the modern world is directly the result of the lack of an auspicious moral environment that can meet the minimal standards and expectations of this governance, then it is imperative to connect this morally based impossibility with the wider problematic contexts that modernity's moral difficulties have engendered. Hence, we argue that this impossibility is merely another manifestation—and a constant companion—of a number of other problems, not the least of which is the increasing collapse of organic social units, the rise of oppressive economic forms, and, most importantly, the havoc wrought against the natural habitat and the environment. All these are seen in this book as philosophical-moral and epistemic issues as much as they are material and physical. Indeed, looking closely at the internal moral critiques within Western postmodernity, we find close parallels, even a virtual identity, between them and the latent meanings of the modern Muslim call for the establishment of Islamic governance.

This book has been written with a view to making its language and arguments accessible to as wide an audience as possible, beyond specialists in law, politics, and philosophy. Much of its subject matter about Islam has been simplified and stripped of most technical detail, though without allowing the discussion to descend to the simplistic. In order to avoid the latter at any cost, I found it necessary to assume, at many points throughout the book, a certain body of knowledge without which we would not be able to proceed in expounding our arguments. Because such knowledge is necessary for an adequate appreciation of the latter, I have adopted the practice of providing various accounts of knowledge in those places in the book where they are absolutely essential and most relevant and have then referred the reader to these during other discussions where they are necessary, even indispensible, as background information. Needless to stress, then, that these cross-references are not to be seen as merely a convention of scholarly writing but as essential tools providing the necessary amount of knowledge for each of our arguments to be properly appreciated and assessed. However, an alternative to this cross-referenced approach would be to digest my earlier writings, especially *Sharīʿa: History, Theory, and Practice* or, less preferably, the much shorter *Introduction to Islamic Law*.

Finally, a word of caution. Despite the extensive and detailed historical narrative proffered throughout the following chapters, this book is not merely a history of Islamic law. While it represents no significant departure from the substance of narrative I have expounded in *Sharīʿa*, *Introduction*, and elsewhere, it does adopt a distinctive narrative form, which is to say that while it acknowledges and accounts for diversity, messiness, and violations in Sharīʿa's long history, it capitalizes on the concept of paradigm in order to retrieve, from a paradigmatic structure, the moral dimension that nonetheless pervades these complex and messy realia.[16]

THE IMPOSSIBLE STATE

1

Premises

> The paradigmatic case becomes such by suspending and, at the same time, exposing its belonging to the group, so that it is never possible to separate its exemplarity from its singularity. . . . The paradigmatic group is never presupposed by the paradigms; rather, it is immanent in them.
>
> —Giorgio Agamben, *The Signature of All Things*

> Humanism is not a science, but religion. . . . Humanists like to think they have a rational view of the world; but their core belief in progress is a superstition, further from the truth about the human animal than any of the world's religions.
>
> —John Gray, *Straw Dogs*

> In a narcissistic society . . . the cultural devaluation of the past reflects not only the poverty of the prevailing ideologies, which have lost their grip on reality and abandoned the attempt to master it, but [also] the poverty of the narcissist's inner life. A society that has made "nostalgia" a marketable commodity on the cultural exchange repudiates the suggestion that life in the past was in any important way better than life today. . . . Our culture's indifference to the past—which easily shades over into active hostility and rejection—furnishes the most telling proof of that culture's bankruptcy. The prevailing attitude, so cheerful and forward-looking on the surface, derives from a narcissistic impoverishment of the psyche.
>
> —Christopher Lasch, *The Culture of Narcissism*

The proposition that a modern Islamic state is impossible and even a contradiction in terms contains at least two hidden questions that must be stated at the outset. First, if this state is inconceivable, then, one might ask, how did Muslims, having in the past commanded a great civilization and built many empires, rule themselves? What form of governance did they practice? And second, with this impossibility in mind, what type of political rule are Muslims presently adopting or likely to adopt in the future? The second part of the latter question, with the predictions it involves, is not integral to our argument and constitutes a separate field of enquiry for another book and decidedly another author. But the question also makes reference to the present, representing the culmination of nearly two centuries' worth of history shot through with colonial rule and postcolonial nationalist reaction and continuity.

Elsewhere, I have suggested that the postcolonial nationalist elites maintained the structures of power they had inherited from the colonial experience and that, as a rule and after gaining so-called independence for their countries, they often aggressively pursued the very same colonial policies they had fiercely fought against during the colonial period.[1] They inherited from Europe a readymade nation-state (with its constitutive power structures) for which the existing social formations had not been adequately prepared. The paradigmatic concept of the citizen, without which no state can last, has been slow in coming,[2] and the political lacunae left after the collapse of the traditional structures have not been properly filled. The nation-state thus sits uncomfortably in the Muslim world, as evidenced in the rise of the Islamic Republic of Iran, where the state apparatus has subordinated and disfigured Sharīʿa's norms of governance, leading to the failure of both Islamic governance and the modern state as political projects. Nor have the other Muslim countries fared any better, because the political organization they adopted from—and after—colonialism has been and remains authoritarian and oppressive and because their integration of Sharīʿa as a mode of governance has hardly paid anything more than lip service to the original. The failure, in other words, has shown itself at nearly all levels.

We are therefore compelled to dismiss the modern experiment in the Muslim world as a massive political and legal failure from which no lessons can be positively learned as to how Muslims may govern themselves properly. Their states have not successfully met any serious challenge, while the "Sharīʿa" that they often constitutionally enshrine as "a" or "the" source of law has proven, as I suggested elsewhere, institutionally dead and politically abused.[3] To take the present-day call for a restored Sharīʿa seriously, we cannot look at present-day legal and political practices as worthy of consideration, as a model or a discursive field that can instruct. The modern state in the Muslim world can hardly inspire, and *its* so-called Sharīʿa is in shambles.[4] We therefore would do well to overlook the modern Islamic experiment with the Sharīʿa, leaving it entirely out of consideration and focusing instead on what the Sharīʿa meant for Muslims throughout the twelve centuries before the colonialist period, when it existed as a paradigmatic phenomenon. The Sharīʿa practices of the modern states in Islamic countries are simply irrelevant to the arguments of this book and *cannot—and thus must not—be invoked as a measure by which premodern paradigmatic Sharīʿa is understood, evaluated, or judged.*[5]

We are therefore left with the first question that we posed above. How did Muslims rule themselves during twelve centuries of precolonial history? If it is our argument that a modern Islamic state is impossible, then any such form of governance in premodern Islamic history must be deemed never to have existed; it would be a fortiori precluded as a conceptual possibility. This preclusion would rest on the obvious fact—whose implications we will discuss in the next chapter—that the modern state's genealogy is exclusively European. For given the geographic, systemic, and epistemic genealogy of the modern state, then it could not have, ipso facto, been Islamic. But the preclusion is also determined by a nonhistorical consideration, namely, that there was a *qualitative difference* between even premodern prototypical "states" and premodern Islamic forms of governance. To see these Islamic forms, as some political scientists have,[6] as belonging to an indistinctly grouped constellation of premodern "states" is not only to engage in uneducated guesses but also to be unaware of the driving, *paradigmatic* forces that gave form and content to what we will henceforth call "Islamic governance."

The political, legal, and cultural struggles of today's Muslims stem from a certain measure of dissonance between their moral and cultural aspirations, on the one hand, and the moral realities of a modern world, on the other—realities with which they must live but that were not of their own making. In one sense, the entirety of this book seeks to substantiate this claim. The West (by which I mean here mainly Euro-America) lives somewhat more comfortably in a present that locates itself within a historical process that has been of its own creation. It lives in an age dictated by the terms of the Enlightenment, the industrial and technological revolutions, modern science, nationalism, capitalism, and the American-French constitutional tradition, all of which, and much more, have been organically *and internally* grown products. The rest of the world has followed or, if not, has felt the pressure to do so. There is in effect no other history but that of Euro-America, not even pre-Enlightenment European history.[7] Minor segments of earlier history may have been rescued or "retrieved"—e.g., Greek "democracy," Aristotle, the Magna Carta, etc.—but these remain subservient, if not *instrumental,* to the imperatives of the modern historical narrative and to the progress of "Western civilization." Africa and Asia, in most cases, continue to struggle in order to catch up, in the process not only foregoing the privilege of drawing on their own traditions and historical experiences that shaped who they were and, partly, who they have become but also letting themselves be drawn into devastating wars, poverty, disease and the destruction of their natural environment. Modernity, whose hegemonic discourse is determined by the institutions and intellectuals of the powerful modern West, has not offered a fair shake to two-thirds of the world's population, who have lost their history and, with it, their organic ways of existence.[8]

But this is not all. Even if we accept, for the sake of argument, the modernists' claim that poverty, disease, and famine have been the lot of humanity since time immemorial, these same advocates of the virtues of the modern project must face two, possibly three, counterclaims. The first and least evincive of the three is that whereas poverty, famine, and disease were in premodernity mostly the work of nature and therefore could not be helped, they are nowadays mostly manmade.[9] Capitalism, industrialism, and the resultant destruction of natural habitat are not the work of nature; they are the effects of so-called progress. The second, a more secure counterclaim, is the modern fragmentation—within a system of state capitalism—of what were once organic and familial social structures.[10] There is no denying that the collapse of the traditional family and community has in part created the disenchanted, fragmented, and narcissistic individual, the subject of commentary by so many a modern thinker, sociologist, psychoanalyst, and philosopher.[11] This collapse is integral to the modern project and is one that defines it in fundamental ways.[12] Third, and most importantly, there can be no question whatsoever of the disastrous effects of the modern project on the natural world we live in, an unprecedented project that is, in the strongest sense, the "Ultimate Measure of Man." Perhaps there is nothing more damning of modern man and woman than this Project of Destruction. It is a disaster for which we must all be judged, not as a scientifically determined *homo economicus* or as merely irresponsible consumers but as morally accountable beings.[13] The moral and other implications of this project are quintessentially epistemological, for they bear upon and interrogate our philosophies, sociologies, sciences, technologies, politics, and everything we do. To insist that this Project of Destruction be evaluated on a moral and ethical basis is to cut, in profound epistemological ways, through politics, economics, law, and much else.

None of these substantive counterarguments is inseparable from our constitution as moral subjects, and all three must, in the final analysis, rest on moral accountability. Therefore, and as we will see in the final chapter, ethical and moral human responsibility cannot, even by Enlightenment standards, and especially by their Islamic counterparts, be abdicated. On account of social injustice, social fragmentation, and the Project of Destruction, the modernists are left with little choice but to accept that if ethical human agency is to be retained, as the Enlightenment has preached and as the long history of Islam has insisted, then that agency did not—and could not—give rise to these three consequences in the premodern world. I say "could not," because a proper definition of morality is not simply to treat a person—who is unknown to you and whom you are not likely to meet again—as you would treat yourself, but, more importantly, it is being unable to commit or refrain from committing an act, not because you intrinsically cannot but because you cannot live with—or cannot allow your*self* to face—its consequences. This latter definition, widely neglected, sums up the problematic of the modern project and one that constituted the paradigm of the premodern world, including that of Islam. As we shall see in due course,[14] the relegation of the moral imperative to a secondary status and its being largely divorced from science, economics, law, and much else has been at the core of the modern project, leading us to promote or ignore poverty, social disintegration, and the deplorable destruction of the very earth that nourishes humankind, in terms of both material exploitation *and* value. And let us state the obvious, though it need not be stated: that in this project, the state has been a most significant player.[15]

If this much, or any close approximation thereof, is accepted, then we have a good reason to search for moral resources in other traditions, resources that may support us in our social, economic, political, and legal ventures. The search for moral resources in the manner that we shall propose here is certainly not a new proposal but one that has been the constant preoccupation of a number of thinkers, such as Alasdair MacIntyre, Charles Taylor, and Charles Larmore, to cite only three.[16] However, whereas these thinkers understandably limited themselves to the so-called European tradition,[17] seeking answers to their queries in Plato, Aristotle, Aquinas, and their like (as if Neo-Platonism and Aristotelianism were unfamiliar to premodern Muslims and as if Aquinas were not a thoroughgoing "student" of Averroes and other Muslim philosophers of his kind), we focus our enquiry here on the Muslim moral resources,[18] by virtue of the fact that Muslims possess their own tradition—extensive, rich, and rooted in centuries of cultural achievement.

The continuing deep effects of this tradition on modern Muslims lends credence to MacIntyre's critique of the Enlightenment concept of autonomous rationality, where ethical values are assumed to issue from noumenal reason. Rational enquiry and thus ethical values are embedded, MacIntyre rightly observes, "in *a tradition, a conception* according to which the standards of rational justification themselves emerge from and are part of *a history* in which they are vindicated."[19]

Accordingly, when all things have been said and done, the thematic similarities between our project and those of Taylor, Larmore, and especially MacIntyre will become patently evident.[20] They may indeed turn out to be too evident, if only because the moral resources that we will unearth in the premodern Islamic tradition are not only reflective of shared theoretical and philosophical enquiry—as these three philosophers have undertaken—but also, and more significantly, of a paradigmatic way of *living*. In other words, while the traditions on which these philosophers have drawn consisted of theoretical and philosophical concepts (and some would say a notion of community that no one "has ever lived in"),[21] the Islamic tradition on which the project of retrieval can draw is a composite one, combining the theoretical-philosophical with sociological, anthropological, legal, political, and economic phenomena that have emerged in Islamic history as paradigmatic beliefs *and* practices.[22]

To speak of this paradigmatic way of living as a full-fledged phenomenon is in effect to speak of paradigmatic Islamic governance. I employ the compound expression "Islamic governance" in order to draw a qualitative—but not necessarily quantitative—distinction between living life in, under, and with the modern state, on the one hand, and living life in, under, and with premodern Sharīʿa, on the other. These two modes of existence had a similar hegemonic *range*, hence our exclusion of the quantitative. However, they differed from each other dramatically in almost all other respects.

In order to speak of these two phenomena in a comparatively meaningful way, we must recognize what stands in them as paradigms, a recognition that can allow us to identify parallel systemic features whose comparison makes for a rationally valid undertaking. But paradigms also serve a more important function, namely, the identification within systems, relations, and conceptual structures of what might be called "driving forces," which give systems and structures a particular "order of things," to borrow one of Foucault's titles.[23] We shall now therefore elaborate this sense of paradigm, keeping in mind that while such thinkers as Schmitt,[24] Kuhn,[25] and Foucault[26] are for us central in formulating a definition of the concept,[27] our account may at certain points be somewhat different from theirs.

A starting point toward a definition of paradigm is Carl Schmitt's notion of "central domain." If a domain becomes central, "then the problems of other domains are solved in terms of the central domain—they are considered secondary problems, whose solution follows as a matter of course only if the problems of the central domain are solved."[28] In illustration of this notion, Schmitt offers the example of European technical progress during the nineteenth century, an arena of progress that, to use our term, was paradigmatic. The massive upsurge of "technical progress" affected all "moral, political, social, and economic situations." Its overpowering effect gave it the status of "a religion of technical progress which promised [that] all other problems would be solved by technological progress." It became "a religion of technical miracles, human achievements, and the domination of nature."[29] Whereas in an age of traditional religion the central domain is moral upbringing, moral education, and worldly moral desiderata, in the "technical age" what counts as progress, as a true achievement, is "economic and technical progress." Similarly, in "an economic age, one needs only solve adequately the problem of the production and distribution of goods *in order to make superfluous all moral and social questions*."[30] Thus, all concepts, including "God, freedom, progress, anthropological conceptions of human nature, the public domain, rationality and rationalization, and finally the concept of nature and culture itself derive their concrete historical content from the situation of the central domains and can only be grasped therefrom."[31]

The Enlightenment, highly relevant to our concerns here,[32] provides yet another example of a paradigm. There is no doubt that this project encompassed intellectual and political movements that ranged across a wide spectrum of intellectual difference. Suffice it here to cite the philosophical divergences of, and dramatically opposing weltanschauungs between and among, Hobbes, Voltaire, Rousseau, Hume, Spinoza, Kant, Hegel, J. S. Mill, and Marx, to mention only a few. It would thus seem impossible to lump them—and many others—together, much less the thought systems and movements they generated, under any single identifiable category. Yet it is eminently arguable that the Enlightenment in its totality—and despite its Kierkegaards and Herders, for example—exhibits a paradigm, one featuring a shared substrate of assumptions and presuppositions, that bestows on it a certain unity, despite its internal multiplicity. As John Gray has aptly argued, the core project of the Enlightenment "was the displacement of local, customary, or traditional moralities, and all forms of transcendental faith, by a critical or rational morality, which was projected as the basis of a universal civilization."[33] This new morality, secular and humanist and "binding on all human beings . . . would set universal standards for the assessment of human institutions." Under the command of human reason finally divorced of traditional principles of morality, the project would aim to create a universal civilization. "This is the project that animated Marxism and Liberalism in all their varieties, which underpins both the new liberalism and new-conservatism. . . . [And it] is this core project that is shared by all Enlightenment thinkers, however pessimistic or dystopic they may sometimes be as to its historical prospects."[34] This core project constituted the central domain, one by which all major and central problems were solved and which gave and continues to give direction, for better or worse, to our ways of life.[35]

But central domains as paradigms have more to them than Schmitt's account allows for. Calling, after Schmitt's own linguistic usage, the noncentral domains "peripheral," we must acknowledge a dialectical relationship between the central and peripheral domains. The "solutions" provided for the latter do not just "follow as a matter of course" and only "if the problems of the central domain are solved." In our account of paradigm, what is involved is a system of knowledge and practice whose constituent domains share in common a particular structure of concepts that qualitatively distinguish them from other systems of the same species. While it is true that the problems in the central domain acquire priority and subordinate the other domains to these priorities, all these domains function within a system of knowledge that shapes the very priorities within the peripheral domains themselves. If I understand Schmitt correctly, his account seems somewhat linear, because his concept of the political[36] required marshalling and single-mindedly subordinating all forces within the modern structures of power in favor of privileging his neo-Hobbesian concept. In our account of paradigm, the peripheral domains are not so much peripheral as subsidiary and supportive, their relegation to this status being not the function of logical or ontological precedence of the central domain but rather the entrenchment and anchoring of this domain within a system constituted no less by the subsidiary domains. The privileging within a culture of a particular domain is therefore a perspectivist act, one that is a function of the culture's placement of a particular value (or set of values) that appears more prominent in that domain than in others. But that value must, perforce, pervade the subsidiary domains, which at once partake in producing and are produced by it.

While Schmitt is right in insisting on the central domain as a driving force, our account of paradigm emphasizes the centrality of the values adopted in the central domain as ideal values that remain the distinctive desiderata and the locus of purposive action and thought, even when their application and realization are not always achieved and even when the competing forces within the domains constituting the paradigm undermine such application and realization. For paradigms represent fields of "force relations," encompassing opposing and competing discourses and strategies. This is what led Foucault to declare that these discourses of power, in their oppositional trajectories, are inseparable, for discourses "are tactical elements or blocks operating in a field of force relations; there can exist different and even contradictory discourses within the same strategy; they can, on the contrary, circulate without changing their form from one strategy to another, opposing strategy."[37] If power is to deserve the name it bears, if it were to produce effects over its subjects, then its processes and strategies—in their confluence and opposition—must yield such effects that both directly and obliquely flow from these processes and strategies. The full materialization of these effects amounts to the production of a central domain. Thus, while the supreme values reigning in the central domain might operate against competing and subversive strategies within this domain itself, as well as those within the subsidiary domains, a central domain remains central as long as the balance of force relations allows for those values to dictate the rules of play and relations of power within the system. Equally important, however, is the recognition that within both central and subsidiary domains there always exist subversive discourses and resisting strategies that constantly challenge the paradigmatic discourses, i.e., the discourses that constitute, reflect, and advocate the central domain and its values.

Our account of paradigm then allows for diversity within unity, for exceptions and violations, and for irregularity and "abnormality." But if these are subversive forces, as they are by definition, then they are so precisely because they are not *positively* determinative of the central domain, although they may *negatively* be so by virtue of the responses the central domain provides to meet their challenge. However, once any of these forces is able to subvert the existing paradigm, replacing it as the locus of supreme value(s), then what has now become a former paradigm or former central domain will join the ranks of the subversive forces or just vanish altogether.

This paradigm shift finds attestation in nearly all modern phenomena, beginning with the creation of a distinction between fact and value and Is and Ought and ending with the modern bureaucratic state, modern capitalism, and nationalism (all of which will directly concern us throughout the book). We can therefore speak not only of a paradigm of the modern state (constituted by a central and subsidiary domains) but also of that of Islamic governance. We shall address the former in the next chapter but must now attend to the latter.

The fuller characteristics and implications of the paradigm of Islamic governance will emerge in chapters 3 through 6, but for now we must assert that the defining emblem of this paradigm is the Sharīʿa. The Sharīʿa, as will become clear in due course, represented and was constituted by a moral law, hence its significance for us as a moral resource for the modern project (equivalent to Aristotle and Aquinas in the MacIntyrean proposal). Its paradigmatic status for us lies in the very fact of its being a moral system in which law (in the modern sense) was a tool and a technique that was subordinated to and enmeshed in the overarching moral apparatus but was not an end in itself. In the Sharīʿa, the legal is the instrument of the moral, not the other way around.[38] As a central domain, the Sharīʿa was the measure against which the subsidiary domains were judged, and its solutions largely determined the solutions of those domains. In the intellectual spheres, the structure of Muslim education was determined by priorities laid down in the Sharīʿa. Such fields as language, linguistics, hermeneutics, logic, rhetoric, dialectic, and epistemology were created, developed, and refined within the purview of the Sharʿī domain. Even mathematics and astronomy—which became the foundations of early modern European science[39]—evolved to impressive degrees as responses to Sharʿī stimuli. In whatever field a scholar or an intellectual ultimately specialized, his or her basic "undergraduate" training was always Sharʿī. In its formal discourse, the Sharīʿa generally did not account for problems and solutions in other domains,[40] having, as a rule, assumed them to be subsidiary and requiring solutions as such. These latter domains catered to the demands and priorities of the Sharīʿa and were often designed and organized to serve its needs.[41]

In the practical sphere, economic life, however messy, was regulated not only by technical Sharʿī rules but also by a pervasive Sharʿī ethic. The economic domain was Sharʿī minded because society, the subject, object, and predicate of Sharīʿa, was Sharʿī. And political governance, while being less organic to the social than the economic domain, was constrained by a culture and society that by and large knew and accepted nothing other than the Sharīʿa and its paradigmatic ethical stature.

This is of course not to say that the paradigmatic status of the Sharīʿa ensured an ideal life. As we have emphasized earlier, paradigms or central domains are not only supported by subsidiary domains; together with the latter domains, they embody exceptions, irregularities, and violations, all of which amount to subversive discourses, often contingent and ephemeral but at times not. The Sharīʿa was no exception, in that it had to *live in* a society that was, like any other, messy and in constant need of certain forms of order and organization. That society no doubt witnessed the overtaxed peasant, the criminal, the insolvent debtor, and the unhappy and abused wife. Like any society (and without analogizing with the excessively violent, oppressive, and church-abused Europe of the Middle Ages), Muslim society from North Africa and Muslim Spain to Java and Samarkand had its share of misery. It obviously had its own invaders and conquerors, its rebels, larcenists, petty thieves, highway robbers, and even the occasional corrupt judge.[42] But the moral law, as we will see, consistently and unquestionably ruled the day, its paradigmatic discourses and practices persisting in the continual re-creation of a particular order.[43] The mess of social reality—the victimized child, the robbed trader, the overtaxed peasant—could always rely on a hegemonic moral system that did its best to address this reality. That it was not always successful is a fact that we should take for granted—for perfect success is the lot of no society, past or present—but the *paradigmatic* efficacy of the moral disposition cannot be questioned.[44]

The paradigm, like its particular and technical legal rules, always strove toward the realization of this moral end, sometimes failing but most often succeeding, which is precisely what made it a paradigm. The entirety of the system rested on the concept of *jihād* (much maligned nowadays because it has become, especially in late modernity, almost exclusively defined by the influential Schmittian idea of the political).[45] The concept dictated, at every turn, the indispensability of "striving" (the literal meaning of the term *jihād*) toward the accomplishment of the moral end. This *systemic* and profound psychological meaning of *jihād* will become clearer as the argument of this book unfolds, but for now we must take care to separate the signification of the moral resource we are trying to identify from any accusation of nostalgia, for this is precisely the charge leveled—unjustly, though expectedly—against MacIntyre (and to some extent Taylor).[46] To do so, we must address two issues, each represented in a question: First, what components of a now institutionally dead Sharīʿa can be identified with such moral resources? And second, how would such an identification escape the charge of nostalgia?

The first question obliges us to define the relationship between the modern Muslim subject and the Sharīʿa, a system that in its day was at once moral, legal, cultural, and deeply psychological. Modern Muslims obviously possess the right and the empowered agency to claim for themselves a secular subjectivity, one that acknowledges Islam as a nominal religious affiliation and without it entailing a particular system of practices and obligations that we will refer to in due course as the technologies of the self. In fact, this project of secularization had already been adopted and tried during the first three quarters of the twentieth century.[47] But the project, to judge by the overwhelming evidence, has proven to be largely unsuccessful, this evidence being, among other phenomena, the failure of Nasserism and socialism and the subsequent rise of Islamism after the 1960s.[48] Islamism is not just about social justice and profound resentment of the political and military practices of the Western countries in the Islamic world: it is a moral movement that—however politicized—offers critiques of social injustice, political corruption, and Western political domination in moral terms (however lacking in philosophical articulation these have so far been). For the Islamists, the moral, to use Schmitt's scheme, is the declared central domain[49]—that latent desideratum providing the core impetus for the overall conception of this book.[50] The problems of all other domains, including the economic and political, "are solved in terms of the central domain—they are considered secondary problems, whose solution follows as a matter of course only if the problems of the central domain are solved." In the context of the moral, Schmitt's declaration could just as easily have been uttered verbatim by any Islamist intellectual.

This is precisely why the moral resources of paradigmatic Islamic governance, i.e., of the paradigm that was Sharʿī minded and thus morally dictated, become relevant. Just as the modern West drew and continues to draw on its last five centuries of experiences and traditions, on its Renaissance, Enlightenment, and liberal thought, Muslims nowadays are challenging this traditional narrative and are increasingly developing their own history—as a discursive moral practice—in such a way as to provide a source of their own. This is not to say that any of their major discourses calls for the restoration of the Sharīʿa in its traditional form, in its traditional institutions, practices, and hermeneutical conceptions of life, for all these, as anyone can see, have vanished without hope of return. But it does mean that Muslims still find in their history—just as the West finds in the Enlightenment—a resource on which they can capitalize while facing the challenges of the modern project, a project that has proved incapable of solving even those problems of its own making.[51] Pitting the Sharīʿa against the Enlightenment obviously does not work for every purpose, but as the central domain of the moral, the Sharīʿa is not only a match for the Enlightenment and its resultant moral system but is potentially an immeasurably instructive moral font.

While the Sharīʿa is now institutionally defunct (including its hermeneutics, courts, discursive practices, educational systems, and the entire range of its sociology of knowledge), much that is psychologically and spiritually latent has survived, hence the preserved memory of it as a moral resource. While Islamic contract law, commercial dealings, penal law, and much else in terms of applied procedural and substantive law have extensively been replaced by Western laws, Western courts, and modern legal practices, the "pillars of Islam" and their overpowering effects have not.[52] They continue to define what it means to be a Muslim. Therefore, we largely but not exclusively delimit the moral resources in terms of the technologies of the self, and these are provided for amply in the discourses and practices of the pillars. The entire domain of the pillars has been left by the modern state mostly untouched, because it is regarded as belonging to the private sphere. Yet this domain extends well beyond the private sphere, as this book will show in the course of its discussion, especially, and most directly, in chapter 5. Capitalizing on the technologies of the self thus in no way involves a retrieval of premodern Sharʿī institutions, practices, or even education. It is a moral project of the first order, an attempt to draw on the historical self for moral guidance. It is a project of moral critique, moral deliberation, and moral substitution, which is to say that it is a project that aims to find a moral space for the Muslim subject in the modern world, a subject who has grown no less disenchanted by modernity than his or her Western counterpart. The retrieval of Islamic moral resources is therefore as much a modern project as modernity itself. And as a modern project, it is also postmodern to the core.

Postmodernity, let us be clear, both assumes and attempts to transcend modernity, but modernity nonetheless.

Many observers, especially those habituated to the Western liberal tradition and its values, will no doubt question this project, charging it, at the very least, with the sin of nostalgia.[53] I think much has been said in the foregoing paragraphs to dispel this notion, at least for those who believe that the liberal project does not have a monopoly on truth. But the doubters remain legion. Their predictable response to the Muslim project of moral retrieval, including those who expound it as a scholarly enquiry, is that this project remains nostalgic, that it has no place in the modern world. Therefore, we must now address this charge, unpacking its conceptual and doctrinal implications.

The charge of nostalgia rests on two misconceptions. First, our invocation of historical moral capital does not amount to an attempt to restore premodern practices and institutions but rather to draw upon a conception of the world that features the virtues and competence of moral instruction. It is not one of attempting to "roll back" the modern project, as John Gray seems to think of MacIntyre's proposal,[54] but instead of seeking to retrieve the overarching and encompassing values that paradigmatically defined Islam and its ways of life for over a millennium. This becomes all the more urgent in light of the fact that these values continue to provide answers to the environmental, social, and psychological-spiritual problems that modernity has created (problems that will occupy us throughout the present book). Any claim to the effect that we cannot learn from others is one that indulges in self-diminution or narcissistic hubris, for the assumption is that we are either incapable of learning from any source outside of ourselves or are very capable but think that our unsurpassed progress made us superior to all preceding moralities and moral beings.[55] Obviously, the two assumptions are plainly false. Second, the charge of nostalgia is intrinsically baseless because it implicitly presupposes a doctrine that itself cannot withstand scrutiny. That doctrine is modern progress.

Whenever and wherever there is a charge of nostalgia there is a virulent presence of a doctrine of modern progress. Their association is one of entailment, just as the concept of "mother" logically and ontologically entails the existence of "child." Engaging in the discourse of progress, so our argument goes, is an ideological position, one that fixes the rules of discourse in favor of that position, therefore precluding rival views from consideration *ab initio*. It is not so much an exclusion of history itself from consideration, for history is invoked by everyone at every turn. History is not only in our language but *constitutes* this language.[56] The ideological position is rather *defined* by an *ab initio* preclusion of any claim in history that *contravenes* the progressivist outlook, an outlook that has found a discursive weapon of defense in the strategic doctrine of progress. There is, as we shall see, a contradiction in this doctrine's conception of history, since it itself arises from a historical weltanschauung, using history to justify itself, but it simultaneously denies history when history is bestowed with an interpretation that contravenes its own. By an illiberal straitjacketing of history, this doctrine therefore justifies and rationalizes the practices of the present, wearing the latter's supremacist authority to pronounce on anything and everything deemed to stand outside of its parameters. Thus, for instance, the invocation of an ethic in a historical tradition that can instruct in reevaluating the modern project's indulgence in the destruction of nature is usually dismissed as nostalgic, since the progressive tools of modernity, materialized in its technical sophistication, are themselves said to possess the capabilities to cure these destructive effects.

Modernity, in other words, can always take care of itself *on its own terms*, and it is in no need of an old sage who can instruct. It can take care of itself on its own terms, yet, with all its impressive and unprecedented canvass of knowledge and technical sophistication, the destruction of the natural order continues unabated and beyond its control. "We always know better," even better than what we ourselves knew just a while ago. The idea of progress rests not on eternal truths but on technical science, whose ultimate reference of truth is itself. We always know better, because science and technicalism have laid the foundations of truth and dictated its rules. Whatever they say, at any point in time, is the truth. A scientific cure for a disease becomes the truth until it is found to cause as much harm as the benefits it was supposed to provide and until another cure—also the result of progress—is invented. The doctrine of progress never asks why the disease exists in the first place, nor does it ask profound existential and *moral* questions about the system that produces such ills, about its structures and modes of operation. For once the system in its entirety is questioned, the very science that produces the cures will be, perforce, questioned and ultimately undermined. The doctrine therefore lives in the moment, an uncertain moment whose truth is as ephemeral as the alacrity with which the next truth is introduced. It cannot seek guidance from the past because the past, despite its "comparative simplicity," imposes on it the duty to ask the larger questions that it is not equipped to handle.

Nor can it guarantee its own truth against the future, which always has the ultimate power of repeal.

The doctrine of progress has therefore neither foundation nor reference, except, respectively, in and to itself. It is its own source of authority, and in this way, it is a god. Being rationally autonomous, as we all are supposed to be, this god has determined, through science and reason, that the big questions of the past cannot be given a hearing because they are outmoded and irrelevant to the advances of modern civilization, modern science, and reason, the latter being of course universal. But the fact of the matter remains that the concerns of the past remain unheard because there is nothing in the doctrine of progress that equips it to contemplate the profound moral questions dominating what is supposed to be the *central* domain. This incapability is not only intrinsic to the doctrine; it is also the result of the doctrine being itself the consequence of the faltering status of this moral domain. The latter domain, if it is a domain at all, is barely subsidiary. Its problems are identified and their solutions provided only when the problems of the central domain, whatever it may be, are solved, and this latter domain is decidedly not moral. This is precisely why the doctrine of progress refuses to engage these questions by casting them as nostalgia, as attempts to retrieve the tyranny of morality, turning a blind eye to the fact that its own doctrinal position is intellectually no less oppressive.

As we have intimated, the doctrine of progress is the brainchild and handmaiden of the modern conception of history.[57] Made to encompass all human experience from the beginning of time (whenever that may have been), history was endowed with a new structure by the Enlightenment. Whereas in many cultures history is structured eschatologically, providing a narrative of moral choices intended to instruct, the Enlightenment structure was determined by the essentially liberal universalist postulate that the experiences of countless societies and cultures of the past represent a collective phenomenon (indeed a monolith) driven by a certain intent (or Spirit or *Geist*) and directed toward a particular purpose, namely, progressive improvement.[58] This improvement is couched in the interrelated and integrated terms of material advance, scientific knowledge, technical and political development, material enrichment, maturity (in both the Kantian and Comtean senses),[59] and even, as Walter Benjamin has noted, "the infinite perfectibility of mankind."[60]

"Dogmatic" and lacking adherence to reality,[61] the theory of progress is founded on the assumption that time has a homogeneous teleological structure, that this structure is inevitable, and that therefore the earliest phases of history were preparatory for the later phases, which were in turn simply the means to reach the intended summit of real human progress: Western modernity. As Adorno observed, this structure of time was not merely a logical requirement for the theory of progress; rather, it effectively justified and validated the events and developments of the present, because these latter were regarded as predetermined and therefore inevitable.[62] Yet there is another important dimension to this notion of predetermination, namely, that all history—itself intended to "prepare" for the dawn of modernity—is insufficiently developed and, in Hegelian and Comtean terms, not yet "mature." The logical conclusion of this line of thinking is that no culture or "civilization" outside of and prior to modern Europe possessed the same validity, competence, and moral and intellectual development. Whatever these civilizations had possessed of value, culturally or otherwise, was *consumed* in the process of preparing for a higher goal, outside and beyond themselves. The only way for them to escape their fate as fodder for the historical march was, and remains, to join "true," "mature" civilization.

Pervading what Scheler has termed the Western thought-structure of domination,[63] the idea of progress[64] came, in almost all of its variants, to structure history in specifically Eurocentric ways. Condorcet viewed even setbacks in history as instructive "mistakes," so to speak, which Europe, the highest of all civilizations, could learn to avoid.[65] The reader of Condorcet's famous work on the subject is struck by its tenor, by the overall notion that, for Condorcet (despite his deep commitment to so-called *égalité* and *fraternité*), all societies of the past, irrespective of geography or time, lived and died for the sake of, and in preparation for, modern Europe.[66] Meinecke came to a similar conclusion regarding Voltaire, arguing that the "governing motives of his historiography" were to utilize "the whole of world history for the service of the enlightenment."[67] Hegel predicated individual freedom on his theory of the Spirit (*Geist*): wars, violence, and the horrors of history are in fact conducive to the improvement and refinement of the *Geist*. In Hegel's theory, "there is something distinctive and superior about the period of modernity, a period for which all previous history has been somehow preparatory."[68]

The Enlightenment theory of progress shapes not only history, but also, as we intimated, *the very structures* of modern language, a language that in turn not only reflects the weltanschauung of the domination of nature and man but also *constitutes and conveys* domination itself. There is perhaps no idea or doctrine as powerful in the modern mind as this theory. It has been declared "a law of historical development, a philosophy of history, and as a consequence also a political philosophy."[69] "No single idea has been more important in Western civilization," it being "one of the hardiest of Western ideas or values."[70] In his introduction to Bury's important work on this theory, Charles Beard was able to declare that "among the ideas which have held sway in public and private affairs for the last two hundred years, *none is more significant* or likely to exert more influence than the concept of progress."[71] For the past two centuries it has stood, and continues to stand, paradigmatically, as the language of the new gods.[72] It acknowledges no principles except its own, which is to say that it spurns any moral and ethical standard that it itself does not fashion. Being "a receptacle for ideology," the doctrine of progress creates faithful followers "who believe themselves to be absolutely in the right," always finding themselves "confronted by others whom they regard as absolutely in the wrong."[73]

With the foregoing in mind, we now proceed under the assumption that it is legitimate to invoke any central domain of the moral, from past or present, that may provide us with a resource of moral retrieval. While the past is materially and institutionally defunct, its moral principles are not. Thus invoking the paradigm of Islamic governance is as plausible and legitimate a project as invoking Aristotle, Aquinas, or Kant. It is this invocation that will occupy us in the following chapters.

2

The Modern State

"There is nothing greater on earth than I, the regulating finger of God"—thus the monster bellows.

—Nietzsche, *Thus Spoke Zarathustra*

The notion that modernization means repeating the Western experience of modernity, and so of converging upon Western institutions and cultural forms, is itself one of the principal illusions of the modern age, subverted by many of the most decisive developments in modern history. At the same time, this deceptive self-image of modernity passes over and leaves unremarked the one sense in which modernization has meant Westernization—namely, the adoption by other cultures of an instrumental perspective on the earth which is ultimately nihilistic.

—John Gray, *Enlightenment's Wake*

Kant once said that even a band of devils can found a state, "provided that they have only the necessary intelligence."[1] Despite Kant's legitimate point about the requirement of reason, he can still be corrected on this count, to judge by the empirical evidence in both recent and historical political experience. A state of this minimalistic nature, whether or not led by a misguided or devilish band, can never be modern in the true sense of the word. It cannot be paradigmatic, nor can rationality be its sole prop. The modern, whatever meaning we assign it, is always connotative of complex structures, most notably in the case of the state. Kant's aforementioned standards at least presuppose that one can speak of the state as the site of political engagement, if not, as Carl Schmitt vehemently insisted, as an analytical category. But even this much is not conceded by some political and sociological theorists who spurn the concept of the state as a useful analytical field.[2] I shall side with Brian Nelson and others who do not subscribe to this view and who counter by ascribing ideological motives to its proponents.[3] I therefore join the majority of writers who have viewed the state as both an ontologically meaningful and analytically viable entity. The question then is: What constitutes the phenomenon of the modern state?

It has often been noted that the state is different things to different people. A survey of the relevant literature immediately imparts the distinct impression that every original thinker has seen the state in a unique way, ranging from imputing to it an organic ethical impulse (Hegel, Otto Gierke) to founding it on natural law and a state of nature (Hobbes, Schmitt). Marx saw the state as a function of economic domination of one class by another, Kelsen as a primarily legal phenomenon, Schmitt as the embodiment of the political, Gramsci as a hegemonic system, and Foucault and the poststructuralists as significantly pervasive of the cultural. After Schmitt in the 1930s, the Hegelian viewpoint of the ethical has largely dropped out of the scene, but great controversy still rages over the definitional limits and analytical value of the state. Some commentators regard the state as "the central explanatory variable," it being an actor "with interests of its own which do not necessarily reflect those of society."[4] Others take the position that the state cannot be understood on its own but rather as it stands in a relationship with the social order within "specific socioeconomic and sociocultural contexts."[5] Still others navigate a path in between, often emphasizing one over the other. It would then be no exaggeration to say that there are nearly as many ideas of what the state is as there are prominent scholars writing about it.

A careful reading of the various theories of the state—excluding those of Hegel and the Hegelians—suggests that at the heart of this vast disagreement is little more than perspectivism: each view is occasioned by the fact that it adopts a particular perspective that has been, for one reason or another, privileged over others. The cases of Marx, Weber, Kelsen, Schmitt, and even the Foucauldians—whose vantage point is, relatively speaking, the widest—are all emblematic of this. It is therefore possible to approach the matter synthetically, weaving certain perspectives into a more or less coherent narrative. The Weberian bureaucratic, the Kelsenian legal, the Schmittian political, the Marxian economic, the Gramscian hegemonic, and the Foucauldian cultural can all be brought to bear upon a conception of the state. And we are not obliged to accept the delimitations of any of them. One can, for instance, accept much of Kelsen's theory of law and constitutional theory but reject his condition that this sphere must remain uncontaminated by ethics, politics, or sociology. From our perspective, Kelsen fits within both a Schmittian theory of the political and a Foucauldian theory of power and culture. For our purposes, perforce also perspectivist, all these and several other theories remain highly useful and will therefore be drawn upon.

Furthermore, our account of the state need be neither comprehensive nor exhaustive, although it is important that we not overlook features of the state that are either inherent to it or necessary for our query about the Islamic state. For the absence from our account of any such feature could obviously be detrimental to evaluating the possibility or impossibility of this state. Accordingly, I will distinguish between the form and content of the state, regarding the content as a variable or a set of variables and the form as *consisting of fundamental structures or properties that the state has in reality possessed for at least a century and without which it could never be conceived of as a state, being that essential.* As noted in the previous chapter, our benchmark is the real, existing, and paradigmatic state, not one that is utopian or futuristic.

In our account, it is content that is changeable or potentially changeable. For example, the state may be dominantly controlled by liberals, socialists, communists, oligarchs, or any such brand, but these, despite their varied influence on the state and its society, cannot (and, more abstractly, do not) change its forms. The form is not only essential to the existence of the state but is also what shapes it into a state.

This distinction requires some justification. The content/form typology must not be allowed to impute to the state an ahistorical character, as if the modern state emerged out of a vacuum—as is often projected in political science. In fact, the contrary is true. The state is as much a historical product as any institution or concept we know, including—as we will see in due course—modern versions of metaphysics. Even more, I shall argue in the next section that this very historical provenance is an integral part of the state's quiddity and that without it we will never understand it completely or even adequately. A state's history is the process by which the state, *as both an abstract concept and a set of practices,* unfolds. And for a body politic to adopt the paradigmatic features of the modern state, it must come to possess the means to penetrate society and culture, to shape them in ways conducive to the formation of the state's subjects. In other words, for an entity to form itself in the image of a fully realized state, it must presuppose a particular subject/subjectivity, viz., the citizen. The state and its fully realized citizen are possible only by virtue of a historical process, one that is not always integral to many states that we would nowadays call "weak," "rogue," or "underdeveloped."

But that which made the state what it has now become does not necessarily remain integral to its form. It is now well understood and acknowledged by the vast majority of historians that the state has always been, even in its premodern forms, heavily engaged in economic policy planning, economic ventures, capital, and industry (however these last two may be defined).[6] Countless historians have argued that the connection between the state and capitalism was at one time organic.[7] Yet this particular connection is mutative, as evidenced in the many decades of rule in so-called communist countries, as well as in the various and at times very different economic policies that characterize the economically developed countries (the United States, Canada, Sweden, and Italy are cases in point). Thus, different economic or state-class arrangements can arise within the bounds of the modern state. The point remains that if such a state as the former Soviet Union could diverge so drastically from Euro-American economic organization and its philosophies (on which Euro-American countries in turn differed among themselves), then it would be difficult to argue that a particular economic policy or ideology is a fixed attribute of the state. As David Held has argued, the theory that essentializes the state as the sum of class relations sits in tension with the necessity of seeing the state as a "set of collectivities concerned with the institutionalized organization of political power," thus failing to separate out these sui generis institutional elements of the modern state and its politics from the variables of class relations.[8]

What, then, are those features without which a modern state could not and cannot exist and, in the foreseeable run, without which will not likely be able to exist? Before addressing the question in both of its variants, I wish to emphasize, yet again, that the question does not presuppose a fixed concept of the state or a concept of a fixed notion of state, one that is ahistorical and therefore unchangeable. The question—again posed from the perspective of concern about the Islamic state—rather posits a particular trajectory in which the paradigm of state requires certain constitutive features that *happened to remain essential* for the regular operation and existence of the modern state. This is not to say that a form-property in the present day cannot or will not become a content attribute, a mutative quality, at some point in the future. This is clearly possible, just as the issue of capitalism, essential to the rise of the state, proved to be after the Bolshevik Revolution. The future obviously can admit a wide range of possibilities, all responsive to the progressively rapid changes of and in the modern project. But if we are to speak of what an Islamic state would look like in the present or foreseeable future, we must consider the facts on the ground as they have *actually* existed for a century or longer. If and when one or more of our form-properties is reduced to a content attribute or eliminated altogether, then someone might reconsider the issue and might want to write another book asking questions of the sort the present book poses.

As things stand today and have stood for a long while—and, importantly, as far as our question about the possibility of an Islamic state is concerned—there are five form-properties possessed by the modern state without which it cannot, at this point in history, be properly conceived. These are: (1) its constitution as a historical experience that is fairly specific and local; (2) its sovereignty and the metaphysics to which it has given rise; (3) its legislative monopoly and the related feature of monopoly over so-called legitimate violence; (4) its bureaucratic machinery; and (5) its cultural-hegemonic engagement in the social order, including its production of the national subject. As we will see, the nation as a political community and political concept, as well as the nation's education and educational institutions, are integral to this cultural hegemony.

Although these five attributes will be discussed under separate headings, they are substantively, methodologically, and theoretically inseparable from one another; one may issue from, impinge upon, or be the consequent of the other. Frequently, as we will soon see, they all stand in dialectical relationship with the others.

1. *The State Is a Specific Historical Product.* All things in the world are historical, including, in one important sense, God himself. But this is not quite the sense in which the state is historical, for its historicity is far more concrete than metaphysics requires. The modern state represents a process of becoming, the unfolding of a novel and particular political and politicocultural arrangement that is distinctly European in origin.[9] This is to say that no other part of the world produced, on its own, this particular political arrangement. Europe, defined in geographical and human terms, was the near exclusive laboratory in which the state was first created and later developed,[10] and Euro-America remains until today the location of the paradigmatic state.[11] The mild qualification "near exclusive" is intended to make allowance for a second-order dialectic between the paradigmatic socioeconomic and sociopolitical developments in Europe and those in its colonies, especially during the nineteenth century. For there is no doubt that the colonial powers learned some lessons from their political and legal experiments

in colonized lands, particularly the British in their conquest of India.[12] But this, as noted, was subsidiary to the paradigmatic transformations that Europe was undergoing in the eighteenth and nineteenth centuries, transformations that were occasioned by rapid shifts in its own economies, technologies, societies (in city, town and countryside), political structures, and, indeed, epistemologies.[13] Within this last category there must be included not only new forms of governmentality (where the political intermeshed with the sociocultural, producing new forms of subjectivity) but also the massive intellectual movement of the Enlightenment, which has had tremendous influence, within an extensive dialectic, on the state. The Enlightenment, also of European provenance despite its early massive indebtedness to the Islamic sciences,[14] not only conduced to the making of the modern state but also, and just as importantly, provided the requisite ideological justification for this new form of political and politicocultural system. To say, therefore, that "the modern Western state is *above all* the product of historical contingency"[15] is not only to offer a sound historiographical description but also to define an essential characteristic of this modern institution.

Partly as a result of ideological legitimation, the state in much of political science discourse appears as an abstraction, as a universal and timeless subject. The trend promoting this timelessness and universality began early in the eighteenth century, when the concept of the state was connected with the theories of progress, rationalism, and civilization.[16] It was widely believed throughout Europe that fully civilized human beings lived within the bounds of state systems and that those who did not (and they happened to live outside Europe) belonged to inferior "tribal" societies who "were scarcely human."[17] This belief took various forms, one of which, the Hegelian, went so far as nearly to mythologize the state and attribute to it a pervasive moral fiber,[18] an attribution that was rejected as spurious by successive generations of European philosophers and political scientists. Its positivist nature and "purely matter-of-fact realities"[19] fully accepted, the state instead came to be associated with a "value-free" scientific method that was presumably based on universally valid laws. The product of this sort of conceptual association was the distorted view that, because the state lends itself to empirical examination and thus to the "scientific" method, it is subject to universal scientific principles that must by definition be as timeless as reason itself.

While this ideological construction of the modern state may readily qualify as a form-property[20] and therefore as utterly indispensable for the existence of any enduring state, it remains, like all other form-properties, a byproduct of historical evolution and historical context. And it is precisely here that the apex and backbone of this property comes to the fore. The history of the state *is* the state, for there is nothing in the state that can escape temporality. It is therefore a historical product of a particular, culture-specific location: Europe, central and Atlantic—not Latin America, not Africa, not Asia. As Carl Schmitt averred, the "state has been possible only in the West."[21] In one important sense, this book is a continuous attempt to tease out the implications of this form-property.

2. *Sovereignty and Its Metaphysics.* Inasmuch as it is inescapable for the modern state to be a historical contingency and thus of a context-specific provenance, it is also—if we speak of it as we must—a constructed entity; that is, it must consist of something or things, whether these are real or fictional, material or conceptual, mythical or symbolic.[22] The concept of sovereignty is one such form-property that remains, despite the changes the state has undergone over the last two centuries or so, one of its hallmarks.[23] While all premodern rule was sustained by certain political and ideological structures, the modern state is unique in its impersonal character,[24] an abstract concept that lies at the heart of its legitimacy.[25] The abstractness of sovereignty therefore requires the evaluation of the state not only as an empirical set of differentiated institutions but also as an ideological structure that both pervades and orders the state's social matrix.[26]

Politically and ideologically, sovereignty is constructed around the fictitious concept of will to representation. European in origin (which is to say, specifically European *conditions* had produced it), the concept of sovereignty is constituted by the idea that the nation *embodying* the state is the sole author of its own will and destiny.[27] For it to come into existence, for it to become ontologically conceivable, the will must presuppose a break from an enslaving agency, a tyranny, or some such dominating evil. The break from tyranny—historically, paradigmatically, and narratively exemplified by the American and French Revolutions[28]—represents a quintessential requirement without which sovereignty would then have no meaning. To speak of the modern state is thus by necessity to subsume—as if it were a minor premise in a syllogism—the form-property of sovereignty and in turn to include perforce the popular will as the master of one's own collective destiny. The will, popular and collective, does not presuppose actual and active individual participation[29] but claims its collective force precisely because it is a fiction. The concept loses none of its force even when nondemocratic powers come to rule, for even in the absence of traditional democratic practices, any state (read: nation-state) comes to expect its sovereign will to be embodied in the acts and speech of its rulers, even when they happen to be a band of devils. That the elision from democratic will to tyranny and vice versa remains protected by sovereignty is an accurate expression of the historical transitions from absolute monarchies to democratic rule under the trenchant concept of the sovereign state.

Sovereignty has domestic and international dimensions. Internationally, sovereignty means that other states recognize one another's authority within their respective borders and that each state legitimately represents its nation in its dealings with other states, individually or aggregately. The fiction has proven so successful and powerful that even when everyone knows that a regime is unrepresentative and even oppressive, it is still deemed to speak *legitimately* on behalf of its citizen/nation. Only a revolution or a fundamental *constitutional* change in a country can presume to replace an earlier tyranny with a government accepted internationally as the bearer of sovereignty. But although violence makes and breaks the representation of sovereignty, it is insufficient to constitute a state as a legitimate member of the international community. For sovereignty must be literally constituted, legally speaking, through a politicojuridical constitution.[30] Otherwise, it will remain nothing more than an act of arbitrary violence.[31] Violence, therefore, is the direct route to sovereignty when it is an expression of a juridically constituted popular will.[32]

This international arrangement, mapped out in principle in the aftermath of the so-called Peace of Westphalia (1648), is structurally connected with the internal, domestic dimension. Within a nation's borders there is no order higher than that of the state. Its law is the law of the land, so to speak. It cannot be countermanded and cannot, as a law, be appealed to any higher order,[33] for it is, after all, the expression of sovereign will. Any such challenge would lack a claim for moral support. As Geoffrey Marshall has argued, in today's world, "it is held that there is no moral right, generally speaking, to disobey the law."[34] To challenge the law is to challenge that very will, which is to say that for a citizen or a group of citizens to challenge the law of their own state is either a contradiction in logical terms (for that would amount to challenging their own will) or an act of extreme and radical violence representing an alternative popular will, an alternative sovereignty. What is profoundly characteristic of this challenge and its reception in a positivist world of states is that the legitimacy of this challenge depends entirely on the success of violence to displace the previous order,[35] for without this step no alternate constitution can ever be possible. Violence and the threat of its use are not only essential to the constitution of sovereignty internationally but also, and more importantly for us, internally. As a pure logic of might, violence is indispensable, and it constitutes a necessary condition for the internal sovereignty of the state as representing and represented by its legal will.

To come into existence, sovereignty needs not only a state but also the general prerequisite of an imagined construct, the nation.[36] Being sovereign, the nation-state is thus "the product of no subject's actions apart from its own self-creation,"[37] for it is by virtue of the constructed notion of constitutional violence that it both comes into existence and continues to implement its regular law-based practices. Paul Kahn has aptly argued that the sovereign state is "conceived as the efficient agency of its own construction . . . comparable to the divine Creation ex nihilo" and "capable of having or expressing such an act of will." In its full implications, sovereignty has in common with monotheism a host of attributes:

> First, it is omnipotent: all political forms are open to its choice. Second, it wholly fills time and space: it is equally present at every moment of the nation's life and in every location within the nation's borders. Third, we know it only by its product. We do not first become aware of the popular sovereign and then ask what it has accomplished. We know that it must exist, because we perceive the state as an expression of its will. We deduce the fact of the subject from the experience of its created product. Finally, we cannot be aware of this sovereign without experiencing it as a normative claim that presents itself as an assertion of identity. We understand ourselves as a part, and as a product, of this sovereign. In it, we see ourselves.[38]

Thus, the identification of the self with the sovereign amounts to conceiving and fashioning the subject through the sovereign will, in turn conceived as the source of both the law and the nation, which, as a collectivity, is in turn fashioned in the mirror of the law. The law as reflecting sovereign will, and thus the will that creates the subject and fashions him in its own image, is little more than a replacement and substitution for the Christian conception of will. Like a great many modern concepts, pre-Enlightenment, Christian forms of authority are largely retained with a substituted set of sources that are of equal authoritative force.[39] Carl Schmitt cast the matter incisively when he wrote:

> All significant concepts of the modern theory of the state are secularized theological concepts not only because of their historical development—in which they were transferred from theology to the theory of the state, whereby, for example, the omnipotent God became the omnipotent lawgiver—but also because of their systemic structure.[40]

In due course, we shall address the impossibility of a nation-state as an Islamic order of divine sovereignty, but for now we must briefly note a single characteristic that has been inseparable from the practices and ideology of the nation-state as a representation of sovereignty, namely, the sacrifice of the citizen.[41] If the nation-state is conceived as an expression of sovereign will, then the Aristotelian final cause of its existence is nothing more than its perpetual existence. The nation-state exists for its own sake. It is a means to no other end. It is "not an end among others; it is that end for which all others can be sacrificed."[42] Carl Schmitt argued that, as a sovereign being, the state's "decision has the quality of being something like a religious miracle: it has no reference except the fact that it is."[43] The supremacy of the state as the highest value, which the citizen must always privilege, is not a value outside of, or external to, the citizen. There is nothing in the will of the paradigmatic citizen that is outside the will of the sovereign, since the latter will—as we have seen—subsumes not only individual will but also all other wills. But that is not all: the citizen himself is not above being sacrificed for the highest end. Indeed, the citizen is the archetype and fullest manifestation of sacrifice, because there is nothing more precious than life except the nation-state, the sui generis cause that can legitimately demand and receive that ultimate sacrifice.

To be a citizen therefore means to live under a sovereign will that has its own metaphysics. It is to live with and under yet another god,[44] one who can claim the believers' lives.[45] (To anticipate our arguments below, this attribute alone, with its grave implications, would suffice to render the modern state an anathema to any form of Islamic governance.)

3. *Legislation, Law, and Violence.* It is, then, a truism that sovereign will gives birth to the law. The law constitutes the very expression of that will, it being sovereignty's most paradigmatic manifestation in the practice of governance. If sovereignty constitutes one of the essences of the state, then the capacity to produce law is another cognate essence, an attribute without which no state can continue to be conceived of as a state. In the next chapter, I will detail the location of law within the modern state system, a location that is of significance to our enquiry into the Islamic state. But the fact that the modern state, as an *integrated and integrating* system (i.e., integrating branches of government, departments, agencies, administrative and military functions, etc.), by necessity produces law is an attribute that we, in this context, cannot and must not take for granted. As an expression of sovereign will, the state is the godlike Law-giver par excellence. The demonstrative entailment between sovereignty and legal production explains why a state must claim ownership of its law in the sense that what it adopts becomes *its own.* Sovereign will ceases to be operative should a state formally declare that *its* law is to be found provided by another country, another state, or another entity. This does not mean that legal transplantation cannot occur (for indeed it does, and extensively at that), but transplantation amounts to appropriation of the law from another country or legal culture through the deliberative *choice* of sovereign will. By virtue of sovereignty, appropriation becomes an act of naturalization.

Kelsen argued that the state consists of three elements: territory, people, and power.[46] If we are to accept his definition, we must interpret power as at least encompassing (1) law as political will and (2) the violence necessary to implement that law both internally and internationally. Seen from a juristic point of view, the state is a particular form of community created by a *national* legal order, where the community is defined as the regulation under a normative order of mutual behavior of a group of individuals. The state is the juristic person that represents that community both as a sociological and legal entity. To speak of a distinction between the state and its law amounts to isolating an essential attribute of a thing and then speaking of it as being able to stand apart autonomously from that thing. Of strictly logical necessity, the essentialness of the property, being relational, would cease to exist, just as no bodily organ can exist in the world independent of a body of which it is a natural part. Kelsen is right to insist that we have no reason to assume the existence of two different normative orders, one of the state and the other of "its" legal order. We "must admit," he argued, "that the community we call 'State' *is* 'its' legal order"[47] and nothing less.[48]

If the modern state is constituted by sovereign will, and if sovereign will manifests itself through law, then the enforcement of law becomes the realization of that will.[49] Will without the coercive instrument to back it up is no power at all: it is, in political terms, nothing. We have seen that the state (now also read: law) is its own end, that it knows, by virtue of its very constitution, only itself and its own metaphysics. The boundaries of violence therefore are set only by the state, and it is its own measure that determines the type and level of violence to be applied against transgressors of its will.[50] Put more clearly, the state is the supreme agent in the sanctioning of violence, for even if it were supposed that some divinely ordained punishment should be implemented or adopted, it would be so adopted as a choice of the state, as an expression of its will. Here, it is the state that ratifies divine will, not the other way round. Here, put more explicitly, the state stands as the God of gods. If, as we saw, sovereign will is the new god, then there is no god but the state. Therefore, the exclusive right to exercise violence and to use its threat to implement sovereign legal will is one of the most essential features of the modern state. The emphasis here is not so much on the millennia-old technique of the ruler's capacity to mete out violence but rather on the unique relationship between violence and the metaphysics of sovereign will.

4. *The Rational Bureaucratic Machine.* There is perhaps to date no language used by any commentator on the state that has been less controversial, and indeed the locus of general consensus, than the following statement of Weber:

> The primary formal characteristics of the modern state are as follows: it possesses an administrative and legal order subject to change by legislation, to which the organized activities of the administrative staff, which are also controlled by regulations, are oriented. This system of order claims binding authority, not only over the members of the state, the citizens . . . but also to a very large extent over all action taking place in the area of its jurisdiction. It is thus a compulsory organization with territorial basis. Furthermore, today, the use of force is regarded as legitimate only insofar as it is either permitted by the state or prescribed by it. . . .

> The claim of the modern state to monopolize the use of force is as essential to it as its character of compulsory jurisdiction and of continuous operation.[51]

In Weber's political sociology, the administrative order, both an integral part and an extension of the legal order, exhibits a characteristically rational type of domination. The central features of this domination are the principles of voluntarism and systematization. Voluntarism is said to be a rationally based and thus deliberately created political organization that precludes it from being determined by tradition or religious decree. This rationality justifies not only reform and alteration of any existing order but even, at least theoretically, its total removal from existence by and through political will. Within the political, therefore, rationalism amounts to the creation and reproduction of contingency and its concomitant attribute: arbitrariness.[52]

On the other hand, systematization entails not only the calculability of the administrative order as an empirically measurable and measuring entity[53] but also—and more important for our purposes—its standardization. In the impersonal structure of bureaucratic rule, all is treated equally, and rationality here is seen in the image of the blind lady of justice. Weber is right to emphasize this aspect and to hold what I think to be a largely correct view that this standardization implies equal treatment not only of the general populace but the members of the state apparatus themselves. But unlike Marx and several others, Weber does not equally nor adequately emphasize the complex relationship between the ruling and dominant elites on the one hand and legal and bureaucratic structures on the other. To state the case minimally, no reasonable/*rational* argument can be made that this (structural) relationship creates equality between this rational bureaucratic order and the disadvantaged multitudes in the social order. This is why Marx believed that bureaucracy should disappear from the future communist world, since it is, like the state, an "irresponsible" and exploitative institution that subjugates one class by another.[54] A premodern Muslim jurist would, though for somewhat different reasons, endorse Marx's view with enthusiasm.[55]

The more important point here is that, even for Marx, there shall always exist a dominating bureaucratic structure as long as the state exists, for this structure constitutes its essence.[56] On this essentiality of the bureaucratic, Weber and nearly every other theorist agree. The history of the last two centuries has fairly consistently shown that revolutions and regime changes have managed to alter significant features of rule and even social structures, but bureaucracy was never one of these. Indeed, if anything, bureaucracy and administration have not only become consistently paradigmatic components of the state but continue to experience progressive growth in both complexity and pervasiveness, raising, as we will see in the next chapter, profound constitutional questions in any modern state. On the exponential growth of state bureaucracy there is an equally vast agreement among scholars and theorists. To say that it has been and will continue to be—at least in the foreseeable future—"indestructible"[57] is merely to state the obvious.

It need not be overemphasized that bureaucratic structures are diverse and multifaceted even within a single state or province. By the nature of their jurisdictions, they even tend to compete. State bureaucracies for immigration and labor are, for obvious reasons, a case in point; so are the educational and military bureaucratic fields. Their competitiveness also manifests itself along the lines of so-called separation of powers, where legislative, judicial, and executive bureaucracies tend, by their very raison d'être, to protect their respective domains. Yet, although they are differentiated, they are simultaneously bound up within a controlling paradigmatic structure, what is often euphemistically called centralization. All bureaucratic divisions, even at the lowest levels, are supervised and controlled by higher unifying administrative units, which in turn tend to accumulate under their jurisdiction various bureaucratic divisions that exhibit the feature of competition, if not turf protection. Put differently, the more bureaucracy expands, the more it falls under unified organizational rules,[58] thereby creating a hierarchical structure of administration. If centralization means anything (and certainly it does not mean the center of a periphery of equidistant points) it is a top-down, pyramidal structure. It is the top of the pyramid that rules and administers, and it does so through the bureaucratic technique. Thus, bureaucracy is the tool and instrument of administration, and administration, in the modern state, is the organization of control, governing, governmentality, and violence.

State bureaucracy therefore has a wide range of influence exceeding that of any other political organization (corporations, political parties, NGOs, etc.). State bureaucracy in fact regulates such sub-bureaucratic structures, orders them, and renders them subordinate to its rational imperatives. It also goes further to regulate civil society, from registration of birth to the certification of death—and almost everything in between: schooling, higher education, health, environment, welfare, travel, labor, safety at work, taxes, public hygiene, parks and entertainment, etc. In other words, bureaucracy not only intrudes on the private sphere and civil society, but it also—and importantly for us—orders and sets the standards for the community. We will later see how, as an extension and integral part of the law, bureaucracy fashions and continually refashions the community and the individual subjectivities of which it consists. Bureaucracy therefore breeds its own community, the community of the state.

5. *Cultural Hegemony, or the Politicization of the Cultural.* As noted at the beginning of this chapter, differences and even opposition between and among theories of state are mostly a function of perspective, which is to say that seemingly different theories are often reconcilable. Accordingly, from our perspective, there is no contradiction, for example, between the Kelsenian and Foucauldian approaches to the state, despite Foucault's desire to "cut off the king's head" in political science.[59] Cutting off the king's head did not mean for Foucault abandoning the prerequisite of looking first at the "king's law" and the changes it induces at the level of state operation, be these empirically verifiable or not. He takes this as self-evident and as a point of departure. Nor did it mean to dismiss the immediate actions of the state insofar as law, bureaucracy, and violence are concerned. I read Foucault, despite the claimed contradictions in his position,[60] as saying that it is high time to look beyond, that is, to uncover the implications of not only how the state or each of its organs operates but also (1) how we must demythologize the discursive structure conducing to the ideological justification of the state itself (i.e., deconstructing the object as subject and vice versa) and (2) how the limits of analysis must be stretched to the realm of culture, where state and culture/society dialectically produce each other ("governmentalization") and where the state's progressively expanding influence on the cultural order has produced and reproduced particular kinds of subjectivity.[61]

In one important and here relevant respect, even Kelsen is Foucauldian. But the Kelsenian perspective, being juristic and political in the conventional positivist sense, did not require cutting off the king's head, for the "king" and his law remained most central to his analysis. Nonetheless, Kelsen would not have disagreed with Foucault on one essential phenomenon, namely, that society is not to be seen as separate or distinct from the state. Any claim that they are so separate, he argued, "can be substantiated only by showing that the individuals belonging to the same state form a unity and this unity is not *constituted* by the legal order but by an element which has nothing to do with law. However such an element . . . cannot be found."[62]

Kelsen, here, would be in even greater agreement with Foucault if he were to bestow on the term "constituted" a performative value.[63] If law as a set of discourses is seen as performative in the full sense of the term and not only in the limited sense that court decisions, for instance, are performative, then Foucault's analysis would necessarily follow from, and upon, Kelsen's above-stated view. It would and should be seen as integrating Kelsen's analysis and expanding its range to the subsuming and subsumed realm of the cultural.

We shall address the state/culture dialectic in more detail in the fourth and fifth chapters, but for now the argument must be limited to this dialectic as an essential form-property of the state. For there cannot be a full-fledged and stable state without the presence of this dialectic. One may even say that the internal coherence and strength of any state significantly depends on its ability not only to organize society, which it does by its very constitution, but also to penetrate it culturally.[64] If the Islamic state is to be treated as a state, properly so defined, then it must come to acquire the dynamics of this dialectic, for there is no stable and paradigmatic state (e.g., Euro-American states) that can be deemed sustainable without it. If it is true that sovereign will is constitutive of the state,[65] then no autonomous authority can be imputed to any unit or entity within the state. This is why the European state destroyed all such internal entities and why many of the " 'third-world' states today are states in name only. Created as legal fictions by colonizing powers in the last century, they are states attempting to rule essentially segmental societies based on tribal or other local units that are the locus of political loyalty and that strive to function independently of the state."[66] Of course, the destruction of such internal entities is the first concrete step in the state's "cultural" penetration, as classically exemplified in the rise of the English and French states since the early eighteenth century. Cultural penetration presupposes the destruction (and reconstitution) of traditional prestate sociocultural units, and both are thus successive stages through which sovereign will comes to manifest itself.

Some analysts have rightly capitalized on the distinction between two types of power, one of which involves the capacity of an agent to force another to do or not do something, thereby reducing the relationship to a unilateral form of coercion. The other generates the reception of, and cooperation with, power on the part of the very subject that is subordinated to that power. Thus, under this second type of power, the state's ability to work through the various units of civil society increases state autonomy by virtue of its success in generating the greatest sum of social and cultural consent. Those analysts who see in this "sharing of power" a negation of the position (expressed by Michael Mann, for one)[67] that state power is held *over* society are themselves subject to the very paradox they create, for they *also* argue that this sharing of power "increases state autonomy."[68] This sort of analysis "never doubts enough," to use Pierre Bourdieu's phrase,[69] for it thinks the state through the state. As much political science does, it conduces to the legitimization of the state and its ideological apparatus while studying—or claiming to study—the state. This legitimizing scholarly project exemplifies the very issue at hand: that through state schools and an education regulated by state law (which destroys earlier forms), a paradigmatic scholarly elite is created and re-created as a cultural domain responsive to the state's overall penetration of the social order.[70] Arrogating to the social order an agency that stands autonomous from the state denies, indeed contradicts, both the essence and ramifications of sovereign will, i.e., a state political order that knows only itself, its law, its bureaucracy, and its violence. If we accept the historical contingency of the state, as we must,[71] then we must also accept its contingent yet ever-present foundation as the locus of sovereign will. To impute an autonomous agency to the cultural domain is not only to deny the material and conceptual effects of this will as destructive of earlier forms but also to sanction its arbitrariness as natural. As Bourdieu has persuasively argued, the cultural domains are "constituted as such by the actions of the state which, by instituting them both in things and in minds, confers upon the cultural arbitrary all the appearances of the natural."[72]

The deconstruction of these appearances must also interrogate the fundamental paradox that the autonomy of the cultural entails the fact that the cultural possesses the capacity to sanction its own destruction. If we accept that the state knows only itself, that it is its own end, that it knows no other end,[73] and that therefore it is inherently incapable of sanctioning its own destruction, then the implication that the cultural domain sanctions its own destruction would make total nonsense of any claim for the autonomy of the cultural.

Later chapters of this book will further explore the foregoing themes as well as their implications within the structures of the modern state and its society. In conclusion to this chapter, however, I stress two points: the first is that the five form-properties we have discussed are indubitably ones possessed by the state; that is, no paradigmatic state can exist or be sustained without any single one of them. As earlier noted, these attributes have been form-properties, and thus any change in them as form-properties will, by necessity, require not only a reevaluation of the assumptions of our thesis (and therefore the thesis itself) but also nearly all the discourse on the state that has been engaged in from the eighteenth century until the present. This is because the disappearance or deletion of any of these form-properties from the present picture will necessarily change the archaeology, architecture, structure, organization, and overall makeup of the state as we have come to know it. This includes the first attribute, which, by definition, implies and effectively entails all the others. Second, and following from the previous point, is the compelling fact that these form-properties are structurally and organically interrelated, that a change in one will *entail* a change in the others. That they stand in a mutually dialectical relationship is not only obvious but also essential for the continuing existence of the modern state and its regular operation. One particular dialectic of wide-ranging importance will constitute the focus of the next chapter, this time considered in the light of a comparative Islamic component.

3

Separation of Powers

Rule of Law or Rule of the State?

The pure doctrine of the separation of powers is based on the view that there are three functions of government: to give laws, to implement the laws and to interpret the laws. To each of the three functions corresponds a branch of government: laws are given by a legislature, implemented by an executive and interpreted by a judiciary. . . . The doctrine . . . has become so riddled with exceptions that it must be scrapped.

—Mogens Hansen, "The Mixed Constitution Versus the Separation of Powers"

Still, we cannot seem to solve the problem of separation of powers. We are not even close. We do not agree on what the principle requires, what its objectives are, or how it does or could accomplish its objectives.

—M. Elizabeth Magill, "Real Separation in Separation of Powers"

The post–New Deal administrative state is unconstitutional, and its validation by the legal system amounts to nothing less than a bloodless constitutional revolution. . . . The destruction of this principle of separation of powers is perhaps the crowning jewel of the modern administrative revolution. Administrative agencies routinely combine all three governmental functions in the same body, and even in the same people within that body.

—Gary Lawson, "Rise and Rise of the Administrative State"

From nearly the start of the American republic, the separation of powers as the Framers understood it, and as contemporary constitutional law continues to understand it, had ceased to exist.

—Daryl J. Levinson, "Separation of Parties, Not Powers"

Because we rightly believe in the basic ideal of democracy we feel usually bound to defend the particular institutions which have been for long accepted as its embodiment, and hesitate to criticize them because this might weaken the respect for an ideal we wish to preserve. . . . It seems to me that the disillusionment which so many experience is not due to a failure of the principle of democracy as such but to our having tried it in the wrong way.

—F. A. Hayek, *Law, Legislation, and Liberty*

If sovereign will is a historically produced phenomenon, and if its expression is the law, then the modern state, in important structural ways, is historically the embodiment of the law. In order for law to represent this will, which is its end, it must be backed up by coercion.

We have also seen, and it will become increasingly obvious in the following chapters, that through the sovereign will's legal manifestation the state does not stand independently of culture. In other words, the state produces and thus possesses its own community. By these definitions, Kelsen (who argued for the identity of state/law)[1] would have to agree with Foucault that if the law is *everywhere* in the state, then law as a manifestation of the state's will must operate upon culture. We will leave this last cultural issue aside for now, making the sole point that the paradigmatic modern state, in its politics, law, and society, represents a closely knit unity. The claim that the modern state is a unity brings with it grave ramifications, some of which will be increasingly obvious in the second half of this chapter, when we introduce Islamic governance as a comparative dimension.

The argument of this chapter is that this unity does not meet the standards of Islamic governance. I say "governance" precisely because of the fact that the Islamic "units" regulating the political and the social were not as closely intertwined as they are in the modern state. This is despite the full acknowledgment—variously emphasized throughout this book—that the modern state is not a homogenous entity, constituted as it is by various interest groups that challenge and compete with one another. This *relative* heterogeneity—which we have theoretically accounted for[2]—must be recognized fully. But this is exactly where law is embedded in politics, since law "neither operates in a historical vacuum nor does it exist independently of ideological struggles in society."[3] It is precisely these "struggles" and their ultimate evolution into political society that created modern sovereignty and its law, the very crux of the Hobbesian-Schmittian thesis.[4] Structurally, therefore, law is "an integrated part of a wider political context."[5] The structural, internal unity of the modern state means that if law as representation of sovereign will is everywhere, then the distribution of legal power crosses not only "every individual life-plan"[6] but also all units constituting the state. If law, defined as normative order, pervades these units vertically and horizontally, then it is right to interrogate the relationship between this normative order and the institutions that embody it, especially those whose specialization is to adjudicate and execute its particular norms.

We therefore turn to the theory and practice embodied in the so-called separation of powers. The aim, it must be stressed, is not to give an exhaustive account of this subject (on which a vast body of literature already exists) but rather to highlight briefly the structural problems that constitutional scholars have identified. If objection is made here to setting aside the blessings of the system of separation of powers, I plead that it is the problems, not the blessings (which surely exist), that must be, for obvious reasons, evaluated in an enquiry of the type we are conducting. If it turns out that the problems in the Western concept of separation are structural and multiple, then we can with justice say that Muslims, as well as other non-Western others, might want to approach the concept with due caution.

1. Separation of Powers in the Nation-State

Both popular belief and much visionary political and constitutional theory advance the narrative that the separation of the three state powers or "branches of government"—the legislative, judicial, and executive—constitutes the backbone and foundation of liberty and democratic rule.[7] The vesting of power in three distinct, separate, and independent groups of institutions is said to be indispensable to the constitutional state, the site where the rule of law is deemed both most sustainable and meaningful. Likewise vital to this concept of separation is the notion that these three powers ought to be exercised by separately staffed departments, each being constitutionally equal and mutually independent. This mutual independence dictates—and this is particularly important to our argument—that the legislative branch must not ipso facto only enjoy total independence but that it also must not delegate its powers, especially to the executive.[8] This ideal has become a universal truism, endlessly repeated by political reform movements around the globe. Article 16 of the Declaration of the Rights of Man and the Citizen states: "A society in which the observance of the law is not assured, nor the separation of powers defined, has no constitution at all," the implication here being that only by clearly defining this separation can a state be constitutional and thus democratic. (Let it be at once stated that this common conception of the relationship between democracy and the state's rule of law never manages to account properly for such phenomena as the Third Reich, Israel, and South African apartheid, all of which represent strong forms of the rule of law.)

If this theory holds water, then it would be a promising place from which Muslims can begin thinking about constructing an Islamic state along such lines. The theory would also, as we shall see, be sufficiently compatible with premodern Islamic practices of government as to encourage the installment of this separation in a new state that would have the added advantage of drawing on the Islamic indigenous tradition.[9] As it turns out, however, this does not seem to be a possibility, because the rhetoric about and theory of separation not only lacks significant support from the facts on the ground but also masks a reality in which this separation appears as problematic as the claim that it is the basis of democratic government.[10]

Constitutional scholarship has come to recognize the conceptual problems involved in the theory and practice of separation of powers and, as a result, in the idealistic narrative it has promoted.[11] It is striking, however, that the full implications of these problems have not, to my knowledge, been sufficiently teased out,[12] although, for our purposes, enough has been acknowledged. The concept of the separation of powers has been seen as "most confusing,"[13] "riddled with so many exceptions,"[14] and infected with "notorious difficulties" and "much imprecision and inconsistency."[15] It "may be counted little more than a jumbled portmanteau of arguments for policies which ought to be supported or rejected on other grounds."[16] One scholar declared it a "failure,"[17] while others dismissed it as "unconstitutional"[18] and an unconvincing theory,[19] a mere "page" from Montesquieu.[20] It has been acknowledged as an arena of deep controversy where even the consensus on some of its basic tenets is "confused" and "possibly incoherent," one that "must be abandoned" as "the first important step toward formulating a new set of ideas about separation of powers."[21] In the United States, constitutional thought and practice have been described as pathological and dangerous.[22] In this country, "the doctrine about the separation of these powers has been considerably modified by a network of checks and balances, and in Europe the doctrine has been destroyed first by the parliamentary system and after the Second World War by the new constitutional courts."[23] The best argument for it satisfies the minimal and not so hopeful standard that, among all possible ways of rule, it is the "most successful of the twentieth-century State."[24] But many of these scholars argue, often vehemently, that this minimal standard is no sufficient reason for its acceptance.[25]

The difficulties in the concept and practice of separation stem from the structural unity of the nation-state we have described,[26] a unity that premodern Islamic governance never developed. The idea that each of the three powers should constitute checks upon the others created the dilemma of the *degree* of separation. Since complete separation in the structures of the modern state is obviously impossible, the challenge would then revolve around the determination of that point in the separation where too much or too little of it renders it meaningless or problematic. Obviously, the problem affecting all rule is concentricity of power, and so it is the overlapping, imbalance, and delegation of power between and among the three branches that become the issue.

Like many critics, Kelsen has vehemently argued the case that the concept of separation is highly inaccurate and that the architecture of the three powers is rather one of distribution,[27] for "one can hardly speak of any separation of legislation from the other functions of the State." The appearance of separation, Kelsen seems to say, is a matter of naming, because the legislature, for example, specializes only in legislating, but its functions are also "distributed among several [other] organs." If the legislature is referred to as such, this is merely by virtue of a "favored position."[28] The legislative has no monopoly over lawmaking; it only *specializes* in creating general norms. But even here, in the creation of general legal norms, the legislature is not the only active agency, since this function—i.e., the production of *general* norms—is also delegated to the other two powers. Like many others, Kelsen argues that the label "legislative" is a mere historical convention given to that branch which specializes in legislation.[29] In both the United States and Europe, there has been such "a merging of legislative and executive functions" that political practice in these regions stands "contrary to the doctrine of the separation of powers,"[30] in effect amounting, particularly in the United States, to a constitutional revolution.[31] Similarly, although much legislation occurs within the judicial and executive branches, they are not named legislative because they specialize in their respective functions. It is an "impropriety" and "particularly unsound" to refer the function of legislation to the judiciary and, especially, to the executive.[32] The "progressive breakdown" of the principle of separation is nevertheless particularly "obvious" in the case of the legislative and the executive, where the latter chips away at the prerogatives of the former.[33] For example, the amalgamation of judicial and legislative functions at the hands of American administrative departments, done in the name of "public convenience, interest, or necessity," is not only "a standing violation of the separation of powers" but might have in earlier times been struck down "as an abdication of legislative responsibility."[34] This much is openly recognized by American courts themselves on the grounds that the modern administrative state might be incapacitated if Congress were to be required to oversee legislatively all policy and administrative decisions.[35] Nonetheless, it is arguable that "any law that attempts to vest legislative power in the President or in the courts is not 'necessary and proper for carrying into Execution' constitutionally vested federal powers and is therefore unconstitutional."[36]

The emergence of administration as a virtually autonomous entity magnifies the problems of the administrative state and points to how it inherently undermines the rule of law. As Morton Horwitz argued, the "rise of the administrative state raised the most basic questions about the meaning and continuing viability of the 'rule of law' in situations where unelected officials exercised enormous and unprecedented power to affect the lives and property of citizens."[37] And as if this is not enough of a problem, the administrative state has produced further problematic effects, at least in the American case. Much vigorous debate—suggesting nearly a state of crisis—has been generated about the fragmentation of the executive, where the president, who is expressly and (it seems) exclusively mandated by the Constitution—on behalf of "We the People"—to execute and superintend all federal laws, has been shorn of what many view as his unitary capacity. Administrative independence and a lack of presidential control over a considerable portion of the executive is said to have created out of administrative and certain executive agencies a "headless fourth branch of government,"[38] one that appears to possess an autonomous status.[39]

That the American president is in practical reality far from being the exclusive "Chief Executive magistrate" stipulated in the Constitution is in little doubt, but whether or not this sharing of executive power is constitutional—or whether or not it "distorts" the text of the Constitution[40]—is a controversy that, ipso facto, appears to call into question not only the cogency of the American political institution (and "what has gone wrong with" it)[41] but also its epistemic structure. However calculated, it must be the case either that the bifurcation in the executive into a presidential branch and a headless fourth branch is right and the Constitution wrong or that the Constitution, in assigning executive power to none other than the president, is right and executive governance is a misapplication and deviation from the founders' intent. It must be either, as it cannot be both.[42]

Furthermore, and still pertaining to the American constitutional arrangement (routinely presented to the world as a model of democracy to be emulated),[43] it is still unclear whether separation of powers has not been "destroyed" under the weight of party politics. As Daryl Levinson has convincingly argued, the notion of political competition built into the structure of American government is "frequently portrayed as the unique genius of the U.S. Constitution, the very basis for the success of American democracy. Yet the truth is closer to the opposite."[44] The dynamics of party politics, Levinson avers, have "overwhelmed the Madisonian conception" of separation of powers nearly from the start of the American republic, preempting the dynamics of that conception, which rests on the presumption that the separation and balance of powers would structurally set off political "ambition" to "counteract ambition." It was Justice Jackson who seems to have been the first to note that only a fanciful observer would overlook the fact that the president heads both a political system as well as a legal system and that party politics and interests, "sometimes more binding than law, extend his effective control into branches of government other than his own and he often may win, as a political leader, what he cannot command under the Constitution."[45]

Thus politics could override constitutional precepts, including the Madisonian interbranch competition, depending on whether or not the House, Senate, and presidency are controlled by a single political party. "Recognizing that these dynamics shift from competitive when government is divided to cooperative when it is unified calls into question many of the foundational assumptions of separation-of-powers law and theory," because when unified, political competition "often tracks party lines more than branch ones," thereby creating in practice at least one more system of separation (a practice that American constitutional theory does not account for in the least).[46] The effects of this duality are numerous, as Levinson shows, but two such effects are worth noting. First, presidents tend to accumulate too much power and enjoy too free a range on a number of important political issues under unified government. And second, Congress tends to delegate significantly more authority to the executive branch and further to lift constraints designed to curb the discretion of executive agencies when government is unified. In a country where the president's party is traditionally in control of both the House and the Senate most of the time (at least since 1832) this does not make for easy compliance with the Madisonian model.[47]

But these and other constitutional problems are not exclusively American. There is in fact no nation-state in which the legislative power is the sole organ producing *general* legal norms. Nor, conversely, is there any state in which the executive and judicial branches are expressly barred from creating such norms, which they produce not only on the basis of statutes but also directly on that of the constitution.[48] In most nation-states, and aside from the profound questions that the administrative state raises, the head of the executive is authorized by virtue of his or her office to legislate on a variety of matters related to war, martial law, economic contingency, and much else—all this without implicit or explicit authorization from the legislative. In the United States, for instance, the presidency "was transformed into a kind of plebiscitary principate with despotic tendencies toward arbitrary, ruthless, and self-aggrandizing exploitation of power."[49] Furthermore, in most liberal democracies, the executive frequently performs the function of the courts, in that public administration is based on administrative law, which is as coercive as civil and criminal law. Exactly like regular courts, offices of public administration, within their jurisdiction, are exclusively competent to decide infractions and to determine particular sanctions, notwithstanding the fact that one is called "judicial" and the other "executive." What the judiciary and executive powers produce is usually termed "regulations" or "ordinances," but these in effect often possess the same character as general norms created by the legislature.[50] This distribution of power could perhaps be justified if the capacity of the judicial and executive powers to create such general norms were delegated to them by the legislative branch, but it is not always clear that this is case. Nor is it clear, even in the case of presumed delegation, where exactly the lines of separation between the respective competences lie.[51]

Nor is the separation between legislative and judicial powers all that clear.[52] The courts perform a legislative function by virtue of their competence to annul constitutional laws or administrative regulations on a variety of grounds that range from public interest to reasonableness.[53] They can even strike down laws of the legislature on the grounds that these laws are contrary to the law or constitution, although the former is in part created by the legislature itself. The courts also create law through the doctrine of precedent, a law that stands on a par with laws created by the legislative (and executive) powers.

The competence of the courts to review legislation (as well as executive orders) is another "obvious encroachment upon the principle of separation of powers."[54] What this separation means is that the judges are independent and guaranteed security in discharging their offices, but their role as reviewers of the work of the legislature "invades the principle that each department has an independent sphere of action and a right to take its own review on matters of constitutionality."[55] This competence simply means that courts can and do legislate, and it is precisely here that a certain distrust of the legislative power can be observed.[56]

That the courts may express distrust of the executive is understandable, since history everywhere, and especially in Europe, has taught a universal lesson: an unchecked executive is an arbitrary power on the loose.[57] Historically, the courts during the phase of constitutional monarchy in Europe came to provide an independent check on the executive and legislative powers of the monarch, but when the monarch ultimately lost his legislative power to the parliament, the courts continued to provide such a check as a matter of tradition. But perhaps there is more to this continuity of judicial review than just tradition, for a fuller answer may lie in the absolute sovereign will that itself is the rule over any other rule, including the rule of law. We recall that sovereign will knows only itself, deferring to nothing but itself.[58] When it undergoes a change of mind, so does its law.[59] Which is to say that the unity of the state as sovereign will allows this will to be represented even in a potentially arbitrary site, the executive. We shall later briefly return to the issue of incompatibility between this across-the-board representation of the will and democratic rule.

There is yet another less formal and deeper dimension to the matter of judicial independence, a dimension intimately tied to the concept of separation. As Miliband has noted, socioeconomic considerations further increase the dependence and therefore mixture of the judiciary with other powers of the state. Judges in lower and higher courts are never independent of factors such as class, education, privilege, professional association, and much else that contribute to their social formation and political loyalties. As we will see later, the educational system and, therefore, forms of social and academic knowledge are not only intimately related to the state apparatus but are also formed and re-formed by the state and its national will.[60] Needless to say, within the generally—and necessarily—conservative nature of the legal profession, judges routinely uphold the interests of the state, the highest end of all. There is no modern judiciary that operates outside of the state's legal or political parameters, sanctioning this loyalty upon itself as well as upon the citizen, whose "highest duty is to the state."[61] If the state serves the interests of dominant elites, then the judges—as citizens and by virtue of what they are meant to do as judges—bolster the conception of favoring privilege, capital, and property. By the nature of things, they are circumscribed by the state and its law.

This is not to say that the court does not at times consider the plight of the unprivileged, but *structurally and paradigmatically* the judges and their discretion navigate a spectrum of legal choice that has been predetermined by the law. Even when a state legislates harsh or oppressive measures, the judges must not only apply the law, by which they are bound as judges, but also bestow on the state, in the very act of application, a structure of legitimation. Resignation from the bench or exercising judicial discretion to reduce some malevolent effects of the law are admittedly the very rare exception rather than the norm, since judges as a rule and on average have proven "more commonly . . . willing to strengthen the arm of the state in its encounter with dissent."[62] This argument will become all the more poignant once we discuss the counterpart to this brand of judiciary: Muslim judges (*qāḍīs*).

This embeddedness of the judiciary in the state system also explains its relationship to the executive. A strict separation between the two powers is said to be impossible, since the judiciary in fact performs functions as an executive of general legal norms. The act of determining obligations and rights, the essence of the judicial function, must be taken for granted, but the jurisdiction of the judiciary extends further. It does not merely decide on claims for rights and obligations but also engages in establishing delict and the ordering of sanctions.[63]

Furthermore, and as we have discussed earlier, administrative-executive orders and contracts may be settled by the executive itself, acting independently both as legislature and executive at once. One might expect that administrative orders, upon the commission of infractions, are prosecuted by regular courts, where the violation is determined and a sanction is decided. But this is not always the case,[64] since administrative authority prosecutes, judges, and executes, all at once, even in the realm of contracts. Proper allocation of powers in this context "has never been completely realized" in the modern state.[65]

The foregoing characteristics we have described resolve themselves into two main points. First, the legislative power does not create all the general norms of the state order. It is called legislative only because it is an organ that specializes in the creation of general norms. Second, much legislation of general and particular norms originates outside the realm of the legislative power, namely, in the executive and the judiciary. The products of the legislative power are therefore impinged upon by both executive legislation—which often delimits and reinterprets legislative norms—and judicial review, which has just as much power to quash norms created by the legislative branch. That this latter branch is independent in the paradigmatic nation-state is obvious, but its independence must be construed as such in highly relative terms within the context of political structure. If sovereign will is embodied in the law, then the legislative (presumably the organ that legislates the expression of this will) is not its mouthpiece in the full sense of the term. For, under this system of sovereign will, the executive, for example, is imbued with an incompatible duality: to legislate and to execute its own legislation. In this respect it shares much with the judicial power, which performs a similar role: it creates norms by precedent, quashes legislation through judicial review (what has been called "negative legislation")[66] and then turns around to adjudicating cases on the basis of law partly of its own making and proceeds further to issue sanctions.[67]

To sum up: The practice and even the theory of separation raise profound questions. If the legislature is the representative of popular sovereignty and of sovereign will, then why can't it be the exclusive legislating organ of the state? Why allow an organ, whose declared function is to apply the law, to legislate? But perhaps most importantly, why arrogate the power of legislation to an executive organ whose declared function is to execute judicial orders? Even if we accept the standard claim that the separation between the three powers is not so much a separation as a way to prevent concentricity of power in any one of them, how do even satisfactory answers to the questions posed here provide an adequate explanation for the very problem of concentricity? For one, the distribution of legislative power over three organs is a nonsolution to this problem. Again, if the legislature is a legitimate and competent body that expresses the will of the popular sovereign, why abdicate its legislative powers in favor of an organ that is supposed to execute decisions on the basis of legal norms? On this account, the theory of concentricity prevention may be deemed incoherent, because by arrogating so much power to the executive, not to mention the judiciary, it promotes the very opposite of its declared intention: it leads to the concentration of too much power in the hands of the executive[68] and a consequent reduction of the powers of the legislative. The fundamental question then is: How can there be a rule of law when an executive and a judiciary are empowered to legislate general norms? At a minimum, the claim for the rule of law must be called into question, and with it the claim for democracy.[69] Perhaps no one has captured this paradox better than Hans Kelsen, who must be quoted at length here both for the extraordinary poignancy of his statement and because of its direct relevance to us in the remainder of this chapter:

> The principle of a separation of powers understood literally or interpreted as a principle of division of powers is not essentially democratic. Corresponding to the idea of democracy, on the contrary, is the notion that *all power should be concentrated in the people*; and where not direct but indirect democracy is possible, that all power should be exercised by one collegiate organ the members of which are elected by the people and which should be legally responsible to the people. *If this organ has only legislative functions, the other organs that have to execute the norms issued by the legislative organ should be responsible to the latter, even if they themselves are elected by the people, too.* It is the legislative organ which is most interested in a strict execution of the general norms it has issued. Control of the organs of the executive and judicial functions by the organs of the legislative functions corresponds to the natural relationship existing between these functions. Hence *democracy requires that the legislative organ should be given control over the administrative and judicial organs.* If separation of the legislative function from the law-applying functions, or a control of the legislative organ by the law-applying organs, and especially if control of the legislative and administrative functions by courts is provided for by the constitution of a democracy, *this can be explained only by historical reasons, not justified as specifically democratic elements.*[70]

2. The Paradigm of Islamic Governance

There never was an Islamic state. The state is modern, and by modern, I do not mean a particular unit of time located at some point in the trajectory of human history. The modern is a specific structure of relations that distinguishes itself as a unique phenomenon. It is a particular quality. Therefore to resort to such a usage as "Islamic state"—as an entity having existed in history[71]—is not only to indulge in anachronistic thinking but also to misunderstand the structural and qualitative differences between the modern state and its "predecessors," especially what I have called Islamic governance.

Islamic governance (that which stands parallel to what we call "state" today) rests on moral, legal, political, social, and metaphysical foundations that are dramatically different from those sustaining the modern state. In Islam, it is the Community (Umma) that displaces the nation of the modern state. The Community is both abstract and concrete, but in either case it is governed by the same moral rules.[72] In its abstract form, the Community is also a political formation delimited by moral-legal concepts. Generally, in whichever territory the Sharīʿa is applied as the paradigmatic law, the territory is deemed an Islamic domain, Dār al-Islām.[73] Wherever the Sharīʿa does not operate, or in whichever territory it is relegated to a secondary, inferior status, the territory is deemed Dār al-Ḥarb,[74] a territory that is potentially subject to conversion by peace or by war. The ultimate purpose of this conversion is to bring non-Muslims to accept Islam's law,[75] which is primarily a set of moral principles sustained by legal concepts. Thus, the boundaries and defining concept of the Community is the Sharīʿa. Islam, unless eviscerated, stands or falls on the Sharīʿa.

Whereas the nation-state is the end of all ends, knows only itself, and therefore is metaphysically the ultimate foundation of sovereign will,[76] the Community and its individual members are a means to a greater end. This implies that the Community itself neither possesses sovereignty nor does it have—in the sense the modern state has—an autonomous political or legal will, since the sovereign is God and God alone. Of course, the Community as a whole, and as represented by its chief jurists, does have the power of decision, this being the crux of the doctrine of consensus. But this power is an interpretive one, bounded—as the final chapter in this book makes clear—by *general moral principles* that transcend the Community's control. These principles may have been sociological at one point in history, but they soon emerged as a representation of divine moral will. Before being transcendental and theological, divine sovereignty was moral. An expression of this sovereign will, the Sharīʿa came to articulate the moral principles through a morally constructed law.

Paradigmatically defined, the Community consists of the totality of believers who are, as believers, equal to each other in value and thus stand undifferentiated before God.[77] If God prefers one member over another, it would be not by virtue of belonging to a more powerful class or having a particular skin color but rather by virtue of the quality of his or her belief. Thus, the premium of social relations—that is, the interaction between and among the members of the Community as well as their relations to the outside world—is determined by the quality of this belief. But most importantly here is the knowledge that, in the determination of the moral values upon which belief is erected, God is the only sovereign. He is the end of ends, earthly existence being an ephemeral and ultimately transient reality to be always seen as embedded in a creative cosmic context.[78]

The Community and its members thus come before the sultanic executive, both historically and logically, just as the Sharīʿa takes precedence, at both levels, over that executive. Sherman Jackson sums up the matter well when he states that government's intervention in society and law is

> the exception rather than the rule. The state (= sultanic executive), even as executive, is not the repository of religious authority. Nor does the individual exist for the sake of the state. It is rather the state . . . that exists to promote the welfare of the individual. The individual, who again actually precedes the state, is beholden, in the final analysis, only to God. In the end, the state is justified only to the extent that it promotes the efforts of the individual to obey and worship the Creator.[79]

God is the sovereign because He literally owns everything. Human ownership of any kind, including the absolutely unencumbered ownership of property, is merely metaphorical and ultimately unreal. It is at best derivative of the original state of sovereign ownership.[80] (This explains, for instance, why in Islam the care for the poor is legislated as "their right" against the wealth of the well-to-do,[81] since the wealth of the latter is God's, and God's compassion is *first and foremost* bestowed on the poor, the orphans, and the wretched of the earth.)[82] If the physical world in its entirety is derivative, then it cannot have any real form of original possession, including possession of a law or a moral code. It is God therefore who is the sole Legislator, and it is with Him *and Him alone* that sovereignty and sovereign will lies. If the modern state's sovereign will is represented in the law, so is God's sovereign will. The law of the Muslim God is the Sharīʿa, pure and simple. And the Sharīʿa is the moral code, *a representation of His moral will*, the first and final concern. The rest is details, including the technical body of the law and, more importantly, any form of worldly political rule. The Sharīʿa, God's Law and Will, precedes any and all such rule both logically and in time.[83]

The Sharīʿa consists of the hermeneutical, conceptual, theoretical, practical, educational, and institutional system that we have come to call Islamic law.[84] It is a colossal project of building a moral-legal empire whose foundational and structural impulse is summed up in the ever-continuing attempt to discover God's moral will. We shall speak later of the dialectic between the sociological and the metaphysical, between the Community *as a worldly society* and its persistent attempts to locate itself in a particular moral cosmology. But this realism about the world was always placed in a metaphysical context, just as this metaphysics was constantly teased out in the realism of mundane existence. The transcendentalism that disturbed the British Empiricists,[85] Muslims, including their intellectual elites, thought to be perfect common sense.

Now, the few preceding paragraphs suffice for us to make a decisive point: There can be no Islam without a moral-legal system that is anchored in a metaphysic; there can be no such moral system without or outside divine sovereignty; and, at the same time, there can be no modern state without its own sovereignty and sovereign will, for no one, I think, can reasonably argue that the modern state can do without this *essential* form-property of sovereignty. If all these premises are true, as they ineluctably must be, then the modern state can no more be Islamic than Islam can come to possess a modern state (unless, of course, the modern state is entirely reinvented, in which case we must, as we are entitled to, call it something else). As important and foundational as this conclusion may be, it is only the beginning of a longer story with multiple and multifaceted profound implications.

One such implication relates to the constitutional capacities of the Sharīʿa. As a representation of God's sovereign will, it regulates the entire range of the human order, either directly or through well-defined and limited delegation. Whereas the modern state rules over and regulates its religious institutions, rendering them subservient to its legal will,[86] the Sharīʿa rules over and regulates, directly or through delegation, any and all secular institutions. If these institutions are secular or deal with the secular, they do so under the supervising and overarching moral will that is the Sharīʿa. Therefore, any political form or political (or social or economic) institution is ultimately subordinate to the Sharīʿa, including the executive and judicial powers. The Sharīʿa itself, on the other hand, is the "legislative power" par excellence. Unlike the modern state, in Islamic governance the Sharīʿa is unrivaled in this domain, and no power other than it can truly legislate. There is no judicial review in Islam, and so the judiciary could never directly contribute to legislation, as we shall see in more detail later.[87] The executive power was mandated by the Sharīʿa to legislate in limited and restricted spheres, but this right was *derivative*, *subsidiary*, and—compared to the modern state—*relatively marginal*. On these grounds, Kelsen's critique of the separation of powers in the modern state would have been, in principle, satisfied by the Islamic forms of governance. Let us indulge here in a little speculation: had he come to understand the Sharīʿa as a bottom-up system of governance (a subject we later discuss in some detail), and had he been able to free himself of the presupposition that the only democratic form possible is the Western, Kelsen might well have declared the Islamic system a democracy of the first order, superior, at any rate, to its modern Western counterpart.[88] Let us look at this issue closer, at least insofar as the separation of powers—and therefore the rule of law—is concerned.

To do so, we must understand something about the manner in which the Sharīʿa functioned, indeed, how it lived. And to tell the story of the Sharīʿa, we must begin from the beginning, from the common social world. We must ask the question: If the Sharīʿa is not the work of the Islamic ruler or the Islamic state (which we a priori precluded), then what and who made it? The answer is that the Community, the common social world, *organically* produced its own legal experts, persons who were qualified to fulfill a variety of legal functions that, in totality, made up the Islamic legal system.[89] The jurists of Islam lived with and in the norms and values of the common social world and on average hailed from the lower and middle social strata. Their mission was defined by these norms and values, which were heavily inspired by the pervasive egalitarianism of the Qurʾān, which is to say that they saw themselves and were seen as advocates of society, the weak and disadvantaged having first priority.[90] They were called upon to express the will and aspirations of those belonging to the nonelite classes, interceding on their behalf at the higher reaches of power. The jurists and judges thus emerged as the civic leaders who found themselves, by the nature of their "profession," involved in the day-to-day running of civic affairs. Jurists and judges felt responsibility toward the common man and woman and, on their own, frequently initiated action on behalf of the oppressed without any formal petition being made by these social groups or their individual members. As a product of their own social environment, the legists' fate and worldview were inextricably intertwined with the interests of their societies. They represented for the masses the ideal of piety, rectitude, and fine education. Their very "profession" as guardians of religion, experts in religious law, and exemplars of the virtuous Muslim lifestyle made them not only the most genuine representatives of the masses but also the idealized "heirs of the Prophet," as one influential and paradigmatic Prophetic report came to attest.[91] They were the locus of legitimacy and religious and moral authority.[92]

As jurists, they fulfilled many functions, from the pedagogical and professorial to the judicial and notarial. For our concern here, we shall focus mainly only on two functions, those of the *muftī* and the *qāḍī* (judge). The *muftī*ship, among other things, is a supreme social-legal function because of the central role it played in the early evolution of Islamic law and the important contribution it made to the continued flourishing and adaptability of the Sharīʿa throughout the centuries and in many regions of the world.[93] The *muftī* was, as a rule, a private legal specialist who was legally and morally responsible to the society in which he lived, *not to the ruler and his interests*. His defining duty was to issue a *fatwā*, namely, a Sharʿī legal answer to a question he was asked to address. Consulting him was free of charge, which meant that legal counsel was easily accessible to all people, poor or rich.[94] Questions addressed to the *muftī* were raised by members of the community or by judges who found some cases brought to their courts difficult to decide.[95] The first legal elaborations that appeared in Islam were the product of this question-and-answer activity. With time, these answers were brought together, augmented, systematized, and eventually transmitted in memory as well as in writing as "law books."[96]

The *muftī* stated what the law was in a particular factual situation. As he was considered to have supreme legal authority,[97] his opinion (*fatwā*), though nonbinding, nonetheless settled many disputes in the courts of law. Thus regarded as an authoritative statement of law, the *fatwā* was routinely upheld and applied in the courts. A disputant who failed to receive a *fatwā* in his or her favor was not likely to proceed to court and would instead abandon his or her claim altogether or opt for informal mediation. *Muftī*s, however, did not always physically sit in court, but this did not change the fact that they were routinely consulted on difficult cases, even if they resided several days' distance from the court. It was a frequent occurrence for a judge, say in Cairo, to send a letter containing a question to a *muftī* who lived, for instance, in

Muslim Spain or Syria. The court, in other words, could not make law, and its ultimate reference was neither itself nor an executive authority. The law of the Muslim court, as a judicial organ, was entirely under the authority of the private legal experts, the Sharīʿa-anchored, Sharīʿa-minded, and socially embedded *muftīs* and jurists.[98]

The authority of the *fatwā* was decisive. When on occasion a *fatwā* was disregarded, it was usually because another *fatwā* on offer constituted a more convincing and better-reasoned opinion. In other words, and to put it conversely, it was rare for a judge to dismiss a *fatwā* in favor of his own opinion, unless he himself happened to be of a juristic caliber higher than that enjoyed by the *muftī* from whom the *fatwā* was solicited (in which case the judge would not seek a *fatwā* in the first place). All this is to say that the *fatwā* is the product of legal expertise and advanced legal knowledge, all grounded in a deep concern for the society and for its general moral principles and not for a state or a top-down law.

The central role of the *fatwā* in the Muslim court of law explains why the decisions of judges were neither kept nor published in the manner practiced by common law courts. In other words, law was not to be found in precedents established by courts of law but rather in a juristic body of writings that originated mostly in the highly reasoned answers formulated by *muftīs*.[99]

Thus, emanating from the world of legal practice, it was the *fatwās* rather than court decisions that were collected and published, particularly those among them that contained new law or represented new legal elaborations on older problems that continued to be of relevance. Those *fatwās* that were collected usually underwent a significant editorial process so as to fit within the textual world of technical legal language. Once edited and abstracted, the *fatwās* became part and parcel of legal doctrine.[100]

The great majority of Islamic legal works, however, were not written by the *muftī* but rather by the author-jurist, who depended in good part on the *fatwās* of distinguished *muftīs*. The author-jurist's activity extended from writing the short but specialized treatise to compiling longer works, which were usually expanded commentaries on the short works.[101] It was these works that afforded the author-jurists the opportunity to articulate, each for his generation and region, a modified body of law that reflected both the evolving social conditions and the state of the art in the law as a technical discipline. It is also instructive that the *fatwās* that formed the substance of later doctrine were those that answered contemporary needs and had at once gained currency in practice. On the other hand, those opinions that ceased to be of use in litigation and practice were either excluded altogether or designated as "weak."[102]

Many of the works written and "published" by the author-jurists were standard references for the judges, who studied them when they were students and consulted them when they assumed the judicial functions. Since the authority of the law resided in the *muftīs*' opinions and the author-jurists' treatises, the judge—unless he himself was simultaneously a *muftī* or an author-jurist—was not expected to possess the same level of expert legal knowledge. This is to say that a person who was a *muftī* or an author-jurist could usually function as a judge, although a judge who was trained only as judge could not serve in the capacity of a *muftī* or an author-jurist (or, for that matter, a law professor). But this is also to say, by implication, that the *muftī*, the author-jurist, and the judge operated in their respective functions under the authority of the Sharīʿa, not under a state law, state order, or statute. *And they did so in their own social world for the sake of that world.*

One final matter must be noted, namely, the inextricably close ties between law and society (we must do our best to avoid casting the matter in the language of "social order" and "legal order," since the highly porous relationship between law and society precluded meaningful distinctions between them).[103] In terms of judicial practices, litigants and consumers of the law appeared before the *qāḍī* without ceremony and presented their cases without needing professional mediation, for the Sharīʿa had no lawyers. The litigants spoke informally, unhampered by anything resembling the absolute discipline of the modern court (the very disciplinarian notion of contempt of court did not exist).[104] They presented their cases in the way they knew how, without technical jargon. This was possible because in the Islamic system of justice no gulf existed between the court as a legal institution and the consumers of the law, however economically impoverished or educationally disadvantaged the latter might have been. Yet it was not entirely the virtue of the court and *qāḍī* alone that made this gap nonexistent, for credit must equally be given to these very consumers. Unlike modern society, which has become estranged from the legal profession in multiple ways, premodern Muslim society was as much engaged in the Sharʿī system of values as the court itself was embedded in the moral universe of society. It is a salient feature of that society that it *lived* legal ethics and legal morality, for these constituted the religious foundations and codes of social praxis. To say that the moral law of premodern Muslim societies was a living and lived tradition is to state nothing less than the most obvious.

If law was a lived and living tradition, then people knew what the law was. In other words, legal knowledge was widespread and accessible, thanks to the *muftī* and other legists who were willing to impart legal knowledge free of charge and nearly *at any time* someone wished to obtain it. The social underdogs thus knew what their rights were before approaching the court, a fact that in part explains why they won the great majority of cases when they happened to be plaintiffs. Their counsel were not lawyers who spoke a different, incomprehensible language nor were they higher-class professionals who exacted exorbitant fees that often made litigation and recovery of rights as expensive as the litigated object.[105]

But the spread of a legal ethic and legal knowledge in the social world of Islam was also the function of a cumulative tradition transmitted from one generation to the next and enhanced at every turn by the vibrant participation of aspiring law students, the greater and lesser *muftīs*, the imams, and by the occasional advice that the judge and other learned persons gave while visiting acquaintances, walking in the street, or shopping in the market. Thus when the common folk appeared before the court, they spoke a "legal" language as perfectly comprehensible to the judge as the judge's vernacular "moral" language was comprehensible to them. Legal norms and social morality were largely inseparable, the one feeding on and, at the same time, sustaining the other. As much a social as a legal institution, the Muslim court was eminently the product of the very community it served and in the bosom of which it functioned.

Now, it is true that the Sharīʿa developed certain apprehensions (or, in American constitutional parlance, "distrust") toward executive political power, apprehensions that are testimony to Sharīʿa's ability to command loyalty to the society and morality in which it functioned and lived. It is by no means an exaggeration to say that the Sharīʿa and its jurists emerged from the midst of society and continued to serve that society until the Sharīʿa was effectively dismantled. If it cooperated with political powers, it did so as a mediator between these powers and the masses, while keeping its eyes fully open on the interests of the people. And if the political elite sometimes used it to accomplish their own ends, they used it under its terms, not theirs. That they were constrained by it while embarking on their own ventures there is little doubt.[106] The Sharīʿa was not only the law of the land but also the law of the heavens and everything lying in between, including politics and rule.

If the "legislative power" in Islam was entirely embedded in a socially based, divine body of law (and no contradiction must ensue from this), and if the Sharīʿa was an independent "legislative power," then in what sort of relationship did it stand with judicial power? Before proceeding to answer this question, we must observe that adjudicating disputes was only one of the many duties that the Sharīʿa court and its judge had to undertake. The *qāḍī*, like the *muftī*, was a member of the community he served.[107] He was trained by his fellow *muftī*-cum-law-professors[108] and belonged to the guild of ulama, the scholarly religious "class" that emerged from the midst of the ordinary social ranks. Islamic law itself insists that a *qāḍī*, to qualify for the position,[109] had to be trained in Sharīʿa and to be intimately familiar with the local customs and ways of life in the community in which he served.[110] With the help of his staff, he was in charge of supervising much in the life of the community. He oversaw the building of mosques, streets, public fountains, and bridges. He, or his deputies, inspected newly constructed and dilapidated buildings, the operation of hospitals, soup kitchens, and charitable endowments (which constituted between 40 and 50 percent of all real property in the great majority of Muslim lands).[111] He looked into the care afforded by guardians to orphans and the poor and himself acted as guardian in the marriage of women who had no relatives capable of functioning as legally competent guardians.[112] Moreover, the *qāḍī* oftentimes played the exclusive role of mediator in cases that were not of a strictly legal nature. Not only did he arbitrate disputes and reconcile husbands and wives, but he listened, for example, to problems dividing relatives and friends who might need no more than an outsider's opinion. Furthermore, the Muslim court was the site in which important transactions between individuals were recorded, such as the sale of a house, the details of the estate of a deceased person, or a partnership contract concluded between or among merchants.[113]

Just as important was the social context in which the *qāḍī* and his court functioned. Judges invariably sought to understand the wider social context of the litigating parties, often attempting to resolve conflicts with full consideration of the set of present and future social relationships of disputants. Like arbitrators but unlike modern judges, the *qāḍī* tried hard, wherever possible, to prevent the collapse of relationships so as to maintain a social reality in which the litigating parties, who often came from the same community, could continue to live together amicably.[114] Such a *judicial* act required the *qāḍī* to be familiar with and willing to investigate the history of relations (and relationships) between the disputants.[115] The Muslim court thus was not only a legal forum but also an anthropological, social, and moral site.[116] Thanks to its remarkably low fees (incomparable with the exorbitant costs of litigation in the modern court) and by virtue of the nature of the Islamic notions of justice, it was highly accessible, providing a venue for poor and rich alike, women[117] and men, Muslims, and even Jews and Christians ("minorities" who often favored the Muslim court over their own denominational tribunals).[118]

Now, it is crucial to understand that the law applied by *qāḍīs* was the result of a centuries-long, cumulative hermeneutical project undertaken by the jurists themselves, both as individual believers and members of the Community.[119] They developed methods of thinking about and interpretation of the law that came to be known as *uṣūl al-fiqh*, a body of theory that brings into a systematic amalgam a number of advanced fields: logic, theology, language, linguistics, rational-textual hermeneutics, legal reasoning, and much else.[120] On the basis of this theory and the principles it offered, those jurists who attained the highest intellectual standards (and they were numerous in every age) exercised these faculties in order to arrive at solutions to legal questions, from issues of "ritual" and inheritance to equally complex and complicated matters of contract and damages. These interpretive methods constituted the tools of *ijtihād*, the processes of creative reasoning that the accomplished jurist employed in order to arrive at the best guess of what he thought the law pertaining to a particular case might be. With the exception of a relatively few Qurʾānic and Prophetic statements that were unambiguous and contained clear and specific normative rulings, the rest of the law was the product of *ijtihād*. Thus, whereas such unambiguous textual rulings were deemed certain and hence not susceptible to *ijtihād* (because the mind cannot see any other meaning in the language in which they were stated), this latter involved inferences and was the domain of probability.[121]

In the majority, therefore, the laws, rules, and regulations of the Sharīʿa are largely the result of *ijtihād*, a domain of interpretation that rests on probability. Every accomplished jurist could exercise *ijtihād*, and two or more could arrive at different conclusions on the same problem with no one knowing but God which *mujtahid* (i.e., the jurist conducting *ijtihād*) had arrived at the truth. This extensive relativism gave rise to the famous tenet that "Every *mujtahid* is correct," a maxim that proved operative and became sanctified.[122]

Ijtihād thus gave Islamic law one of its unique features. For every eventuality or case, and for every particular unique set of facts, there may be anywhere from two to a dozen highly reasoned opinions, if not more, each held by a different jurist but all belonging to the same school (which is to say that the opinions are reasoned on the basis of a shared set of principles that in fact give the school its identity as a particular "legal" method or way of thinking about the moral law).[123] In other words, there is no single legal stipulation that has monopoly or exclusivity, as law is designed by the modern state (which is also to say that in this system it would have been impossible for the legislative to be "unruly" and potentially "tyrannical," as the American framers had feared the Congress might become).[124] Islamic law is one of legal pluralism, not only because it acknowledges local custom and takes it into serious account but also because it offers an array of opinions on one and the same set of facts.[125] This pluralism gave Islamic law three of its fundamental features. First, it equipped it with a great deal of flexibility and adaptability in governing drastically varied societies and regions, from Morocco to the Malay Archipelago and from Transoxiana to Somalia. Second, this pluralism was constitutive of an inner juristic structure that allowed substantive law to undergo piecemeal change throughout the centuries, thereby accommodating new developments in social and economic life.[126] Finally, this great multiplicity of legal opinion reflected, over time and space, the endless varieties of societal interests and concerns, particularly those within the common social order. Overwhelmingly in the interest of the population, this "popular" representation was both legal and political, for its legally expressed will was also politically binding on the ruler in his dealings with the civil population. And it was this law that the Muslim judges applied, a law that was not the product of a state or a few distinguished jurists but of hundreds of socially anchored specialists who flourished across time in culturally disparate regions.

The Muslim judiciary therefore was not in the service of applying a law determined by the dominant powers of a state or a peremptory ruler but rather of safeguarding a Sharīʿa law whose primary concern was the regulation, on moral grounds, of social and economic relations. It was a law of the people, although one that served equally to circumscribe the ruler in his treatment of the population. But while the jurists' values and the laws they applied were of societal and Sharʿī inspiration, they themselves were appointed by the ruler, who could dismiss judges from office and limit the purview of their jurisdiction (i.e., confining them to adjudicate disputes in family law, criminal law, or a particular district or part of a city, etc.).[127] The ruler, however, could play no role whatsoever in the work of the judge between appointment to, and dismissal from, office. The law and procedure of the court was the judge's business, and his business was wholly the business of the Sharīʿa, in which he had trained and to which he was morally, legally, and culturally faithful.

The appointment of judges by the ruler operated by virtue of the concept of delegation. The historical origins of this appointment went back to the early days of Islam, when the caliph represented both religious and "secular" authority. As a deputy of the Prophet, he was assumed to be a jurist of some sort, and so as a deputy and jurist he appointed the *qāḍīs*. Initially, therefore, the *qāḍī* was an extension of the caliphal office insofar as supervising society and its affairs were concerned. Later on, and after the ninth century A.D., the effective rulers were not the caliphs but sultans who mostly hailed from Central Asia. The sultans were political and military leaders who ruled through a dynasty and who displaced the worldly powers of the caliphs. Normally after consultation with local jurists and ulama, the sultans or their governors appointed *qāḍīs* in various locations in the sultanate.[128] However, it must be reiterated that whoever they appointed as *qāḍī* was expected to apply the Sharīʿa and its norms and regulations. The Muslim judiciary was entirely independent of the executive (i.e., the sultan and his men), no matter how often judges were appointed and dismissed and no matter which sultan ruled. No judge presiding in a Sharīʿa court, the default court of the land, could apply any other law. It was unheard of.

Nevertheless, the famous Lebanese Orientalist Émile Tyan argued, and his argument enjoyed authority for many decades, that one "consequence of the concept of delegation was the complete lack of separation between the judicial and executive powers."[129] This view is ill informed and entirely erroneous, on at least three grounds. First, as we have seen, the law of the Sharīʿa court is not dependent on the legal will of the ruler but the contrary: the ruler—what we have called the sultanic executive—stood under the Sharīʿa law, not above it, and no ruler could dispute the established fact that it was the Sharīʿa that reigned supreme in the courts no less than in society at large. According to this scheme, the Sharīʿa court applied the law as formulated by the "legislature," i.e., the moral law of the Sharīʿa, not that of the ruler, the sultanic executive.

Second, the paradigmatic discourse of the Sharīʿa views the *qāḍī* not as the true but merely as the nominal delegate of the sultan or caliph. In this Sharʿī juristic-political discourse, the ruler is deemed a representative of the Community,[130] and his appointment and dismissal of *qāḍīs* is no more than a function of his representation.[131] This is precisely the reason why the *qāḍīs*' tenures were not terminated when the ruler who appointed them was dethroned, abdicated, or died.[132] To this category of appointments belongs other so-called public servants, such as the secretary of the public treasury (*amīn bayt al-māl*), the superintendents of charitable foundations (*nuẓẓār al-awqāf*), and the commander of the army (*amīr al-jaysh*).[133] All these were regarded as public appointments and the ruler as merely the mediator. This also explains why the sultanic judicial appointments were usually made after extensive prior consultation with the juristic class of the locale to which the *qāḍī* was appointed, not to mention the chief jurists sitting—regularly—at the royal court,[134] this having been a fixed and longstanding feature of sultanic justice as well.

Finally, the concept of delegation could also be taken to mean control of the judiciary by the executive, since dismissal from office is generally regarded by modern observers as undermining judicial independence and consequently separation of powers.[135] In the modern legal system this is certainly the case, but not so in its Islamic counterpart. Today's job-based economy and the concept of expertise have obviously created the notion that securing a career or a professional job is essential for the individual's economic independence. Threatening the job necessarily means threatening independence. But this economic conception did not exist prior to the nineteenth century, be it in the Islamic world or elsewhere. Jobwise, Muslim jurists did not specialize in their field because they routinely performed other tasks, meaning that income from their *qāḍī*ship was merely one of several sources of livelihood. In the first centuries of Islam, *qāḍīs* and their fellow legists had other "professions," mainly artisanal.[136] Later on, they came to perform a variety of functions in the field of education, including tutoring, teaching, and copying manuscripts, which were always flourishing trades. Some worked as scribes, secretaries, and record keepers, while others were small merchants or, still fewer others, merchants on a larger scale. In other words, the Muslim judge as an economic man did not depend exclusively or even significantly on his income from a judgeship. But this is half the story. The normative average tenure of a judge was two or three years, often renewed after an interval.[137] Dismissal was a fact of life and a taken-for-granted matter. It was expected and done with such natural frequency that it threatened no one. In fact, it is precisely this frequency and its naturalness (not to mention the unquestioned commitment to the Sharīʿa) that made judicial independence not only possible but also gave it a strong character.[138]

It should be noted that the three factors I have enumerated are practical or functional explanations as to why Tyan was wrong. A fourth factor mitigating executive-judicial collusion may be added, namely, the paradigmatic moral force of the Sharīʿa, which, as a rule, compelled judges and rulers alike to respect judicial independence. Put differently, judicial independence was integral to culture. That the moral argument plays no role in Tyan's account says less about the system being described than about Tyan's own modernist and positivist conceptions.[139]

We have so far given an account of the Sharīʿa-based "legislative" and judicial powers. The former was entirely independent and sovereign, whereas the latter implemented the Sharʿī moral law in accordance with the will of the "legislative" power. The question that poses itself now is: How did these two powers stand vis-à-vis the executive? One way to begin an answer is to describe the executive as a hired class that was under the obligation to fulfill certain functions. This class consisted of a dynastic ruler (typically supported by slave-soldiers who, like those who brought them, were not original inhabitants of Muslim lands) who mainly executed the Sharīʿa ordinances and generally complied with its order and wishes in exchange for a rent that he levied on the populace. The rent essentially took the form of taxes, which often exceeded Sharīʿa specifications, although to what precise extent we do not yet know.[140] Nevertheless, we do know that the benchmark of taxation was the Sharʿī-stipulated rates, universally acknowledged to be extraordinarily low, especially by modern standards.[141] In other words, taxation could be determined by fixed and objective criteria, and thus overtaxation was relatively easy to evaluate and dispute in a Sharʿī court.[142] Even in the most statelike of all Islamic empires, the Ottoman, the "sphere of action of the sultan was at all times confined within the parameters of a [Sharʿī] concept of justice which ensured the rights of the proprietor."[143]

The relatively tentative nature of executive sultanism is reflected in the standard vocabulary of Islam. The term reserved for dynastic rule was *dawla*, a term that has come to refer to the *totality of the modern state* of the late nineteenth century and thereafter. But before then, it meant nothing of the sort. The term *dawla* essentially connoted a dynastic rule that comes to power in one part of the world, Islamic or non-Islamic, and then passes away.[144] This idea of rotation and of the successive change of dynasties is integral to the concept.[145] Thus the Community remains fixed and cannot come to an end until the Day of Judgment, whereas the *dawla* that governs it is temporary and ephemeral, having no intrinsic, organic, or permanent ties to the Community and its Sharīʿa.[146] It is a means to an end. Just as one hires a housekeeper to maintain a home according to certain standards, so did the *dawla* and its somewhat mercenary sultan function to uphold the Sharʿī social world on the Community's behalf. And just as the housekeeper is replaceable, so is the *dawla*. The difference is that the end of the *dawla* is not brought about by an autonomous decision of the Community. If the *dawla* was brought to an end, this was because of the rise of another, more powerful *dawla*, which becomes the newly hired protector and keeper of the Community's House (literally, Dār al-Islām). The more powerful dynasty succeeds and gains Sharʿī legitimacy by virtue of the fact that it is a more effective and efficient servant and executor of the Sharīʿa and its norms.

This tentative nature characterizing dynastic rule, which stands in stark contrast with the enduring permanency of the Community and its Sharīʿa, is fundamental to an understanding of the Islamic concept of separation of powers and therefore of Islamic constitutional theory and practice. The significance of this contrast is further bolstered, in profound ways, by the fact that throughout the twelve centuries of Islamic history (until colonialism destroyed Islamic political, educational, and social structures), the Community and its Sharīʿa witnessed a relative stability that is rarely attested in human history. This may be contrasted with the dynastic rotation, over this same period of twelve centuries, in which Arabia and Asia Minor each experienced some eighteen dynasties (*dawlas*), Iran no fewer than twenty-four, and Egypt eight (an exceptionally low number).

Generally, the rulers of Islamic lands were foreign to the regions that they dominated. Frequently, they were non-Muslims who eventually converted at a later point of time, and it often took them one or two generations before they were habituated to the local Islamic values, customs, and language. Lacking the bureaucratic machinery that the modern state enjoys, they could not administratively penetrate society,[147] and they resigned themselves to this, finding in the Sharīʿa a ready-made tool of governance and in the jurists important middlemen in their capacity as representatives of the Community. Thus, they accepted the Sharīʿa's dictates, conducting their duties toward the Community accordingly and reaping what financial benefits they could, often within reason.

Not all rulers, of course, complied with the Sharīʿa norms in the same way or to the same extent, but compliance as a whole was paradigmatic. An illustrative analogy exists in our own modern politics. No one can foretell how an American president or a Canadian prime minister, on just being elected, will conduct the affairs of his or her state. Some end up ruining the national economy, others will drag their countries into intractable wars, some are more peaceful and less trigger-happy than others, and some will protect fundamental rights while others will callously erode them. But all of these presidents and prime ministers—despite arguments that their powers may constitute "a serious threat" to their country's "constitutional tradition"[148]—will have to operate by the general rules and standards of a liberal democracy, which the United States and Canada are. The same variations existed in Islamic dynastic rule, with two main constitutional differences, however: namely, (1) that the Sharīʿa dictated the law of the land and provided the standards of executive political management (*siyāsa*), whereas the legislative branch in modern liberal democracies has comparatively lesser powers; and, as we have seen, (2) that the executive and administrative powers in liberal democracies enjoy much greater privileges of legislation than the sultanic executive did. It may also be added that, just as there is a sense among some constitutional scholars that the American presidency has become a threat to the constitutional tradition and even "a principal agent of destruction,"[149] there were certain periods in Islamic history that were described in similar terms, as exemplified, for instance, in the last three or four decades of Mamlūk rule.[150]

All this is to say that the executive ruler stood apart from the "legislative" and even the judicial powers, being in many respects subservient to their commands. Islamic juristic-political theory and practice (*siyāsa Sharʿiyya*) demanded this much, and the theory was largely put into practice. An essential constitutional fact here is that it was the Sharīʿa itself that arrogated certain powers to the ruler. While not every ruler complied with every single dictate of *siyāsa Sharʿiyya*, it remains the case that the paradigmatic law was just that, paradigmatic, meaning that the ruler's actions were always judged by this Sharʿī-minded and Sharʿī-based standard. Betrayal of the principles of *siyāsa Sharʿiyya* was bad government.

The foregoing permits a further comment on the widespread Western-Orientalist imagining of the concept of "Oriental despotism." The concept was given added weight by the spurious Prophetic report proclaiming that "sixty years of tyranny are better than one day of civil strife."[151] This was taken to be evidence that "Orientals" are inherently submissive and therefore possess a natural capacity to endure tyranny and oppression (needless to say, a doctrine necessary to justify colonialism past and present). While the Prophetic report does reflect an accurate understanding by Muslims of their own political-legal systems and practices, the Orientalist interpretation of it is entirely erroneous. The key terms here are "tyranny" and "civil strife." If "tyranny" is defined by pre-nineteenth century European standards, the period in which the concept of despotic Orientalism was fashioned, then it becomes clear that we are dealing here with the projection of the European concept of monarch—who was absolutist and an arbitrary legislator and executor—onto the Islamic scene. But this projection is unjustified because "Oriental tyranny" at its worst could not accomplish two goals that the European monarch successfully and easily achieved: namely, (1) sultans and kings could never penetrate the societies they came to rule but could only govern from the "outside," and, more importantly, (2) these rulers were severely constrained by a law that they did not create and that was largely out of their control. Thus, whatever tyranny they practiced could not, as a rule, have affected the integrity of the communities they ruled, communities that were the basis and defining parameters of life. In the Orientalist definition, the meaning and range of "tyranny" has been wildly amplified, whereas the paramount significance of "civil strife," where the all-important Community is split asunder, has been dramatically deemphasized. On the other hand, and given the nature of Islamic constitutional organization, the Muslim conception privileges the community as the cradle of life and the locus of meaningful living, deeming tyranny and its political sultanic source as comparatively far less pernicious than its European counterpart.

The fallacy of the concept of "Oriental despotism" becomes even clearer if we ask: What were the powers and functions of executive sultanism? First, the sultan possessed no real sovereignty. Although mainly controlling the tools of violence, he represented no popular will beyond the legitimacy that the jurists (and, to some extent, Ṣūfīs) bestowed on him on behalf of the populace. He was not the source of law and thus had no significant legal will. He served the "Noble Sharīʿa," whether he liked it or not.[152] The bartering terms were exceedingly clear: The sultan levied taxes in exchange for the legitimacy the jurists bestowed upon him, a legitimacy that could not be given away without him implementing the ordinances of the Sharīʿa, including the maintenance of social and communal harmony (a sacred concept in Islam). Sovereignty always remained with God, as represented by the Sharīʿa.[153]

As we saw, the sovereign will of the modern state is, by contrast, represented in its own legal will and therefore in the state's law. There is no modern nation-state that does not have *its own* law. In constitutional terms, the Muslim ruler did not possess a sovereign will that was inherently represented by his law. He was under the duty to enforce a Sharīʿa that was not of his making. In fact, in a world where several dynasties could and did exist simultaneously in Muslim lands, all rulers had to apply the same law, the Sharīʿa. Thus the Sharīʿa, being pronouncedly extraterritorial, was the common law of all these dynastic empires.

The Sharīʿa, through the doctrine of *siyāsa Sharʿiyya*, requires the ruler to "manage worldly affairs" and to uphold the Sharʿī world on behalf of the Prophet, a mandate that translates into observing the norms of the Sharīʿa. This in turn entails the maintenance of the Community's interests (repeatedly expressed in the language of "*riʿāyat maṣāliḥ al-Muslimīn*").[154] All Muslims and protected non-Muslims living in Dār al-Islām were assumed to stand in a permanent contractual bond with the ruling dynasty, a bond whose terms are the protection of life, limb, and property for a consideration. Any attack on these rights was tantamount to an attack on the Muslim polity and, by implication, on the bond it has established with the Community. As Johansen argues, this would be regarded as an attack "on the authority of the government, which through its response [i.e. defense] has to reestablish it."[155] Therefore, the executive stood vis-à-vis the Community in a contractual relationship, but this was a relationship constitutionally defined by the Sharīʿa and its jurists and no one else.

In fulfillment of this contractual bond, the ruler was obligated to (1) enforce and execute the Sharīʿa court judgments in his domain; (2) implement punishments for the Qurʾānically prescribed *ḥudūd*, these latter having been rules also determined by the Sharīʿa; (3) maintain the capacity to raise an army; (4) defend the frontiers and improve safety of the roads; (5) divide booty after war; (6) collect and redistribute the alms tax; (7) appoint, supervise, and dismiss *qāḍīs*, market inspectors (*muḥtasibs*), and officers of the mint (*sikka*) who conduct their duties according to the Sharīʿa;[156] and (8) attend to the orphaned minors and those who have no legal guardians.[157] Note here the boundaries of these obligations. The first five—which in both Sharʿī theory and practice constituted the most important duties—involve the capacity to exercise legitimate violence. The sixth involves taxation, which the Sharīʿa arrogated to the ruler as a matter of course. The seventh captures the ruler's most important duties in administering justice. The eighth is a set of duties usually delegated to the *qāḍī* and thus in effect subsumed under the seventh. It would not then be an exaggeration to say that the ruler's duties, compensated for by taxes, consisted of "tools" hired for the purpose of maintaining the Community's security and public order. The abstract notion of the Community becomes here concretized: the ruler is the keeper of the safety of and maintainer of order in that Sharʿī community or communities which he rules.

On the other hand, *siyāsa Sharʿiyya* also equipped the ruler with the legal power to supplement the religious law with administrative regulations that mostly pertained to the regime's machinery of governance, including—as we have said—powers to limit the *qāḍī*'s jurisdiction to certain areas of the law or to particular types of cases, as well as to curb and discipline abuses by the government's officials.[158] In addition to taxation, *siyāsa Sharʿiyya* regulations normally included matters related to land use and at times criminal law and some aspects of public morality that could affect social harmony. In theory, and largely in practice, the powers conferred upon the ruler through *siyāsa Sharʿiyya* were not only consistent with the dictates of religious law; they were, as we will soon see, an integral extension of this law. As such, their proper exercise could in no way constitute an infringement thereof.

Thus, in order for the ruler to exercise effective powers in accomplishing his tasks, *siyāsa Sharʿiyya* required that a supplement consisting of administrative regulations be made. (Note here that for all the rules and regulations of *siyāsa Sharʿiyya*, none of this juristic or any other discourse amounted to a theory of state).[159] Oftentimes, administrative regulations merely asserted the provisions of religious law in an effort not only to place emphasis on such provisions but also to depict the sultanic will as Sharʿī minded. In these instances, the bid for legitimacy is unmistakable. But administrative regulations did supplement some provisions of the Sharīʿa, especially in areas having to do with public order, the bedrock of any successful regime. Among the most important of these areas were highway robbery, theft, bodily injury, homicide, adultery and fornication (and accusations thereof), usury, taxation, land tenure, and categorically all acts conducive to disturbance of public order and peace. All of these areas, it must be stressed, were covered by the Sharīʿa, but administrative regulations came to enhance them, *mutatis mutandis*. With a view toward a strict enforcement of these religious and sultanic laws, the regulations at times permitted torture (mainly to extract confession from habitual thieves) and the execution of highway robbers upon the sultan's orders. Legalizing usury, extrajudicial taxes, and torture were perhaps the most objectionable pieces of legislation in the view of the jurists, and the jurists and *qāḍīs* often militated against them. These objections notwithstanding, administrative regulations—in their thin but diverse substance—were mostly seen and accepted as an integral part of the legal culture and as an extrajudicial element that was required—after all—by the *siyāsa Sharʿiyya* itself. On the whole, they had far more commonalities than differences.[160]

While the civilian population was subject to the law of the Sharīʿa, the government's servants—including the army, police, government administrative-secretarial class, and *qāḍīs*—were by contrast subject to another code, one that may aptly be called sultanic.[161] In other words, while no man or woman, Muslim, Christian, or Jew in the civilian population could be punished without a Sharīʿa court trial—standing largely independent of the sovereign's will—the sultanic code was absolute with regard to the ruler himself and his men, including the Sharīʿa judges.

The ruler himself was also expected to observe not only his own code but, more importantly, the law of the Sharīʿa. As a private person, he remained, like any common Sharīʿa subject, liable to any civil claim, including debts, contracts, and pecuniary damages. Likewise, he was punishable for infractions of the Sharʿī penal laws and Qurʾānic *ḥudūd*[162]—the reasoning in all these domains being grounded in the assumption that all Muslims, weak or strong, are equal in their rights to life and property and in their obligations toward one another.[163] In the Sharīʿa, the sultan and his men enjoyed no special immunity.

On the "political-moral" plane, forbearance, mercy, and near infinite forgiveness were expected standards of governance that, when violated, could result in his dismissal or even assassination. For political power to acquire any legitimacy, it had to meet these standards and conduct itself in a morally and legally responsible way.[164] Even highly unsympathetic European observers of the Islamic legal system felt compelled to acknowledge this feature. The Sharīʿa "circumscribed the will of the Prince" who "observed [the law]; and the practice of ages had rendered some ancient usages and edicts so sacred in the eyes of the people, that no prudent monarch would choose to violate either by a wanton act of power."[165]

Therefore, ruling in accordance with *siyāsa Sharʿiyya* was in no way the unfettered power of political governance but in a fundamental way the Sharʿī exercise of wisdom, forbearance, and prudence by a prince in ruling the Sharīʿa's subjects. In the case of the civilian population, these qualities manifested themselves in the recognition of the *qāḍī* as the final judge and as representative of the religious law, for in each and every case referred by the sultan to the *qāḍī*, it came with the unwavering sultanic command to apply the Sharīʿa law and the administrative regulations. While the imperial servants, on the other hand, also frequently benefited from the sultanic virtue of forgiveness—especially upon first or less grave infractions—they were ultimately subject to the sultanic code, which was absolute, swift, and harsh. The right of summary judgment was reserved for the sultan against his own men and, by extension, their official representatives, all of whom owed complete allegiance to him. For, after all, the sultan's men, who were brought up from childhood as the servants of the state, literally belonged to the *salṭana* (sultanship). They themselves, and all the wealth that they would accumulate in their lives, were the property of the *salṭana*; upon death or the commission of a grave infraction, this property was to revert to whence it came.

As the overlord, the ruler was responsible for any commission of injustice by his appointees and civil servants. Misconduct of government servants and of *qāḍīs* could be referred directly to the ruler or to the *maẓālim* courts. What is remarkable about this conception and practice of governance is that, far from depending on a formal ethic of desirable and fair conduct of institutions (such as constitutions or bureaucratic reasoning, which is largely independent of the moral accountability of individuals), it was grounded in a different ethic seen as *indispensable* for political legitimacy and for the well-being of society and dynasty alike. In other words, it was a culture that was permeated by the political concept of moral accountability. This was the paradigm of executive governance, and like all paradigms (as explained in chapter 1), occasional minor or major violations did not change the fact of its being a paradigm.

It was thus by design that a line of communication was always left open between the tax-paying subjects and the dynastic order. This is why the ruler's and his governors' assemblies, which met regularly, included the *qāḍīs*, tax collectors, the notables, the leading *muftīs*, the neighborhood representatives, and a host of other figures from the populace. These local officials were therefore subject to intersecting interests whereby the loyalties they might have otherwise shown to the sultan and empire would be mitigated and counterbalanced by their local stake in maintaining their own social, economic, and moral networks. Indeed, the local *qāḍīs*, *muftīs*, representatives of the neighborhoods and of professional guilds, and even tax farmers sat in the assembly as defenders of their communities' interests, which latter had justified their appointment to that assembly in the first place.

3. Comparisons and Conclusions

The discussions of this chapter offer us at least two conclusions that pertain to four out of the five form-properties of the state that we outlined in the previous chapter. First, as a world civilization, Islam developed a historically grounded paradigmatic moral-legal ethic that defined its identity. Obviously, there can be no Islam nor any specifically Islamic moral-legal culture outside of history, for it is history and its forces and circumstances that gave rise to this legal-moral identity. To be a Muslim individual today is to be, in fundamental ways, connected with that Sharīʿa-defined ethic, for it is this ethic that shaped what Islam is and has been. The following chapters will illustrate and demonstrate this claim in detail, but it suffices for now to say that the formation of Muslim identity means the paramountcy of Sharīʿa as the ruling ethic of human behavior. *There is no Muslim identity without this ethic*. To claim that modern Muslim identity, so defined, can be stripped of this history or of the ethic that pervaded it to the core amounts to claiming that the citizens of Euro-America could still be who they are but without their historical roots, without their socioeconomic history, without their legal history, without their political history, and without the Enlightenment and its values. Thus, inasmuch as the modern Western state and its citizen are the product of a historically determined phenomenon, the Muslim identity of today is inextricably connected with a particular moral-legal ethic that was historically determined by the supremely central values of the Sharīʿa.

Second, in this history and the identity it generated, the Sharīʿa was the expression of God's sovereignty, for the paradigmatic invocation "*lā ilāha illā Allāh*" ("There is no god but God") sums up the foundational knowledge and religious and discursive practice that God is the only sovereign. This knowledge was structural: it permeated the fabric of Muslim life, from social-practical ethic to political governance.

Finally, the concept of God's sovereignty in Islam shaped a particular paradigm of separation of powers. The "legislative" power was manned by private jurists who lived *in* and *with* society and its communities. They themselves, as private, unpaid scholars, constructed the law and were its guardians only by force of erudition, piety, religious charisma, and moral strength. The Sharīʿa therefore was more amenable to the average social ranks—including its poor, orphaned, and unprivileged—than to the higher reaches of power. In fact, it was suspicious of the mighty and the politically powerful. In these senses, then, the jurists and their Sharīʿa represented the populace to the high political powers just as well as any known system of representation does today. This is true not only because the jurists (and their affiliates, local leaders, and other learned Sharʿī-minded men) represented their communities in the fashion that an elected representative speaks for his or her constituency but also because the very substantive law of the Sharīʿa was far more accommodating to the common social classes than is the law of the modern state. If the Sharīʿa was the unchallenged law of the land (and it certainly was), then the law itself spoke on behalf of the weak and the disadvantaged even when they had no legal or political representation. But they had. And so to add the representation of the jurists to the privileged position of the common social strata in the law is to secure representation in intensive, extensive, and substantive ways.

It was this paradigmatic law that was applied in the courts of the Islamic world, and it was applied, as a rule, faithfully by a judicial order committed to the letter and spirit of the law's moral and just constitution. If it is true, as Kelsen argued, that "democracy requires that the legislative organ should be given control over the administrative and judicial organs,"[166] then the Islamic form of governance amply provides for such a democratic system, since the Islamic judicial and executive branches remained—insofar as society was concerned—under the control of the "legislative" power. But we have also seen that there is more than one reason to claim this system to be highly representative. However, the point here is even more emphatic. Islamic governance separated the executive power from the legislative by degrees, making the former wholly subservient to the will of the latter, the supreme moral law. The law of the courts was also independent, despite the executive's prerogative to appoint and dismiss *qāḍīs*. This prerogative was more nominal than substantive, for notwithstanding judicial appointments and dismissals, the *paradigmatic* law applied by the *qāḍīs* always remained that of the Sharīʿa.

In sum, the supremacy of the Sharīʿa meant a rule of law that stood superior to its modern counterpart, the present form of the Western state that has come to be fused, in the majority of instances, with a claim to democratic legitimacy (or popular sovereignty) that "sits very awkwardly with its practical realities."[167] For Muslims today to seek the adoption of the modern state system of separation of powers is to bargain for a deal inferior to the one they secured for themselves over the centuries of *their* history. The modern deal represents the power and sovereignty of the state, which we have seen—and will continue to see in the following chapters—to be working for its own perpetuation and interests. By contrast, the Sharīʿa did not—because it was not designed to—serve the ruler or any form of political power. It served the people, the masses, the poor, the downtrodden, and the wayfarer without disadvantaging the merchant and others of his ilk.[168] In this sense it was not only deeply democratic but humane in ways unrecognizable to the modern state and its law. If the test is "what ought to constitute inalienable rights *beyond the reach of any government*," to borrow Robert Dahl's words,[169] then the Sharīʿa passed that test, privileging the rule of law over that of the state. Accordingly, we may now also recognize a certain homonymy in the meaning of the formula "rule of law." In the Islamic context, the formula acquires a "thick" conception of what "rule of law" means, whereas in the Euro-American context—the location of the paradigmatic modern state—the conception is not only "thin" but also teeming with problems to boot.

We may say that the paradigmatic Sharʿī structures provided for what John Rawls called—in a different context—"a well-ordered society," a society that, he thought, was conceivable yet, as things stand at present, "highly idealized." Little did he know that every detail of his description of "a well-ordered society" not only obtained, *mutatis mutandis,* in paradigmatic Islamic governance but was also taken for granted:

> To say that a society is well-ordered conveys three things: first (and implied by the idea of publicly recognized conception of justice), it is a society in which everyone accepts, and knows that everyone else accepts, the very same principles of justice; and second (implied by the idea of the effective regulation of such conception), its basic structure—that is, its main political and social institutions and how they fit together as one system of cooperation—is publicly known, or with good reason believed, to satisfy these principles. And third, its citizens have a normally effective sense of justice and so they generally comply with society's basic institutions, which they regard as just. In such a society the publicly recognized conception of justice establishes a shared point of view from which citizens' claim on society can be adjudicated.
>
> This is a *highly idealized* concept. *Yet any conception of justice that cannot well order a constitutional democracy is inadequate as a democratic conception.*[170]

Here, Rawls could easily have been a distinguished Muslim jurist describing the *reality* of his own legal culture, perceptively commenting on the inadequacies of modern constitutional democracy.

4

The Legal, the Political, and the Moral

> A truly positive science could never apprehend moral truths because its own premises had eliminated their ontological foundations. In a world of primary qualities, "is" and "ought" simply fell apart. . . . All the empirical investigation in the world could not overcome this fundamental problem. No matter how many trips you make to the well, you won't bring up water with a sieve.
>
> —Thomas A. Sprangens Jr., *The Irony of Liberal Reason*

> The political begins when I can imagine myself sacrificing myself and killing others to maintain the state. The modern state has fully arrived not when it defends me against violence, but when it conscripts me into its armed force.
>
> —Paul W. Kahn, *Putting Liberalism in Its Place*

> Yes, a cunning device of Hell has here been devised, a horse of death jingles with the trappings of divine honours! Yes, a death for many has here been devised that glorifies itself as life. . . . I call it a state where everyone, good and bad, is a poison-drinker: the state where everyone, good and bad, loses himself: the state where universal slow suicide is called—life.
>
> —Friedrich Nietzsche, *Thus Spoke Zarathustra*

In the previous chapter, we saw that the claim of good government within the bounds of the modern state is weakened upon a closer examination of its constitutional organization. Insofar as the rule of law is concerned, paradigmatic Islamic governance has little to learn from its modern counterpart, given that the nature of the separation between and among the legislative, executive, and judicial powers in Islam was a more accurate embodiment of the meaning and purpose of such separation and clearly superior to what obtains in the paradigmatic modern state. When considering the effects of this highly meaningful rule of law in Islam, combined with the fact that the jurists and their law were grassroots products woven fully into the fabric of their civil society, the system of Islamic governance emerges, in comparative terms, as a distinctly more favorable expression of just and democratic rule.

This conclusion, evident to anyone familiar with the Sharīʿa and modern constitutional theory, invites further inquiry into constitutional organization and furthermore calls the Muslim desire for a modern state based on Islamic principles into serious question. But this is only one among several other cardinal difficulties that Muslims must deal with as they eagerly set out on the path to emulate the Western state. In this chapter, we introduce two more vexing problems, aggregately—and even severally—sufficient to cause serious alarm if not immediate abandonment of this journey.

The first problem is represented in the rise in modern Europe of the distinction, indeed separation, between Is and Ought. I shall call this problem the rise of the legal, the latter term bearing a particular significance. The second problem has to do with the rise of the political, articulated most effectively by the neo-Hobbesianism of Carl Schmitt. These phenomena are interrelated, both historically and substantively, and their context is one that relates to a particular conception and practice of domination. I will argue that the rise of the legal and the political in the modern project renders them incompatible with the constituent forms of *any* Islamic mode of governance, because they contravene even the minimum degree of moral fabric that *must* exist in any such governance in order for it to be meaningfully called Islamic.[1]

1. Morality and the Rise of the Legal

In his *Problems of a Sociology of Knowledge*, the German philosopher and sociologist Max Scheler avers that an essential characteristic of the modern West is "its obsession with gaining knowledge of control."[2] Science and learning are given a new trajectory, whose aim is to explain nature in a *detached* way, but this ultimately serves to channel their energies for the "utilization and control" of nature and all that is in it.[3] The characteristic is *structurally* tied to the Enlightenment notion of the autonomous self, captured as a modern paradigm by Kant's "What Is Enlightenment?"[4] For Kant, as for the emerging modern paradigm, individual and civilizational "maturity" is defined in terms of a profoundly autonomous impulse lodged in the Self, an impulse or will that not only directs one's moral and rational behavior but also, and more importantly, ensures autonomy. As Paul Guyer has argued, Kant's moral philosophy must be anchored in his foundational notion of freedom, which he regarded as "the quintessence of humanity":[5] freedom, that is, from the burdens of history, forms of authority, political oppression, material depredation, serfdom, corruption, and all those things we now know to have characterized European history for over a millennium prior to the Enlightenment. This freedom from authority, by reason of its detachment, is easily translated in practice into freedom to control and dominate.

Modern man, for Scheler, possesses an a priori will, an inherent "struggle for knowledge" that "grows out of an innate drive impulse."[6] What was seen as a disenchanted world by Weber[7] was taken by Scheler as proof that this "innate drive"[8] culminated in an all-inclusive "thought structure which has been the basis of all realistic thinking since the Renaissance," one that "sprung from an underlying, *a priori* will- and value-structure centred upon the desire to dominate the material world."[9] Compared with Eastern thought structures, Scheler argued that (and this is quite relevant for us) Western "metaphysics rests on an entirely different consciousness of self and entirely different interpretation of man himself, viz. as sovereign being *above* all of nature."[10] This inhering attribute of domination—having become "the decisive *axiological* element"; a "*systematic*," "not only occasional"[11] phenomenon; and a "*central value attitude*"—was the basis "from which the study of reality was undertaken."[12]

Scheler's theory, anticipating in this respect the work of the Frankfurt School[13] and Foucault's theories of discipline and power,[14] extended the modern Western trait of control and domination to the Self, which, together with nature, is "*conceived* as being controllable and manipulable . . . through politics, education, instruction, and organizations."[15] Domination thus was the paradigmatic attitude not only toward "brute" and "inert" matter[16] but also toward the Self, the human subject.[17] Scheler argued, furthermore, that

> the more recent history of the west and its independently developing cultural annexes (America, etc.) exhibits a systematic, increasingly one-sided and almost exclusive propensity to cultivate knowledge which aims at a possible practical transformation of the world. Cultural and religious knowledge has been pushed more and more into the background. . . . Internal life- and soul-techniques, that is to say the task of extending the power and domination of the will . . . over these processes of the psycho-physical organism[18] . . . has undergone a far-reaching involution. . . . Positivism and pragmatism are merely the honest, very one-sided philosophical expressions of this real state of modern Western culture.[19]

If Scheler—along with Bacon, Vico, Nietzsche, Foucault, and the Frankfurt School thinkers, among others—is right that the modern system of Western knowledge is programmatically geared to the service of power, discipline, domination, and transformation of the world, then to know, *stricto sensu*, is to engage in power and in transforming the world.[20] It was indeed the seventeenth-century Bacon himself who was the first to fashion the statement "knowledge is power."[21] No form of modern knowledge, including the legal and the political, can escape engagement with the dynamics of *this* type of power.

The organic connection between this thought structure of domination, on the one hand, and morality and values, on the other, is of immediate concern to us. The connection was forged early on in the Enlightenment, when the so-called mechanical philosophers, such as Boyle and Newton, began to emerge. Until then, but increasingly less and less, Europe was dominated by (that is to say, Europe's discursive formation was grounded in) modes of thought and conduct stemming from scholastic and Aristotelian ideas of matter driven by an intelligent, value-laden plan of motion. Bodies were thought to move by virtue of a world design animated by intent and infused with passion—an *anima mundi*. The seventeenth century produced a group of natural philosophers who reacted to the mechanical view of the world by asserting that nature has its own way of operating, which God had laid down in a working plan, after which he then left the scene, so to speak. Importantly, although God established this plan, He cannot be credited with an *ex nihilo* creation of the world. Nature just exists, is what it is, and is separated from actual creation, which is to say that the direct Catholic connection between creator and created had been erased, along with any connection between matter and spirit. But the mechanical philosophers went far beyond this position, arguing that matter is "brute," "inert," and even "stupid."[22] All spiritual agencies, or the *anima*, had been banished from the universe, rendering matter spiritually meaningless but still relevant in an anthropocentric, materialistic sense. If matter exists in a "brute" and "inert" form, then the only reason for its existence must be that of its service to man. Robert Boyle, a leading mechanical philosopher, represented his movement well when he elaborated the view that "man was created to possess and to rule over nature."[23]

Enlightenment mechanical philosophy emerged as paradigmatic, which is to say that modernity's attitude of domination toward nature led to the canonization of the notion of "natural resources,"[24] now thoroughly normalized in modernity's industrial social structures and government institutions and policies, not to mention every geography textbook taught in modern primary and secondary schools. "Natural resources"—a highly exploitative and violent discourse and practice—necessarily followed from denuding nature of all value. If nature is "brute" and "inert," then one can deal with it without any moral restraint, which is precisely what has happened since the early nineteenth century.

This is not all, however. The more important point in the isolation of matter as "brute" and "inert" is the resultant crucial phenomenon of separating fact from value, which is yet another major and *essential* factor in the modern project. If matter is, in itself, devoid of value, then we can treat it as an object. We can study it and subject it to the entire range of our analytical apparatus without it making any moral demands on us.[25] This separation allowed for the emergence of what has been called objective and detached science, which finds parallels in the academic fields of science, economics, business, law, history, etc.—all of which pretend to some sort of objectivity, always with the aspiration to be as detached and thus as "scientific" as pure science. In all of these disciplines, *fashioned and nourished by the modern state*,[26] the scholar can study the Other dispassionately, without it making any value-laden or moral demands on him. For to allow such demands to be made would contradict the weltanschauung,[27] the thought structure of domination in the first place.[28]

The modern state and its sovereign will, represented in the law, was not only an integral part of this weltanschauung but also one of its chief architects. By the beginning of the nineteenth century, when John Austin was writing his famous lectures on jurisprudence,[29] the state had become such a dominant legal reality that any respectable consideration of jurisprudence had to take serious account of the state's politicolegal project. This accounting for the state's role was of course already present in Hobbes,[30] who had argued that the only source of the law is the will of the sovereign. Law can achieve validity only by virtue of a government that has the power to command and to declare the law to be valid. If English judges make law, Hobbes asserted, it is by virtue of the fact that their legal findings and discoveries unravel the sovereign's will to power.[31] This was the beginning of the notion of political sovereign will. Furthermore, and as added background to the later rise of analytical positivism—generally regarded as having been founded by Austin himself—Hobbes considered the standards of ethical judgment to turn on man himself, not on an active agency of a cosmic order or divine plan. Moral rules are discovered by human reason, dictated by considerations of the well-being of society, of the importance of preserving life, and of curbing violence by one man against another.[32] To say that Hobbes' theory—i.e., that morality and ethics must rest on objective laws discovered by human reason, not on tradition or scriptural authority—ushered in the modern conception of the relationship between law and morality is to state what is now taken for granted in philosophical circles.

Transcending Hobbes—and even Hume and Bentham[33]—Austin brought the sovereign's law to the forefront of the debate over law and morality. He took strong exception, for instance, to Sir William Blackstone's thesis that no human law can be deemed valid if it should conflict with divine or natural law. "The existence of law," Austin declared, "is one thing; its merit or demerit is another. Whatever it be or be not is one enquiry; whether it be or be not conformable to an assumed standard, is a different enquiry. A law, which actually exists, is a law."[34] Blackstone, Austin writes, may have meant

> that all human laws ought to conform to the Divine law. If this be his meaning, I assent to it without hesitation [because] the obligations they impose are consequently paramount to those imposed by any other laws, and if human commands conflict with the Divine law, we ought to disobey the command which is enforced by the less powerful sanction; this is implied in the term *ought*; *the proposition is identical, and therefore perfectly indisputable*—it is our interest to choose the smaller and more uncertain evil, in preference to the greater and surer. If this be Blackstone's meaning, I assent to his *proposition*, and have only to object to it, that *it tells us just nothing*.[35]

What Blackstone must have meant, Austin writes, is that no human law that contradicts divine law *is* law. And if this were Blackstone's intention, Austin asserts, then it was nothing but "stark nonsense." As Austin points out, the most pernicious laws standing in opposition to the divine law "have been and are continually enforced as laws by judicial tribunals."[36]

Austin's sharp conceptual separation between the law of the sovereign and the moral law reflects the most fundamental tenet of legal positivists—such as the influential J. C. Gray, Justice Holmes, and others—who take it that law, irrespective of how immoral it may be, remains the valid law of a commanding sovereign.[37] The essential epistemological character of legal positivism is, then, the denial of a logical entailment or of any necessary connection between law as it *is* and law as it *ought* to be.[38]

This important distinction between Is and Ought is by no means uniquely Austinian. It has indeed permeated, in the most complex of ways, the fiber of modern moral philosophy. As Charles Taylor has cogently argued, "the fact/value split" has become "a dominant theme in our [twentieth] century" and has undergirded "a new understanding and valuation of freedom and dignity."[39] Representing a cornerstone of the Enlightenment project and expressed powerfully by the Kantian notion of autonomy,[40] freedom ceases to denote God's omnipotence and the capacity of absolute choice and becomes instead an expression of man's own natural powers of reasoning. Human reason, in the here and now, becomes the sole arbiter in the project of objectifying the world, of submitting it to its own demands, which are instrumentalist in the first order. The pursuit of happiness, utility, and much else that is subservient to these imperatives—such as preservation of life and protection of private property—become natural rights derivable from the natural order by what is/was seen as far-sighted, calculating reason. Formerly restricted by the power of revelation, reason now becomes free, expanding to overtake the authority of all scriptural competitors.[41]

The most central theme here is that the sources of reason—and thus of obligation, duty, and such notions as the Kantian categorical imperative[42]—now reside within the self, an inner human power,[43] not an intellectual emanation of a cosmic order (be it Aristotelian, Platonic, or otherwise) or an anthropological, Protagorean reality,[44] whence freedom, much like reason, breached its relations with an external world to become part of the self, originating and operating entirely within its confines. Human dignity now also attaches to the notion of sovereign reason, for dignity can be attained only by the realization of this sovereignty in the regulation of human affairs. This, I think, is the appeal of Kant's categorical imperative, an appeal that has absurdly persisted in Western philosophy overall, despite the fact that this same philosophical tradition simultaneously and effectively debunked Kant's arguments, showing them to be at best vacuous and at worst groundless.[45]

The Is/Ought dichotomy is therefore representative of the conflict between the instrumentalist manifestations of reason and, to a great extent, of the remnants of the Christian legacy of morality and virtue. This is precisely why, in an influential article, G. E. M. Anscombe made (and rightly so) the grave charge against Kant's notion of duty, that it is a Christian intrusion, a leftover from religious Europe that was surreptitiously allowed to wear an Enlightenment garb of reason within his notion of the categorical imperative.[46] What Anscombe argued in philosophy, Carl Schmitt, as we will see, argued in politics.[47] The Is/Ought distinction, as Nietzsche recognized,[48] is the outcome of particular historical circumstances, of a certain philosophical development that has given new meaning to the notions of dignity, freedom, and reason.[49] This is also why Charles Taylor asserted, along with Alasdair MacIntyre, that "the modern meta-ethics of [the] fact/value dichotomy does not stand as a timeless truth, at last discovered" in the way we have come to discover the "circulation of blood. It makes sense only within certain ethical outlooks."[50] But the fact is that it was—like much else in modernity—made to be a sort of timeless and, moreover, universal truth designed to "outrageously fix the rules of discourse in the interests of one outlook, forcing rival views into incoherence."[51] The outrageousness of this state of affairs stems not only from the biases involved and the suppression of competing philosophical narratives but also from the distinct likelihood of its being entirely false. Both Taylor and MacIntyre have advocated the contingent, contextual nature of the split and have argued that no moral reasoning can "do without modes of thinking which the split rules out."[52] Moreover, in some juristic circles it is now recognized that the nearly absolute distinction between Is and Ought—the result of Cartesian dualism—has generated and aggravated the crises in American and European legal theory.[53]

If the split between Is and Ought was initially and rudimentarily occasioned by Hobbes and Descartes, philosophically problematized by Hume,[54] and translated into legal positivism by Austin, it was Nietzsche who raised the positivist bar by effectively denying the validity of the split altogether, a denial not effected by harmonizing the two or at the expense of the fact side of the equation; rather, the denial was accomplished by sacrificing value, the Ought, which appears in his philosophy to be deprived of all worth. Nietzsche's concept of truth as it relates to his doctrine of the will to power makes the Ought entirely vacuous and illusory.[55] As Raymond Geuss has argued, Nietzsche thought it impossible to have a hold on "what 'ought' could conceivably mean at all," on "what non-illusory sense it might have for anyone to think that something 'ought' to be the case which in fact is not. . . . The world is just what it is, a huge, historically and spatially extended brute fact."[56]

Nietzsche, in other words, has taken Descartes' dualism to its most extreme conclusion. In many ways, Nietzsche turned European

Christian morality of the Thomist type right on its head: the organic connection between Ought and Is in Christendom was bifurcated in Descartes and Kant and obliterated altogether by Nietzsche. True, Austinian legal positivism did not go so far as Nietzsche's scheme, but it certainly allocated no real place for the moral in the law (a position slightly modified later by H. L. A. Hart's critics, who advocated what they called "internal" moralistic interventions in the law).[57]

Now, the distinction between Is and Ought in modern law, a flagrant standard, can never obtain in any form of Islamic governance if we insist on even a minimal moral definition of what Islam is or can be. As we will see, this minimum, however relative, far exceeds in density and texture the "internal" moralistic interventions in modern law.

In premodern Islamic tradition and its discourses, including its Qurʾān (obviously *the* founding text), the legal and the moral were not recognized as dichotomous categories, Is and Ought and fact and value being one and the same. The distinction did not exist in any of the ways we have come to draw them in the modern world. Nor did such a distinction exist in pre-Enlightenment Europe. The leading moral philosopher Alasdair MacIntyre has aptly observed that in Latin, the *lingua franca* of pre-Enlightenment Europe, as well as in ancient Greek, "there is *no* word correctly translated by our word 'moral'; or rather there is no such word until our word 'moral' is translated back into Latin," i.e., *moralis*.[58] The same is true of pre–nineteenth century Arabic—also the *lingua franca* of Sharīʿa and Islam—and, insofar as I know, of all other major premodern Islamic languages: the word "moral" has no precise equivalent and bears none of the major connotations we now associate with the term in moral and legal philosophy. Nowadays, many insist that the term *akhlāq* (as used by the ethicist Miskawayh and his ilk and also in semijuristic works)[59] is equivalent to our modern term "moral." On both historical and philosophical-linguistic grounds,[60] however, this claim may easily be falsified. As MacIntyre has observed with regard to the post-Enlightenment context, the same process of projecting the present onto the past and of retrieving a modernized past into the present took place in Islam as well. The "moral" was brought to bear upon the linguistic (not conceptual) repertoire of medieval Islam, retrieving from it *akhlāq* as an equivalent, if not as a synonym.[61]

If the term "moral" as we understand it in modernity did not exist in premodern Islam, then the distinction between the "moral" and the "legal" could not have existed, either in the Sharīʿa at large or in the Qurʾān in particular. One can argue even further, as I have done elsewhere,[62] that the very term "law" is ideologically charged with Foucauldian notions of surveillance, inconspicuous punishment, and hegemony over and subordination of the docile subject, all of which mechanisms of control (at the very least) make our modern notion of law, and therefore of morality, quite different from any earlier legal system and therefore from earlier notions of "law"—those of pre-sixteenth century Europe included. What is "legal" in the Qurʾān and in the Sharīʿa that was based on it is also equally "moral" and vice versa. In fact, we might even reverse the modern bias and argue (conceding for the moment to modern vocabulary)[63] that the legal was an organically derivative category of the moral, the latter being the archetype. Accordingly, to understand this moral archetype, we must uncover the massive legal contributions of the Qurʾān to the formation of Sharīʿa and hence to the fashioning of Muslim subjectivity.[64] We must understand and appreciate its moral message and moral structure as integral to, and as enveloping, its "legal" conception and discursive practice.

The Qurʾān, singularly retaining immense religious value for modern Muslims, has from the beginning provided Muslim believers with a cosmology entirely grounded in *moral* natural laws, a cosmology with perhaps far more persuasive power than any of its Enlightenment metaphysical counterparts and one that had powerful and deep psychological effects.[65] The Qurʾānic moral arsenal was thus embedded in a holistic system of belief, in a cosmology that *comprised* a metaphysic. In fact, it may be argued that this cosmology was itself part of an enveloping moral system that transcended the categories of theology, theosophy, and metaphysics. In this broadest sense of cosmology, we might argue that the Qurʾān offers no less than a theory of *cosmological morality* of the first order, which is to say that Qurʾānic cosmology is not only profoundly moral but is also itself constructed, both in form and content, out of a moral fiber. Everything that this universe contains was created for humans to enjoy, not in a utilitarian manner but rather in ways that show *deep*[66] moral accountability, translating into an acknowledgment that what we do we do for ourselves—certainly as individuals but, *more importantly*, as members of a social group. Actions, therefore, have universal consequences despite our, and their own, ephemeral existence.

The Qurʾānic narrative of creation, which bears upon the modes of human action and behavior, is single-mindedly geared toward laying down the foundations of moral cosmology. The heavens and the earth were brought into being according to the divine principle of Truth and Justice (*ḥaqq*), Sūrah 39:5, among many others, announces. Here, a strong conceptual connection is forged with the profoundly significant declaration, made in the same Sūrah two verses earlier, that the Qurʾān itself was likewise revealed on account of the same principle of Justice (39:2). The message of the Qurʾān, destined to a human society, is therefore an extension, if not an integral part, of the entire project of creation, sanctioned, moreover, by the same rules and principles.

Yet God's creativity is not only about bringing into existence the colossal and magnificent universe *ex nihilo* but, more often and ultimately, about His secondary laws of generation and corruption.[67] The marvel of macroscopic creation is posited largely as the background against which colorful and lively microevents of creation and "creative" destruction are elaborated in a nearly infinite manner. Here, the physical world is not a scientific site subject to cold and bland rational explanation and calculation but rather a natural world saturated with spirituality and psychology, one wholly subservient to moral actions taken by the very humans that were created by God.[68] If mountains tremble,[69] seas split,[70] and "nations" are abruptly wiped from the face of this earth,[71] it is all because of moral failure or, at least, because of morally precipitated laws of nature. The same is true of the rise and setting of the sun,[72] the boon of plowed fields and good earth,[73] famines,[74] earthquakes,[75] storms,[76] and the consequent devastation of the earth's produce. *Everything* in the universe "runs with an appointed term" (*kullun yajrī ilā ajalin musammā*),[77] a term whose end arrives with the Day of Judgment, the Day of Reckoning, when the Divine Scales will weigh, for everyone, even the smallest acts one had performed, those "atoms of good" that will be measured against the "atoms of evil."[78]

The Qurʾānic laws of nature are thus moral and not physical. They are set in motion for explicable, rational reasons, but these reasons are ultimately grounded in moral laws. If things come into being or evaporate into nothingness, it is because the moving force—the philosophers' Prime Mover—is determined by the moral design. The entire enterprise of creation, re-creation, and death—that is, the series of laws governing the operation of the universe—is specifically designed by divine munificence and power for the *single purpose of challenging humans to do good.* This Qurʾānic narrative of "doing good" is all pervasive, and it is captured most potently in the opening verses of Sūrah 67 (aptly titled Sūrat al-Mulk, or Sovereignty), where God's omnipotence is causally and exclusively tied to the natural project of generation and corruption, which is in turn causally connected to the challenge God poses to humans to undertake good works: "Blessed is He the possessor of

Sovereignty, the Omnipotent, He who created death and life that He may try you: which of you is best in conduct; and He is Almighty, All-Forgiving."[79] The Qur'ān, before any Sharī'a came into being, had already succeeded in establishing an extraordinary benchmark by which all human conduct is evaluated with exclusive reference to a divinely grounded moral principle.[80]

In commenting on Sūrah 30, M. Pickthall observes that the prophecies in this Sūrah are

> only the prelude to a proclamation of God's universal kingdom, which is shown to be an actual sovereignty. The laws of nature are expounded as the laws of Allah in the physical world, and in the moral and political spheres mankind is informed that there are similar laws of life and death, of good and evil, action and inaction, and their consequences—laws which no one can escape by wisdom or by cunning. . . . Those who do good earn His favor, and those who do ill earn His wrath, no matter what may be their creed or race; and no one, by the lip of profession of a creed, is able to escape His law of consequences.[81]

The law of consequences is thus the law of nature, put in the service of accomplishing the greatest grade of good. *Life and living are in effect the ultimate test*, for the Qur'ān is abundantly clear as to why man was created: "We have placed all that is in the earth as an ornament thereof that We may try them: which of them is best in conduct."[82] Ignorance may lead some people away from this truth, rendering them—despite the fact that they are always given a second chance to repent and join the Straight Path[83]—incapable of comprehending the test's importance. The laws of nature are designed to serve the promotion of good in, as well as the elimination of evil from, this world: good-doers (*muṣliḥūn*) are blessed with God's bounties, which range from abundantly productive land—naturally irrigated—to pleasant living and healthy and happy families and children. The abundance of the earth and good family and social surroundings are replaced in the Hereafter by equally wondrous existence. In other words, the Hereafter is the continuation of this life,[84] with a difference: this life continues to be a long test aimed at persuading the evildoers (*mufsidūn, mujrimūn*) to change their ways, to repent, unless, of course, they belong to the hopeless and hapless wrongdoers who invite an immediate judgment in the Here and Now. The Hereafter, on the other hand, awaits the results of this test; it is the place where people are classified once and for all. The fire of Hell is the perfected equivalent of storms and earthquakes that destroyed hopeless "nations," while Paradise represents the actualized supreme ideal of good earthly living. The laws of nature are thus everywhere, operative both in this life and in the hereafter, although they may present themselves in various forms according to need. But whatever the laws of nature may be, they are ultimately God's laws that He designed and installed with a view to accomplishing a moral purpose in the world. Nothing other than doing—and being—good seems to matter.

If God's laws of nature are grounded primarily—if not entirely and exclusively—in conative moral principles, then the universe is imbued with, and woven from, a moral fiber whose warp and woof are designed to promote good and suppress evil (*al-amr bil-maʿrūf wal-nahy ʿan al-munkar*).[85] This conativeness dictates that, as part of the indefinable omnipotence through which God created the World, there must be, and therefore there is, an omniscience whose main trajectory and ultimate task is the implementation of the moral laws of nature. If the laws are intelligent, so are the forces by which they are set in motion and operation. If it is important for God to be *the* All-Listener and *the* All-Knowing, it is precisely because He has an omnipresent net of surveillance that knows of and evaluates the smallest act, although He does so not only in accordance with moral laws but also, and primarily, for the sake of the human social order.

But what exactly does God want from His human creatures? Why does He repeatedly urge them to believe in Him? What does it mean to believe, or to be a believer (*muʾmin*), in the first place? Answers to these questions are answers that the Sharīʿa jurists arrived at, which explains the obvious fact that the ethic of the Qurʾān not only pervaded the Sharīʿa *but also constituted it.* To begin with, being Self-Sufficient and All-Powerful, God does not really need humankind, although, strikingly, He is explicitly grateful (*shakūr*)[86] for their good deeds. This gratefulness, which stems from His kindness and mercy (*raḥma*), should not be mistaken as a reflection of any favors that human beings do for Him. If anything, He is the Bounty-giver (*Razzāq*)[87] Who has "honored the children of Adam" and Who "carried them on the land and the sea, giving them distinct preference over many of those whom [He] created."[88] All forms of human subsistence, indeed, their very existence, are owed to Him, to His boundless mercy and giving. The Qurʾānic God expects humankind to be appreciative of His blessings and all that He created for humanity to enjoy and cherish. What He dislikes is not only a lack of appreciation but also misconduct and abuse (*ṭughyān*) of these gifts and blessings.[89] Such misconduct and abuse are indeed expressions of this lack of appreciation. Those "abusers" and, therefore, deniers of God's graces and bounties are the oppressors (*ṭāghūn*, *kāfirs*). As Izutsu has convincingly argued, the conceptual derivatives of *K.F.R.* are among the most outstanding vocabularies in the Qurʾān, with a "semantic field" that engenders the deepest and richest relationship to the concept of "belief" (*īmān*),[90] another central Qurʾānic concept. To be a *kāfir*, a nonbeliever, is to deny God's good works in nature, to deny the blessings (*niʿam*; sing., *niʿma*) that humans live by and experience in every moment of their existence, and to behave badly toward other people and things, which is to say that one is behaving badly toward God's work and creation. Human beings thus owe God the duty of *genuine* appreciation (*shukr*), the indicant and measure of belief.

Thus, to be a true believer (*muʾmin*), a genuine Muslim (*min al-muslimīn*), is to appreciate the facts of having been born (*khuliqa/khalq*); of having been given family solidarity, family love, and compassion (*dhawī al-qurbā*); of having received the gifts of food and pleasant beverages, especially the simplest boon of life-giving water; in sum, of enjoying all the blessings of the world that surround humankind by virtue of God's infinite generosity. To behave badly toward any of these God-given gifts is not only to be thankless or to deny (*yakfur/kāfir*) God's Signs (*āyāt*) but also to transgress (*mujrim*, *ẓālim*).[91] And the Qurʾān makes it all too obvious that a transgressor's final lodging is in less than a pleasant abode (*yuṣlā nāran . . . wa-sāʾat maṣīrā*).[92]

We have thus far remarked on the Qurʾānic conceptual dichotomy and antonymic distinction between believing/*īmān* and disbelieving/*kufr*. He who does not deny God's blessings and His sole sovereignty is a believer. But what is it that constitutes the Qurʾānic believer, the *muʾmin*, beyond his or her full acknowledgment of, and gratitude for, God's blessings? Any perceptive reader of the Qurʾān will immediately note the heavy emphasis placed throughout the text on the "act of performing good" (*yaʿmalūn al-ṣāliḥāt*).[93] In its different variants, it occurs at least 120 times, without counting other conceptual cognates such as *khayrāt* and *aḥsana/ḥasanāt* (e.g., "*taṭawwaʿa khayran*," "*mā yafʿal min khayr*," "*man jāʾa bil-ḥasana*," all of which mean "to do good").[94] It is one of the most common and oft-repeated expressions in the Qurʾānic repertoire.

Ṣāliḥāt is conceptually associated with *ajr*, the latter meaning a "fee," "reward," "remuneration." Those who perform *ṣāliḥāt* will enter paradise, as many verses attest.[95] But the conceptual relationship here is also significantly contractual. *Īmān* must be proven, and only good works can be the effectual means. Once performed as solid proof of *īmān*, the *ṣāliḥāt* will yield an *ajr*, resulting from performance. Thus, God in effect makes a contractual offer (amounting to calling the individual to Islam), and the believer enters into a covenant/contract/*ʿahd* with God should he accept God's offer. The entitlement to the *ajr*, the consideration, is the very fact of performance, but the consideration itself is a ticket to Paradise. Hence the inviolability of the logical and epistemological connection between belief/*īmān* and good works/*ṣāliḥāt*. Izutsu, who conducted the most detailed and serious research on Qurʾānic semantics, avers that "the strongest tie of semantic relationship binds *ṣāliḥ*[*āt*] and *īmān* into an almost inseparable unit. . . . Where there is *īmān* there are *ṣāliḥāt* or, 'good works,' so much so that we may almost feel justified defining the former in terms of the latter, and the latter in terms of the former."[96] There is thus an inextricable organic and structural relationship between "belief" and "good conduct." If one entails the other, then there is also an immediate logical and epistemic connection between them, which is to say that the presence of belief apodictically entails the presence of good works and vice versa. To believe in God as the sole sovereign is at once to accept, as Izutsu soundly puts it, a "whole practical code of conduct"[97] that is heavily geared toward "good works."

As intimated earlier, the Qurʾānic ethic centering on good works did not only pervade the Sharīʿa to the core, shaping its warp and woof, but also remained central for Muslims' popular practice throughout the centuries and until today. Yet the Qurʾān does not constitute law in a technical sense, which the Sharīʿa most certainly does. It consists of a relatively plain narrative, devoid of any intricate lines of legal reasoning that were created and developed by the later jurists of Islam. But this is in no way to say that this body of legal reasoning, as impressive as it may be, created a distinction between the legal and the moral. We must always bear in mind that the modern distinction was occasioned by a particular view of domination and power, as we have already seen. It reflected the recognition of the "Is-ness" of the political, earthly sovereign. The "Is-ness" was a political and sociological construct, not a divine will, squarely anchored in and calculated by cosmic moral design. Even if Sharīʿa's law at times looks and sounds as if it treats the world with technical, razor-sharp legal rigor, the master principles that such technical reasoning served were ethical ones. This is not to say that there is a perfect identity between the Qurʾānic ethic and that of the Sharīʿa, but it is to say, emphatically, that if it is true—as many philosophers have already noted—that the distinction is modern, then the Sharīʿa could not have known it. But this is an argument by implication. More directly, there is absolutely nothing in the Sharīʿa and in premodern Islam as a whole to give rise to this distinction. And any argument that such a distinction existed in the Sharīʿa is one that ignores not only the thrust of the Sharīʿa as an ethical project but also both the quality and significance of the modern European political and legal divide between Is and Ought,[98] thus navigating at the surface of this profoundly, and now universally, systemic distinction.

Paradigmatic modern law is positive law, the command of the fiction of sovereign will. Islamic law is not positive law but substantive, principle-based atomistic rules that are pluralistic in nature and ultimately embedded in a cosmic moral imperative. For Muslims today to adopt the positive law of the state and its sovereignty means in no uncertain terms the acceptance of a law emanating from political will, a law made by men who change their ethical and moral standards as modern conditions require. It is to accept that we live in a cold universe that is ours to do with as we like. It is to accept that the ethical principles of the Qurʾān and of centuries-old morally based Sharīʿa be set aside in favor of changing manmade laws, laws that have sanctioned nothing less than the domination and destruction of the very nature that God has given humankind to enjoy with moral accountability. Whether to accept or not to accept is a question that only Muslims can answer for themselves. Our own point, however, is that—observed from a distance—Muslims have very little reason to opt for the modern state's law, when they have enjoyed a legal culture that has insisted for more than twelve centuries on a law paradigmatically structured and fleshed out by an overarching moral source.[99]

2. Sacrifice and the Rise of the Political

The rise of the legal state (with its positivist outlook) was accompanied by the rise of the political, a distinctly Schmittian concept that has both disturbed and captivated political and legal thinking for over half a century.[100] Fundamentally, Schmitt was Hobbesian in his overreaching and controlling doctrine that power, earthly political power, was the new God.[101] The genealogy of the political, like that of the legal, lies at the moment when Is was divorced from Ought,[102] when politics began to exist and strove for its own sake. Power and positivist norms became inseparable, just as the political and the legal became a near, if not total, identity within the state. "In the world as it is, the final arbiter of things political is power and not morality."[103]

The political is not a distinct field of power relations, nor is it just a matter of politics, economy, ethics, or science. The political is an all-encompassing, pervasive phenomenon that intrudes upon all fields, upon existence itself. The political is the name of an age, just as other ages are characterized as "bronze" or "technological." It is a field of action that "pervades the whole of life,"[104] and any enquiry into it amounts to an enquiry about the modern "order of human things."[105] The violent nature of the political, exclusively and specifically framed within the theoretical context of killing or being killed, allows it—nay forces it—to draw on all other fields for support, subsuming them in the process.[106]

Violence constitutes the main and most reliable source of power in the realm of the political.[107] The political is therefore the highest manifestation in the modern project of the separation between Is and Ought and between fact and value. More than the modern legal and ethical spheres—two fields that struggle, however unsuccessfully, with notions of justice and moral good—the political is exclusively and adamantly concerned with "what is,"[108] with a Nietzschean world just as it is, "a huge, historically and spatially extended brute fact."[109]

The quintessentially defining feature of the political is the distinction between friend and enemy, a distinction that shapes the form and content of politics. The distinction also gives the political its status as an autonomous sphere and a central domain,[110] subordinating all else, since it is about life and death. In other words, the political arises precisely at the moment the distinction is born, when a society begins to conceive of its existence as one of violence and war, as being in a "state of nature" where survival is constantly at stake. "The political is the most intense and extreme antagonism, and every concrete antagonism becomes that much more political the closer it approaches the most extreme point, that of the friend-enemy grouping."[111] Violence and enmity are the substrates of the political as well as its potential, but the distinction of friend-enemy is its ever-present and realized constitution. Violence and enmity may subside and rise, but the distinction is both omnipresent and *always* materialized. That violence and war erupt at times but not always does not make the exception any less an overarching and imminent reality. For it is from this state of exception that the political not only derives its meaning but finds its own raison d'être. Political behavior is thus shaped under the spell of this state of exception, and, being autonomous, the political defines and colors all other spheres of human action.

Although Schmitt's concept of the political is profoundly Hobbesian, he differs from Hobbes in one important respect. Whereas Hobbes was largely concerned with the internal body politic and with developing a theory of earthly sovereignty, Schmitt is mainly interested in the outer realm of the body politic, where "one fighting collectivity of people confronts a similar collectivity."[112] The state for him is only one player in the field of the political, although he does not doubt that it remains the most central one.[113] The state is not only the "sole subject of politics" but also its "bearer."[114] This being the case, the Schmittian political is a fruitful site of analysis, especially in the context of the relationship between the state—as the most significant location of the political—and the citizen.

The citizen is a multilayered concept. We will deal with one significant (psychological) aspect of the concept in the next chapter, but another (political) aspect we must discuss now. We take it for granted that no one can live outside of citizenship, for no one can find an independent space outside of the state. There is no neutral site between one state and another and nothing that allows a human being to be just a human being, one without political, state-based affiliation. The citizen therefore is as much of the state as the state is of the citizen; they are as conceptually linked with each other as the implications residing in the concepts of "parent" and "child," since one demonstratively entails the other. Furthermore, while it is immaterial for us to decide on whether nationalism is the cause or effect of the Schmittian ontological distinction, it does matter for us that if the nation-state is by definition made of the nation, then the citizen, who makes and is made by the nation—at least logically and fictionally—squarely belongs to the state.

It is a key concern of ours—in this chapter and the next—that the modern subject is by definition a nationalized entity, a subject that identifies with the nation as a way of life.[115] If the state is the location of the nation, and if nationalism is a defining form of politics,[116] then the citizen must be comfortably located within the political. To be a citizen therefore is to conceive of oneself as the site of the political as a way of life. It is also to identify the self with the state as the sovereign representation of one's nation. The citizen constructs the political meaning of his or her citizenship by virtue of accepting and absorbing, well-nigh as a second nature, the meaning of the state, of territory, and of the greater family—the nation.[117] One implication of this epistemic-psychological assimilation is that it is inherent to the citizen to view the self, his own *citizenship*, as possessing the capacity to sacrifice himself for the state. The conception of this capacity is inextricably tied to the Schmittian distinction, since, as Kahn put it, "only the political has the power over life and death. . . . The political begins when I can imagine myself sacrificing myself and killing others to maintain the state. The modern state has fully arrived not when it defends me against violence, but when it conscripts me into its armed forces."[118] The full meaning of citizen and citizenship is therefore not one that emerges by virtue of birth or a formal affiliation with the state and its nation but rather one that constitutes itself by the readiness for self-sacrifice. This readiness is taken for granted by the state; it is a potential that is embedded in the nation qua nation and in its members as citizens. Schmitt summed it up in horrifying terms when he wrote: "With each newly born child a new world is born. God willing, each newly born child will be an aggressor."[119]

The haunting image of the Schmittian state of exception arrogates to the state the license to kill or have its citizens killed for its own sake. But this killing, as Kahn argued, can never be

> justified on the grounds of any moral calculus. The fundamental moral message of the West is that there shall be no killing: "Thou shalt not kill." But the politics of the West has been a long story of killing and sacrifice. This was not just the story of colonization of non-Western populations, but also of the mass sacrifice by Western states of their own political communities in the wars of the nineteenth and twentieth centuries. As Michael Waltzer writes, "surely there has never been a more successful claimant of human life than the state."[120]

It is the state as "a successful claimant of human life" that generated this massive level of violence. It is the conceivability of the conscription of "each" of Schmitt's "newly born children" that created both the possibility and reality of this violence. And all this is, in effect, for the purpose of the state and for the purpose of its self-perpetuation.

If the modern state is also the embodiment of the legal and its positivism, as was argued in this chapter; if its constitutional structures in their best form are no more than a weak representation of the rule of law (chapter 3); and if it is the new God that commands life and death by virtue of a positivist, sovereign legal will, then dying for it presents a significant conceptual problem in the context of an Islamic state. In other words, how can Muslims aspiring to build an Islamic state justify sacrifice for a state that could not and cannot subscribe to the moral, that could not and cannot commit except, at best, to an amoral way of being, to positivism, facticity, and Is-ness?

As a moral entity, the modern state has proven unsupportable even in theory. The failure of Hegel's theory of the ethical state and the oblivion to which it was sent by political scientists and most philosophers is a case in point.[121] Such theories fly so much in the face of state realities that they have no place except for providing intellectual play. The modern state cannot be constructed on ethical grounds, nor can it ontologically operate as a moral entity. It "does not seek to enter the moral realm,"[122] nor is it its duty "to make us good."[123] Any moral argument adduced in politics and in the framework of state domination is, in the final analysis, nothing but a political argument, a way to legitimize "political ambition."[124] Nietzsche went as far as to describe it as "the coldest of all cold monsters . . . whatever it says, it lies—and whatever it has, it has stolen."[125] If half of this much is accepted, then how can the concept of the citizen's sacrifice be reconciled with the paradigm of Islamic governance that we charted earlier? (The question, the reader will note, assumes that the concept of citizen is posited as acceptable to the modern Islamic state, but as we will discover in the next chapter, this concept is itself riddled with serious problems and therefore can in no way be taken for granted.) In other words, how does the concept of sacrifice for the sake of an amoral entity fit within a context of Islamic governance? The answer, relatively simple, is that Islam never knew the concept of conscription. Nor did it, in any effective way, command life and death for anyone's sake, *not even for the sake of God.* The very concept of conscription as potential sacrifice was unknown. And as we will see shortly, there was nothing in *jihād,* the chief theory of war and peace, to command this sacrifice.

Executive sultanism, effectively the military branch, depended on slave-soldiers whose lives and careers were consecrated to the business of war and violence. These soldiers were purchased or snatched from their families; trained according to individual capability as foot soldiers, cavalry, military scribes, or commanders; and spent their lives in the service of the sultan as paid employees (through stipends, land allocation, etc.). They also generally lived apart from the civil population, leading a different lifestyle, and many did not even speak the local language. On the other hand, the ordinary Muslim normally did not engage in war, and the only venue by which he was permitted by the Sharīʿa to do so was through *jihād*.

The Sharīʿa juristic works, long and short, always insisted on the distinction between two types of *jihād* (commonly translated as "holy war"): mandatory and optional (respectively, *farḍ ʿayn* and *farḍ kifāya*).[126] However, in the conception of the Sharīʿa, not every war or battle was one of *jihād*. Since Muslim sultans and kings (*mulūk*) warred on each other more often than they did on non-Muslims, many wars and battles never qualified as *jihād*, and they remained the business of these sultans, kings, and their slave-soldiers. In fact, the great majority of times, they occurred at quite a distance from the civil populations. But when the war was launched on non-Muslims as an offensive act, the jurists insisted that participation in the *jihād* be optional;[127] that is, those who could and wanted to join might do so, bringing with them their own weapons.[128] The option to withdraw from the *jihād* campaign remained valid until the moment the call for battle was announced—but not after, for once preparation for battle was initiated, the *jihād*ist was bound to stay and fight.[129]

However, if *jihād* is defensive—defined as a situation in which non-Muslim armies conquer or attempt to conquer Muslim populations (not just vacant land)—then it becomes an individual duty.[130] The duty does not extend to all Muslims (who must be male and of age) within the dynastic territory but only to those living close by the threatened area.[131] Underlying this conception of *jihād*—especially after the eighth century—is always the tacit assumption that the mainstay and core military forces are not the civilians who join the *jihād* effort but the ranks of the slave-soldiers in the paid service of executive sultanism. (This historical reality comes to full life in the multivolume works of Islamic history, one example being the accounts of the repeated efforts of Egyptian sultans to curb the Crusading armies invading Cairo and Damietta.)[132]

While acknowledging *jihād* as an important obligation, the Muslim jurists, without exception, did not privilege it over mundane obligations. Debtors, for instance, could not join the *jihād* campaign, whether defensive or offensive, without permission from the lender.[133] Here, a private obligation clearly overrides the duty to partake in *jihād*. Moreover, men wishing to join the campaign had to obtain the permission of their parents.[134] Respect and deference to one's parents "has priority over *jihād*,"[135] because "if *jihād* is in principle an optional duty, then someone else can substitute for him who could not [secure the permission of parents]."[136] In other words, as "private" persons, parents could veto the right of *jihād* (and thus any governmental order) to claim their son. Not only that, but if the parents change their mind after granting permission, their son must still withdraw and return home if preparations for battle have not started.[137] Furthermore,

> fighting the non-Muslim enemy was not ordained in the Sharīʿa for its own sake, because in essence fighting is a cause of harm and damage. Rather, it was decreed for another reason, namely, rendering victorious the Word of God and rebuffing the aggression of the enemy. Thus if fighting is accomplished through the participation of some Muslims, then the others are absolved of this duty. . . . For if *jihād* had been imposed as an incumbent duty upon every Muslim individual, then both religion and worldly affairs will come to utter ruin. This has been the practice since the days of the Prophet and until these days of ours.[138]

Moreover, if Muslims were to fight every power who transgressed against them and every enemy who has remitted Muslims into bondage, then "we [Muslims] will be preoccupied by fighting all of our lives, and will inevitably neglect our worldly affairs. This is why there is consensus among Muslims throughout [the centuries] that such [an endeavor] will not be pursued . . . and consensus is the most evincive of legal proofs."[139]

Two final points must be made: First, *jihād* is not a state law but a morally anchored set of prescriptions whose violation is a matter of conscience, and second, even when *jihād* is deemed obligatory on every adult male Muslim, the obligation remains a moral one, and thus there is no prescribed earthly punishment in the Sharīʿa for refusal to join the war effort, except for the threat of losing credit in the Hereafter.[140] This is a far cry from the modern state's punitive measures intended for those who refuse conscription, not to mention deserters. In this latter context, it is instructive that leaving the *jihād* battle (so-called deserting) was legally permitted if certain conditions obtained, including tiredness, the collapse or death of the cavalryman's horse, or even in cases where the enemy forces outnumber Muslim fighters.[141]

3. The Moral Dimension: A Concluding Remark

We cannot sufficiently emphasize the importance of the conclusion, to be further elaborated in the next chapter, that it is the modern state that fashions the identity of that historically unique subject, the citizen; Islamic governance, significantly defined by Sharᶜī values, fashions a drastically different identity of its subject, one that does not know the political and therefore the political meaning of sacrifice. Sacrifice in paradigmatic Islamic governance was a moral duty imposed exclusively in the context of self-defense and unfettered by stern conscription laws. It was largely a matter of individual choice. When it was undertaken, it did not derive its meaning from a love for the nation or even for the Community as the site of the political but rather from a moral meaning whose anchors were the moral subjectivity of the individual, the atomic unit that makes up the aggregate of the Community as the central domain of the moral.[142] The Sharīᶜa, the paradigm of Islamic "legislative" power, did not possess a political will, at least nothing comparable to the will of the state. The Sharīᶜa was about society and far less about politics; it was about the moral social character, not political society, one of many secondary concerns. The modern project represents and constitutes, in the living realities of the contemporary Muslim world, a profound transformation from the age of legal morality to the age of the political. In modernity, politics and the political are everywhere, and they rule the day.[143]

Whereas the discursive world of Islam and its forms of knowledge were pervaded by moral prescriptions and by Sharīᶜa-prescribed ethical behavior, it has now become permeated by positivism, politics, and the political, by concepts of citizenship and political sacrifice. While the law of the modern state forces the citizen to "give his energy and life for the state," he "could not be under any moral obligation to do so. The glory of a high ethical ideal, that has always transfigured the death for the fatherland, then would fade. Why should the individual sacrifice himself for the welfare of others who are equal to him?"[144] The answer to this question cannot yield any sense without seeing the citizen as a subjectivity fashioned in the service of a state that was not only made of war[145] but also one that perpetuates it, in the process marshalling the citizen to offer the most precious sacrifice. The controlling interrogative syllogism here is: If the state can only recognize "facts" and the Is, constituted as it is by a world largely devoid of value and moral impulse, and if the state draws, through the law, on its citizens' lives and energy to fight for, and in, this valueless *mundus*, then does it mean that the citizen sacrifices himself for the sake of a state that knows no value, no moral imperative, and no good beyond its own? This is a question that contemporary Muslims must face, squarely and without mitigation, although Muslims—as we will continue to see—do not face this question alone.

5

The Political Subject and Moral Technologies of the Self

> Technologies of the self . . . permit individuals to effect by their own means, or with the help of others, a certain number of operations on their own bodies and souls, thoughts, conduct, and way of being, so as to transform themselves in order to attain a certain state of happiness, purity, wisdom, perfection, or immortality. . . . *For us now, this notion is rather obscure and faded.*
>
> —Foucault, "Technologies of the Self"

> What did you learn in school today
> Dear little boy of mine?
> I learned our government must be strong!
> It's always right and never wrong!
> Our leaders are the finest men!
> And we elect them again and again.
> I learned that war is not so bad.
> I learned of the great ones we have had.
> What did you learn at school today . . .
>
> —Tom Paxton, "What Did You Learn at School Today?"

> The state . . . robs men of themselves.
>
> —Johann Gottfried Herder

Every society, be it tribal, urban, or otherwise, knows and integrates into its structures one form of discipline or another. No society can live without an ordering apparatus that, by necessity, requires some type of discipline. But disciplinary forms are as numerous as the societies that live by them. Their multiplicity notwithstanding, all but one share a common characteristic, namely, their organic constitution. All but one developed over many centuries or even millennia, allowing social, spiritual, moral, economic, and "political" factors to blend in slowly and even imperceptibly, creating in the process internal systems of checks and balances that were driven by an internally developing and socially based logic. Even when war devastated such communities, they in time regrouped and resumed their ways of living more or less as these existed before. Premodern societies—i.e., prestate social formations and outside of Europe—were largely autonomous and self-regulated in social terms and rarely and thinly penetrated in bureaucratic terms. Apart from the distant presence of the ruler and his unsystematic attempts to tax them, societies practiced self-rule.

It is undeniable that these traditional societies differed from one another significantly, yet for all their dissimilarities, they still differed considerably more from the discipline and order of the modern state's social creation. Our concern in this chapter lies in these differences only insofar as they contribute to the formation of particular subjects. From this angle, we contend that the modern state systems of order and discipline are unique in human history, producing individuals whose subjectivities are unprecedented. If the state is a uniquely European product (as is almost universally agreed), and if the state is overarching in its control over its population (and here a few would disagree), then the subjectivities produced by the state systems must also be unique. It is precisely the quality or qualities of these subjectivities and whether they are compatible with those produced by Islamic governance that is our concern here.

1. The Production of State Subjects

Like the separation of powers, positivism, and the Enlightenment's distinction between Is and Ought, the form of discipline produced by the European state was unique, geared as it was toward fashioning the subjectivity of the new citizen who recognizes himself in the state and is willing to die for it. If, in origin, the state was a uniquely European phenomenon, so was its offspring, the citizen. Distinctively and exclusively European, the genealogy of European state discipline was inextricably tied to the rise of powerful monarchs whose main concern had been to tighten their hold over their populations while enriching their coffers. They had sponsored and promoted colonizing ventures that brought home much gold and silver—wealth that later supported an Industrial Revolution that capitalized on these gains, exponentially increasing profits and the accumulation of capital. Corollary with these developments, the urban populations grew by leaps, leaving wide segments of the population impoverished, all this while the upper classes watched their wealth grow with the support of, and in partnership with, the now emerging constitutional monarch. This was precisely the context that allowed Marx to insist that the state represents the rule of the bourgeoisie over the proletariat, the impoverished, rights-deprived laborers.[1]

Flagrant social and economic disparities, working conditions beyond appalling, and monarchical rule barely emerged from the age of absolutism all gave rise to mob violence and unruly urban populations, which in turn induced the state to introduce an organized and well-staffed police apparatus that not only maintained a presence in these urban areas but extended its sway into the countryside, which had formerly been beneath the radar of rulers. By the later part of the nineteenth century, no village, town, or city could escape the watchful eye of this apparatus. And to reinforce the policing apparatus, an unprecedented, colossal prison system was created.[2] But crude physical force was not enough, and this the European rulers understood. The population had to be educated in the ways of good conduct, and good conduct meant social order and, in a thoroughly capitalist system, an ability to work and produce. Discipline thus translated into a site in which the subject was corralled into a system of order and instrumental utility. The system that was adopted to accomplish this regulative mechanism was the school, which began to spring up everywhere in various forms, and concurrent with the consolidation of the police apparatus, the school became a standard social fixture by the end of the nineteenth century. Legislated as mandatory (literally coercing parents to send their children to schools on pain of imprisonment), primary education forced the great majority of Europe's children into a regimented system where certain ideas and ideals were drilled into their minds. The days of learning within the family or church were gone forever. Still, policing and schooling were not enough: poverty in the wake of the Industrial Revolution intensified, and social discontent became ever more evident. Vividly remembering the French Revolution and its causes of discontent, reformers, politicians, and rulers quickly realized that poverty could lead to another revolution, one that might snatch both political power and economic privilege from under their feet. Quickly enough, state welfare systems began to be established in all of the European countries, creating a social safety net and, even more importantly, public health institutions and specialized hospitals.[3]

On an epistemic level, the institutions of coercive surveillance, education, and health (prisons, schools, and hospitals) were neither distinct from one another nor neutral in any sense. They each worked in a specialized domain, but they worked together, having come into existence in the wake of a pervasive bureaucratic machinery that possessed distinct ideological claims. Schools, armies, hospitals, and prisons constituted systemic manifestations of an elaborate and highly specific way of doing and ordering things,[4] which explains why the techniques used to implement them were rapidly circulated from one institution to the next and, in fact, from one European country to the next.[5] Extensive regulations, shaped by empirical, calculated (not to mention calculating) methods, were applied to these institutions for the purpose of disciplining the operations of the body. They reflected the two major concerns of submission and utility, that is, submission to a regulating technique that engenders docility and, on the other hand, utility as a materially productive performance. From both perspectives, the body was not only a site of empirical analysis but also of intelligibility. It had become colonizable and as such capable of manipulation and analysis, of being shaped according to a particular will so that through it certain desired effects could be produced.

This particular will was novel, for it issued not from the internal volition of the subject or the local community (a characteristic of the premodern world) but from an external force, a political will that located itself outside it. As Foucault noted, the

> human body was entering a machinery of power that explores it, breaks it down and rearranges it. A "political anatomy," which was also a "mechanics of power," was being born; it defined how one may have a hold over others' bodies, not only so that they may do what one wishes, but so that they may operate as one wishes, with the techniques, the speed and the efficiency that one determines.[6]

The pervasive techniques of surveillance and the administrative regulations thus flowed from an external order with a view to dictating the very processes of the body's activities, not only the results of its performance. This was training, not just control; it was a process-based rather than simply consequentialist project. It falsely resembles ascetic training, because discipline, in both cases, is harnessed in the formation of a controlled body. But the differences, important for us, are both profound and significant, since the ascetic's achievement lies in maximizing mastery over the body as an *internal exercise*; i.e., the operations he or she conducts are techniques applied by the self to the self, techniques that seek the *renunciation* of the material world, holding in low regard utility as a materialist performance. This is perhaps the decisive difference between the qualities of the premodern and modern disciplinary types we noted in the opening paragraph to this chapter, a difference pregnant with significant implications.[7]

With the maturation of educational, bureaucratic, and discipline-based institutions, the initiation of the state subject was completed. Now, the state can use the trained subject as a fully developed skill or even as a tool whose performance is backed by self-imposed loyalty and efficient utilitarian enthusiasm. Put differently, it is no longer a monarch or an identifiable group that governs but the totality of social and bureaucratic—though always state-based—institutions. This is the background of the argument, often made with a view to explaining the success of Western democracies, that power shared is power increased,[8] the argument itself being a part of the ideological justification of modern democratic forms. The argument fails on account of omitting from consideration the processes within the modern Western state through which the subject is tamed and rendered politically innocuous. For it is through these processes that massive institutions can be relied upon to do the bidding of the state, institutions that also represent the state insofar as the latter embodies a collection of deliberately trained personnel.

This bidding is no more obvious than in academia, a field that prides itself on intellectual independence and on conducting research and generating knowledge through the so-called scientific method—knowledge that is regarded as resting on a dispassionate examination of the world. The fact remains that paradigmatic academia is a state institution in at least three senses. The first is its nearly unqualified and unquestioning adoption of the positivism of the state;[9] indeed, the scholarly paradigm of academia remains thoroughly, if not entirely, positivist.[10] The second is the overwhelming acceptance of the state as a taken-for-granted phenomenon, this being presupposed in the discourses of the social sciences and the humanities. On the whole, academia thinks the state—nay, the world—through the state. The third is the role academia plays in state governance, and by this I do not mean only its direct involvement in the production of research with military and political implications (itself a phenomenon worthy of separate consideration).[11]

Frequently drawing on the help of academia, the modern government portrays itself as a problem-solving machine, a characteristic always implied in government's self-declared goal of being in the "service of the people." This, of course, is not a mere slogan: it reflects actual reality, especially in the modern Western state. However, the genealogy of this phenomenon is not always clear. The state is not an organic society in the same sense that traditional societies were constituted over a long stretch of time. In fact, the state is antithetical to such a society.[12] The long history of human sociopolitical organization teaches us that organic societies did perfectly well without states, which is precisely why the state never made an appearance until Europe invented it. Hence, the very notion of the state is synonymous with the disruption, dismantling, and rearrangement of the social order. The rearrangement and continuous reengineering of society (through economic policies; unceasing—even crushing—reforms in education; changes in the laws of personal status, health care, and social insurance, etc.)[13] no doubt solve perceived problems, but they often create many new ones, mostly unpredicted, of course. The perception that a "problem" exists and that it therefore needs a solution must also be seen in relation to the knowledge forms of the state, which is to say that "problems" become ontologically possible only when the state becomes possible. It so happens that a great majority of these "problems" were the normal and even natural order of premodern societies, "problems" with which these societies had lived (without conceiving them as problems) from time immemorial. The attribute of "problem-solving machine" is thus one that is essential to the paradigmatic state.[14]

Governing in the modern state means addressing these and many other subsequently emerging "problems" ranging from crises in the family and depopulation and lack of economic competitiveness to urban poverty and the destruction of natural habitat. Task forces, investigative committees, research projects, proposals, and reports are all integral to the processes of the "problem-solving" machine, and the personnel directly involved in them are academicians, invariably scientists, social scientists, and philosophers of sorts. They all must accommodate this reality, which is to say, a reality that the state must face and thus, by definition, a reality positivist in nature.[15] This is not to say that these academicians, especially the philosophers and their ilk, never engage with the moral Ought, for they at times do. But what is sought after in government circles and what therefore receives emphasis in academic disciplines (through funding opportunities among several other forms of leverage) are those patterns of research and intellectual production that first recognize and then accommodate positivist realism. This accommodation must first obtain for any proposed solution to win a chance at being heard.

To make itself relevant, as it must, academia—*which educates the nation and its elite*—exercises upon itself a particular discipline that seeks, among other things, to develop expertise in fields relevant to the interests of the state, although the porosity of state and society often clothes these interests in the garb of social and societal concerns. Governing, a business divided among countless departments and institutions, presupposes that the sphere under the purview of each of these units is capable of representation, that each sphere is known or at least knowable and therefore can be subjected to deliberative political calculation. Accordingly, "theories of the social sciences, of economics, of sociology and of psychology, thus provide a kind of intellectual machinery for government, in the form of procedures for rendering the world thinkable, taming its intractable reality by subjecting it to the disciplined analyses of thought."[16] If we think of education in the modern state—and in effect there is no formal education worth speaking of outside of its purview—as the site in which various strands of discipline intersect (bureaucracy, science, technology, political science, nationalism, etc.), then it is a field that "takes care" of the subject during the most crucial, formative period of his or her life. It begins by instilling in the child skills and knowledge of utility and efficiency, of love for the homeland and its goodness, proceeding incrementally with the adult student to inculcate state interests, state priorities, state programs, nationalism, and state "problem-solving" ideology. This is not a unidimensional power imposing a set of alien rules on an externally situated object but rather a power that inscribes itself in the subject who has been endowed, through education and training, with the ability to be regulated, politically, willingly.

To say that the paradigmatic state produces the paradigmatic citizen and vice versa is virtually to state a scientific axiom. To say that the modern state can live and be reproduced without its citizens is to say that the body can live without the circulation of blood. The point in all of this is that for the individual to be *in* and *of* the state, which the citizen almost wholly is,[17] calls for a totalizing subjectivity, one reflecting—on a micro, sociopsychological level—several essential features of the state. It means the introduction of a subjectivity in the human subject, as the state is relatively new. It means the production of the unique *homo modernus*.

The subjectivication of academia, the elite pedagogical machine of the state, finds a parallel in a more essential social unit, the family. Here, the state is everywhere. It lays claim not so much on the family as an organic social unit, a sacred collective that nurtures happy and content individuals, but on the family as a production unit, namely, a unit that produces the citizen, the national subject. There is no nation-state that does not claim a monopoly over lawmaking, and there is no lawmaking that does not devote a good part of its attention and energy to legislating the family. The family, integral to the concerns of sovereign legal will, has been redefined to serve the state,[18] a redefinition that was accomplished in the name of a program of priorities pertaining to the interests of the child, interests that nearly always come prior to those of parents, especially the father.[19] The child becomes the site in which the authority of the state unfolds as a program of reform inhabited by law,[20] psychologists, psychiatrists, social workers, and technicians. The patriarchy of the family is replaced by that of the state: it is the magistrate, the school, the psychiatrist, and the social worker that largely displace the parent.[21] The concurrence of the juridical and the psychiatric professions marks the collaboration of two disciplines that are geared to produce the state subject, the national citizen. Adorno, as we shall see later, would add to this mix the "culture industry" that shapes the young (and old) into narcissistic, fragmented individuals.[22]

In his important work *The Policing of Families*, Donzelot characterizes the situation of the modern family as one of crisis, having changed from "being a pillar of society to being the place where society constantly threatens to come unglued." This loosening of the family structure is the direct result of state policies, where the family appears fully integrated into the disciplinary apparatus installed by the state. The family "thus appears as the troubled site of social subjection, of the impossibility of social autonomy."[23] Just as the state has given rise to the realm of the political, it has also, through its discipline-based social engineering, created the realm of the social, where society unfolds in the image of the state. As Deleuze has argued, the crisis of the family and the rise of the social are the twofold political effect of the confluence of discipline apparatuses of the state.[24] The social has thus become a hybrid domain where the political shapes society, particularly its children, according to a certain model. And the model is that of the national citizen, the citizen of the nation-state, with all the attributes that this identity comprises and implies.[25]

It is noteworthy here that the institutional, epistemic, and bureaucratic forms producing the docile subject of the state first preceded and then coincided in their operation with the rise of nationalism. In other words, nationalism not only presupposed these forms, which were instrumental in constructing the modern state, but also represented their correlative result. Patriotic speeches, ethno-"national" literature, public festivals, and much else of the sort pervaded history, recent and remote, but their new location and context within the boundaries of these new forms acquired new meanings, producing qualitatively effective means to enhance the subordination of the subject.[26] The nation, therefore, is not some random group formation but rather a recently invented discursive and potent political practice that is "fundamentally related to the modern state form."[27] Although as an identity the concept of nation(alism) is never fixed, and although it is a continuous project and therefore represents an unceasing process of self-reproduction, it remains a constant paradigm that constructs, on behalf of the state, particular subjects who perceive themselves and who perceive the world in highly characteristic ways.[28] More importantly, these are *politically integrated* subjects, which is to say that they are not integrated in a metaphysical or cosmic-moral order but instead in the metaphysics of the state and its nation.

Nationalism is perhaps the most significant source and groundwork of meaning available to its subjects. If we live in a world of states, and if out-of-state existence is impossible,[29] then we all must live as national citizens. We are the nation, and the nation is us. This is as fundamental as it is an inescapable reality. Nationalism engulfs both the individual and the collective; it produces the "I" and "We" dialectically and separately. Not only does nationalism produce the community and its individual members: *it is itself* the community and its realized individual subjects, for without these there is no nationalism.

Leading sociologists and philosophers have emphasized the pervasive presence of the community in individual consciousness, where the social bond is an essential part of the self.[30] It is not only that the "I" is a member of the "We" but, more importantly, that "the 'We' is a necessary member of the 'I.' "[31] It is an axiom of sociological theory, writes Scheler, that all human knowledge "*precedes* levels of self-consciousness of one's self-value. There is no 'I' without 'we.' The 'we' is filled with contents prior to the 'I.' "[32] Likewise, Mannheim emphasizes ideas and thought structures as functions of social relations that exist within the group, excluding the possibility of any ideas arising independently of socially shared meanings.[33] The social reality of nationalism not only generates meanings but is itself "a context of meaning";[34] hence our insistence that nationalism constitutes and is constituted by the community as a social order. "It is senseless to pose questions such as whether the mind is socially determined, as though the mind and society each possess a substance of their own."[35] The profound implications of the individual's embeddedness in the national community is that the community's ethos is prior and therefore historically determinative[36] of all socioepistemic phenomena. And if thought structures are predetermined by intellectual history, by society's inheritance of historical forms of knowledge, then these structures are also a priori predetermined by the linguistic structures in which this history is enveloped, cast, and framed.

Like law, nationalism is everywhere: it creates the community and shapes world history even before nationalism comes into it. There is no contradiction involved here, because nationalism is a metaphysic. It not only overrides history; it makes and rewrites it at will. The nature and power of nationalism could not be otherwise, because, as we said, nationalism and the state are not mere twins; they are embedded in each other, nationalism being one side of the coin that is the state. And no wonder that it is a metaphysic, for what else could it be if it is integral to the state and its own metaphysics? The state and its nationalism, conscribing the community both as politically sacrificeable and sociopsychologically devout members, are two gods in one. This is the political framework and metaphysic within which the citizen is born. They shape him in their image so he can reproduce them, perpetually, for their own sake.

The training of the subject extends beyond nationalism, although this latter is more or less present in all state training projects. Training in instrumentalism and efficiency, whose substrate is profoundly materialistic, has created what Weber called the "iron cage,"[37] a set of cultural values and perceived opportunities that are constrained by material acquisitiveness and the particular outlook of rational choice. These two have, like nationalism and much else, come to constitute the state subject, creating a personality that cannot rest on or be shaped by spirituality. They are based on a technique of self-knowledge, what Foucault has called "know yourself," not a technology of "taking care of yourself."[38] The distinction here is between rationality and practical ethics.[39] The trained modern subject finds "it difficult to base rigorous morality and austere principles on the precept that we should give more care to ourselves than to anything else in the world. We are more inclined to see taking care of ourselves as an immorality, as a means of escape from all possible rules. . . . We also inherit a secular tradition that sees in external law the basis for morality."[40] The efficiency and instrumentalism that have been pedagogically inculcated in the nurtured citizen would here come full circle. They would meet, within the confines and limits of regulated autonomous rationality, the law of the state, which represents as much a reflection of their will as they are a reflection of its will. And, to extend Weber's metaphor, it is within this "iron cage" of law, regulating bureaucracy, mechanization, materialism, and instrumentalism that the morality of the modern subject finds itself.

The "iron cage," a structure of interrelationships that is made of all these modern characteristics (sanctioned by the state), is also the site in which modern pedagogy conflates technical training with free intellectual enquiry. The systematic and systemic refinement of mechanisms and techniques geared toward regulative and instrumental mechanization has created a class of technical and "intellectual" experts whose talents are usefully put to the service of the bureaucratic and capitalistic machinery instead of nurturing truly free personal enquiry.[41] For Weber, who saw capitalism as a "compulsive apparatus rather than a locus of freedom," modernity, with its bureaucratic machine, heralded "the decline of the cultivated man as a well-rounded personality in favor of the technical expert, who, from the human point of view, is crippled."[42]

Individual freedom and a rationally autonomous determination of destiny—relabeled by Marcuse as "democratic unfreedom"[43]—amounted for Weber to a titanic tension between the moral/spiritual order and the world of matter and materialism, between the morality of taking care of the self and the morality of self-gratification. The premium of life-value is now external rather than internal. It assigns supreme importance to discipline, efficiency, and work, three of the many lessons that the state came to inculcate, as second nature, in its citizens. Work for the sake of work, just as capitalism's money is made for the sake of garnering wealth,[44] just as the state exists for its own sake and perpetuates itself for the sake of perpetuating itself.[45] Weber saw in modernity's claim of progress a concept that amounts to the "production and accumulation of wealth and the mastery of nature . . . as well as the idea of emancipating the rational subject."[46] But the price of progress was what he called "disenchantment," a deep sense of loss, the loss of the sacred, of a state of wholeness, of the spiritual anchoring of the self in the world, in nature, and in what I have called a moral cosmology.

It is precisely this disenchantment that compelled Adorno and others to speak of the emotional impoverishment of the modern subject, of the standardization and automation of his psychology. The modern subject is isolated and fragmented, having fallen prey to a "culture industry" that has shaped for him and her a new type of identity. "Sequestered from key types of experience," the "self is energized against a backdrop of moral impoverishment" and "under conditions of substantial moral deprivation."[47] The divisions of the inner self has resulted in a narcissistic individual whose frame of reference and meaning derives from the impersonal, from the ideal power types (represented in nationalism, fascism, Nazism, etc.) that delude him into a sense of containment.[48] In these power types the narcissistic ego finds refuge, stability, and even contentment. "Modern capitalist society not only elevates narcissism to prominence, it elicits and reinforces narcissistic traits in everyone."[49]

But Adorno problematizes this downward turn as a "curative," in the sense that the nation and its meaning become the antidote to the fragmentation of the modern subject and to the Weberian sense of loss and disenchantment. Taking over the past and the future and creating a universal historiography of its own, the nation becomes a natural ontology that retains not only values that displace and replace all values but also, as we have seen, a historical transcendence, a metaphysic. *Nationalism thus developed as a necessary and integral component of the state phenomenon because it served as a curative against the malaise of state effects: the destruction and reengineering of the social order, the subject's fragmentation, general instability, fragility, narcissism, etc.* The metaphysical dimensions of nationalism and its psychological investment in the social order create for the subject not only a frame of reference but a world of meaning that replaces the world now lost. This is why there cannot be a state without a nation, and this is why the modern state must always be a nation-state, because without nationalism the state would have as much chance to survive as a cancer patient has the chance of surviving without treatment. But as with any modern treatment, the cure has side effects. In the case of nationalism, these have been so grave that it is impossible not to conclude that the genocides and atrocities of the twentieth century (and the present one) are the direct product of the phenomenon of the nation-state.[50] As a dialectic of modernity, nationalism is

> the pay-off for a disenchanted world, the mythic, naturalised, non-rational fantasy produced by the demythologising, "rational" development of the state. . . . It comes to stand in for a guiding force of social and individual life. This in turn leads to identification with the nation and its figureheads as the grounding for subjectivity. Nationalism offers autonomy (self-determination)

> and particularity in the form of subjugation to a universal. It is an instituting moment for the self, society and the state. . . . Humanity no longer worships gods but rather itself as the transcendental nation. *We become nationalised narcissists.*[51]

2. The Moral Technologies of the Self

The paradigm of the modern state and its inherent capacity to produce subjects can find no common ground with the paradigm of Islamic governance. The two stand worlds apart. A central comparative dimension here is the controlling phenomenon of historical experience. The European experience that generated the modern state is just that: European. Islamic governance was squarely the product of Islamdom, of the total historical experiences of Islamic culture, values, and weltanschauungs, however varied within the tradition these experiences may have been. Constitutive of the difference is the absence from the Islamic paradigm of a monarch or state that controlled legislation. The "legislative" in Islam did account for the ruler and for a certain reality of politics, but it was not the product of politics or the political. The political absolutism that Europe experienced, the merciless serfdom of feudalism, the abuses of the church, the inhumane realities of the Industrial Revolution, and all that which made revolutions necessary in Europe were not the lot of Muslims. On the whole, and despite the inescapable cruelties of human life and its miseries (which obviously are not the preserve of premoderns only), Muslims, comparatively speaking, lived for over a millennium in a far more egalitarian and merciful system and, most importantly for us, under a rule of law that modernity cannot fairly blemish with critical detraction.[52]

Nor did Islamic governance know anything like the scale of surveillance generated by the modern state's police and prison systems. These, so normalized and a matter of fact today, would have been horrifying to Muslims as specters of domination and cruelty. Nor, still, did Islamic rule so much as tamper with the sphere of education, which remained not only private but also nonformal and highly accessible, accommodating the entire spectrum of social strata.[53] Sultans, emirs, and viziers did establish institutions for higher learning (*madrasas*), but like the judges they appointed and dismissed, they had no influence over what was taught and how. The subjects of education—mostly taught outside of royal *madrasas*[54]—long remained those that were essential for the law and for satisfying the needs of society, i.e., for leading to the desideratum of the good life. They invariably consisted of language (grammar, syntax), Qurʾān studies, Prophetic traditions, law, mathematics, medicine, chemistry, logic, hermeneutics, dialectic, rhetoric, and the like. These were intended for the development of skills utilized within the social order, including primary education, law courts, hospitals, market transactions, commercial dealings, etc. Certain skills, such as the scribal and the secretarial, were utilized at the royal court at the level of executive power, but these were skills largely devoid of political-ideological content and remained squarely grounded in the established civil, mostly Sharīʿa-controlled, network of education. In brief, like the Sharīʿa itself, education was significantly independent of executive will, the latter having no control over either its substance or its religious-moral constitution. Which is to say, still briefly though emphatically, that the capabilities of political power to produce subjectivities that would *recognize themselves* in that power did not exist. (The slave-soldiers we had earlier mentioned[55] were almost always "educated" by the dynastic elite and the men of arms, so their education was relevant for the business of rule and war; they lived in relative seclusion from the population and its civil order.)

Yet, Islamic governance was productive of subjectivities that were paradigmatically Sharʿī based. If the Sharīʿa represented an expression of God's sovereignty on earth, then it was par excellence the context in which such subjectivities were fashioned. The Sharīʿa subject was therefore drastically different from the subject produced by the modern state. Paraphrasing Foucault, one might say that the Sharīʿa subject was the site of care for the self, while knowing the self, though not entirely unknown, was relegated to a distant second place. Let us now turn to this matter, although, before proceeding, and in order to minimize our incapacities as modern observers of spatially and temporally distant cultures, we must briefly address a methodological issue that has a bearing on what it means to study the Islamic notion of care for the self.

Central to modern moral philosophy is the question "Why be moral?"[56]—a question that presupposes a particular state of affairs in which consciousness of the moral as a distinct, distinctive, and integral category takes center stage and where the moral is not to be taken as a matter of course. In the way the question "Why be moral?" is specifically posed, in the way it is predicated upon a particular set of assumptions that places restrictions on acceptable answers to it, and in the way it rests—together with these assumptions—on both genealogy and societal formation, the question is both unprecedented and unique. It echoes a fundamental quandary of modernity and the modern condition; it is a question that the mainstream Islamic tradition, in any of its premodern variants, never asked, at least not in the way modern discourse has posed it. Nor, as far as I know, did any other premodern culture.[57] In its forcefulness, formulation, and conceptual origins, the question is modern, arising from and assuming the modern condition.[58]

It was the common understanding that the Sharīʿa constitutes the path to the good life, a path that claimed to guarantee well-being in this world and in the hereafter, hence the implication—which remains no more than that—that morality-cum-law possess a teleology whose very fulfillment is their own raison d'être. But in saying so, in separating the two realms and assigning to them two different concepts—our only way of expressing it—we have committed the first fallacy in examining the Sharīʿa as outsiders. The imposition of a foreign vocabulary, by which discrete conceptual and organic units are identified and segregated, immediately becomes the first impediment to understanding, the first act by which the object of our epistemic inspection is contorted and defined in ways alien to its natural and native habitat. This is another way of saying that once the observer's language intrudes with its own repertoire of creating conceptual distinctions relevant and suitable only to itself, the subject is fundamentally altered upon the genesis of that epistemic inspection, that is, at the first discrete moment of its coming into existence. But in this act of inescapable linguistic play we do not merely alter meanings; we in fact reconstitute our objects.

The distinction between—and the segregation of—the legal and the moral indeed constituted the first act in the emergence in nineteenth-century colonial Europe of the academic subject of "Islamic law." This "law"—another misnomer[59]—was described and continues to this day to be viewed as having "failed" to distinguish between the moral and the legal. This perceived failure—a conceptual judgment whose standard was the paradigmatic model of European law—amounted to an indictment issued on grounds of both deficiency and inefficiency, an indictment resting securely on the ideological foundations constructed by the modern state. The scholars who created the knowledge that is "Islamic law" and whose measure of a legal culture is one imbued with the intrusive and ubiquitous agency of the state found incomprehensibly deficient a "law" that not only seamlessly meshed with morality but depended on morality for enforcement. For, in their legal weltanschauung, enforcement through morality counted for little, if at all. (It is analytically tenable to predicate this mistrust on the history of the modern philosophical question "Why be moral?" but the problematic of such predication is not our concern here.)[60]

The indictment also issued from a gross underrating of the "moral" force that was regarded within the Islamic tradition as an essential and integral part of the "law." At the foundation of this underrating stood the observer's ideological judgment about religion (at least the Islamic religion), a judgment of repugnance, especially when religion as a moral and theological force is seen to be fused with law.[61] The judgment, in other words, undercuts a proper apprehension of the role of morality as a legal form, of its power and force. Historical evidence was thus made to fit into what makes sense to us, not what made sense to a culture that defined itself—systemically, teleologically, and existentially—in different terms. This entrenched repugnance for the religious—at least in this case to the "Islamic" in Muslim societies—amounted, in legal terms, to the foreclosure of the possibility of considering the force of the moral within the realm of the legal, and vice versa. Theistic teleology, eschatology, socially grounded moral gain, status, honor, shame, and much else of a similar type were reduced in importance, if not totally set aside, in favor of other explanations that "fit better" within our preferred, but distinctly modern, countermoral systems of value. History was brought down to us, to the epistemological here and now, according to our own terms, when in theory no one denies that it was our historiographical set of terms that ought to have been subordinated to the imperatives of historical writing.

It is therefore the unimpeded integration of the moral force within the Islamic legal world that commands our attention here. Whereas the answer to "Why be moral?" was—and rightly so—too obvious to Muslim legists to warrant much reflection on their part, *our* question must be: How was the moral subject fashioned? The immediacy of this question stems from a reality in which law fed on morality, *in its multilayered social constitution*. The Sharīʿa, historically speaking, emerged out of a fundamentally spiritual and religious Near Eastern background and continued to evolve in ways that accommodated societies whose "law" was enmeshed with, and enshrined in, social and spiritual morality. In other words, the Sharīʿa historically did not invent social morality but rather enlisted it in its own service and systematized it, feeding on its force and power in order to sustain its own moral concepts, practices, structures, and institutions. By capitalizing on the social substrate of morality, by giving direction and method to the force of social morality, the Sharīʿa generated its own "legal," but socially based, system of moral values. Hence the fundamental importance of the question: How did this system work, and how was the moral subject, *the discrete unit of the Community and communal life*, fashioned?

Obviously, Sharīʿa's integration of the sociomoral force may be studied from a variety of perspectives: The legal historian and legal anthropologist, for instance, may approach the court and its functioning with a view to examining the dialectic between morality and law in the jural reproduction of the social order. These scholars may focus on the court as the arena of moral claims,[62] where formal legal doctrine metamorphoses into applied practice, modified, shaped, and reshaped by the actors involved, including the disputants, their witnesses, the court's own witnesses and examiners, the audience present in the hearing (e.g., the community's representatives), and the *qāḍī* himself, among others.[63] The focus would be on the functioning of the court within the moral community and how the one influences and shapes the other. Another perspective, our chief concern here, is to examine the production of the moral subject from a schematic perspective, one that has the advantage of explaining the production of that subject before arriving at the court of law or before engaging with "law" in any of its worldly concerns. Put differently, the court, by virtue of the boundaries within which it operated, generally lacked the foundational underpinnings that fashioned the Sharʿī moral subject by means that were spatially and temporally prior to its involvement. For the moral subject was assumed to have *already* been fashioned *qua* moral subject within the "law" at the moment of the judicial event, at the moment, that is, when the "law" took for granted—as it always did—the presence of the moral force. If morality indistinguishably located itself within the habitat of "law," it was because the subject of this "law," in its individual and collective forms, was unqualifiedly assumed to be a moral agent.[64] Otherwise, the Sharīʿa's overall injunctions would have had no meaning within the contexts of social relations and would have been no more than a figment of the jurists' imagination.

Our schematic account assumes a theoretical and practical interaction between legal doctrine and the individual Muslim subject as a member of the community. It is taken for granted that the Sharīʿa as it manifested itself through legal doctrine (in its substantive *as well as procedural and due process* provisions) had acquired in Muslim societies the highest form of legitimacy, that it was accepted as exemplary of what the "law" should be and *is*,[65] that it was the fully legitimate contextual structure and paradigm in which the "well-ordered society" operated and lived,[66] and that right and good practice was that which conformed to its prescriptions. This interaction, a sociolegal dialectic of the first order, finds ample attestation especially in the way I approach the question of fashioning the moral subject. My emphasis on the so-called ritualistic aspects of the law fortifies assumptions about the historical existence of this dialectic, for, to my knowledge, no one has made the claim that these aspects of the Sharīʿa suffered any disconnection with practice and social reality. Even when skeptical Orientalism (incorrectly) argued for a divorce between Sharīʿa's "substantive law," on the one hand, and social and political practices,[67] on the other, it never questioned the spiritual and religious (and, we may add, practical) importance of "ritual" to Muslims.

It is also posited that inasmuch as social and religious morality sustained the Sharīʿa, the various parts of *fiqh* doctrine reinforced one another in moral ways. The morality that was fashioned in one area of the "law" constituted a moral prop for the enhancement and practical implementation of another area of the "law." Yet since these areas were reflected and elaborated in juristic discourse, their arrangement was by no means haphazard or interchangeable but rather carefully structured to yield a particular effect. The arrangement and form thus impart much meaning to juristic expression as substance and content. This highly structured arrangement of legal doctrine best explains the programmatic efficacy of legal subject matter, an arrangement that has not thus far been subjected to our scholarly attention, much less analysis.

The inattention to the significance of this highly deliberate doctrinal arrangement of subject matter must be tied to another distinction created by those modern disciplines that constructed the field of "Islamic law."[68] For more than a century, modern scholarship has viewed the Sharīʿa's legal domain as comprising two main but distinguishable parts, one related to "rituals" and the other to so-called law proper. "Islamic law proper," it was confidently and repeatedly argued, was that part of the Sharīʿa which dealt with areas of the law that generally corresponded to what is regarded as "law" in the Western conception. These areas of "law proper" had been termed *muʿāmalāt*,[69] indicating those spheres pertaining to legal relationships between and among individuals, such as family law, commercial law, and penal law. *ʿIbādāt*, on the other hand, referred to those laws that were said to regulate man's relationship to God, clearly a religious set of practices. This sphere of ritual would therefore be largely[70] set aside in scholarship until the beginning of the twenty-first century, when a very few writings dealing with ablution and purity finally appeared.[71] But these developments must not be attributed to refinements in mainstream Orientalist knowledge, since these writings clearly represent spinoffs of developments in biblical studies and mainly anthropology.[72] Still, none of these otherwise meritorious monographs appears to approach the "rituals" as an integral part of the "law," namely, to see these ritualistic performances as constituting a web of relations closely tied to the other "strictly legal" parts. None of them, in other words, has treated the "ritual" as *constitutive* of the "strictly legal." It is my contention here that the segregation of the "ritual" from the "legal" was, and continues to be, a function of overlooking the moral force of the law, of failing to appreciate both the legal ramifications of *ʿibādāt* and the moral ramifications of those "strictly legal" provisions of *muʿāmalāt*.[73]

As a rule, legal works of Islam—including those of the Twelver Shīʿites and Zaydites—begin with five major "chapters" or "books" (*kutub*; sing., *kitāb*),[74] each reflecting, in strict order, four of the five pillars of Islam, the *arkān* on which belief in the religion rests. As one important Prophetic tradition announces, Islam

> was built upon five [foundations, pillars]: [1] the double-testimony that there is no god but God and that Muhammad is the Messenger of God (*shahādatayn*); [2] performance of the prayer (*ṣalāt*); [3] payment of alms-tax (*zakāt*); [4] performance of pilgrimage (*ḥajj*); and [5] fasting (*ṣawm*) the month of Ramaḍān.[75]

Apart from the first, a predominantly theological pronouncement of faith accompanied by neither substantive nor procedural rules, the rest (already enshrined as pre-Islamic religious practices)[76] occupy a prominent place in the legal literature, having for the entire history of Islam been regarded as the foundations of religion and religious practice, blending the transcendental with the earthly legal. Together with purification (*ṭahāra*)—a prelude to and prerequisite for prayer—they have come to constitute the opening "books" of legal treatises, occupying as much as one-quarter to one-third of the entire body of these treatises.[77]

Created and constituted by the believers as devotional acts for the purpose of fulfilling a covenant with God, the religious works of the *ʿibādāt* appear to stand apart from the rest of the law, where acts relate to worldly objects and persons and where the intention and raison d'être is to acquire or sell property, marry, divorce, create partnerships, sue for damages, etc. The priority of these "ritualistic" chapters in the overall corpus of the legal works is reflected in their universal placement at the beginning, a longstanding tradition no jurist ever violated. But the placement was not merely an emblem of symbolic importance and priority; it had a function that made this ritualistic grouping a logical and functional antecedent. The function was subliminal, programmatic, and deeply psychological, laying the foundations for achieving willing obedience to the law that follows, that is, the law regulating, among much else, persons and property. The legal treatises, depending on the school and the jurist, began their second installment of exposition with either the contractual and pecuniary subjects (such as sales, agency, pledge, partnerships, rent, etc.) or family law (marriage, various forms of divorce, custody, maintenance, inheritance, etc.). Usually following these rules are sections dealing with offenses against life and limb, some regulated by the Qurʾān (*ḥudūd*), others by principles of retaliation or monetary compensation (*qiṣāṣ*). The last sections of legal works usually treat adjudication and rules of evidence and procedure and often include an exposition of *jihād*, although in some schools or juristic writings, this latter section appears earlier in the treatise. It bears repeating that whatever the arrangement of these chapters/sections/"books," the materials dedicated to the elaboration of so-called rituals are always prior, having universal precedence over all else.

Within this privileged arrangement, prayer still comes first. With its sequential bodily positions, it signals submission to a higher power, and with its recitals, invocations, and incantations, it expresses the need for that power's contentment and pleasure with the deeds and comportment of the believer. In the same vein, fasting compels identification with the suffering of others, generating compassion for, and even humility before, other human beings. It represents an acknowledgment of gratitude to God for the bounties He bestowed and continues to bestow on humankind, enabling them to enjoy earthly and material pleasures. So too does almsgiving engender empathy toward the needy and the poor, reminding the believers of nominal ownership of whatever earthly wealth they possess, wealth whose real Owner can claim it back at His discretion. This cumulative enhancement of the recognition of God's generosity is crowned by the physically demanding act of pilgrimage, exhibiting the believer's humility and patience before God and his creation.

As I have discussed elsewhere,[78] the Sharīʿa cannot be understood, nor could it have operated in any social context, without its moral bearings. The Sharīʿa without a moral community (which assumes morally grounded individuals) was not Sharīʿa. And morality—legal, social, or otherwise—traces its sources in large measure to the performative force of the five pillars. The morality that activated willing submission to the authority of the "law" was *constituted* by these performative acts. That they were given a prime weight and precedence was testimony to not only their ritualistic religious significance but also, if not primarily, their grounding moral force. To oust these pillars from the *fiqh* is to disengage the moral foundations of the law, to render the latter devoid of the most compelling impulse for jural observance. A *muʿāmalāt* law deprived of its *ʿibādāt* foregrounding is thus a law that is not only lacking in moral force but a law that is inapplicable, ineffective, and frequently unenforceable. (It is telling, therefore, that British India's governors—not least Cornwallis and Hastings—found the Sharīʿa lax and too lenient in the sphere of criminal law and in much else.)[79]

Before proceeding, something must be said of the double-*shahāda*, a pronouncement that receives no coverage in legal works. Inasmuch as the Sharīʿa conceptually stood in an intimate relationship with the linguistic, logical, metaphysical, and theological, the double-*shahāda* harks back to a set of theological creeds whose locus is the *ʿilm* (theoretical knowledge), not the *ʿamal* (practice and religious works). This theoretical foregrounding, defining double-*shahāda*'s boundaries, explains its exclusion from *fiqh* works. However, the exclusion is strictly formal, having to do with a particular logic of arranging subject matter and of delineating the lines of separation between various yet interrelated fields of discourse.

As a conceptual compound, the double-*shahāda* is an attestation to the existence of a Higher Order, one that is omnipotent and omniscient, who endures through eternity, who does not sleep, who knows the minutest particulars of worldly occurrences, and who keeps accounts, yet, He is all-merciful, compassionate, loving, and immeasurably forgiving.[80] *He is everything in their contradictions.* Not a single attribute of His being is subject to analogy with other creatures.[81] His compassion, love, punishment, and wrath are only homonymous attributes, the only way humans can understand Him, relate to Him, worship Him, and love Him. Whatever attribute of compassion or punitiveness we assign to Him, it is like no other we know. The statement "there is no god but God" is a banner of surrender to this Higher Order, to everything and all that He is. If we seek nearness to him, we are seeking those attributes we want and avoiding those we do not want. It is not merely a fear of punishment that compels us to do the right thing but the desire for, and allure of, His love, compassion, generosity, peace, and eternal comfort.[82] He is not a unidimensional entity of terror and fear, the Inquisitor, the Inspector of Bad Deeds, awaiting the slightest fault and misdemeanor to jump at the opportunity to punish. Rather, He is forgiving and, indeed before anything else, He is The Compassionate and The Merciful (*al-Raḥmān al-Raḥīm*), the two names by which he is famously and universally known, two attributes that announce him in all mundane and worldly Muslim speech.

Divine punishment may be analogized to the coercion of the modern state, but this analogy is at best imperfect. For those who deserve punishment, God's is horrendous and eternally painful, to an extent and quality that cannot be imagined by the human mind. For the petty and not so petty wrongdoers, He is forgiving and merciful. Repentance pays. Not only can many bad deeds be forgiven, but good deeds are rewarded and have, in their overall weight, an *offsetting effect* against bad deeds.[83] The reward is thus exponential. Doing good and performing beneficial deeds increases one's credit, meticulously noted in one's transcendental ledger. And *everyone* has a ledger. All this is to say that the totality of an individual's deeds are put to the balance and do not stand, one by one, as determinants of God's judgment. This calculus of incentive allows for much latitude in dealing with life's issues and earthly enticements, for engaging with the world and worldly affairs. *What matters is the final accounting of the total sum of the individual's deeds*, accounting being a particular calculus integral to and inherent in the revealed conception of God's justice.[84] Thus, to do good is by definition to be "near God" (*qurba*) in this life and in the hereafter, to be loved and in receipt of His grace and bounty. "There is no god but God" ultimately epitomizes but does not mask the totality of these relationships with the Creator, in their threat and promise.

The second part of the *shahāda*—that "Muhammad is God's messenger"—modulates and cements the connection between the effectiveness of divine powers, the imagining of their actualized potential, and the practical reality of the believer. The "Message," the latent signified in Muhammad the signifier, constitutes the connection, the method of creating the epistemic link between the known and the unknown. It is this Message that announces the Sharīʿa, and it is with the full acknowledgment of this announcement that the subject subscribes to the rules of the order that is the Sharīʿa. Thus containing latent assumptions of theory and knowledge, the double-*shahāda* is, from the *fiqh* perspective, an end in and of itself. There is no more to do about it than to require its physical pronouncement, provided it is done with full intention.[85] The rest is hidden in the cerebral and emotive world of the believer.

Purification (*ṭahāra*), wrote one jurist, is the "key to prayer," the latter being "the most certain of Islam's pillars after the double-*shahāda*."[86] Although it is not itself one of the pillars (*arkān*) of religion, purification as a juristic subject occupies a relatively prominent position, amply attested by the fact that its treatment in legal works occupies space roughly equal to each of the five "pillars" (save the double-*shahāda*),[87] namely, prayer, alms-tax, fasting, and pilgrimage. Juristic works differ greatly on the detailed prescriptions on how to wash and on which surfaces of the body to wash. But whatever jurist's doctrine is adopted, purification must be applied according to that doctrine's prescriptions.[88] Yet purification is not limited to the believer's body but rather extends to her clothing, the place in which she intends to pray, and the very body of water used for washing. Again, ample space is allotted to the discussions of what constitutes ritual purity and impurity, where the latter resides inherently and where and how it can be removed.[89] The overall effect is a multitude of details, each requiring not only close attention by the believer but careful performance. Insofar as they enclose the full range of required acts of purification, they constitute a complete system of orthopraxis that at once prepares the believer for the realization of the act of prayer and drills her inner self and body in programmatic ways. The exercise, repeated for the entirety of adult life and in view of its ultimate purpose, is saturated with both spirituality and psychology.

Be that as it may, the foremost condition for the validity of ablution—as in all forms of worship—is the all-important attribute of intention (*niyya*).[90] The worshipper must have the intention to purify herself when embarking upon washing the face, the first step in the performance. *Niyya* occurs in the heart (*qalb*), the vehicle of rational thinking and abode of reason. It may or may not be accompanied by a verbal pronouncement, although some jurists require it.[91] Operating at a deep psychological level, *niyya* is an internal state whose presence gives each act of worship its identity, separating it from other identical acts that do not belong to the category of worship; e.g., washing the face or giving away money. The latter might be an act of paying alms-tax (*zakāt*, which also requires *niyya*) or merely a payment for a purchased object, while the former might be an act of *ṭahāra* ("ritual purification") or a mundane act of refreshing oneself. *Niyya* constitutes an awareness of, and confidence in, the individual act as fulfilling a particular purpose that is squarely categorized as an act of worship. Acts that cannot be mistaken for any other actions do not require *niyya*.[92]

The presence of *niyya* in the repeated performance of a ritual act is therefore insurance that the act is not constituted through a physically mechanical performance devoid of content but is rather engraved onto the mind and soul, in the rational and emotive faculties, at every individual performance, as if the act is being performed, every time, for the first time. The importance and effect of imbuing every ritual performance with originality of intent was well appreciated by the jurists. Indeed, it was a "self-evident matter" that "acts of *qurba* are entirely based on *niyyas*," which is another way of saying that "an act without *niyya* can never be constituted as one of worship."[93] "Niyya is the heart, soul, and backbone of religious works whose validity and invalidity are predicated upon it."[94] However, to intend an act of worship presupposes an emotive predilection on the part of the individual. It would be meaningless to attempt the fulfillment of a religious obligation if the performer dislikes the performance—if, that is, the *niyya* is caught in an emotive web of reluctance or resentment. Inasmuch as God is to be loved, performance of acts directed toward Him are to be loved as well, for *niyya* presupposes love. A well-known *ḥadīth* announces that "The best of people is he who intensely adores (*ʿashiqa*) worship, he who embraces and loves it (*aḥabba*) with all his heart; he who brings his body in contact with it; he who devotes himself to it; he who has no care in the world as to whether he will wake up the next day poor or rich."[95]

A constitutive element of prayer and a condition for its validity, *niyya* is required to affirm one's consciousness of the obligatory nature of this act and to declare which of the five daily prayers one intends to perform. Another constitutive element is the opening invocation (*takbīrat al-iḥrām*), consisting of the declaration "God is Great," intended to remind the performer of the gravity of this act of worship, of the exalted and magnificent status of He to whom one is praying. It is recommended that the worshiper pronounce the Opening Supplication (*duʿāʾ al-istiftāḥ*), which announces one's monotheistic faith and loyalty to the One and only God. This pronouncement may be followed by another, seeking refuge in God against Satan (*taʿawwudh*), this latter signifying all temptations to do what is less than moral. At this point, and upon every act of bowing down, the *Fātiḥa*, the Opening chapter of the Qurʾān, is recited in full and concluded with the *taʾmīn*, the solemn ratification "Amen." Upon the first and/or second act of bowing down, the believer is encouraged to recite a Qurʾānic chapter, however short it may be. Bowing down, in its minimal form, requires as much bending as one needs to place her palms on her knees, this being followed by a pause, then praise to the Lord (*tasbīḥ*). When standing up, the body's posture must be perfectly straight, so that this position is not confused with bowing. If a straight posture is to be ensured, it is with a view to making unmistakably clear the identity of the act of prostration (*sujūd*), to isolate it as a univocal bodily language of obedience, subordination, and humility. The more upright the body is, the clearer the processes of bending and prostration will be, and the more demonstrable and unqualified the humility is.

Prostration requires the exposed part of the forehead to touch the ground, pausing in this position at least for a moment (again, to ensure the identity of the act as one of submission). To qualify as a prostration, the head must be lower than one's lower back, a posture intended to reinforce humility. As a metaphor, this position precludes the possibility of meeting between the worshipper's eyes and those to whom he is prostrating. Any physical impediment preventing a full prostration, e.g., pregnancy or a back injury, waives the requirement inasmuch as one is unable to perform it.[96]

Intended to establish a certain connection and closeness (*qurba*) between the worshipper and her God, prayer, as I already intimated, is the most important of all religious acts after the *shahādatayn*. Hence, any adult deliberately desisting from praying was to be charged with apostasy. Prayer was so fundamental that it had the distinction of being the only ritual performance claiming to be the constant companion of the believer. Claiming a minimum of five performative acts a day for the entire duration of adult life, prayer exceeds in importance any of the other four obligations: the *shahādatayn*, pilgrimage (required once in a lifetime), fasting (Ramaḍān plus some optional periods), and alms-tax (once a year). Each and every Muslim who is an adult and *compos mentis* must pray, adulthood technically beginning at puberty but practically and for purposes of early training at ten years of age.[97]

It is significant that the obligation to pray in effect begins at this young age. Nowhere outside of the "pillars" is an obligation imposed on individuals who have not reached majority, this latter normatively defined as occurring at puberty, although this physiological state must also be accompanied by full mental competence. Reaching puberty without this competence will not allow for this passage to occur. In every other sphere of the law, majority that gives rise to the full range of obligations and rights is one that must be commensurate with mental maturity (*rushd*), a state of intellect that demonstrates the individual's ability to act prudently and responsibly (*ṣalāḥ*) in the pursuit of life's needs and requirements. A person who has reached the age of puberty but who continues to lack the quality of discernment necessary to manage his or her affairs will be subjected to legal interdiction (*ḥajr*), in which case a guardian is appointed to act on his or her behalf. This normative juristic position is, quite untypically, entirely abandoned in the case of prayer. Thus, at the age of ten, a person may be disciplined for failing to perform this act, the rationale being that by the time they reach majority (i.e., puberty), he or she is expected to be a consummate practitioner of prayer. For while other engagements in the "law" require no prior training and can therefore be accomplished at once upon maturity, prayer constitutes a complex process of outer and inner performances that need to be learned over time. To produce the moral subject of the "law" is to induce in the individual, in every individual, the programmatic effects engendered by prayer. If puberty/majority ushers in legal obligation at large, then the moral subject must have already been fashioned prior to the genesis of these obligations.[98]

Limited to the bodily and spiritual spheres, prayer's inducement of morality does not extend to all vital aspects of the believer's material, social, and psychological universe. Hence the necessity of setting in motion other "pillars," foremost among which is the *zakāt* (alms-tax), which, by Qur'ānic ranking, immediately follows on the heels of prayer in importance. Among all "branches" of the law, *zakāt* is unique in that it has a dualistic character: on the one hand, it is an integral part of religious "ritual," and, on the other hand, it functions as a substantive legal sphere, constituting itself as a "tax law." Inasmuch as socially based financial responsibility merges into rituality, rituality merges into the moral accountability for society's welfare. Like the ubiquitous charitable trust (*waqf*), *zakāt* was one of the most important instruments of social justice.[99]

Literally meaning growth, *zakāt* bears the extended connotation of paying out of the growth on one's property with a view to purifying that property. In one sense, *zakāt* is the financial/material parallel of ritual ablution: just as washing removes ritual filth, *zakāt* removes the moral burden that accompanies the garnering of wealth. In other words, and to state a major Islamic tenet, *to be wealthy is potentially a moral liability that requires dispensation, and the means of such dispensation is the sharing of that wealth with those who are in need.* The sharing of excess in wealth with the Qurʾānically specified beneficiaries (the poor, needy, and wayfarers) is seen not only as such a means of purification but reflects, among other things, the belief that all things ultimately belong to God and that Muslims are the trustees of earthly wealth accountable, furthermore, for the ways in which they dispose of it. Hoarding wealth is a cause for divine condemnation as well as for the eternal punishment of the Hereafter.[100]

The payment of *zakāt* is obligatory upon every Muslim, male and female, including—according to Mālikites, Shāfiʿites, Ḥanbalites, and Twelver Shīʿites—minor and insane individuals.[101] As in prayer, the imposition of *zakāt* on minors has an acculturating effect, engendering a moral impulse at a young age and preparing the individual, once reaching the age of majority, for accountability toward his or her social environment. The obligation imposed on the insane stems from financial aspect of the *zakāt*, the counterpart of that aspect which is ritualistic-cum-moral.

To be valid, *zakāt*, like all ritual performances, must be accompanied by *niyya*.[102] The indispensability of *niyya* draws a thick line of separation between, on the one hand, the voluntary and willing performance for the sake of God and, on the other, the coerciveness that is involved in what might be termed here secular taxation. However, *niyya* precludes a sense, on the part of the subject, of imposed obligation.

Arguably, a duty may be distinguished from an imposed obligation, in that there is a wide margin of difference between asking for the best one *can* give away and what one *must* give away irrespective of willingness or ability. By contrast with the rate (not to mention nearly amoral manner) of taxation in all industrialized countries, *zakāt* is levied generally at the rate of 2.5 percent of growth on one's wealth, after all amounts needed for subsistence have been deducted. This exemption, known as *niṣāb*, represents a size or value of wealth below which no *zakāt* can be levied. A property whose value falls between two *niṣābs*, namely, one that has not reached the next *niṣāb*, is exempt from levy on the differential. For example, if the *niṣāb* of a certain commodity is five, a person who owns nine units of that commodity would be paying *zakāt* on only the first five.[103]

In one important sense, *zakāt* represents at once an extension and an enhancement of prayer, for while prayer applies to the soul and body, *zakāt* transcends the immediate confines of physiological constitution, creating moral accountability for the sphere that lies beyond the self. It is not only the body that is subdued but also that material sphere which falls under its command. Taxing wealth is therefore not only a practical proof of social accountability and responsibility (which translates into "doing the right thing toward the needy and poor") but an indirect way to ensure thorough corporeal subordination.

While *zakāt* is designed to tame the body through excising that material wealth through which bodily pleasure is procured, fasting (*ṣawm*) engages the very body of the believer on another level of excision.[104] It is a tax on the flesh and body of believer, on the very nourishment on which it lives. This sense of bodily taxation is evident in the fact that although fasting is usually associated with the month of Ramaḍān, it plays other important roles, most notably as penance or expiation.

Fasting during Ramaḍān is obligatory, by universal agreement. Exempted from the duty to fast are the sick, pregnant women, nursing women, the elderly, travelers on long-distance and arduous trips, and persons whose health may be threatened if subjected to this performance. All others must fast. To be valid, abstinence must aggregately and concurrently include all food, drink, sex, and sexual play and must begin at dawn and end at sunset. The subject must be a Muslim individual of majority age, without the impediments of insanity or uncleanliness, both of which invalidate fasting. Majority, for purposes of fasting, begins at around ten years of age, the early start—as noted above—being viewed as necessary to inculcate the practice in children who will have to fulfill this demanding obligation in the most complete fashion when they reach puberty. (The implication here, as in prayer, is that, until puberty, some lapses may be tolerated.)[105] Menstruation and postnatal bleeding, among other impurities, invalidate the fast.[106] So is the absence of prior intent (*niyya*), which is indispensable for validity. During Ramaḍān—or any voluntary period of fasting—the intention regarding the next day must be declared each preceding day between *ifṭār* (breaking the fast) and the light of dawn (when fasting resumes). Intent must be present until the end of the fasting day. Failure to maintain intent, even for the shortest duration, is cause for the fast's invalidity.[107] That *niyya* plays here a psychological role as important as it does in prayer need not elicit further comment.

Fasting is not confined to the month of Ramaḍān. During certain other times of the year, fasting is recommended on a voluntary basis (*taṭawwuʿ*), this being both a performative and conceptual parallel to the *zakāt al-fiṭr*. Whereas optional fasting represents an added sacrificial act involving the body, *zakāt al-fiṭr* further complements this sacrifice in terms of external ownership of the body. Thus a spiritual and material link is created between the taxed/fasting individual and the community in which she lives: It is precisely where the individual deprives herself of bodily pleasures that she contributes to the bodily pleasures of others. The food she does not eat is what others who need it will.

Fasting, like *zakāt*, is thus intimately connected to those areas of law that regulate various aspects of social and economic life. Just as *zakāt* engenders notions of charity that sustain philanthropic enterprises (such as the all-important *waqf*),[108] fasting, insofar as it constitutes control over sexual desires, engenders conceptions of social discipline. Inasmuch as the highly commendable "institution" of marriage was intended, at least in part, to restrict *zinā*,[109] sexual fasting provided the psychological substrate of training the soul and body to avoid this abhorrent and criminal practice. Fasting, therefore, represents the tip of the iceberg: a trenchant social ritual, it powerfully and psychologically underlies and in fact constitutes the economic, social, and moral spheres.

Underlying fasting lie various rationales, all of which aim to train the self to acquire and augment compassion, self-discipline, and gratitude toward both the Creator and creation. Experiencing hunger and thirst through fasting restrains the soul and trains the body to control physical and mental desires. It teaches compassion for the poor in whose life hunger is prevalent. *Zakāt*, therefore, comes to complement fasting, for it is only through the latter that the rationale of *zakāt* unfolds and is made comprehensible. Furthermore, the actual experience of thirst and hunger serves as a strong reminder of God's blessings on us, of the bountiful existence He created for us. It is an instrument to thank the Lord-Giver (*Munʿim*). In this way, fasting becomes another rationale for *zakāt*, this time not vis-à-vis the poor but rather vis-à-vis the natural world surrounding us and the very nature that makes us what we are. Abstinence from sex and its pleasures teaches not only self-control but also an appreciation of that nature.

Should fasting be unintentionally interrupted by invalidating acts (including mistakes and forgetting), the believer must make up (*qaḍāʾ*) for those days in their entirety, even if the invalidity had entered fasting shortly before breaking fast. Intentional acts of eating, drinking, and having sex invalidate the fast and require penance (*kaffāra*) in addition to *qaḍāʾ*. *Kaffāra* may be fulfilled by freeing a Muslim slave in good bodily health, failing which, fasting for two consecutive months, failing which, feeding sixty of the poor. Women who engage in sexual acts during fasting must make up the fasting but are absolved of the duty to do penance.[110]

Finally, the last of ritualistic performances that enhance the subduing of both the body and soul is pilgrimage. Classified as a "pillar,"[111] it is incumbent upon each and every believer at least once in a lifetime, the strong implication being that anyone who abjures it may be deemed an apostate. And as is the case in all the other "pillars," the penalty for failure to fulfill it is less because one is abandoning the community of believers and more because pilgrimage is necessary in order to ensure a complete subordination to the set of five performative rituals. This is why there was, to my knowledge, no discussion among the legists about situations where a believer would perform all pillars but one. In other words, abjuring one pillar was not a political marker of religious identity or a marker of an ideological rejection of religion. Rather, the conscious rejection of a single "pillar" was primarily seen—though at the level of underlying fundamental assumptions—as failure to complete the set of religious works and performances that complete the program of fashioning the religious individual, the moral subject. To miss the performances entailed in a single "pillar" is to tamper with the total sum of effects that the set of five pillar-ic performances are intended to accomplish as an aggregate. It is in this sense that abjuring one of the "pillars" constitutes apostasy. (Apostasy, it must be said, is not just an act of rejecting the Muslim God, for, on its own, it is merely a summative declaration that implies and encompasses certain collective and foundational derivatives. It is indeed the moral implication of this declaration that was at the heart of the matter. *Fundamentally, therefore, apostasy is the rejection of the moral instruments that fashion the moral subject.* If it is one side of the coin, *jihād* is the other. Apostasy law intends to curb the moral damage of the Community's inner sphere, and *jihād* intends to protect and, if possible, expand the limits of that sphere.)

The obligation to perform pilgrimage is subject to exceptions, nonetheless. It is not incumbent upon those who are unable to perform it, i.e., those who are not in possession of *istiṭāʿa*.[112] Furthermore, the believer subject to it must be sane, of major age, and free. *Istiṭāʿa* consists of the following elements: (a) the ability to provide sustenance for oneself as well as for the dependent family members whom the pilgrim leaves behind; (b) the means to afford travel costs, food, lodging, etc.; (c) being healthy enough to travel and endure the hardships involved in the journey; and (d) the concomitant feasibility of *a*, *b*, and *c* during the season of pilgrimage.[113] Some jurists added the condition of travel safety and security on pilgrimage routes.[114] The legal duration of pilgrimage extends over the months of Shawwāl, Dhū al-Qaʿda, and the first ten days of Dhū al-Ḥijja. Generally, it is recommended that the obligation be dispensed upon one's fulfillment of all conditions relating to *istiṭāʿa*.[115]

The first of the four essential components of pilgrimage is entering a state of ritual consecration (*iḥrām*). This state begins with the *niyya* to perform pilgrimage in a specific form, namely, to perform *ḥajj* alone, minor pilgrimage alone, or both together. A ritual bath (*ghusl*) is then taken, also accompanied by the *niyya* that the act is performed specifically for the purpose of entering *iḥrām*. Shaving pubic hair, plucking the underarms, clipping the mustache, and trimming nails are then in order.[116] Clothes that have any sewing on them are changed for a white garment, and sandals that must not cover the toes or the heel are put on. The body should be perfumed, for men and women, and for the women it is recommended that they dye their hands with henna. Finally, a prayer consisting of two *rakʿas* is performed, the first requiring the reading of Qurʾān 109 and the second Qurʾān 112. Once all this is done and the believer begins journeying toward Mecca, he or she is said to have entered the state of *iḥrām*. During the entirety of the *iḥrām* period, it is forbidden to wear sewn garments, to remove hair or clip nails, to engage in sexual activity, or to hunt.[117]

The law of pilgrimage, like the law pertaining to the other "pillars," is complex and replete with exquisite detail. Yet the rationale behind this juristic complexity, behind the discursive and actual practices involved, is comprehensible to laymen and jurists alike: Through the performance of *ḥajj*, a relationship of acceptance is reenacted, acceptance of and submission to the greater power of God.[118] The submission to and humbling presence before God are enhanced by the shedding of earthly luxuries; by wearing the most basic of clothing and footwear; by abandoning all worldly concerns; and by focusing the heart (*qalb*), the mind, and soul on the graceful, generous, merciful, compassionate, and creative God. It is the last and final performative "pillar" that crowns the acts of worship and seals them into a cogent, enclosed, and complete body of works that ensures the act of submitting to the will and power of the Lawgiver. In their aggregate force, these performative acts provide the modalities through which the moral foundation and moral dimension of the law are constituted.

A powerful commentary on what Foucault called the technologies of the self was offered by Abū Ḥāmid al-Ghazālī (d. 505/1111), one of the towering intellectual figures of Islam. Indeed, in most ways relevant to our present discussion, Foucault was a thoroughgoing Ghazālian, though a much less engaged one in his assessment of the premodern subject.[119] In any attempt to understand these technologies Ghazālī's value is inestimable, perhaps because his life (at least as a biographical exemplar)[120] and scholarly-spiritual pursuits reflected the synthetic practices of mainstream Islam in its Sharʿī, Ṣūfist, and philosophical manifestations. His consummate exposition of the Sharʿī and the mystical and moderated acceptance of philosophical metaphysics reflected much of what religious culture propounded, practiced, and held dear. His magisterial and influential *Iḥyāʾ ʿUlūm al-Dīn*, in particular, offered an ethic that mirrored the Sharʿī-Ṣūfist orthopraxis, one that defined much of what Islam, as a lived spiritual and worldly experience, was.[121] His *Iḥyāʾ* is a virtuoso exposé of the art of religious practice and, indeed, of living and the good life. It is paradigmatic. If one can say that the modern age is one overshadowed by Kantianism, then the several centuries of middle Islam were overshadowed by Ghazālianism.

A practical guide, Ghazālī's work rests on what we now call a theory of human nature. The essence of his theory is that human beings (*al-insān*) are pliable in their natural constitution—they are neither good nor bad in their original state. Humans are made of different potentialities, which, once given substance, determine what each individual will become. In each of us, there are four potentialities: the aggressive, beastly, satanic, and divine (*sabʿiyya, bahīmiyya, shayṭāniyya*, and *rabbāniyya*, respectively). Anger, animosity, violence, and courage are the preserves of the first; greed, gluttony, caution, and lustfulness, of the second; deception, lying, and trickery, of the third; and knowledge (*ʿilm*), intellect, cognition (gnosis), and understanding, of the fourth. This fourth potentiality also includes a strong innate predilection to command, dominate, and moderate the other three.[122] This is not to say, however, that the fourth potentiality stands in diametrical opposition to the first three, having monopoly over positive attributes and detached from their negative counterparts. The first three potentialities, however, do include attributes that possess the capability of being good or bad, since courage, for instance, is harmful if not restrained, and so is caution if it becomes excessive.

Each human being enjoys a certain measure of these four potentialities, and only the prophets were free of the first three. However, the potentiality of *ʿilm* is both the quintessence and raison d'être of human beings.[123] It is the exclusive venue through which the individual can attain perfection, for the potentiality whose sphere is control and dominance reigns supreme. This human potentiality of *rabbāniyya* was bestowed with the power to exercise complete and absolute mastery over the others, a power to subjugate and vanquish them.[124] It is the master instrument of taking care of the self.

These potentialities are located in two distinct spheres, the first three occupying the sphere of soul (*nafs*), whereas the fourth resides in the sphere of heart (*qalb*). Yet knowledge and therefore intellect (*ʿaql*) do not only inhabit the heart but also constitute it; indeed, the intellect *is* the heart. This latter is defined as a "divine grace" (*laṭīfa rabbāniyya rūḥāniyya*), the true nature and essence of the human kind (*ḥaqīqat al-insān*) as well as the source of all human knowledge. This is an all-encompassing intellective and cognitive faculty that, when exercised, brings under its purview also knowledge of value because the world, suffused with value, can appear to our intellection and cognition in no other way.

On the other hand, the soul is the domain in which the other potentialities gather. The stronger the actualization of these potentialities, the more evil the soul becomes. Thus, under the influence of the commanding heart/intellect, the soul might rebuff and suppress the actualization of the nondivine potentialities. In acting that way, the soul might be elevated into a stage in which it garners consciousness of the divine potentialities, positioning itself in a state of self-blame (*lawm*). This soul (*al-nafs al-lawwāma*) thus represents a middle stage, one of transformation leading to a higher stage, namely, the peaceful soul (*al-nafs al-muṭmaʾinna*) that has succeeded in ridding itself of all negative qualities.[125]

The relation of the commanding intellect over the human body and its soul finds an analogue in the metaphor of a king's rule over his kingdom. Just as he must be the manager (*mudabbir*) of his domains, exercising control over his army and protecting his subjects, so must the intellect restrain desires and whims of the temporal body. The seditious elements in the kingdom, as much as the evil soul in the body, must be defeated for the kingdom, the community, and the constitutive individual to maintain their integrity and peace. Should the king fail to protect his subjects, he will be censured and condemned, just as the body and the intellect that resides in its heart will be consigned to Hell. The political duty of the ruler is thus cast as an analogue of the care of the self; both rest on a bedrock of obligations, not rights. The operative assumption here is that these obligations ought to be fulfilled, and when they are not, failure turns into liability.

Reflecting a pervasive ethic, Ghazālī's discourse places much emphasis on the relationship between man and his physical environment, especially earthly wealth and material abundance. It is up to the intellect to determine the extent of indulgence in such abundance and wealth. True, Ghazālī argues, God created the earth and all that is on it for the enjoyment of humankind, but all this bounty must be put to meaningful use (a notion heavily emphasized in Islamic discourse). The human body is a vessel and a means by which one must reach a destination. Human beings therefore are no more than travelers, and temporal life is no more than the distance of travel. Each day is yet another traversed mile toward the end of the journey, and earthly desires represent nothing less than highway robbers.[126]

The greatest of all desires is ravenousness, the source of all spiritual maladies, followed, in second order, by lasciviousness. Ardently seeking to fulfill these desires inevitably involves one in garnering wealth, in turn leading to indulgence in both spheres. It appears that Ghazālī posits a causal link between these two instincts, on the one hand, and the personal desire to acquire power and influence, on the other. To protect wealth and power, it is inevitable for the covetous individual to engage in competition and envy, which in turn engender greed, hypocrisy, arrogance, and hatred. And once these become habits of the soul, it is a short step for the individual to be implicated in morally repugnant acts.[127]

Nor is this causal link affected by notions of heredity or genetic transmission. Obviously, the kind of discourses propounded by Galton, Spencer, and Gardner were far from being on his mind, leaving him with a notion of human nature that is determined by the intellective faculty of will (*irāda*).[128] The latter, emanating from the heart, stands in opposition to the negative potentialities, since its burden is both the determination of evil consequences and forewarning against them. The will is the abode of both conscientiousness and accountability, and it is found in each and every one of us. Nothing is therefore predetermined;

it is up to the heart and its faculties to succeed or fail in completing the journey of life without falling prey to the highway robbers. Individual responsibility is indeed great.

Ethical conduct is thus entirely acquired and a matter of training, for had it not been so, there would have been no meaning whatsoever to moral exhortation, counsel, and educational instruction.[129] For Ghazālī, as for the tradition that produced him, education was an essential tool of caring for the self. In fact, acquisition of ethical conduct begins with attentive listening of the heart and its will to the narrative of counsel, abundantly available in the Qurʾān and the Sunna of the Prophet. This narrative instructs: "There is no act more dear to God than that of hunger and thirst," and "no one who has filled his stomach to the full will enter Heaven." Hunger, in this narrative, is said to engender "a pure heart," "compassion," "humility," "modesty," "remembrance of the plight of the hungry," and, most important of all, "curbing desires and misdeeds."[130] Once heeded, this narrative has the effect of instilling a kind of conduct that produces benefits. Hunger drives away sleep, for he who overeats oversleeps, and sleep is much like death: it shortens active life and deprives the believer of the opportunity to strive (*jihād*) for self-improvement. Overeating likewise produces sluggishness, another cause not only for neglecting the care of the self[131] but also of bodily ailments.[132]

Care of the self is accomplished through training (*riyāḍa*), a thoroughgoing process of subjecting the self to repeated exercises that shape and form the soul. The process might begin with a cumbersome effort, which tends to evolve gradually into a sort of normal conduct, ultimately becoming a second nature (*ṭabʿ*).[133] Every act of such formation emanates from the heart but spreads its effects into the limbs, extremities, and the outer physical body. The body would be ordered to move or not move and to act according to the heart's intellective orders and directions. Once the body is attuned to the imperatives of the intellective power and becomes automatically responsive to the latter's ways, the body redeploys the same effects back to the heart and intellect. In other words, the body's trained behavior, instilled as a second nature, in turn enhances the heart's predilections. At this point, the intellectual and bodily performances begin to run in harmony, involving a circular, dialectic motion (*dawr*). This reciprocity in turn produces mutual corroboration as well as progressive and exponential effects.[134]

Now, in Ghazālī's conception, the spectrum of training extends over the entire range of human acts. Living, in and of itself, is training. Yet the source of training resides in a set of well-defined acts that have been constituted as paradigmatic: namely, the five pillars we have discussed earlier. They represent the means of attaining *akhlāq*, i.e., the corridor through which foundational ethics can be acquired. Ghazālī's discussion of the five pillars, geared toward teasing out their ethical effects, is passionate, imaginative, metaphoric, and aphoristic, enriched with a quasi-legal and quasi-mystical language. This synthetic articulation appears faithful to the reality on the ground, a reality in which mainstream mystical Ṣūfism and Sharīʿa were entwined, amalgamated, and merged into a unified field of discursive and technological practice.

In the final analysis, then, the training is defined and implemented by the pillars. If the range of life and living must be the object of training, then every aspect of life must be ultimately subsumable and indeed implied by one or more of the five pillars. Prayer is constituted by the "works performed by the heart" (*min aʿmāl al-qalb*), which ipso facto means that the heart must be concomitantly present when it is performed. This presence is represented by *niyya*, amplified and enhanced with a layer of meaning over and above the basic meaning we have already discussed. The presence of the heart (*ḥuḍūr al-qalb*) is of the essence, defining the precondition of prayer. This presence dictates full attention to the addressee, for, after all, prayer is a conversation (*munājāt*) of the heart between the believer and his God. One cannot have a true conversation with another while distracted by other matters. The *niyya* is precisely the guarantee for conversational concentricity around and exclusivity of the Subject addressed. The required purity of this conversation translates into a deeper meaning of *niyya*, one that, Ghazālī says, is not present in any of the other pillars. The very act of detaching wealth from the believer necessarily gives meaning to a level of intent in the *zakāt* even when conscious intent fails to be present, since this extramental act of detachment forces itself on the heart and thus bestows on it a notion of intent, however incomplete. So too do pilgrimage and fasting, for the hardships involved in these performances force the inducement of a certain level of intent. But not so in prayer, because it merely requires speech, kneeling, prostration, and standing up—acts that do not demand extraordinary effort. Without *niyya* in prayer, the act itself does not count, however frequent the performance may be.[135]

Associated with pure intention and exclusive attention is a profound understanding of the import of language used in prayer. Every word has a meaning that must be comprehended, so every word matters. For it is the meaning conveyed in language that permits the performer to genuinely address God as the Great Being (*ʿaẓamat Allāh*), an essential attribute that establishes a particular relation of power between an inferior and a superior. Also integral to this relationship is a deep sense of awe and reverence (*hayba*), accompanied by an equal awareness of one's own shortcomings (*ḥayā*').[136] The latter represents an intellective consciousness of the constant desire for, and pursuit of, the "care of the self," that is, a consciousness of a founding ethic that underlies all other performances. Embedded in prayer (the first pillar of all), the desire of training the self and of improving it lays the logical and chronological foundation for the proper pursuit of other obligations. The seeds of ethical conduct thus lie herein.

A faculty of the soul, desire is a state of will (*irāda*) through which *niyya* is deployed. *Niyya* therefore is an internal act that cannot be expressed through external means. For instance, one cannot be said to be in love by merely declaring: "I intend to fall in love." To be meaningful, love must be emitted from the inner self. Yet genuine love is not just an example of inner acts. Indeed, it is the desideratum and substrate of *niyya*, for love gives *niyya* its fullest manifestation. True love emanates from an inner perception (*al-baṣīra al-bāṭina*), a faculty of the intellective heart. This perception is superior to sense perception in that it is intensely more acute and is thus quicker in registering comprehension and, moreover, at a deeper level. The capability to register abstract meanings operates internally and can thus perceive inner forms superior to any external image. It is only through this means of perception that one can truly love, for no external sense perception can be of help.[137]

Love of God for Ghazālī appears to outweigh fear of divine punishment, for this love dominates his discourse throughout the *Iḥyā*ʾ. The care of the self is therefore entwined with this love and follows as a consequence. *To love God is to care for the self, to train it, and to subject it to a self-reflective and consciously intended routine of performative acts.*[138] Love is pervasive. It permeates prayer and fasting as much as pilgrimage and giving alms-tax. The latter, for instance, has several functions, foremost among which is its power to test love. It is a test that distinguishes and then forces a choice, for love is a homonym that appears to obscure rather than reveal meaning. But its final truth must finally come to light. Ghazālī rejects eliding and confusing different forms of love, insisting on the necessity to identify inferior forms of love and making them entirely subservient to a superior form. Ultimately, it is inevitable that one type of love must be sacrificed to another:

> Pronouncing the double-*shahāda* is a commitment to Unity, a testament to the individuation of Him Who is worshiped. A condition for the fulfillment of this pronouncement is that there be no beloved other than the Individual One, for love is incapable of partition. However, verbal pronouncement [alone] is of little use, and so the lover is tested by taking away from him that which he loves. Material wealth is loved by human beings, for it is a tool with which they enjoy worldly pleasures and because of which they [both] find comfort in this world and fear death, although it is through the latter that one meets the Beloved. *People are tested for the veracity of their pronouncement about the Beloved by means of exacting their wealth to which they aspire and which they love.*[139]

In this paradigmatic conception of mystical Sharᶜism, morality becomes entwined with virtue. As H. A. Prichard once averred, "we must sharply distinguish morality and virtue as independent, though related, species of goodness," because the virtuous act is done "willingly or with pleasure"—what Ghazālī would characterize as an act of love. It is not done from

> a sense of obligation but from some desire which is intrinsically good, as arising from some intrinsically good emotion. Thus in an act of generosity the motive is the desire to help another arising from sympathy with that other . . . an act which is not at the same time an act of public spirit or family affection or the like. . . . The goodness of such an act is different from the goodness of an act to which we apply the term moral in the strict and narrow sense, *viz.*, an act done from a sense of obligation.[140]

The overall effect of the conception of mystical Sharᶜism—exemplified here in the Ghazālian discourses—is precisely to bring the virtuous to correspond to and permeate the moral.

3. Incompatibility of Subjectivities

It was, then, the coming together of the triad of law, morality, and mild mysticism,[141] in their nearly imperceptible interconnectedness, that allowed Ghazālī and a host of others like him[142] to speak of such technologies of the self. Love and fear combine to instill a profound sense of subservience to a higher power that created—and therefore owns—everything in this universe. In Ghazālī's account, as in the Ṣūfist tradition that thoroughly permeated conceptions of the moral law, love acquires a prominent status in the relation between man and God. Caring for the self and training the self are means to express this love, for the very expression represents a guarantee of *qurba*, the gaining of a place near God and becoming His neighbor (*jiwār*).

On this conception, there was no question as to the reason why one should be moral, only how one fashions oneself as a moral being. And the venues of this fashioning were consolidated into a set of mutually enhancing acts performed on the self. The truth of moral conduct and the right things to be done before God and one's fellow human beings were manifested in actions that were moderately ascetic,[143] exercising effective influence on the body of the believer so that the soul can be shaped to obey the intellective moral imperatives of the heart. Here, man's view of his place in the universe is one of an epistemic "relation between asceticism and truth," a truth that has no end, not even with death. That the notion of care for the self is now "obscure and faded," as Foucault tells us, is testament to an epistemic transformation wherein the technologies of the self have turned into technologies of the body—technologies that at best can accomplish the feat of "knowing yourself." As it has been frequently observed, the emphasis on the "I" and on what things "mean to me" is intimately connected to the constant search of the narcissist to relate outside events to the self's own needs and desires, it being the focal point of existence.[144] Thus, the transformation amounts to changing the site of fashioning the individual from the inner self to the outer body, hence the much talked about trend toward modern phenomena of hedonism and self-indulgence. The new technologies of the body heed the imperatives of the material world, of shaping the corporeal, strengthening it and prolonging its temporal residence on earth. The result, as we have seen, is disenchantment, fragmentation of the self, and a thoroughgoing narcissism. If, in the technologies of the self, fasting shapes and trains the soul, in the technologies of the body it strengthens the body itself, the shell without its spirit. Yet, fasting in the two technologies is done with other qualitative differences: whereas one engenders in the self a "peaceful soul" (*al-nafs al-muṭmaʾinna*), the other procures a physically healthy body; whereas in the technologies of the self the relation is "between asceticism and truth," in the technologies of the body, the relation is between corporeality and truth, the truth of value-free science that sees no inherent meaning and value in a mechanical, "brute," "stupid," and "inert" world.[145]

Concomitant with this transformation is another that occurred in the relations of power: Whereas the technologies of the self tend to induce self-restraining notions in these relations and therefore a certain unity with nature and being, the technologies of the body tend to engender the view that the corporeal field of power relations is the ultimate measure of man. This is the man who has come to inhabit a modern world that recognizes very little other than the political, other than the conquest of a world that is normatively mute and devoid of moral directives. This is the man who sees the world "as it is," a positivist being admitting of power and might as the sole logic and law of sociopolitical relations. (It is noteworthy here that this transformation explains not only the emergence but also the strong relevance of Foucault's own power/knowledge theory in recent times, a theory that—I suspect—would be both dubious and irrelevant to a culture whose main prop is the technologies of the self. In one important sense, Foucault's success as a power theorist is predicated on his very diagnosis that the notion of caring for the self is for us moderns "rather obscure and faded.")

The Ghazālian project thus represents not only an intellectual synthesis of morality, law, theology, mysticism, and philosophy but also an "anthropological" foray into Muslim subjectivity, capturing the intellectual, social-communal, and psychological forces that shaped this subjectivity into a paradigm. The juristic discussions of the five constitutive pillars—the indubitable foundations of the concept of what it means to be a Muslim—are not only taken for granted but also turned into socio-psychological tools of cognitive and behavioral construction. Juristic Sharʿism, in other words, becomes a sphere of culture inasmuch as, if not more than, the modern state has acquired a chameleonic social and cultural character. In Ghazālī and in the entire premodern Islamic tradition, law is embedded in a dialectic not only with social and cultural norms[146] but also, preeminently, with psychology as a mildly mystical realm. We can thus comfortably assert that the Sharīʿa, in addition to its trenchant legal-moral character, represents at once a field of practical mysticism, and as such it is thoroughly embedded in the mainstream Ṣūfistic ways of Islam. If we accept this much, then the implications are both profound and serious. If the Sharīʿa was *also* a psychological-mystical enterprise, and if it constituted the paradigmatic and undisputed "legislative" power of Islamic governance,[147] then *this governance was not only about law, morality, and their organic confluence; it was also and equally about a mystical perception of the world, a perception deeply anchored in a society—represented by a class of mystics-cum-jurists*[148]*—that did not distinguish, in the practice of living, between the meanings of the legal, the moral, and the mystical.*

The question that should arise here is: How would our world be if the legislative power in the modern state could indisputably and exclusively determine the law of the land, a law that—within the bounds of the civil population—would be thoroughly honored by the judiciary and the executive? And how, given this genuine separation, would our world be if this law was *at once* both moral and mildly mystical? Western moral philosophy, as we saw, has developed certain critical strands of thought whose effect is a call to draw on the moral repertoire of the European intellectual heritage,[149] but this remains only a rather thin attempt that has not come anywhere close to becoming an emerging paradigmatic force, much less a paradigm. The state and its successfully produced modern subject—and also, as we will soon see, capitalism and the corporation—have all been steadily and increasingly working toward ensuring that no such paradigm can come into existence, including, and especially, an Islamic one. The state's *homo modernus* is, by definition, antithetical to the *homo moralis* of our gaze.

6

Beleaguering Globalization and Moral Economy

Money is everywhere conceived as purpose, and countless things that are really ends in themselves are thereby degraded to mere means.

—Georg Simmel, *The Philosophy of Money*

He who gives (of his wealth) and fears God, and who believes in doing good, We will ease his way unto an easy state. But he who hoards and deems himself independent, and disbelieves in doing good, We will ease his way unto adversity. His riches will not save him when he perishes. . . . Therefore I have warned you of the scorching fire which only the wretched must endure . . . he who denies and turns away. But saved from it is the righteous, who gives of his wealth so that he may grow in goodness.

—Qurʾān, 92:5–18

The Pious . . . in whose wealth the beggar and the outcast have due share.

—Qurʾān, 51:15, 19

You shall not drive the beggar away.

—Qurʾān, 93:10

Let us suppose, for the sake of argument, that Islamic governance has become fully established. Let us suppose that the minimal conditions for such a creation have been satisfied, including, but not limited to, the following: (1) the establishment of a divine sovereignty in which God's cosmic moral laws are translated, as a system of moral principles, into practical "legal" norms; (2) a robust separation of powers where the legislative—the *discoverer* of said practical "legal" norms—is fully independent, genuinely representing the source of all laws of the land; (3) the legislative and the judicial powers are woven from a moral fabric whose warp and woof is a thorough amalgam of fact and value and of the Is and Ought; (4) an executive power is largely confined to the implementation of legislative will and permitted to issue temporary and small-scale administrative regulations consistent with this will; (5) a situation where morally based practical "legal norms" are put in the service of society, nurturing the community *qua* Community and serving its interests as a morally constituted entity (this includes a healthy dose of egalitarianism and a Qurʾānically based system of social justice); (6) educational institutions at all levels are designed and operated by a fully independent civil society that has been formed by a dialectic of conditions 1–5, above; (7) the educational system, lower and higher, asks and answers questions about the meaning of the good life, engaging science and the humanities only insofar as the morally good life requires investigation (here reason is not instrumentalized); (8) the concept of the citizen is successfully metamorphosed into the concept of the paradigmatically moral community, in which each member stands with other members in a moral relationship of mutual ties (here, the Schmittian concept of the political is sent to oblivion and, together with it, the citizen's sacrifice); and (9) the Muslim Community's individual members practice the art of caring for the self, viewing themselves, aggregately and severally, as an extension of a morally imbued universe.

1. A Globalized World

Should we suppose the coming into existence of such a *paradigmatic* form of governance, we must also suppose and, indeed, take for granted, that this governance has to live in a community of *modern* states, ones constituted according to the criteria we have delineated in the previous four chapters. As we have seen, the very concept of popular sovereignty, by definition, both presupposes and entails the existence of other states. A state is defined only by the existence of other states, by virtue of their sanction of each member of their community as a sovereign entity.[1] Our world is not only made up of states, but it is also a place in which there exists no apolitical space between or among these states. A person without a state is a persona non grata. Thus, for Islamic governance to constitute itself as a politically recognized entity, it must be acknowledged as a participant in the community of nation-states, no matter how its weltanschauung may differ from these states.

This is not all, however. This international order of states has been increasingly dominated by a relatively new power relationship that has come to be known as globalization. Although the world has witnessed, for over two millennia, conquests, migrations, and certain forms of transregional commercial activity, modern globalization possesses a different quality.[2] It is not only an economic phenomenon (as the premodern commercial form mainly was, though on a small scale); it is virulently economic, and it is extensively and intrusively political and cultural as well. Essential to the modern form of globalization is an unprecedented dialectic—generated by powerful telecommunications technology—between the local and global, where the import of local events automatically and synchronically present globalized meanings. Which is to say, conversely, that global meanings and events intermesh in localized life, automatically rendering these global meanings, as they unfold, integral to the local.

In substantive terms, political and especially economic transnational networks have asserted their dominance across state boundaries, rendering these boundaries largely permeable. Furthermore, it is abundantly clear that the markets and economies that control and direct this massive movement toward globalization are capitalist and not socialist, egalitarian, or populist. Globalization is clearly the project of the rich and powerful states and the colossal corporations ostensibly regulated by them,[3] a project largely imposed on weaker states.[4] And it so happens that the political-economic paradigm of these powerful states is a liberal one. No other significant economic-political force can be detected.[5] With this dominance, the goal of the liberal order is the creation, to the largest extent possible, of a single or unified world market operating under shared, common—even identical—legal norms.[6] Even though the globalizing liberal order crosses, by definition, state boundaries, it embodies and reflects nearly the same ideology of the liberal state, which has largely conduced to the virulent, most modern forms of globalization. The strong correlation and connection between the two can hardly be denied, and if this much is accepted, then the founding ideology and operative mode of globalization comport, *mutatis mutandis*, with the constitutive ideological features of the paradigmatic modern state.[7]

This comportment, however, does not give rise to a unified interpretation of the relationship between the state and globalization. Political and international relations theory has debated this question for almost two decades, dividing itself along two main theses.[8] The first depicts the state, having conduced to the movement of global capital, as progressively losing its autonomy, power, and centralizing capacity.[9] Because of the heave and thrust of globalization, the state is losing its ability to maintain itself as a unified set of institutions, with executive power and thus sovereignty being affected in the process.[10] Facing the stress of economic globalization, the state is also said to have lost a certain measure of its power to control its internal economic, social, and cultural spheres. Yet the receding power of the state in certain economic and other domains does not mean that its disappearance is imminent. It remains, even on this thesis, a regulatory force that global institutions rely upon for further expansion of markets, both within its borders and outside them. But there is no question that the balance of power has shifted and continues to shift in favor of the global market and away from the state.

The second thesis views the nation-state as capable of upholding its status and strength in the new globalized world. The state, according to this thesis, remains a key political actor that has not only resisted but dictated the forces of the international economic market.[11] It continues to define the concept of territoriality and citizenship, a concept that remains as solid now as it has been for the past century. Above all, the state has maintained its political character despite, if not because of, the increasing range of international regulations. It not only itself plays an important role in the creation of these regulations but also confers legitimacy upon supra and transnational corporations.[12] The state continues to enjoy sovereignty and independent legislation and to have exclusive control over the means of legitimate violence. It also has absolute power over the bureaucratic machinery and continues to expand its cultural penetration in the social order. With its massive power structure and by the logic of the rules of stimulus and response, the state is said to have reacted advantageously to the competitive challenges of globalization, in the process strengthening itself in these and other domains. It is even said to be the "major institutional framework in and through which the contemporary round of globalization is being fought out."[13] Finally, this second thesis, in order to bolster the credibility of its arguments, takes into serious consideration the social and economic disparities that globalization has intensified, indeed created.[14] These disparities are bound to engender, as they have, social and political unrest that only the state can address through its reforms and policies in the spheres of distribution of wealth and social justice.[15] The state, in other words, will continue to be indispensable.

For our purposes, it is possible to subsume under the second thesis the so-called transformationalist school,[16] since this school views the state as able, in the short run, to withstand the overall effects of globalization and, in the long run, to adjust or transform itself into an order in which traditional political and social categories will be replaced by new ones. In other words, the state will be able to reconstitute itself and thereby successfully meet the challenges posed by globalization.[17]

The two theses we have outlined, and the range of views represented in them,[18] essentially offer the position that the state will either persist or be replaced by a new globalized structure of power. The view that the state will adjust and transform itself so as to meet the globalizing challenge is, in our view, somewhat redundant because it apparently does not take for granted the essential premise that change and adjustment are integral to the state as a historical process. The state, let us take it for granted, did undergo transformations in the past and will continue to do so, and this must be the latent, though unarticulated, assumption of the second thesis. Yet the transformations cannot be so drastic as to metamorphose the state into something lacking in resemblance to anything we have known it to be for the past two centuries. For once this occurs, we can no longer talk of the state except to compose its requiem. In this event, we would be left with the first thesis, if any at all, since even this thesis is premised upon an assessment of the state's (in)ability to cope.

We are therefore left with three schematic possibilities: the total victory of globalization, the total victory of the state, or a complex and continuous dialectic of both friction and cooperation between the two. In the foreseeable future, neither victory seems likely to happen, leaving us with the third possibility, which is largely the present reality on the ground, plus any variation on the more or less existing situation. We contend that if Islamic governance—as we have seen—is incompatible with the modern state, it will be even less compatible with (1) the present (or even foreseeable) form of globalization as the sole form of governance and (2) the synthetic result of any dialectic between this form of globalization and the state.

Now, globalization has come to mean several different things, none of which is insignificant or without serious implications. We briefly note three main characteristics, the first being the cultural.[19] The new telecommunication technologies have taken away some of the state's monopoly in the production of culture and cultural forms, now opening this sphere to competing forces that have generally had the overall effect of globalizing certain, but not other, cultural forms. One can safely say that while particular aspects of local traditional cultures have, by virtue of globalization, been subject to protection (think of world heritage sites), these remain museum-like phenomena competing with the rapid, aggressive, and massive advances of generally Western cultural types (think of Western performing arts, the McDonald's diet, Walmart's sweatshop practices, the stiff modern business suit, the culture of consuming alcohol, and the abandonment in Afro-Asian countries of traditional cultural forms—and the vanishing means of their production—in favor of their Western counterparts). The threat of cultural displacement haunts, though to a lesser extent, even some Western regions, as evidenced in the case of Quebec and its continuous struggle against Anglo-American cultural hegemony. The Catalans and the Basques are two other examples in point.

Needless to say, cultural hegemony over the non-West is concomitant with forms of dominant political and military power, which are in turn concomitant with economy and markets.[20] Here, the state remains a significant source of globalization. As Martin Shaw has argued, the contemporary paradigmatic form of the modern state is not just that of a nation-state but also "a massive, institutionally complex and messy agglomeration of state power" that "has undergone further transformations and it is becoming possible to see the western state as a global form of state power."[21] Drawing on Michael Mann's theory (and he might have enlisted Carl Schmitt as well), Shaw argues that globalization is as much a political and military force as it is an economic one in terms of importance and that these "multi-powers" represent the continuing dominance of the West over "more or less the entire world."[22]

There is little doubt however that the economic aspect of globalization is the most pronounced. It remains the first priority of ASEAN, the European Union, NAFTA, MERCOSUR, APEC, CIS, and the OECD, not to mention the WTO, IMF, World Bank, and others.[23] The sheer size of the financial global market is staggering, overshadowing the total costs of global militarism, another instrument of globalization.[24] By the mid-1990s, world exports equaled no less than 17 percent of world output, representing a 10 percent increase over that of the three previous decades combined.[25] The numbers have increased since and are increasing daily. Thus, to say that globalization privileges, as does modern society at large, material wealth and economic prosperity is to state what is most evident. In this respect, we are looking at an economic model that issues from the same logic as that of the paradigmatic state, which happens to be staunchly liberal in orientation.[26] However, the world economy is undoubtedly more intensively pursued and minimally regulated, having little resemblance to a system.[27] It therefore lacks any mechanism similar to what the state has developed in dealing with issues of social justice and wealth redistribution (the United States being a partial exception here, even when compared with far less prosperous countries). In this respect, the state, however impoverished its record, has been more attentive than anything globalization has so far managed or is likely to manage. Yet, where markets and capital are concerned, the state should not be always pitted against globalization, as if the latter were entirely out of its control—as some theories of globalization make it to be. Globalized free markets are largely the work of the state, led, in the current situation, primarily by the United States but also by Europe and Japan (not to mention emerging China).

One prominent example of the state's role, an example essential for our enquiry, is the stark fact that the state-created and state-regulated corporation plays a central role in the globalized economy.[28] Apart from any judgment about the merits or demerits of globalization *qua* globalization, a driving force of globalization has undoubtedly been the corporation.[29] Thus, it is reasonable to assess globalization by one of its dominant features, i.e., its corporate ethic, which has received and continues to receive the endorsement of the state.[30] Despite the fact that the early modern state recognized the moral repugnancy of the corporation and although it had outlawed it for a period on the grounds that it subverts personal moral responsibility, the state has nonetheless allowed it not only to come back but to do so with an enhanced juristic personality, the very quality that initially outraged the government's moral sense.[31] Space does not allow extensive comment on the nature of the corporation, but one aspect is crystal clear. The corporation is created by law for one purpose: to increase its wealth and to prioritize this purpose above all others, including social responsibility, which, when it exists at all, is placed in the service of generating even more profit. Corporate charity and social responsibility thus become strategies to increase profits and hence the economic size of the corporation. This is precisely why corporation-based globalization cannot vie with the state, because the state has developed the means of addressing, however minimally, the human needs of its own citizens. The corporation has, by contrast, not only failed to do the same; it has also been notorious in its inhumane and exploitative practices, destroying the lives of people (so-called externalities) as consumers of their products, as victims of chemical and oil spillages, as abused laborers in their sweatshops, and as inhabitants of a planet being slowly but assuredly destroyed by their callous industrial practices.

We may conclude that none of the features we have attributed to the nation-state in the last four chapters has, under globalization, diminished to an extent sufficient to justify a reconsideration of its nature. All features, or what we called form-properties, have either been minimally affected (e.g., sovereignty and state cultural monopoly) or even enhanced (e.g., legal regulation and bureaucracy). On the other hand, there is nothing in the form-properties of globalization, except for its range, that the state does not already possess. Globalization has no real sovereignty; it has, compared to the state, and independent of it, minimalistic powers to exercise legitimate violence and the threat of its use; its legislative competence is likewise comparatively limited; and its potency, *as an autonomous agency*, to permeate the cultural domain is still in its infancy. In fact, globalization possesses no cultural autonomy, because it derives its cultural thrust—as we have seen—from a Western society heavily influenced by state interference. The educational and the larger cultural spheres—significant arenas of power formation—remain penetrated by and under the direct control of the nation-state, while globalization is chiefly their semiconductor (however rapidly it is increasing its conductive capacity).

Now, isolation not being an option—certainly in the long run—Islamic governance must deal with both the nation-state and a globalized world, both of which operate according to a certain set of parameters. We have noted most of these in the foregoing chapters, having left one out, namely, liberal, free-market capitalism. We shall address this characteristic in the next section and conclude, in a set of brief remarks, with a synthesis that brings in the conditions of Islamic governance we have outlined in the first paragraph of this chapter.

2. Islam's Moral Economy

Just as liberal economics dominating the world today are defined by a set of principles that distinguish them from other economic orientations—such as socialism—so is the Islamic system of economics (nowadays nearly all but forgotten). And just as modern liberal economics rests on a certain conception of the world and a particular form of political life, so does Islam's economy, which is heavily colored, if not fully determined, by a certain conception of the world that was not political but Sharʿī in nature. Whereas liberal economic philosophy, both at the state and globalization levels, is characterized by free trade, free movement of capital, privatization, and the desideratum of maximizing profit and capital accumulation for their own sake (hence the much noted irrationality of capitalism),[32] the Islamic paradigm rests on what might be called a moral economy.

The paradigm of this economy emerged with the Qurʾān itself, the founding document of Islam, its cultures, and its material world. It was further elaborated by the articulation of Prophetic narrative and subsequently by the encompassing system of the Sharīʿa as a discursive and institutional phenomenon. While commercial practices and economic activities varied from region to region and from one century or period to the next, the Sharʿī moral values reigned supreme, creating an overall reality that testified to both its success and prevalence. The success can be measured by the indisputable fact that Islamic material civilization and Islamic regional and international commerce were among the most vibrant and prominent in premodern world history.[33] This (perhaps understated) characterization is not only validated by what we know about Islam and its economic history but is also attested by the fact that European colonialism could not truly dominate Muslim lands during the nineteenth century without first dismantling the economic structures, and these structures depended on Sharʿī regulations, laws, and values to a significant extent.[34] This is one important reason why the colonialist project insisted on rooting out the Sharīʿa, it having been an impediment to Europe's political expansion and, far more importantly, economic domination. This perceived and actual impediment sums it all up, for it speaks to the Sharīʿa's incompatibility, as a moral system, with the ways and values of modern capitalism.

Essential to any account of the Sharīʿa's moral economy is the idea that the protection and promotion of property and wealth represents one of the five "universals" (*kulliyyāt*) according to which the Sharīʿa legal system, and therefore Islamic society as a whole, had been structured and was made to operate.[35] Protection of life, religion, mind, and community were the other four.[36] Accomplished through the laws of homicide and of grievous bodily injury, the universal of protecting life (*nafs*) includes, but is not limited to, criminal compensatory damages and, in the case of homicide, the agnates' right (but not the state's) to seek monetary damages, choose capital punishment, or grant pardon. Protection of religion (*dīn*) is promoted by what we called technologies of the self[37] as well as through the laws of *jihād* and *ridda* (apostasy), amounting, respectively, to defending the rights of Muslims against outside threat and internal religious dissension.[38] Protection of mind or rational faculty (*ʿaql*), quintessential to any "legal" act (including prayer, pilgrimage, etc.), is brought about through various regulations that determine legal capacity and the necessity of interdiction as well as such laws that prohibit the consumption of inebriants. Preservation of the community (*nasl*) is achieved by the laws regulating marriage, illicit sexual relationships, divorce, inheritance, custody, and the like. Although the term *nasl* literally means children or lineage, the "legal" meaning and laws pertaining to this category effectively covered the extended family and, by implication, the community in which it lived and with which every extended family established marriage and other socioeconomic ties.[39]

The five universals, consensually accepted in Islam as defining the purposes of the moral law—and "instituted for serving the best interests of the believers"[40]—emerged in jurisprudence as the result of an inductive project whereby, after the Sharīʿa had reached a level of maturity, the jurists looked back at the whole picture, so to speak, and culled these universals from the full range of legal culture, not limiting themselves to the texts of revelation or the rational methods of legal theory (*uṣūl al-fiqh*).[41] In other words, the overall effect of the Sharīʿa—as a discursive, theoretical, institutional, and practical system—was boiled down to these universals, which, in turn, once unpacked and elaborated to the finest detail, produced nothing but the Sharīʿa, in all that it was. Drawing on at least five centuries of established legal tradition, the universals were inductively identified and later continually elaborated, having become paradigmatic features defining the Sharīʿa as a legal and cultural system. Indeed, they may be said to capture much of what Islam was all about.[42]

None of these five universals is autonomous, however. To be implemented to any reasonable measure and to be meaningful, each universal is bound to draw upon and overlap with the others, maintaining with them a relationship of interdependence. The universal of protecting life is obviously an essential one and provides the basic structure of order without which none of the other four universals can be pursued. The universal of protecting religion is equally foundational, because it determines both the quality and texture of the order that the first principle, that of life, had established. *Jihād* and apostasy do not denote the simplistic and crude political meanings they have come to acquire nowadays but represent deep conceptual structures that tie in with religious works, a mildly ascetic philosophy of life, and the all-important technologies of the self. If the first universal is a mechanical apparatus that lays the "foundations of social order," the universal of religion gives this order its values, meanings, psychology, and spirituality. By this logic, it follows that the universal pertaining to the family and community intermeshes with the universal of religion, because the latter is also the foundation, and productive, of the former.

Yet all of these, including the universal of the mind, constitute the matrix within which the universal of property is made both possible and constructive. It is also this universal of property that engages in a dialectic with any of the other three to promote the remaining fifth. To say that elements belonging to the entire set of universals were put in motion simultaneously whenever one of them was invoked for action is to sum up the matter accurately. Thus, the principle of property was delimited, constrained, supported, and brought out into reality by a structural dialectic of Sharʿī values, practices, and institutions. The very principles of property rights and the acquisition, maintenance, and dispensation of wealth were all at once regulated by a dialectic of spiritual, metaphysical, and worldly considerations.[43]

Seeking material wealth and accumulation of capital was encouraged in Islam and its Sharīʿa.[44] The Prophet himself was a business manager and a trader, having married a powerful woman who was a considerable merchant in her own right. The Qurʾān likewise declares trade and business to be legitimate activities to be pursued once the religious duty to pray is discharged.[45] The Sharīʿa has also come to possess elaborate rules and regulations for sale, contract, and trade. The overall space devoted to such issues, including business partnerships, pledge, transfer, agency, deposit, loans, insolvency, civil misappropriation, leases, rent, hire, and the like constitutes no less than 15 percent of the vast written record of the Sharīʿa. When other financial regulations and laws pertaining to taxation, inheritance, bequests, gifts, charitable foundations, divorce, and the like are included, the percentage rises to about, if not in excess of, one-quarter of that totality.[46] Considering the paramount importance of the "pillars" that constituted the technologies of the self[47] and in view of the sacred place that family and laws relative to the family have come to acquire—not to mention the other nearly countless areas of regulation—allotting a quarter of textual attention to contract, trade, and financial transactions is quite remarkable.

All contractual transactions under the Sharīʿa are imbued with moral values. To be valid, contracts must presuppose, inter alia, *riḍā*, a morally and psychologically charged concept. *Riḍā* is a wholehearted consent devoid of any trace of coercion or even reluctance.[48] It presupposes fair dealing, good faith, and psychological ease by all contracting parties. Commerce and trade, being contractual, must be situated in this framework, one that requires forgiveness, magnanimity (*samāḥa*), rectitude, and avoidance of greed, avarice, and placing oppressive constraints on one's contractual partners. "God will have mercy upon a man who is magnanimous in his selling, buying and settling [debts, lawsuits, etc.].[49] The "honest and truthful merchant accompanies the prophets [to Paradise],"[50] whereas those merchants who cheat and swindle will face the fire of hell for their sins.[51] Trade is suspicious if conducted within a market in which property and money have been corrupted by malpractices, whether these involve misappropriation, risk, or *ribā* (charging usury).[52] The fear that trade, and the money made from it, have been, even unknowingly, corrupted by the market's immoral practices prompted the Sharīʿa to install legal and moral mechanisms that were intended to "purify" that money. Hence the demand to pay the alms-tax (*zakāt*) and to engage in various other charitable practices, including *ṣadaqa* and, indirectly, *waqf* (this latter having commanded nearly half of all real property in Muslim lands by the sixteenth century).[53] It was the presumption that in every sale there is the potential presence of an *ithm*, a moral liability, this because one does not always know—however honest one may be—where his profit came from. This liability is so grave that it is said to raise the fury of God's anger (*ghaḍab al-Rabb*), and the surest way to appease this anger is to engage in charity for the benefit of the poor and even the wayfarers.[54] Those who hoard wealth, who make money for the sake of making money—who, in other words, forgo social responsibility as a genuine act of worship—have one certain fate: burning in hell.[55]

This moral impulse is neither incidental nor does it hover at the margins of the legal culture. It is paradigmatic, surrounding and thoroughly permeating the fabric of the Sharīʿa's rules about property, contracts, investments, commercial transactions, and anything having to do with profit. None of these emanates from a "brute" or "inert" world;[56] rather, they are integral to the bounties that God has bestowed on humankind. He has given this kind all these blessings and comforts without expecting a share in them for Himself, because His profit, the return on His investment in potentially ungrateful humans, is obtaining their gratefulness to Him. Yet, the teleology of the gratefulness to Him Who is Self-Sufficient (*ghanī*) does not finally rest with Him, since gratefulness has an anthropological reflexivity and can be expressed only in one way: giving to the poor, fellow human beings, as a way of appreciating the basic fact that one is alive and enjoys secure sustenance above and beyond one's basic needs. Gratefulness, in Sharīʿa's definition, thus translates, even at this modest level of securing sustenance, into a fully fledged conception of social responsibility.

Earning a living to the extent that one needs to support oneself and one's family and to pay one's debts is a religious obligation[57] and an incumbent duty (*farḍ*).[58] The Sharīʿa's fundamental position is one that adopts the principle of *istiʿfāf*, namely, seeking *whenever possible* economic independence and avoiding financial help from others.[59] However, earnings beyond this basic level of sustenance are recommended (*mustaḥabb*)[60] even though only for the purpose of spending them on the poor or assisting distant relatives in need. It is also permissible (*mubāḥ*) to engage in business ventures that may yield large fortunes, which may be expended in the enhancement of a better style of life and even opulent living. But this permissibility is predicated upon the condition that one's life is conducted according to the virtues of religion, where honesty, modesty, rectitude, good faith, and fair dealings are given first priority and supreme value. Here two sets of obligations must be fulfilled: the rights of God and the rights of one's fellow human beings. Any earnings beyond those necessary for sustenance must be expended; for the first set of rights, they must be spent as alms-tax (*zakāt*), as various other stipulated and unstipulated charities (*ṣadaqāt*, *waqf*, etc.), and as tax on land income; for the second set, any surplus must be used to settle personal debts, fulfill pecuniary agreements, and support the extended family, including distant relatives in need (*nafaqāt*).[61] It should be noted, furthermore, that because all wealth is always assumed to belong to God, the poor are seen to have a natural right to a part of the wealth of the rich,[62] this wealth being defined as income that exceeds the needs for self-sufficiency. The Qurʾān explicitly decrees this right.[63]

Lawful earnings (*kasb*) must fulfill all these conditions, but three others are noteworthy in our context: First, any income or profit made must be conceived, at a psychological level, as coming from God and His grace, this being an integral part of the technologies of the self we have discussed earlier.[64] Second, no excessive effort should be expended in acquiring wealth,[65] this standing in sharp contrast to the principle that "utmost effort" (*jihād*) must be exerted in the struggle to be a better moral subject.[66] Thus whereas moral striving requires total effort, material gain is assigned a lower priority. Finally, in the process of making a living or acquiring wealth, no "creature of God may be harmed."[67]

Acquisition of wealth, permitted and even encouraged, is therefore regulated by and subordinated to higher moral principles that place qualitative constraints on it. These principles are not of the technical legal type but hearken back to the epistemic and psychological technologies of the moral subject. It is simply not enough to avoid engaging in obvious usurious and risk-ridden (*gharar*) business ventures, two pillars on which modern Islamic banking and finance claim to rest, and even then problematically. Conducting business and making profit must be sustained by a holistic view of the world, a view that derives from a system of practices and beliefs constituting and reflecting the entire range of the technologies of the self, which shape and sustain the moral subject. These technologies are utterly absent from any account of modern Islamic banking and finance, a phenomenon that (when coupled with the narrow technical concerns that pervade these accounts) compels the conclusion that both the theory and practice of current Islamic banking and finance are deeply flawed. At the end of the day, they are Islamic merely in name, reflecting nearly nothing of what Islam as a moral system is all about.[68]

3. Concluding Remarks About Predicaments

Having supposed the coming into existence of Islamic governance, we are forced also to suppose that this governance will be subject to the challenges posed by a globalized world. We have identified at least three such challenges: the militarism of powerful imperial states, exogenous cultural intrusions, and a massive liberal-capitalist world market. These challenges are not independent of one another, however, because the centers of military power are nearly identical to the sources that emit cultural and economic hegemony. At times the economic challenge is accompanied by both military and cultural impositions. And cultural domination has also often proven to support economic globalization and its free markets. Our history since the Cold War—from Vietnam and Angola to the occupation of Afghanistan and Iraq—has offered clear proof of the operation of the three forces, acting both severally and aggregately.

While military power and wars have, on their own and without the involvement of cultural and economic hegemony, been integral to human history for millennia, they are now often inseparable from this hegemony. Military defeat in the fashion of Afghanistan and Iraq is, if not imminent, always a possibility facing any form of Islamic governance. As long as the balance of power in the world remains in favor of a Schmittian state, Islamic governance as an existential entity will always be under fatal threat.

Culture is a less tangible and more insidious form of control. An Islamic governance, having reached the consciousness and sophistication that are prerequisites for such self-constitution, will be forced to peruse and evaluate globalized cultural forms. Whether they are performing or visual arts, culinary or dietary habits, commercially manipulated sexual images or sexualizing the body, subliminal or manipulative advertisement, etc., Islamic governance must take a stance with regard to all these issues. It will, we must also assume, understand the sources of such cultural phenomena, its materialism, hedonism, and narcissism, and its structural tendency to separate morality and value, on the one hand, from fact, science, law, and economics, on the other. It will understand what makes for the "disenchantment" of the modern subject and the national narcissism imbuing the modern mind. Every painting, sculpture, and culinary experience must be reevaluated according to different norms and values, asking questions about esthetics as much as about the human mind and body and their purposes in this world. Whatever is deemed unfit for the cultural landscape of Islamic governance must be discarded, and this is where the challenge lies. How will this governance rebuff the forces of globalized culture, forces fully backed by the superior, positivism-grounded powers in the world? How will it stem the intrusiveness of the giant corporations who are backed by these powers and who push their products into the hands, bodies, and minds of teenagers and adults alike? The severity of these challenges is surely undeniable.

Certainly no less crucial is the economic challenge. If Islamic governance is to pursue its economic goals—which promote trade, financial investment, and profit making—it must contend with a global market that is backed by powerful liberal and staunchly capitalist states, a market dominated by the corporation and its endless and amoral pursuit of profit. The question as to why Islam never developed a corporate juristic personality has been debated since the 1960s, but an answer that rests on moral analysis has, interestingly, not been forthcoming.[69] The Sharīʿa's lack of recognition of this personality has been seen as a deficiency, one of the many of which Sharīʿa is accused. It has not occurred to the critics advancing such superficial explanations that it is precisely the moral bent of the Sharīʿa that has precluded this possibility. Sharīʿa's morality may well have recognized that certain things simply cannot be done, not because they intrinsically and objectively cannot be done but because once done, the consequences cannot be tolerated (this perhaps being one of the finest definitions of morality). This intolerance for sacrificing value is precisely the moment of moral sanity that propelled the English government to ban the corporation momentarily during the sixteenth century, but that sanity was not long lived. With its twelve centuries of continuous and extensive experience, the Sharīʿa could not accept the concept of a corporation because it ran in diametrical opposition to its moral principles. The moral and legal accountability of natural persons may be said to have been the deepest-running anchor of the Sharīʿa, perhaps the feature that gave the Sharīʿa its character. The corporation and all that it represents as a virulent capitalist enterprise is not only amoral and often immoral; it is also the epitome of anti-Sharʿism. Even if Islamic governance were to mitigate and tone down its moral imperatives, traces of this morality would still be highly incompatible with modern capitalism and its principal weapon, the corporation.

Furthermore, economists have for long understood that any modern national economy will inevitably experience serious difficulties in maintaining economic growth if at the same time it tried to implement a policy guaranteeing a decent measure of social and economic justice. They have declared that "economic structures and policies that promote growth depress distributional equality."[70] Paradigmatic Islamic governance is by definition geared toward implementing such guarantees, for social justice is one of its constitutive and central features. Within a globalized capitalism, such governance would progressively weaken, becoming less and less competitive, resulting in economic and a host of other social and political problems. It is likely to grow dependent on foreign help, thereby losing its autonomy in favor of IMF or World Bank governance. No doubt, these latter would impose on this type of governance, as they nowadays routinely do, their rules of reorganization and thus frustrate any attempt to build this governance into a meaningful and autonomous entity.

7

The Central Domain of the Moral

> "Love thy neighbor as thyself" is the very soul of the moral point of view, which demands that we regard another's good as having the same direct claim on our attention as our own good expectably does. And those wedded to an instrumentalist approach will naturally refuse to attach any rational sense to the idea, holding that our allegiance to morality has to be grounded in the pursuit of our own interests, and finding themselves therefore unable to explain why our moral attention should extend to strangers and to the weak, as it obviously must if another's good weighs with us independently of our own. Yet though I have quoted Scripture to bring home the import of a non-instrumentalist conception of morality, can one really maintain that it makes sense only within a religious world-view? Do we not judge the worth of a religion by moral principles we know in our heart of hearts to be right, including the very one in question?
>
> —Larmore, *The Autonomy of Morality*

Modern Islamist discourses assume the modern state to be a neutral tool of governance, one that can be harnessed to perform certain functions according to the choices and dictates of its leaders.[1] When not used for oppression, the machinery of state governance can be turned by leaders into a representative of the people's will, determining thereby what the state will become: a liberal democracy, a socialist regime, or an Islamic state implementing the values and ideals enshrined in the Qur'ān and those that the Prophet had once realized in his "mini-state" of Medina. The modern state is then seen by them just as logic was seen by Aristotle and the Aristotelians, namely, as a neutral technique or instrument guiding correct thinking about any issue or problem in the world—until, that is, it was shown centuries after Aristotle, by Muslim intellectuals themselves, that Aristotelian formal logic and the theory of universals on which it rests was *inherently* saturated with particular metaphysical assumptions that predetermined the nature of its premises and therefore its conclusions. The very use of this logic meant an a priori acceptance of a certain brand of metaphysics, one that most Muslim intellectuals rejected.[2]

The modern state is no different, for it comes with its own arsenal of metaphysics and much else. It *inherently* produces certain distinctive effects that are political, social, economic, cultural, epistemic, and, no less, psychological, which is to say that the state fashions particular knowledge systems that in turn determine and shape the landscape of individual and collective subjectivity and thus much of the meaning of its subjects' lives.

As no idea or thought can come into existence outside of a human context, and as no event or act can be conceivable outside time or space, the state—as both abstract thought and concrete practice—is product of a unique historical experience. As a paradigm of governance, it evolved in Europe and was later nurtured by Euro-America, and it subsequently was exported to the colonies and the rest of the world. As we have seen, the modern state is uncomfortably seated in many parts of the world, suffering from lack of legitimacy and unable to rule hitherto unhomogenized subject populations. We often characterize these as "weak" or "rogue" states, euphemisms for the fact that a nonindigenous form of political control has, relatively recently and without "preparation," been violently imposed on colonized societies that never knew or had never on their own or willingly adopted such a form. This perhaps is the most evincive evidence of the foreignness of the modern state, an entity that is—historically, substantively, and conceptually—thoroughly Euro-American.

However, none of this should mean that the modern state is an immutable phenomenon, that it does not and cannot change, that it has not adapted or could not adjust to an ever-changing world. For it is hardly deniable that the state of the nineteenth century had noticeably evolved by the middle of the twentieth, and today's state, as we saw in the preceding chapter, continues to undergo certain changes in response to, inter alia, the emerging challenges of globalization. Yet none of these changes and none of the otherwise persistent structures of the modern state have ever proven themselves compatible with even the basic requirements of Islamic governance. In fact, instead of rendering the modern state less objectionable, the mutations of the last three decades, especially in the direction of so-called globalization, have increased their incompatibility progressively. It should not by now come as a surprise that this incompatibility is ultimately a moral one.

1. The Major Incompatibilities

Let us, by way of summary, count some of the important ways in which this incompatibility manifests itself, while realizing that no single one is mutually exclusive of the others. First, as an anthropocentric entity, the state possesses a metaphysic that resides within its own boundaries as sovereign will. The metaphysic generates its own meanings, which is to say that its particular views of the world are of its own creation and bound by its own standards, however changeable these standards may be. As the highest manifestation of positivism, the state possesses and displays a metaphysic of the here and now, reflecting its own concepts, structures, and practices. What Is for the state is its truth of will, its will to power, all other truths being marginal and subordinate. By stark contrast, no form of Islamic governance can permit positivism, nor is there a place for a metaphysic that issues therefrom. If the autonomy of the moral is the highest of all desiderata, then metaphysics, which foregrounds moral autonomy, cannot descend to positivism. If moral autonomy must lead, if it must be the determinant of all determinants, then metaphysics must necessarily transcend the narrow domain of positivist anthropocentricism. The two metaphysics, therefore, stand in an irreconcilable deadlock.

Second, and flowing from the former consideration, Islamic governance cannot permit any sovereignty or sovereign will other than that of God. If morality is to guide human actions, if it be autonomous, then it must rest on universal and eternal principles of truth and justice, principles that transcend the manipulation and whims of a positivist entity. It must determine the limits of human actions, drawing a line of separation between what can and cannot be done and curbing the domain of the rational when this leads to the violation of its own domain. In Islamic governance, where—as we have seen—the rule of law takes on one of its most supreme expressions, no earthly sovereignty is allowed to compromise the dictates of moral autonomy. If transcendent morality imposes on us the protection of the poor and the weak, if it creates for them an inherently natural right against the wealth of the rich, then no economic development or capitalist principle can be allowed to override this will. If this morality dictates a humane treatment of others, then no political or scientific calculation *whatsoever* can be permitted to reduce another's humanity by any measure, to let her starve or send him to the gas chambers, simply in the name of science and rationality. As Paul Kahn aptly observed, there are no principles of restraint on the use of force in a polity that "understands itself as the expression of popular sovereignty under the rule of law." On the other hand, a "state that understands itself as an expression of a divine or a natural order can look to meanings outside of itself to limit its actions."[3]

Islamic governance is thus bound by a sovereign will outside of and higher than itself, whereas the modern state's sovereignty represents an inner dialectic of self-constitution: sovereignty constitutes the state and is constituted by it. These two opposed conceptions of sovereignty will inevitably stand in a deadlock.[4]

Third, and flowing from the former two considerations, if God is the only sovereign—which is to say, if God is the ultimate source of moral authority—then any system that regulates human behavior must heed the general norms and technical rules and regulations derived from and dictated by the higher moral principles. This, for Muslims past and present, is the true and ultimate meaning of the rule of law. As we saw in chapter 3, the best form of separation of powers in the paradigmatic modern state suffers from defects that render the system, even as an elaborate theory, inconsistent, confused, and even a "failure."[5] If the modern state as a sovereign will inherently bestows on the executive branch powers formidable enough to chip away at the legislative, then the rule of law would have to be defined in terms of executive will as much as of that of legislative will. At the same time, judicial review chips away at the latter will still further, reducing its purview and narrowing its competence. Such a constitutional arrangement, integral to the structures of the modern state, would be unthinkable in any form of Islamic governance, making the two arrangements, both in theory and in practice, largely incompatible.

Fourth, and reflecting the aggregate effects of the former three considerations, the modern state produces subjects that differ from those produced by any form of Islamic governance in profoundly political, social, moral, epistemic, and psychological ways. The microcosmic insistence of the Muslim subject on the unity of the Is and Ought is a faithful representation of the macrocosmic Sharʿī (and Ṣūfist) insistence that fact and value are one and the same, *that all existence is a unity*, and that the term "poor" in Qurʾānic discourse and in Muslim social and economic life is not a statistic or a scientific datum. In the very terms "poor" and "poverty," the *value of an inherent right to aid, assistance, and compassion* is intertwined with and indistinguishably meshed into the *fact* of descending into poverty. There is no "poor" in the vocabulary and conceptual categories of Islamic governance that can be distinguished in any way from the deontological moral value not only of the poor's right to aid but also of a commensurate duty incumbent upon those who can provide it. This type of nondistinction is pervasive, extending to nature and the nature of things. Everything in the world is the work of One Agent who created one and all for a reason. No "atom of a good or bad deed" can be separated from any atom of sand or seed. Everything is interconnected, and all things are but One. Living in the world is living in the Kingdom of God, with all of its fortunes and misfortunes, its good- and evildoers, its trees and rivers, its poor and rich. To live in this world is to accept the majestic wisdom of its Creator, as manifested in His creation. It is to accept humanity with its honorable strengths and dishonorable weaknesses. But it is also to accept the necessity and the *paradigmatic* desideratum of striving to be good and of being thankful for being alive and for the bounties bestowed upon humankind, however small or large they may be. It is to surrender to the majesty of this creation, our transient abode and our test of goodness. There is no reason for humankind to exist other than to prove, in heart and deed, the extent to which they can do good. Doing good is the heart and soul, the core and kernel, and the most pronounced message of the Qurʾān and therefore of Islam and Islamic governance. If there is Hell and Heaven, punishment and reward, and if God is the One, the Punisher, the Compassionate, and the Merciful, it is all deployed for one purpose and one purpose only: To create the good-doer and hence the good community, for there would be no meaning for his Oneness, Mercy, and Wrath without this concept of good.

But the call to goodness is not an ambiguous invocation, a moral injunction devoid of content. To be good is both a defined and defining concept that can be located within the five pillars of religion, pillars that Islam—from the beginning until this very present—never questioned and, more importantly, never abandoned. If the pillars are by definition exclusivist—and they are—it is because everything other than them is subsidiary and subordinate. If these are the pillars, then everything else is not. But since the Sharīʿa and Islamic governance must, by necessity, regulate all human behavior,[6] then that which is not a pillar must conform to the pillars' dictates and aggregate will. Which is to say that the structure and operation of the pillared system predetermines both the subject and subjectivity, preparing them to embark upon that which lies in the nonpillared world. And the pillars, accurately reflecting the tenor of the Qurʾānic philosophy, are anchored in a simple message: understand your place in the world; understand your own transience; understand that you are created as part of a community and of a family that together feed your soul, just as plants and grains feed your body; understand that all this is a gift that comes with a responsibility toward everything around you; understand that you really own nothing, that you will inevitably face your end and that you will take nothing with you to the grave except your good deeds, your good name; understand that you have duties toward the world in which you have been created, toward the community that was created for you and that is your anchor. Take nothing for granted.

It is this *foundational* understanding that underlies a set of performative acts and utterances which have a cumulative shaping effect on the body, soul, and mind. In their entirety, these acts are private, internal, and thus affective. From prayer and fasting—which both locate themselves in that foundational understanding—to pilgrimage and almsgiving, the total effect of these acts tends to shape the Muslim subject, fulfilling the desideratum of the Sharīʿa, of Islamic governance, and therefore of the art of living itself. The remaining Sharʿī laws and rules presuppose such a subject and operate—in one strong sense—as the addendum and annotation of this morally formed subject.

By stark contrast, the subject of the modern state is not wholly formed by the moral imperative. The conventional morality of tradition is constantly contested by a state-oriented technology of the self that systemically and systematically operates to create the national citizen. The contest is summed up with pinpoint precision in the statement that "it is not the duty of the state to make us good. That is *our* business."[7] The duty of the state, fulfilled maximally and most faithfully through education and nationalistic discourse—among much else—is to create the efficient and productive citizen, the subject of "law and order" who is willing to die for his country and nation. Whereas Islam—as we have seen—does not command sacrifice of life, even for the sake of God, the modern nation-state is inconceivable without this requirement. But there is another difference still. Whereas the aggregate effects of Islamic governance are intended to fashion the moral subject who interacts responsibly with an *anima mundi* and with community and family, the subject of the modern state is an exteriorized personality whose soul and spirit are of no concern but whose value resides in a political, materialistic, and efficiency-based conception of life. Put differently, whereas the Muslim subject strives for moral improvement, the state's subject strives to fulfill sovereign will, fictitiously a representation of the subject's own will but realistically the will of a commanding sovereign. The difference is a paradigmatic one between a continuous and unending moral struggle for the Ought and a continuous and unending worldly struggle for the Is, which aims to maintain a hold over the material bounties of an otherwise brute world of fact. The subject of

Is and the subject of Ought are two drastically different human subjects. They stand not only in diametrical opposition but in irreconcilable contradiction.

Fifth and finally, the modern state, in its collaboration and contestation with the globalization project, remains engaged in a preeminently material world of Fact. It depends on and promotes a *homo economicus* whose exclusive and ultimate desideratum is material profit and little else. This stands in sharp contrast with the morally constructed *homo economicus* of Islam and its governance, a species that is subordinated to a higher moral imperative. This latter subject is neither contingent nor a mere accident in the structure and makeup of Islam and Islamic governance: *it is of its essence*. Without this moral *homo economicus* there could hardly be an Islam, Muslims, or a Muslim civilization, at least in the way we have come to know them. It is precisely this *homo economicus* that created, over the course of an entire millennium, a civil society that kept politics and executive power at bay and that defined what Islam was. The paradigmatic Muslim *homo economicus* seeks wealth and profit but remains materially and psychologically committed to social responsibility, as is abundantly evidenced in twelve centuries of Islamic socioeconomic history. Honor, prestige, nearness to God, and the love and respect of family and neighbor all paradigmatically intersect with this ethic of indebtedness to one's own community. As everything is owned by the Ultimate Sovereign, wealth and profit are not possessed by or destined for only the rich. They are made "from" and "for the sake of the Ultimate Sovereign," whose Rights are identical with those of the rights of the poor and unprivileged. In this equation, the poor are integral to God, and He is integral to them. Serve them, and you serve God; serve God, and you serve them. Produced by the state and pushed, though willingly, into a brute world of economic competition and profit, the modern subject is one who will find the true Muslim *homo economicus* a curiosity and an aberration, something belonging to the museum of extinct species. Raised on the moral technologies of the self and imbued with a mild form of asceticism, the Muslim *homo economicus* would similarly regard his modernist counterpart as irrational, greedy, shortsighted, and selfish—in short, a brute. The oppositions between the two and their utter incompatibility are nothing short of staggering.

The totality of these inherent and fundamental oppositions poses a significant problem. If Muslims are to organize their lives in social, economic, and political terms, then they face a crucial choice. Either they must succumb to the modern state and the world that produced it, or the modern state and the world that produced it must recognize the legitimacy of Islamic governance, that is, the Muslim conception of polity, law, and, most importantly, morality and its subordinated political and economic demands. The first option would at first glance seem more realistic, given that at present it is largely accepted by Muslims and even their intellectuals, though often on the erroneous assumption that the system of the modern state can in good time be converted to an Islamic state. As I have argued in the previous chapters, this assumption forgoes a proper understanding of the nature of the modern state, its form-properties, and its inherent moral incompatibility with any form of Islamic governance. The second option seems, to all indications, far less likely, since any form of Islamic governance will have to live within a system of states that itself is under pressure from the imperatives of a globalized world. If the modern state, as so many analysts tell us, must itself compete with and readjust under the pressure of globalization, an Islamic governance would suffer multiple and incremental challenges that will quite likely cause its decline and, as likely, total collapse.

2. A Way Out?

Yet there is something worthy of investigation beyond this *realpolitik*, which by definition rests on a skewed vision of morality. Just as the modern state sits uncomfortably in the Muslim (and much of the Afro-Asian) world, modernity as a whole sits rather problematically in the entirety of this world of ours, including the very Euro-America that originally produced it. Throughout this book, we have alluded to some of these problems, which range from the spiritual vacuousness of the fragmented, hedonistic, and narcissistic self to the destruction of the organic community, family, and natural environment—none of which can be dissociated from the overarching project of the modern state. Thus the interrogations of the modern project cannot do without placing the state at the forefront of critique. Nor can they do without at the same time placing the destruction of the environment and the natural world at the center of our gaze, because, as I have already argued, our attitude to and dealings with this natural world is the measure of our existence, of our estimation of what it means for us to be human beings. The consequence of these attitudes is not, as many think, just a fact of life, a merely unfortunate byproduct of our otherwise good intentions and soundly established acts of progress. Rather, it is the ultimate Measure of Man because it constitutes the lowest benchmark against which our moral accountability toward all things in the world must be gauged and judged. It is, in other words, the *most central question* plaguing what ought to be the *central domain of the moral*, a question whose solution predetermines all other questions, problems, and, in turn, their solutions within the entirety of what we have called subsidiary domains.[8]

I shall take it for granted here that while these problems constitute significant physical and practical challenges that must be met in empirical and concrete ways, they are, as Durkheim argued in a similar context,[9] essentially moral problems, because they ultimately stem from a distortion in our moral vision of nature and because only through implementing a correction to this vision can these problems be solved in satisfactory and genuine ways. And these solutions have direct bearings not only on any possibility of Islamic governance in the modern world but also *and primarily* on the modern state and the modern condition in which it exists. As we shall stress in these concluding pages, the most fundamental problems of modern Islam *are not exclusively Islamic* but are in fact equally integral to the modern project itself in the East *and* the West.[10]

In addressing the issues involved here, we must return to the Enlightenment distinction between the Is and Ought, a distinction whose ramifications have profoundly shaped modernity's prevalent conceptions of the moral.[11] As a way of proceeding, we shall invoke the critiques of H. A. Prichard and Charles Larmore, whose work, combined with those of Taylor and MacIntyre, captures the main issues that concern us here.[12]

As we noted earlier, the distinction between Is and Ought stood in a dialectical causal relationship with the separation of value from a natural world that came to be regarded as "brute" and "inert."[13] When matter is stripped of all value, it ceases to be part of an *anima mundi* and thus can be treated as an object. It can be studied and subjected to the entire range of *our autonomous* rational analysis (and thus to our actions) without it making moral demands on us. But this unprecedented paradigmatic distinction created another significant effect, namely, the isolation of reason from reasons, reason being a tool of thinking about the world and reasons representing the substantive "causes" that generate thought through reason.[14] Whereas before the Enlightenment reason and reasons worked indistinctly together, after the Enlightenment reason, as distinct from reasons, was elevated to an autonomous status and was expected to generate reasons on its own. Hence modern moral philosophy's unwavering insistence that morality must be justified by autonomous and self-legislative reason, the backbone of the Kantian conception that rules over the modern moral paradigm. Although this Kantian position has been subjected to repeated and damaging critiques,[15] it still persisted and has not ceased to prove attractive, the reason being the entrenchment in all modern thinking of the distinction between fact and value, where the world is seen "as ultimately nothing more than the matter in motion . . . normatively mute, [and] barren of any guidance as to how we are to conduct ourselves."[16] Here, reason has reduced reasons to a nullity, and, as Spengler argued, *denied all possibilities outside itself*.[17]

As Prichard and Larmore—and more generally with them Taylor and MacIntyre,[18] among others—have in effect argued, it is impossible to reason our way to morality via autonomous rationality, which rests, as we have seen,[19] on the Kantian notion of freedom. Prichard has argued that this essentially Kantian approach is "doomed to failure" because it rests on "the mistake of supposing the possibility of proving what can only be apprehended directly by an act of moral thinking."[20] But the appeal of autonomous rationality as grounded in freedom is in no way a fortuitous one, for the essence of this brand of rationality is precisely the will to freedom. This freedom, in the final analysis, is not merely our personal and private freedom—which of course it is—but the freedom of man to rule over nature and all that is found in it, including "anything" human that may *come to be defined* as integral to it (e.g., the "noble savage," those beings who live "in a state of nature"). It is the freedom from the obligations of living under the moral demands of this world as a cosmic system of value that imposes, as such, its own constraints on us. The ethics of autonomy, which derives from this freedom, has been so dominant that one philosopher went so far as to declare it "the only one consistent with the metaphysics of the modern world."[21] But as Larmore and Prichard have convincingly argued, this conception of self-legislative reason "makes little sense" because it assumes reason or the Kantian "rational will" to be an agent and a proactive legislator, when reason, in fact, "is not an agent but rather a faculty that we, who are [*the*] agents, exercise more or less well."[22] This faculty is, so to speak, a machine of reasoning that deliberates over what we see as reasons and that, having undertaken this deliberation, adduces the reasons for believing or acting in a certain way. *Reason, in other words, cannot be autonomous, because in order for its dormant potential to be realized, it must be activated, and this can happen only by responding to reasons*. Hence reason entails "receptivity to reasons," and therefore "no principle can count as rational unless there exist reasons that recommend its acceptance."[23]

Thus, for there to be such things as reasons for thought and action, reason must "introduce them to the world from without, by way of imposing principles of its own devising on the neutral face of nature,"[24] that is, assuming that the face of nature is neutral. It is precisely here that this account seems to exhibit a naturalistic conception of the world. Having successfully dislodged the Hobbesian and Kantian arguments and having forcefully and just as successfully elaborated the distinction between reason and reasons, Larmore could conclude that the only way to acknowledge the authority of morality is to focus—"at the outset" and "without any detour through my own good"—on the

> defining value of moral thinking—namely, the fact that another's good is in itself a reason for action on my part. . . . Our moral identity consists not in valuing our own humanity and thereby determining that we ought to value humanity in whatever person it may happen to appear. It is a reason to love our neighbor in no less an immediate fashion than we are naturally moved to care about ourselves. The [Kantian] *ethics of autonomy* needs to be jettisoned, and in its stead belongs what I have called the *autonomy of morality*—by which I mean . . . that morality forms an autonomous, irreducible domain of value, into which we cannot reason ourselves from without, but which we must simply acknowledge.[25]

Just what quality of the world might constitute the context of reasons for this autonomy is a question that Larmore answers in general Platonic terms. Reasons "constitute an intrinsically normative order of reality, irreducible to physical or psychological fact."[26] But where do we go from here so that we can attach specifically defined substance and a particular meaning to reasons? What is it in a world saturated with value that tells us, in concrete, precise terms, what another's good consists of? And how do we define this good in a specific cultural context and in each concrete instance?

Ironically, such twentieth- and twenty-first-century questions and debates,[27] emerging out of formidable modern science and rational thought, intimately echo the very debates in which Muslims engaged more than a thousand years ago. The questions and problems they encountered, substantively the same raised by the Kantians, neo-Kantians, anti-Kantians, and others, were intellectual battlefields for over two centuries. From the middle of the eighth century A.D. to the end of the tenth and beyond, major legal-intellectual movements emerged representing the entire spectrum of intellectual difference on the issue of morality, its autonomy, and the role of reason in determining human actions. The only major difference between the two debates is their contexts: while the greatest number of Enlightenment thinkers—for all their diversity—knew only a disenchanted world, the premodern Muslim intellectuals inhabited a world that was, more or less, "enchanted." These intellectuals, locking their intellectual horns for over two centuries, finally settled on what I have elsewhere called the "Great Synthesis,"[28] namely, the synthesis between reason and reasons.[29] There could be no more a denial of a world saturated with value than of a world in which the human rational faculty, God's own creation, is both ever-present and forceful. And the Sharīʿa, the defining belief and practice of Muslims, was the result of a synthesis between the two.

In fact, from its beginning, Islam has defined itself as al-Umma al-Wasaṭ, the Middle Community, a concept sanctioned by the Qurʾān itself and later elaborated upon in legal, theological, and epistemic ways. The Middle Community, defined in the Sharīʿa by the elaborate and complex discursive field of *uṣūl al-fiqh* (legal theory), became conceived as such precisely because it occupied a middle position between the "Muslim Kantians"—so to speak—and the literalists, those who wished to reduce human reason to a marginal status.[30] If it metaphorically became known as the Middle Community, it was because these two "extreme" camps were relegated to minorities, the majority adopting a middle ground, where reason must be the discoverer of reasons, the latter making their moral demands and constraining the former.

But whence do reasons emerge? In chapters 4 and 5, we have detailed an answer at some length, having characterized the source of reasons as "a cosmic moral order."[31] It is precisely the *paradigmatic* attributes of this order that was the business of the Qurʾān. While fulfilling contracts, distributing shares of inheritance, and punishing the offender constituted a part—however miniscule—of the Qurʾānic corpus, any insightful reader of the text cannot fail to realize that these substantive "judgments" were incidental byproducts of the overarching Qurʾānic message: that we humans do not own the earth; that there is something or someone bigger than us; that being created in communities *concomitantly* creates the obligation on our part to perform good works; *that humanity and morality are concomitant*; that divine omnipotence, however eternal and abstract, is functionally and sociologically laid in the service of these grand moral imperatives. There is no meaning for this omnipotence without the moral imperative, for the very raison d'être of this omnipotence hinges on the demand for, and insistence upon, the moral domain. Should the moral domain one day disappear from this cosmic order, then omnipotence would have no reason to continue to exist. The world was already created by this omnipotence, a faculty that can now be withdrawn or set aside, since the task has been accomplished. But if omnipotence remains, it is by virtue of its twin, omnipresence, this latter guaranteeing the continuity of the former as keeper of the moral domain.

The Qurʾān, the Sharīʿa, and the jurists who represented it for centuries all recognized the permanency of this moral domain. Yet all of them also recognized, and with equal force, the fact that the particular legal norms to be derived from this moral domain are situational, subject to the never-ending *ijtihād*. This latter captures the soul and body of the coextensiveness of reason and reasons, of the constant dialectic between them that allows for the eternal moral domain to manifest itself variably according to time, need, and circumstance. If the Qurʾān was revealed in the idiom of the Arabs, it was, as it repeatedly states, for the purpose of making the moral domain comprehensible to them through their language and customs. The Sharīʿa followed this logic most faithfully, adopting the telling maxim—which it consistently and persistently practiced throughout the centuries—that "the Sharīʿa is good for all times and places."[32] And what made this possible was the concept and institution of *ijtihād*, the constantly renewed effort to reason the moral law, to examine at every turn and in every instance the dialectic between reason and reasons. In this tradition, reason was through and through unfailingly receptive to reasons.

3. Courses of Action

As we saw, Sharīʿa's moral bent was like a thorn in the side of colonialism in the Muslim world, a thorn that had to be extracted. Sharīʿa's decimation in the nineteenth century thus sums it all up: modernity and its state could not and cannot accept the Sharīʿa on its own terms because these terms are profoundly moral and egalitarian, whereas the state and the world that produced it relegated the moral to a subsidiary domain. To state the case minimally, colonialism's central domain was the economic and the political, not the moral. And so the economic-cum-political remains as the central domain of modernity and its increasing globalization.

Yet despite the destructive effects of colonialism, historical Sharīʿa today remains, ever more forcefully, the locus of the central domain of the moral. While its institutions, hermeneutics, and personnel have all vanished without hope of return,[33] its moral effects persist with unwavering stubbornness. This moral system, a capital of immeasurable value, can sustain at least two courses of action, one internal, the other external.[34]

First, in line with the central domain of the moral and its imperatives, Muslims can now begin—especially in light of the "Arab Spring"—to articulate and construct nascent forms of governance that would be in due course amenable to further and more robust development along the same lines. This would require nonconformist thinking and native imagination, because the social units that would make up the larger sociopolitical order must be rethought in terms of moral communities that need, among other things, to be reenchanted. Historical moral resources would provide a blueprint for a definition of what it means to engage with economics, education, private and public spheres and, most of all, the environment and the natural order. It would also provide for a concept of communal and individual rights, which would require a clear understanding of the shortcomings and strengths of the liberal order's concept of rights. An articulate position on rights is of the essence, as we will see momentarily. But internal, indigenous considerations of the community as the central domain of the moral would be the ultimate basis on which an evincive theory of antiuniversalism might be constructed, a theory that advocates the uniqueness of world societies but that also must summon up the intellectual stamina needed to provide a persuasive antidote to the dominating liberal concept of universalism. This initial but sustained process is therefore dialectical, moving back and forth between the constructive efforts of community building and a discursive negotiation with—and of—the modern state and its liberal values, *in both East and West*. As we will see, insisting on the second component of this dialectic is as essential as the steadfastness with which the first component—the raison d'être of the entire project—is pursued.[35] Such a steady and slowly evolving approach has the promise, if not the assurance, of initial success, avoiding (if not evading, thanks to its low-key programmatic) the forces we have identified in this book as antagonistic to and destructive of full-scale Islamic governance.

Second, during the long process of building nascent institutions—which would require a restatement of Sharīʿa rules and a reconceptualization of political community—Muslims and their intellectual and political elites can and must engage their Western counterparts with respect to the necessity of positioning the moral as the central domain, which would in turn require Muslims to develop a vocabulary that these interlocutors can understand, a vocabulary that, among other things, attends to the concept of rights within the context of the necessity to construct variants of the moral order befitting each society. Here, Muslims engaged in this process would be convinced and would expend the utmost intellectual energy in persuading others—including Muslim liberals[36]—that universalism and a universalist theory of rights can have no fate but ultimate failure.

In other words, even during this initial process of building morally based communities, there is much that Muslims can do[37] to contribute to the reformation of modern moralities. Such a proposition may at first glance seem bold and far-fetched, but it is not, for there is at least one important moral strand of Western philosophical and political thought that exhibits a near identity with the current Islamic quest, providing intellectual energy to the postmodern critique, however problematically modern this critique remains. As we have seen, the moral quest of modern Islam, which reflects the continuing commitment of today's Muslims to the central domain of the moral, finds its equivalent in the slim yet resounding voices of the MacIntyres, Taylors, and (even liberal) Larmores of the Western world. But this resemblance, nay commonality, is neither coincidental nor fortuitous, because all these voices—Muslim and Christian, Eastern and Western—are responding to the same moral condition,[38] however much their respective vocabularies and idioms may differ from each other. The paramount questions therefore remain: Can these forces, on all sides, transcend their ethnocentricity and *join ranks* in the interrogation of the modern project and its state? Can the Taylors summon enough intellectual courage to become MacIntyres? Can they all, Western and non-Western, dismantle the pernicious myth of a clash of civilizations? Can they augment their moral power so as to bring about a victory that installs the moral as the central domain of world cultures, *irrespective* of "civilizational" variants? For, just as there can be no Islamic governance without such a victory, there will be no victory in the first place without modernity experiencing a moral awakening. This has yet to happen.

> The political forms which may arise in truly post-Enlightenment cultures will be those that shelter and express diversity—that enable different cultures, some but by no means all or even most of which are dominated by liberal forms of life, different world-views and ways of life, to coexist in peace and harmony. For this to be a real historical possibility, however, certain conceptions and commitments that have been constitutive, not merely of the Enlightenment and so of modernity, but also, and more fundamentally, of the central traditions of Western civilization, must be amended, or abandoned. Certain conceptions, not only of *morality* but also of *science*, that are central elements in Enlightenment cultures must be given up. Certain understandings of *religion*, long-established in Western traditions, not as a vessel for a particular way of life but rather as the bearer of truths possessing universal authority, must be relinquished. The most fundamental Western commitment, the humanist conception of humankind as a privileged site of truth, which is expressed in Socratic inquiry and in Christian revelation, and which re-emerges in secular and naturalistic form in the Enlightenment project of human self-emancipation through the growth of knowledge, must be given up. . . .
>
> *It is in reaching a new relationship with our natural environment, with the earth and the other living things with which we share the earth, in which human subjectivity is not taken to be the measure of all things, that a turn in our inherited traditions of thought can be accomplished*, which opens up the possibility of profoundly different forms of human community dwelling together on earth in peace.[39]

Dwelling together on earth in peace is certainly a tall order, perhaps another modern Utopia, but subjecting modernity to a restructuring moral critique is the most essential requirement not only for the rise of Islamic governance but also for our material and spiritual survival. Islamic governance and Muslims have no monopoly over crisis.

Notes

Introduction

1. See chapter 2.

2. Rawls, *Political Liberalism*, 35. For more on this theme, see the conclusion to chapter 3.

3. For an account of this history, see Hallaq, *Sharīʿa*, 371–499; Hallaq, *Introduction*, 85–139; Zubaida, *Law and Power*, 121–157.

4. Illustrative is a comparison between modern and premodern punishments for fornication/adultery (*zinā*). See Semerdjian's important monograph *"Off the Straight Path."*

5. See chapter 5, section 2.

6. Jackson, *Islamic Law and the State*, 190.

7. Kurdi, *Islamic State*, 53; Maḥmūd, *al-Dawla al-Islāmiyya*, 5; ʿĪd, *al-Niẓām al-Siyāsī*, 50–68; Qurashī, *al-Niẓām al-Siyāsī*, 143, 152. On the history and composition of the so-called Constitution of Medina, drafted around A.D. 623, see Serjeant, "'*Sunnah Jāmiʿah*,'" 1–42; Arjomand, "Constitution of Medina." Also note here Arjomand's anachronistic use of the term "state."

8. Kurdi, *Islamic State*, 57, 64, 69.

9. For an average expression of such anachronisms in modern scholarship, see Mohammad Fadel, "Tragedy of Politics," which imagines a concept of a premodern "Islamic state" that must fit into the parameters of the modern state. Such apologetics charge political ideology with pseudoscholarly narrative, thereby elevating dogma and pseudohistory to a scholarly status. On the modern Islamist writers, see Euben and Zaman, *Princeton Readings*.

10. On such views, see Jackson, *Islamic Law and the State*, 190; for Iran, see Hallaq, *Sharīʿa*, 486–493; Schirazi, *Constitution of Iran*, 230. Oliver Roy, *Failure of Political Islam*, xi, accurately describes the preoccupation of political Islamism with the state as an obsession.

11. In this context (and for a definition of "Islamists"), see Hallaq, *Sharīʿa*, 443–499. See also Zubaida, *Law and Power*, 158–219.

12. On the ulama in the modern context of law and politics, see Zaman, *Ulama in Contemporary Islam*; Hallaq, *Sharīʿa*, 473–499.

13. "Al-Sharīʿa wal-Dawla fī al-Mafhūm al-Islāmī," http://www.ikhwan.net/wiki/index.php?title (February 1, 2011; emphasis mine). The fuller text runs as follows: "wal-dawla al-madaniyya ka-taʿbīr ʿaṣrī ʿan al-dawla al-ḥadītha bi-mā yatalā'am maʿ al-mutaghayyirāt al-jadīda lā yataʿāraḍ maʿ taṭbīq al-Sharīʿa al-Islāmiyya, li'anna al-Islām huwa al-marjaʿiyya al-ʿulyā lil-awṭān al-Islāmiyya *aw hākadhā yajib an yakūn al-ḥāl*; fal-dawla al-ḥadītha bi-mā fīhā min āliyyāt wa-nuẓum wa-qawānīn wa-ajhiza idhā lam yakun fīhā mā yataʿāraḍ maʿ thawābit al-Islām al-qaṭʿiyya fa-lā yūjad mā yamnaʿ min taṭwīrihā wal-istifāda min tajārib al-umam al-mutaqaddima ka-muntij insānī ʿāmm yajib al-ifāda minhu li-ṣāliḥi taqadduminā wa-taṭawwurinā." See also Faḍlallāh, *al-Ḥaraka al-Islāmiyya*, 315–316.

14. See also Bannā, *Mā Baʿd al-Ikhwān al-Muslimīn?*, where he not only speaks of the "State of Medina" (186–187) but also insists, as do the Muslim Brothers (whom he criticizes) that the Islamic state is necessary. Of the Muslim Brothers he says that they have "made it clear that as an all-encompassing religion, Islam cannot be realized except under the shadow of an Islamic state that imposes the alms-tax on the rich and gives it away to the poor. . . . For the state to be Islamic is a matter that the intrinsic nature [*badāha*] of Islam requires" (64–65). See also the declarations of the newly founded Salafist party in Egypt, al-Nūr. The party insists on implementing the Sharīʿa (without discussing what this term would mean and imply), on the one hand, and declares that the final goal is to establish an "Islamically based democratic nation-state," on the other. See " 'Al-Nūr' Awwal Ḥizb."

15. As we shall see in the course of this monograph, our argument will unfold in various directions, since it depends on and therefore is determined by larger phenomena and structures of the modern project as a whole. Skeptics should take note that I advocate no view whatsoever to the effect that Islamic law or Islamic governance has no place in the world in which we or, hopefully, our children will live. Only a dogmatic, narrow, and myopic vision can allow for such an interpretation (see, e.g., Mohammad Fadel, "Tragedy of Politics"). Thus, it must be stated once and for all that the argument of this book rests on the premise that a creative reformulation of the Sharīʿa and Islamic governance may be one of the most *relevant* and constructive ways to reshape the modern project, one that is in dire need of moral reconstitution (see the concluding paragraphs to chapter 7). This reconstitution and its political and legal *spin-offs* cannot be conceivable for Muslims without a correct diagnosis of the problem of the "Islamic state," this also explaining why a robust proposal for such a future reconstruction must await a genuine

understanding of the multilayered contradiction inherent in any concept of "Islamic state."

16. See also chap. 1, n. 22.

1. Premises

1. Hallaq, *Sharīʿa*, 443–499. For an insightful analysis in this context, see Massad, *Colonial Effects*.

2. An index of this is the absence in modern Islamic discourse of such conversations as those reflected in Balibar, "Subjection and Subjectivation."

3. Hallaq, "Can the Shariʿa Be Restored?" Note that much in my views has changed since writing this article.

4. For a background and further readings on this issue, see Hallaq, *Sharīʿa*, part 3.

5. Such an approach as that of K. Vikør ("Sharia and the Nation State," especially at 231–250) is precisely what this book tries hard to avoid.

6. Hall and Ikenberry, *State*, 23–34; see also Gill's critical commentary, *Nature and Development*, 184–191.

7. Dawson, *Making of Europe*, 19.

8. For a similar critique from a different angle, see Gray, *Enlightenment's Wake*. See also Amin, *Liberal Virus*, 32 and *passim*.

9. See, for instance, Stiglitz, *Globalization and Its Discontents*.

10. Giddens, *Modernity and Self-Identity*, 144–208.

11. On this, briefly, see chapter 5, section 1. See also Lasch, *Minimal Self*; Giddens, *Modernity and Self-Identity*, 7–9, 171–174; Touraine, *Critique of Modernity*.

12. Bourdieu, *Practical Reason*, 71. See also chap. 5, n. 18.

13. See, in this context, Bookchin and Foreman, *Defending the Earth*; Gorke, *Death of Our Planet's Species*; Naess, *Selected Works*, 13–55.

14. Mainly in chapter 5, but also *passim*.

15. Mann, "Has Globalization Ended . . . ?" 489–490.

16. MacIntyre, *After Virtue*; MacIntyre, *Whose Justice? Which Rationality?*; Taylor, *Sources of the Self*; Taylor, *Malaise of Modernity*; Larmore, *Autonomy of Morality*; Larmore, *Morals of Modernity*. In this context, see also the insightful and highly instructive work of Euben, *Enemy in the Mirror*.

17. "So-called" because Plato and Aristotle were no more "European" than they were "Islamic," a matter evident to any scholar of Islam and its philosophical/theological traditions.

18. Many of which resources assimilated Aristotelianism and Neo-Platonism to what had already been developed internally.

19. MacIntyre, *Whose Justice? Which Rationality?*, 7 (emphasis mine).

20. This is despite the fact, fully recognized here, that the liberal Larmore stands apart on many, if not most, issues from Taylor and MacIntyre.

21. Gray, *Enlightenment's Wake*, 7. Gray writes, referring to such communitarian critics as Taylor, MacIntyre, and Michael Waltzer: "The community

invoked by these writers is not one that anyone has ever lived in, an historic human settlement with its distinctive exclusivities, hierarchies and bigotries, but an ideal community, in its way as much of a cipher as the disembodied Kantian self the communitarians delight in deflating." Our account in this book would then meet Gray's valid requirement.

22. It must be made as clear as possible here that my narrative of premodern Islamic law derives from what I have expounded in *Sharīʿa* and *Introduction*. To regard the present work as a departure from these two books or as representing a shift toward reducing the complexity of this narrative is a temptation that should be resisted. If the reader who is familiar with my earlier work detects such a qualitative difference in narrative, she is strongly advised to think of this in terms of the theory of paradigms expounded here. It should become clear that our narrative of premodern Islamic law is cast in a manner that is suitable to the present project, namely, what we have called moral retrieval. Therefore, the present volume is not a history of Islamic law and should not be regarded as such.

23. Although the original French title is *Les mots et les choses*, the English title seems a better description of the book's arguments.

24. Especially in his "Age of Naturalizations and Depoliticizations."

25. Kuhn, *Structure of Scientific Revolutions*.

26. In his various writings, including *History of Sexuality*, *Les mots et les choses*, and *Archaeology of Knowledge*. See also Agamben, *Signature of All Things*, 9–16; Hallaq, *Sharīʿa*, 6–15.

27. See, in addition, Agamben, *Signature of All Things*, 9–32. Here, we are interested in the concept only insofar as it is of aid to us in unraveling our subject, although obviously much more can be said of it.

28. See Schmitt, "Age of Naturalization," 84–87; quote at 86.

29. Ibid., 85.

30. Ibid., 86. Emphasis mine.

31. Ibid., 87.

32. This relevance is most evident in chapters 4 and 7.

33. Gray, *Enlightenment's Wake*, 123.

34. Ibid., 124. See also Hayes, *Historical Evolution*, 13–14.

35. Thus, such an argument as that of Gordon Stewart, "Scottish Enlightenment," is blind to the concept of paradigm (even structure) and prone to an atomistic vision of reality.

36. See our discussion of this concept in chapter 4, section 2.

37. Foucault, *History of Sexuality*, 101–102.

38. The implication being that, while the general moral norms, or "moral universals," are fixed and thus cannot be changed, the legal norms, which must necessarily occupy a second *and* subservient rank, can be modified in accordance with the demands of place and time. Here, a constant dialectic exists between the demands of the moral universals and those of life and legally regulated acts. And it is here that Ought continuously regulates and restrains the Is. For an extended analysis of this and related issues, see chapter 4.

39. See Saliba, *Islamic Science*; Lyons, *House of Wisdom*; Hobson, *Eastern Origins of Western Civilization*; Goody, *Theft of History*.

40. Such as language, Qurʾānic studies, *ḥadīth*, theology, logic, and mysticism.

41. The most obvious of these are *ḥadīth* and *aḥkām al-Qurʾān* studies, including the interconnected subdisciplines of *asbāb al-nuzūl* and *tafsīr*.

42. From the perspective of such violations and exceptions within the paradigm, one may add the legal stratagems known as *ḥiyal*, a minor body of legal methods (that never found acceptance in mainstream legal literature) through which the Sharīʿa rules and principles and their moral intentions were evaded. On *ḥiyal*, see *Encyclopaedia of Islam*, III, 510.

43. We must always bear in mind that the occasional abuses of the system, whether by men of political power or by men of law, were almost always recorded in our sources because such conduct was seen to violate the norm. Biographers and historians were not interested in recording the day-to-day routine of the judiciary or of legal life, these being taken for granted (for example, a distinguished judge who served in this capacity for decades and who performed his duties as expected would normally be described in the biographical literature [*ṭabaqāt*] as *fāḍil* [virtuous] or *ṣāliḥ* [good], and little more). Thus, the sources passed in silence over the tens of thousands, if not millions, of cases processed by the legal system. But when violations and abuses occurred, they routinely found their way into these historical records. See Hallaq, *Origins*, 190.

44. On this theme in some detail, see Hallaq, *Origins*, 178–193; Hallaq, *Sharīʿa*, 146–158, 197–221; Jackson, *Islamic Law and the State*; Peirce, *Morality Tales*.

45. See chapter 4, section 2.

46. MacIntyre, *After Virtue*, xi; James, "Internal and External," 7.

47. For a penetrating analysis of secularism and its meanings in Euro-America and Islam, see Asad, *Formations of the Secular*.

48. Zubaida, "Islam and Secularization."

49. The most powerful attestation to this claim is the intellectually formidable work of the Moroccan philosopher Ṭāha ʿAbd al-Raḥmān. See his *Rūḥ al-Ḥadātha, Suʾāl al-Akhlāq, al-Ḥaqq al-Islāmī fil-Ikhtilāf al-Fikrī, Fiqh al-Falsafa*, and *al-ʿAmal al-Dīnī wa-Tajdīd al-ʿAql*.

50. Again, it is this moral desideratum as pitted against the ontology of the nation-state that forms the core problem I want to investigate here, a problem we had identified in the introduction as having the feature of an aporia.

51. It is in this sense that my argument in "Can the Shariʿa Be Restored?" should be construed.

52. See chapter 5, section 2.

53. On the genealogy of nostalgia, see Naqvi, "Nostalgic Subject."

54. Gray, *Enlightenment's Wake*, 152–153, 155.

55. Lasch, *Culture of Narcissism*, xvi–xvii; see also the incisive critique of Parekh, "Superior People."

56. Benjamin, "On Language as Such," 315–316.

57. Dawson, *Making of Europe*, 16: "Modern historians . . . have frequently tended to use the present as an absolute standard by which to judge the past, and to view all history as an inevitable movement of progress that culminates

in the present state of things. . . . This way of writing history is fundamentally unhistorical, since it involves the subordination of the past to the present, and instead of liberating the mind from provincialism by widening the intellectual horizon, it is apt to generate the pharisaic self-righteousness of the Whig historians or, still worse, the self-satisfaction of the modern Philistine."

58. Gray, *Enlightenment's Wake*, 64–65; Parekh, "Superior People."

59. Comte, *August Comte on Positivism*, 34–42. See also Rossi, "Bacon's Idea of Science," 39; Hayes, *Historical Evolution*, 169–170.

60. Benjamin, "Theses on the Philosophy of History," 260.

61. Ibid.

62. Adorno, *History and Freedom*, 3–9, 138–141; O'Connor, "Philosophy of History," 181.

63. A theme we discuss in chapter 4, section 1.

64. Comte, *August Comte on Positivism*, 33–34, 496–497; Staude, *Max Scheler*, 167–168.

65. Baker, "On Condorcet's '*Sketch*,'" 56–64. Condorcet believed that progress is a never-ending process, but he also believed that the process will continue to unfold on European and mainly Revolution-based, French civilizational terms.

66. Condorcet, *Sketch for a Historical Picture*, 8–13 and *passim*; see also Stark, *Sociology*, 133, for Meinecke's evaluation of Voltaire on this point.

67. Stark, *Sociology*, 133.

68. O'Connor, "Philosophy of History," 181. On the British notions of progress within the context of colonialism, see Ferro, *Colonization*, 20–23.

69. See Stanley's introduction to Sorel, *Illusions of Progress*, xiii.

70. Nisbet, *History of the Idea of Progress*, 4, 7.

71. Bury, *Idea of Progress*, xi (my emphasis). An index of this theory's pervasive influence is also to be found in Charles Taylor's work. Despite his recognition of the "barbarism" of modernity and the twentieth century, he still succumbs to a sort of Western civilizational march. See the insightful commentary of Quentin Skinner on Taylor's work, in his essay "Modernity and Disenchantment," 42–43.

72. Bauman, *Intimations of Postmodernity*, xiv; Hayes, *Historical Evolution of Modern Nationalism*, 13–14. Here I insist on the theory of progress's paradigmatic status despite the exceptions and irregularities in the Enlightenment's multiplicity of voices, as the nonprogressivist Hobbes and Hume exemplify. As asserted earlier, our theory of paradigms accounts for such divergences.

73. Meier, *Greek Discovery of Politics*, 190; Lasch, *Culture of Narcissism*, xvii.

2. The Modern State

1. Schmitt, *Political Romanticism*, 111.

2. Marinetto, *Social Theory*, 3–5.

3. Nelson, *Making of the Modern State*, 5, 129. Hans Kelsen even went further, arguing that political theory in general has often been an integral part of the ideological machine of the state. Kelsen, *General Theory*, 185–186.

4. Barkey and Parikh, "Comparative Perspectives," 524–525.

5. Ibid.

6. Spruyt, *Sovereign State*, 61–76; Frank, *ReOrient*, 80, 206, and *passim*.

7. Hall and Ikenberry, *State*; Giddens, *Capitalism*, *passim*, esp. 179.

8. Held, *Political Theory and the Modern State*, 208.

9. van Creveld, *Rise and Decline*, 209.

10. For a history of the modern European state, see Poggi, *Development of the Modern State*; van Creveld, *Rise and Decline*; Gill, *Nature and Development*.

11. Kahn, *Putting Liberalism*, 280, although his emphasis is on the United States as the paradigmatic nation-state.

12. See Cohn, *Colonialism and Its Forms of Knowledge*; Dirks, *Scandal of Empire*; van der Veer, *Imperial Encounters*; but also B. Fuchs who, in *Mimesis and Empire*, treats imperial identity formation through mimesis.

13. Some of the best work on changes in the forms of knowledge perhaps remains that of Foucault. See bibliography.

14. See Saliba, *Islamic Science*; Lyons, *House of Wisdom*. For a wider perspective, see Hobson, *Eastern Origins of Western Civilization*; Goody, *Theft of History*.

15. Nelson, *Making of the Modern State*, 6 (emphasis mine).

16. For the historical context of rationality and reason in Enlightenment thought, see Larmore, *Autonomy*, 1–7.

17. van Creveld, *Rise and Decline*, 185. See also Mill, *On Liberty*, 81; Ferro, *Colonization*, 22.

18. Vincent, *Theories of the State*, 119–146.

19. Poggi, *Development of the Modern State*, 90.

20. Which we need not account for here, since Islamic governance also depends on certain sets of belief that play similar roles to those that ideology plays in the modern state.

21. Carl Schmitt's position, as discussed in Bolsinger, *Autonomy*, 124; see also Hay and Lister, *State*, 4–7.

22. For a rich debate on these state themes, see Anderson, *Imagined Communities*; Abrams, "Notes on the Difficulty of Studying the State"; Mitchell, "Society, Economy"; Marinetto, *Social Theory*, 107–109; Finlayson and Martin, "Poststructuralism," 162–163.

23. Gill, *Nature and Development*, 4–5.

24. van Creveld, *Rise and Decline*, 127.

25. Nelson, *Making of the Modern State*, 127.

26. Kahn, *Putting Liberalism*, 266: Popular sovereignty has no "form, place, or time apart from the state itself."

27. Hay et al., *State*, 4–6; Grosby, "Nationality and Religion," 103.

28. Bolsinger, *Autonomy*, 29.

29. Nagel, "Ruthlessness in Public Life," 87.

30. Poggi, *Development of the Modern State*, 90.

31. Kahn, *Putting Liberalism*, 268–269.

32. Iraq under American occupation is an excellent case in point. Even when the dictatorship of Saddam Hussein was removed by the violence of a foreign power, no one was willing to credit "Iraq" with a political voice, much less sovereignty, without and until a government was first constituted on the basis of what was presumed to be an Iraqi constitutional law.

33. Gill, *Nature and Development*, 4–5; Poggi, *Development of the Modern State*, 88–89.

34. Marshall, *Constitutional Theory*, 207.

35. Poggi, *Development of the Modern State*, 90.

36. Anderson, *Imagined Communities*. Drawing on Richard Ashley, Finlayson and Martin ("Poststructuralism," 164) argue that the "figure" of the sovereign state "'is nothing more and nothing less than an arbitrary political representation always in the process of being inscribed within history, through practice, and in the face of all manner of resistant interpretations that must be excluded if the representation is to be counted as a self-evident reality.' This is not meant to suggest that the state does not really exist or is a mere charade; only that its existence as a sovereign entity in an international environment is a kind of myth dependent upon ongoing processes that define and redefine its 'inside' and 'outside' through practices of exclusion that create the very environment within and through which the state is then deemed to act."

37. Kahn, *Putting Liberalism*, 267.

38. Ibid., 267–268.

39. See also Grosby, "Nationality and Religion," 97–104.

40. Schmitt, *Political Theology*, 36; Amin, *Liberal Virus*, 54. For a nuanced analysis of this theme, see Asad, *Formations of the Secular*. But even for Asad, qualifying Schmitt's arguments does not diminish their force in the least.

41. See a more expanded discussion of this question in chapter 4, section 2.

42. Kahn, *Putting Liberalism*, 276.

43. See Strong's forward to Schmitt's *Concept of the Political*, xiv.

44. It is instructive that, for Schmitt, the sovereign is he who decides on the exception, that moment of decision to step outside the rule of law. For Schmitt, this absolute power of decision, once belonging to God and theology, is now translated into a political vocabulary. The traditional God is replaced in modernity by the state. This is essentially the theme and argument of his *Political Theology* (see, in particular, 5–15, 36–52).

45. This is in no way to deny an identifiable multiplicity within the "subject." The citizen is only one part of this multiplicity. See further on the subject the insightful commentary of Balibar, "Subjection and Subjectivation."

46. Kelsen, *General Theory*, 207.

47. Ibid., 182. "To describe the State as 'the power behind the law' is incorrect, since it suggests the existence of two separate entities where there is only one: the legal order. The dualism of law and state is a superfluous doubling or duplication of the object of our cognition" (191). For Kelsen, the political character of the state means that it is a coercive order and this order is itself the

law (192). Especially pertaining to the last point, see also Foucault, *History of Sexuality*, 144; Foucault, *Foucault Reader*, 266.

48. But this is not to deny the cultural and other effects of this "legal order," effects significantly appreciated by the Foucauldians and poststructuralists.

49. Foucault, *History of Sexuality*, 266: "Law cannot help but be armed, and its arm *par excellence* is death; to those who transgress it, it replies, at least as a last resort, with that absolute menace. The law always refers to the sword."

50. Nelson, *Making of the Modern State*, 107; Bolsinger, *Autonomy*, 181; Kahn, *Putting Liberalism*, 277; Hall and Ikenberry, *State*, 1.

51. Weber, *Economy and Society*, 56.

52. Bolsinger, *Autonomy*, 130.

53. Rose and Miller, "Political Power," 183–186.

54. Giddens, *Capitalism*, 237; Peffer, *Marxism, Morality*, 12, 153.

55. Even the modern Khomeini is vehemently critical of bureaucracy, although for different reasons. See Euben and Zaman, *Princeton Readings*, 176.

56. Giddens, *Capitalism*; Peffer, *Marxism, Morality*.

57. Bolsinger, *Autonomy*, 134.

58. Gill, *Nature and Development*, 4.

59. Foucault, "Governmentality," 219–222; Rose and Miller, "Political Power Beyond the State," 174; Finlayson and Martin, "Poststructuralism," 166–170.

60. Steinmetz, *State/Culture*, 28–29.

61. The topic of chapter 5.

62. Kelsen, *General Theory*, 183 (emphasis mine).

63. On performativity, see Austin, *How to Do Things with Words*; Austin, "Performative Utterances"; Butler, *Excitable Speech*.

64. Which is the meaning I take in Hall and Ikenberry, *State*, 13.

65. As argued under the second subheading.

66. Nelson, *Making of the Modern State*, 9; Gray, *Straw Dogs*, 12. The Indian case is one of the rare exceptions. See Kaviraj, "Enchantment of the State."

67. Hall and Ikenberry, *State*, 13.

68. Ibid., 14. It is highly likely that Hall and Ikenberry's positions on this point are heavily colored by the fact that their main concern is limited to the state's relationship to economy and capitalism. The state's success in generating consent with regard to free market and private ownership is no sufficient measure of analysis when compared, say, with the state's educational policies, which cannot capitalize on the individual's sense of choice and freedom. Capitalism, on the other hand, can.

69. Bourdieu, "Rethinking the State," 54.

70. The educational-cultural domain, it must be noted, replicates the transformation of theological concepts into modern political categories—as we have earlier seen in Schmitt's thought. As Sorel has argued (*Illusions of Progress*, 104), it was "from the church that the philosophers borrowed their ideas on the power of education to change society." Just as the missionaries were out to educate the Indian "savage," there were, within Europe, proposals of action that were "exact imitation of the clerical proposals" to educate the European

public, with a view to forming, as Turgot announced, "in all social classes virtuous and useful men, just souls, pure hearts and zealous citizens."

71. See subsection 1 of this chapter.

72. Bourdieu, "Rethinking the State," 55.

73. See subsection 2 of this chapter.

3. Separation of Powers: Rule of Law or Rule of the State?

1. Kelsen, *General Theory*, 191.

2. See our discussion of paradigms/central domains in chapter 1. I have also dealt with the concept of paradigm twice before, looking at it from somewhat different perspectives. See Hallaq, *Sharīʿa*, 6–17, 357–370; Hallaq, "Orientalism, Self-Consciousness, and History."

3. Hutchinson and Monahan, "Politics and the Critical Legal Scholars," 206.

4. Mansfield, "Separation of Powers," 4.

5. Zamboni, *Law and Politics*, 53.

6. Ibid.

7. On this topic generally and on Montesquieu and the *Federalist Papers* in particular, see Marrow, *History of Western Political Thought*, 241–247; Carey, "Separation of Powers and the Madisonian Model," 151–153; Vile, *Constitutionalism and the Separation of Powers*.

8. Marshall, *Constitutional Theory*, 100.

9. This, after all, is Noah Feldman's main argument in *Fall and Rise of the Islamic State*, namely, that an "Islamic state" cannot succeed until the powers of the legislative branch are "balanced" off against and brought to bear upon those of other branches, most notably the executive. Insofar as this issue is concerned, Feldman's work represents a contribution to the liberal critique of Islam and modern "Islamic" politics. But the work deals with none of the profound moral dilemmas that the modern state poses to any project of Islamic governance. It remains thoroughly premised upon a liberal approach that does not recognize the moral as the central domain. Nor does this account recognize the constitutional problems discussed in the present chapter, problems that pervade the liberal order of the state and that Islamic governance largely precludes.

10. A point to be argued in due course. See also Kelsen, *General Theory*, 269, 282. It is also worth emphasizing that a critique of the *practice* of democracy may be leveled from other quarters (not our concern here), including the very process of elections and voting, a process that may be regarded as hampered by the very law that purports to promote democracy. On this see, for instance, Abu El-Haj, "Changing the People."

11. Kelsen, *General Theory*, 269; Calabresi and Prakash, "President's Power to Execute the Law," 544.

12. In this regard, Hayek's statement quoted at the head of this chapter is revealing.

13. Marshall, *Constitutional Theory*, 97.

14. Hansen, "Mixed Constitution," 509.

15. Saunders, "Separation of Powers," 338.

16. Marshall, *Constitutional Theory*, 124.

17. Magill, "Beyond Powers and Branches in Separation of Powers Law," 605.

18. Lawson, "Rise and Rise of the Administrative State," 1231.

19. Mansfield, "Separation of Powers," 15.

20. Vanderbilt, *Doctrine of the Separation*, 3,

21. Magill, "Real Separation in Separation of Power," 1129, 1197.

22. Ackerman, *Decline and Fall*, 3: "The pathologies of the existing system are too dangerous to ignore. We can't limit our critique to details. We must ask whether something is seriously wrong—very seriously wrong—with the tradition of government that we have inherited."

23. Hansen, "Mixed Constitution," 514.

24. Vincent, *Theories of the State*, 8.

25. See sources listed in notes to the present section and to the exordium.

26. Further on this "unitary" nature of the state in relation to the separation of powers, see Wilson, "Separation of Powers."

27. Ibid., 486, calls it no more than an "administrative convenience."

28. Kelsen, *General Theory*, 272–273.

29. See next three notes.

30. Hansen, "Mixed Constitution," 514–515, 528: "It is a breach of the separation of functions that a majority in the parliament by a vote of no confidence can force the government to resign or call for an election, and that the government is accountable to the parliament. In these cases it is the legislature that encroaches upon the powers of the executive. Conversely, in many parliamentary democracies the government possesses the right to dissolve the parliament and call for an election. Also the executive has extended its proper sphere of power by arrogating legislative powers to itself. It is a breach of the separation of persons that the prime minister and most of the ministers are members of parliament and at the same time the heads of the executive branch of government. It is a breach of the separation of functions that almost all laws are initiated and drafted by the government and the civil servants working in the various departments of government. The result is that the role of parliament in most cases is restricted to ratifying or rejecting what the government proposes. Furthermore much legislation takes the form of framework laws that leave important details to be filled in by subsidiary government regulations. . . . There is no longer any separation of powers, each with its own function. Today legislation is divided between *the executive*, namely the government and all the civil servants in the ministries who initiate and prepare almost all new laws, *the legislative*, namely the parliament, which has the power to ratify or reject the bills submitted by the government, and *the judiciary*, namely the constitutional court which in most European democracies has set itself up as a second or third legislative chamber."

31. Lawson, "Rise and Rise of the Administrative State," 1233: "Congress frequently delegates . . . general legislative authority to administrative agencies,

in contravention of Article I (of the Constitution). Furthermore, those agencies are not always subject to the direct control of the President, in contravention of Article II. In addition, those agencies sometimes exercise the judicial power, in contravention of Article III. Finally, those agencies typically concentrate legislative, executive, and judicial functions in the same institution, in simultaneous contravention of Articles I, II, and III. In short, the modern administrative state openly flouts almost every important structural precept of the American constitutional order."

32. Kelsen, *General Theory*, 256–257. See also Saunders, "Separation of Powers," 340, where she argues that especially in the United Kingdom, the "intermixture of institutions is such that it is almost impossible to describe it as a separation of powers. . . . This is most obviously the case with the relationship between the legislature and the executive, famously claimed by Walter Bagehot as fusion of powers."

33. Marshall, *Constitutional Theory*, 113–114; Ackerman, *Decline and Fall*.

34. Kelsen, *General Theory*, 114. See also Marshall, *Constitutional Theory*, 113–114; Vanderbilt, *Doctrine of the Separation*, 95.

35. Lawson, "Rise and Rise of the Administrative State," 1241: The "majority in *Mistretta v. United States* declared that 'our jurisprudence has been driven by a practical understanding that in our increasingly complex society, replete with ever changing and more technical problems, Congress simply cannot do its job absent an ability to delegate power under broad general directives.' When faced with a choice between the Constitution and the structure of modern governance, the Court has had no difficulty making the choice."

36. Ibid., 1238.

37. Horwitz, *Transformation of American Law*, 214.

38. Calabresi and Prakash, "President's Power to Execute the Law," 559–560, 663; Lawson, "Rise and Rise of the Administrative State," 1242–1243.

39. Further on this, see Bruff, "Constitutional Status of the Administrative Agencies"; Lawson, "Rise and Rise of the Administrative State."

40. Calabresi and Prakash, "President's Power to Execute the Law," 664.

41. Fisher's review of *Decline and Fall of the American Republic*, 58.

42. Otherwise, the entirety of the vast academic discourse on this and related issues, which has attracted some of the best constitutional scholars in the United States, would be both meaningless and a figment of the human imagination.

43. Speaking of the "pathologies of the existing [constitutional] system," which "are too dangerous to ignore," Bruce Ackerman tellingly writes that the "great struggle for constitutional democracy will not be waged in Iraq and Afghanistan or some other distant land. It will be waged closer to home, and it will be a spiritual struggle: Will we continue to celebrate our great tradition in a chorus of self-congratulation? Or will we take a hard look at emerging realities, and rise to the occasion in a movement for constitutional renewal?" *Decline and Fall*, 3, 188.

44. Levinson, "Separation of Parties," 2313.

45. Cited in ibid., 2314–2315; also more generally on the American presidency as a "dangerous branch," see Ackerman, *Decline and Fall.*

46. Levinson, "Separation of Parties," 2315: "Recognizing that party competition *can either create or dissolve interbranch competition,* depending on whether government is unified or divided by party, suggests that the United States has not one system of separation of powers but (at least) two." This dynamic has not "received much notice by legal scholars" nor by "the Supreme Court nor any other federal court" (emphasis mine). See also 2329.

47. Ibid., 2322, 2330–2331, 2341. From an entirely different angle, it can also be argued, as Hayek did, that "party legislation leads to the decay of democratic society. A system which may place any small group in the position to hold a society to ransom if it happened to be the balance between opposing groups, and can extort special privileges for its support of a party, has little to do with democracy or 'social justice.' " See his *Law, Legislation, and Liberty,* III, 31.

48. Kelsen, *General Theory,* 270.

49. Dahl, "On Removing Certain Impediments," 249. Dahl continues: "What is more, the other major political actors, including the Congress, the Supreme Court, the parties, the electorate, and the most active and attentive political strata all collaborated in that transformation." See also Ackerman, *Decline and Fall,* 15: "But over the course of two centuries, the most dangerous branch has turned out to be the presidency—requiring a fundamental reworking of our thinking and practice, an overhaul that may come too late if it comes at all." It is not entirely fortuitous that Ackerman capitalizes the expression "Most Dangerous Branch" (63).

50. Kelsen, *General Theory,* 257, 270.

51. Saunders, "Separation of Powers"; Wilson, "Separation of Powers," 481–486.

52. Lawson, "Rise and Rise of the Administrative State," 1246–1247.

53. Stewart, "From 'Rule of Law,' " 10.

54. Kelsen, *General Theory,* 269.

55. Marshall, *Constitutional Theory,* 103–104.

56. Kelsen, *General Theory,* 281.

57. See the citations in Hansen, "Mixed Constitution," 509.

58. See chapter 2, subsection 2.

59. It is in this context that Hayek perceptively wrote: "Civilization largely rests on the fact that the individuals have learned to restrain their desires for particular objects and to submit to generally recognized rules of just conduct. Majorities [in Western democracies], however, have not yet been civilized in this manner because they do not obey rules," meaning that there are no rules or law higher than their will. See his *Law, Legislation, and Liberty,* III, 7. Hayek's statement carries extraordinary significance for our arguments in the next two chapters.

60. See chapter 5, section 1.

61. Miliband, *State in Capitalist Society,* 142, citing the Lord Chief Justice of England.

62. Ibid., 143.

63. Kelsen, *General Theory*, 273.

64. Lawson, "Rise and Rise of the Administrative State," 1247.

65. Kelsen, *General Theory*, 277; also Vanderbilt, *Doctrine of the Separation*, 95.

66. Marshall, *Constitutional Theory*, 108.

67. Lawson, "Rise and Rise of the Administrative State," 1248–1249 and *passim*; Magill, "Real Separation in Separation of Power."

68. Vanderbilt, *Doctrine of the Separation*, 95; Vile, *Constitutionalism and the Separation of Powers*, 385–420; Dry, "Separation of Powers," 82–83; and Schultz, "Congress and the Separation of Powers," 190 and *passim*, despite Schultz's all too charitable approach.

69. Stewart, "From 'Rule of Law,'" 6; Hardin, *Constitutional Reform*; Dahl, "On Removing Certain Impediments" (as annotated in the next note).

70. Kelsen, *General Theory*, 282 (emphasis added). See also Dunn, "Political Obligation," 24. Speaking of the American constitutional experience, Dahl ("On Removing Certain Impediments," 235–236) states the following: "the elaborate system of checks and balances, separation of powers, constitutional federalism, and other institutional arrangements influenced by these structures and the constitutional views they reflect are both adverse to the majority principle, and in that sense to democracy, and yet arbitrary and unfair in the protection they give to rights. . . . In their effort to protect basic rights, what the framers did in effect was to hand out extra chips in the game of politics to people who are already advantaged, while they handicapped the disadvantaged who would like to change the status quo. From a moral perspective, the consequences seem arbitrary and quite lacking in a principled justification."

71. See introduction.

72. On the Community as a particular, concrete construct, see Hallaq, *Sharīʿa*, 159–221.

73. Ramlī, *Nihāyat al-Muḥtāj*, VIII, 184; Baghdādī, *Uṣūl al-Dīn*, 270.

74. Ibn al-Sāʿātī, *Majmaʿ al-Baḥrayn*, 794.

75. ʿAynī, *Bināya*, VII, 100–101; Māwardī, *al-Ḥāwī al-Kabīr*, XIV, 152; Nawawī, *Rawḍa*, VII, 440–41, 462; Ibn Māza, *Muḥīṭ*, VII, 90, 94, 102.

76. See chapter 2, section 2.

77. Obviously, a critique can be leveled against this statement from a liberal-democratic perspective, at least insofar as the status of women is concerned. Two counterarguments can readily be advanced: First, the critique generally assumes the application of the Sharīʿa in the modern nation-state to be representative of how the Sharīʿa operated, and stood for, in premodernity. This is a deeply flawed assumption, since the pre-nineteenth century Sharīʿa shares very little (if anything at all) with its present forms as remanufactured at the hands of the modern nation-state. And second, the critique, even when conscious of the qualitative difference between the modern and premodern forms of Sharīʿa, is oblivious to the anthropological/sociological system of checks and balances that makes the status of women in premodern Islam comprehensible and in fact impressive when compared to any contemporaneous legal and cul-

tural system, especially the European. Once these anthropological and social checks and balances are understood properly, what seems a disadvantage to women ceases to be so. This is not to deny the patriarchal nature of premodern Islamic society but merely to question the modernist reading of history, which equates the present status of Muslim women with a legal value made inherent to the Sharīʿa, past and present. Further on these themes, see Hallaq, *Sharīʿa*, 184–196; Fay, "Women and Waqf"; Tucker, *In the House of the Law*; Tucker, "Marriage and Family in Nablus"; Tucker, "Revisiting Reform"; Marcus, "Men, Women, and Property"; Meriwether, "Rights of Children and the Responsibilities of Women"; Meriwether, "Women and Waqf Revisited"; Moors, "Debating Islamic Family Law"; Moors, "Gender Relations and Inheritance"; Gerber, "Social and Economic Position of Women"; Peirce, *Morality Tales*; Seng, "Standing at the Gates of Justice"; Seng, "Invisible Women"; Zilfi, "We Don't Get Along"; Hélie-Lucas, "Preferential Symbol for Islamic Identity"; Jennings, "Women in Early Seventeenth-Century Ottoman Judicial Records"; Zarinebaf-Shahr, "Women, Law, and Imperial Justice"; Zarinebaf-Shahr, *Crime and Punishment in Istanbul*; Semerdjian, "*Off the Straight Path.*"

78. See the discussions in chapter 4, section 1; and chapter 5, section 2.

79. Jackson, *Islamic Law and the State*, 224 (needless to say, I take exception to Jackson's use of the term "state" in the premodern Islamic context, although the meaning of his language remains crystal clear); see also Gibb, "Constitutional Organization," 3; Abou El Fadl, "Islam and the Challenge of Democratic Commitment," 14–19. In Ṭurṭūshī's *Sirāj al-Mulūk*, 301–309, obeying the Sharīʿa and enforcing its ordinances were so much taken for granted that they did not make it to the list of qualities the sultan must enjoy to qualify as a just ruler. On the other hand, fairness in levying taxes occupies an elevated position on the list of virtues.

80. Hallaq, *Sharīʿa*, 296–297.

81. Qurʾān, 51:15–20; 70:24–25. This is to be contrasted with the modern state's relatively poor record on the poor. See Ashford, "Constitution of Poverty," 166: "Thus, after nearly two centuries of Poor Law struggles, the legal status of the poor remains undefined." Also see Simon, "Theoretical Marginalization of the Disadvantaged."

82. See the aggregate effect of the following verses in the Qurʾān, 2:82–83, 215, 271–273; 4:8–10; 17:26; 51:15–19; 57:5; 70:24–25; 93:9–10; see in addition chapter 6, section 2; and chapter 7.

83. Gibb, "Constitutional Organization," 3; see also Jackson, *Islamic Law and the State*, 217–224.

84. For a sketch of this system, see Hallaq, *Sharīʿa*; Hallaq, "Islamic Law."

85. See, e.g., Ayer, *Language, Truth, and Logic.*

86. Weber, *Economy and Society*, 56.

87. On law-finding in the Sharīʿa, see Hallaq, *Authority, Continuity, and Change*, 166–174.

88. It is insufficient merely to assert, and keep repeating, that one should move "beyond the question of whether Islam and democracy are compatible" (Rabb, "We the Jurists," 577 and *passim*). Our account is just one way of

demonstrating this compatibility, although there are other ways as well. See also the insightful article of Abou El Fadl, "Islam and the Challenge of Democratic Commitment"; Roy, *Failure of Political Islam*, 11–13.

89. For an account of the early rise and formation of Sharīʿa, see Hallaq, "Groundwork of the Moral Law"; Hallaq, *Origins*.

90. In this context, one may develop another (perhaps Weberian) argument that would constitute a sequel to the arguments of this book, namely, that adherence to and insistence upon general moral principles would affect not only social behavior but also the types of institutions (material and not so material) that a society chooses to adopt and build for itself. This argument becomes necessary as an antidote to the claim that moral retrieval (see chapter 1) is impossible because the source of all value exclusively lies in a present social order. With this claim, we return to the prejudiced position upholding the fact/value and Is/Ought distinctions.

91. Ibn al-Ṣalāḥ, *Adab al-Muftī*, 72. Thus, the Muslim jurists and ulama *were* the "People" and not just "a part of the 'We the People,'" as Rabb, "We the People," 577, correctly claims them to be at the present.

92. See Ibn ʿAbd al-Barr, *Jāmiʿ Bayān al-ʿIlm*, I:30–63; Ghazālī, *Iḥyāʾ ʿUlūm al-Dīn*, I:21–50; Māwardī, *Adab al-Dunyā wal-Dīn*, 24–30; Hallaq, *Sharīʿa*, part I.

93. Hallaq, *Authority, Continuity, and Change*.

94. On the principles regulating the *muftī*'s activities, see Ibn al-Ṣalāḥ, *Adab al-Muftī*; Hallaq, *Authority, Continuity, and Change*.

95. In fact, it was an obligation on the *qāḍī* to consult *muftī*s on difficult cases. See Ibn Qudāma, *Mughnī*, XI, 395–400; Kāsānī, *Badāʾiʿ*, IX, 126–127; Ibn al-Ḥājib, *Jāmiʿ al-Ummahāt*, 464.

96. Hallaq, *Authority, Continuity, and Change*, 174–208.

97. See Hallaq, "*Iftaʾ* and *Ijtihad* in Sunni Legal Theory"; Hallaq, *Authority, Continuity, and Change*, 1–23.

98. Messick, *Calligraphic State*, 135–151; Hallaq, *Authority, Continuity, and Change*, 2–23, 75–85, 166–194; Hallaq, "From *Fatwā*s to *Furūʿ*"; and, more generally, Masud et al., *Islamic Legal Interpretation*, 3–26; Tucker, *House of the Law*, 1–36.

99. Hallaq, *Sharīʿa*, 178, 381–382.

100. On this process, see Hallaq, *Authority, Continuity, and Change*, 194–208.

101. On the significance of the tradition of writing commentaries, glossaries, and superglossaries, see Hallaq, "*Uṣūl al-Fiqh*: Beyond Tradition."

102. Hallaq, "From *Fatwā*s to *Furūʿ*."

103. Here, the contrast with the modern state is highly instructive. As Kelsen noted, there is no reason to assume the existence of two separate orders, one of the state and the other of its legal order. We "must admit," he argued, "that the community we call 'State' *is* 'its' legal order" (*General Theory*, 182, 207). The contrast here is instructive because "law" in Islam is a primarily social, not a political, phenomenon. It is identified with society, not the "state," regardless of how the "state" is defined.

104. On what contempt of court meant in the Sharīʿa, see the illustrative discussion in El-Nahal, *Judicial Administration*, 40–41.

105. Hallaq, *Sharīʿa*, 164–176. Nelly Hanna, who studied the courts of Ottoman Cairo, observes that "the procedures of the courts of Cairo were simple and easy to understand; almost unimaginable today, they generally handed down decisions or notarized documents the very day the case or the document was brought before them. Even the local doctrines of the four schools of law seem to have been understood by the people. What we regard today as a very formidable and specialized area of knowledge—the various distinctions between the Ḥanafite, Shāfiʿite, Mālikite, and Ḥanbalite schools of law, in matters, for instance, of personal status or transactions—seems to have been common knowledge all that time. It was not unusual for one person to buy a house one day according to Ḥanbalite law and get married next day according to Mālikite or Shāfiʿite law. By assessing the specific differences between the schools of law . . . people deliberately chose the school that best defended their interests in any particular case or transaction." Hanna, "Administration of Courts," 53. Compare this, for instance, with the present condition of civil courts in the United States; see, in this regard, Kourlis and Olin, *Rebuilding Justice*.

106. Zaman, *Religion and Politics*; Hallaq, *Origins*, 178–193; Hallaq, *Sharīʿa*, 146–158, 197–221; Jackson, *Islamic Law and the State*; Peirce, *Morality Tales*.

107. Until the seventeenth century in the Ottoman Empire and until the early nineteenth century almost everywhere else, the *qāḍīs*, in terms of social origins, belonged to the area or district in which they held courts. Even after the seventeenth century, a majority of run-of-the-mill Ottoman *qāḍīs*, often called *nāʾibs*, served in their own area of origins and were not rotated throughout the empire, as the more senior *qāḍīs* were.

108. The scholarly and legal qualifications of the *muftī* were of such a standard that they permitted him to be a law professor. See Hallaq, *Authority, Continuity, and Change*, 173–174.

109. For the characteristics the legist must possess in order to qualify as a *qāḍī*, including the attribute of moral rectitude, see Kāsānī, *Badāʾiʿ*, IX, 93; Ghazālī, *Wajīz*, 479; Ḥiṣnī, *Kifāyat al-Akhyār*, 267; Ibn al-Humām, *Sharḥ Fatḥ al-Qadīr*, VII, 255; Ibn Qudāma, *Mughnī*, XI, 380–384; for the rectitude of the *qāḍī*'s staff (court personnel, especially the scribe), see ibid., 428–429.

110. Ibn Qudāma, *Mughnī*, XI, 378; Ibn al-Humām, *Sharḥ Fatḥ al-Qadīr*, VII, 259–260.

111. Hallaq, *Sharīʿa*, 401–404, and *passim*; Sabra, *Poverty and Charity*, 69–100; Singer, *Charity in Islamic Societies*, 90–113; Bonner et al., *Poverty and Charity*; van Leeuwen, *Waqfs and Urban Structures*.

112. Ibn al-Humām, *Sharḥ Fatḥ al-Qadīr*, VII, 313–314; Ibn Qudāma, *Mughnī*, XI, 378–379.

113. On the nature of court records, see Hallaq, "The Qāḍī's *Dīwān* Before the Ottomans."

114. Hallaq, *Sharīʿa*, 164–176; Rosen, *Anthropology of Justice*; Rosen, "Justice in Islamic Culture," 39–40.

115. Pierce, *Morality Tales*; Rosen, *Anthropology of Justice*; Rosen, "Justice in Islamic Culture"; Antoun, "Islamic Court, the Islamic Judge."

116. Peirce, *Morality Tales*.

117. On the sociolegal position of women in premodern Muslim societies, see sources listed in n. 77, above.

118. See Al-Qattan, "Dhimmis in the Muslim Court: Documenting Justice in Ottoman Damascus"; Al-Qattan, "*Dhimmīs* in the Muslim Court: Legal Autonomy and Religious Discrimination"; Al-Qattan, "Litigants and Neighbors"; Jennings, *Christians and* Muslims; Jennings, *Studies on Ottoman Social History*.

119. On how the law developed and on the various juristic roles in this development, see Hallaq, *Introduction*, 7–37; Hallaq, *Authority, Continuity, and Change*.

120. Hallaq, *History of Islamic Legal Theories*, 125–153.

121. Weiss, "Interpretation in Islamic Law"; Hallaq, *History of Islamic Legal Theories*, 82–124.

122. Hallaq, *History of Islamic Legal Theories*, 155–156.

123. Hallaq, "Regional to Personal Schools of Law."

124. McClellan, *Liberty, Order, and Justice*, 337–341.

125. When explained to Western lawyers, this feature usually proves confusing, if not incomprehensible, because the very idea of a pluralistic legal doctrine (encompassing a multiplicity of juristic voices) is foreign to the comparatively unitary and absolutist modern law. On how this worked in actual reality, see Hallaq, *Authority, Continuity, and Change*, 121–165; Jackson, *Islamic Law and the State*.

126. Hallaq, *Authority, Continuity, and Change*; Johansen, "Legal Literature and the Problem of Change."

127. Ibn Qudāma, *Mughnī*, XI, 480–481; Nawawī, *Majmūʿ*, XXII, 325; Ibn al-Ḥājib, *Jāmiʿ al-Ummahāt*, 462.

128. Thus, city and town quarters and often large villages each had a *qāḍī*. With the increase in populations and expansion of cities, the *qāḍīs* became more numerous. Thus, for instance, Cairo would witness an increase in the number of its *qāḍīs* from a handful in the eighth century to at least two dozen by the middle of the Ottoman period.

129. Tyan, "Judicial Organisation," 239. Orientalist discourse became so pervasive that Muslim writers (and the Christian Tyan) took to repeating this discourse without exercising critical scrutiny. See, for example, the virtually identical statements made by Ḥasanī, *al-Dawlah al-Sulṭāniyya*, 24.

130. Further on this, see Abou El Fadl, "Islam and the Challenge of Democratic Commitment," 18–28.

131. Ibn Qudāma, *Mughnī*, XI, 479; Ibn al-Ḥājib, *Jāmiʿ al-Ummahāt*, 463. The distinguished jurist Kāsānī (*Badāʾiʿ al-Ṣanāʾiʿ*, XI, 138) argues that "the *qāḍī* may be dismissed on all grounds on which a principal may terminate the agent in a contract of procuration (*wakāla*; agency) . . . with only one difference, namely, that if the principal dies or loses his legal competence, the agent will be terminated, but if the ruler dies or is deposed, his *qāḍīs* and appointees will not be dismissed. The reason for the difference is that in the case of procura-

tive contracts, the agent is appointed by the principal and works exclusively for him; so upon death, the contract is rendered null and void and the agent [herewith] dismissed. But the *qāḍī* does not become a *qāḍī* by virtue of the appointing power of the ruler, nor does he work for him. Rather, he becomes a *qāḍī* by virtue of the appointing power of the [Community of] Muslims, for whom he works. The ruler represents a messenger (*rasūl*) acting on behalf of the [Community of] Muslims . . . and so the *qāḍī*'s appointment continues to have effect subsequent to the death of the ruler. . . . Similarly, when dismissed by the ruler, the *qāḍī* is not so dismissed by virtue of the ruler's own power of dismissal, but rather by that of the common people (*ʿāmma*), for they are the appointees of the *qāḍī* in the first place." Note here that the concepts of "Muslims" and "common people" (*muslimūn/ʿāmma*) are equated.

132. In addition to sources cited in the previous note, see ʿAbd al-Rāziq, *al-Islām wa-Uṣūl al-Ḥukm*, 22–23; *al-Mawsūʿa al-Fiqhiyya*, VI, 227; XXXIII, 321.

133. On the other hand, the mandate of the ruler's vizier is terminated because this office is delegated in the truest sense, that is to say, the ruler appoints the vizier to help him with his tasks, those with which he is directly charged. This means that the vizier does the work of the ruler on behalf of the ruler, but not so the *qāḍī*.

134. Hallaq, *Sharīʿa*, 126–135, 197–216; Qalqashandī, *Ṣubḥ al-Aʿshā*, IV, 37; on the general importance of consultation as an attribute of the just ruler, see Ṭarsūsī, *Tuḥfat al-Turk*, 31; Ibn Taymiyya, *Siyāsa Sharʿiyya*, 414–416; Ibn Jamāʿa, *Taḥrīr al-Aḥkām*, 389–392; Ibn ʿAbd Rabbih, *al-Luʾluʾa fī al-Sulṭān*, 180–183.

135. Marshall, *Constitutional Theory*, 103–104.

136. Cohen, "Economic Background and Secular Occupations."

137. In the post–seventeenth century Ottoman Empire, the intervals were shorter, but the logic of job economy remained the same.

138. During the seventeenth and eighteenth centuries, a "legal aristocracy" developed in Istanbul within a number of families, although they did not work as *qāḍīs* "on the ground." But even these, who represented a minor exception, did not waver in their commitment to the Sharīʿa until the age of so-called reform (after the middle of the nineteenth century, when the Sharīʿa system collapsed altogether). See Hallaq, *Sharīʿa*, 216–221.

139. In his classical study of Ottoman Egypt in the seventeenth century, El-Nahal (*Judicial Administration*, 73) observes that given "the stereotypes of Islamic despotism, the courts were surprisingly free of executive intervention, remarkably even-handed in the administration of justice." This conclusion is thoroughly corroborated by the work of Ottomanists and others. See the works of Jennings, Gerber, and Jackson listed in the bibliography.

140. We scholars of Islamic history still do not adequately understand this phenomenon of taxation and overtaxation (or, for that matter, undertaxation). In any event, see Ibn Khaldūn, *Muqaddima*, 218–221, who notes that overtaxation was often occasioned by the fact that the Sharīʿa-stipulated taxes, conservative in nature, did not, on the whole, generate sufficient income for the ruler (218). Ṭurṭūshī (d. 1126) seems to regard proper collection of taxes as a "pillar" of just rule (*Sirāj al-Mulūk*, 306), suggesting that this "attribute of

the ruler" was not an always-realized condition. On the other hand, certain locals do not seem to have paid taxes, as evidenced in the Damascus riots of 1831–1832, in good part occasioned by the imposition of taxes. Shop owners, among others, are said to have declared their civil disobedience and marched in the streets "because they were not used to paying taxes" ("*wa-lam yakun li-sukkān hādhihi al-balda iʿtiyād bi-dafʿ al-ḍarāʾib*"). Cited in Kawtharānī, *al-Sulṭa wal-Mujtamaʿ*, 58. For a fourteenth-century account of Sharʿī and extra-Sharʿī taxes, see Qalqashandī, *Ṣubḥ al-Aʿshā*, III, 519–540. On the view of legal taxation in the modern state as a form of theft and slavery, see Nozick, *Anarchy, State, and Utopia*, 169–174, as well as p. xi. An even less charitable view is that of Nietzsche, *Thus Spoke Zarathustra*, 75.

141. See previous note. Whereas Sharʿī taxes *in combination* ranged, roughly speaking, between 2.5 and 15 percent, the average individual income tax *alone* in Western countries ranges, as is well known, between 30 and 60 percent (at least in such countries as the United States, United Kingdom, Sweden, Norway, Belgium, Denmark, France, Germany, Greece, Spain, Mexico, Australia, Canada, and Japan).

142. See, e.g., Johansen, *Islamic Law on Land Tax*; El-Nahal, *Judicial Administration*, 51–64; Khoury, *State and Provincial Society*, 178–187.

143. Khoury, *State and Provincial Society*, 179.

144. The lexical meaning of the term is "the occurrence of something consecutively," especially in war and victory in it. Thus, the winning side in war is said to have "a *dawla* over and against" the other side. The term also means "alteration from one state to another" or "a change from one situation to another." This is eloquently illustrated in Qalqashandī, *Ṣubḥ al-Aʿshā*, IV, 3–4. See also Ibn Manẓūr, *Lisān al-ʿArab*, XI, 301–303; Maqrīzī, *Sulūk*, I, 115, 129, 136, and *passim*; Ibn al-Athīr, *Kāmil*, XI, 112–113, 562.

145. See, for example, Ibn Khaldūn, *Muqaddima*, 184–185, 218–238, 259, 260, 261; Ibn al-Ṭuqṭuqā, *al-Fakhrī*, 18, 28, 30. A less frequent usage of the term *dawla* connoted the Islamic dynasties as a generic or collective notion (*al-dawla al-Islāmiyya*), standing in contrast with other non-Islamic rule, such as Persian or Byzantine rule. The referent here is still effective power that emanates from successive dynastic rule in a particular tradition of governance.

146. This may explain the phenomenon that the juristic works of Islam (*fiqh, uṣūl al-fiqh, qawāʿid, al-ashbāh wal-naẓāʾir*, etc.) have, for eleven centuries, introduced into their discourse neither the term *dawla* nor any of its derivatives. The reference is usually to *sulṭān*, here not the ruler as a personal-political figure but rather to government or executive power as an abstract concept, one that is a constant in Islamic governance.

147. On the various forms of separation between Community (Umma) and *dawla*, see Kawtharānī, *al-Sulṭa wal-Mujtamaʿ*, 33–37.

148. Ackerman, *Decline and Fall*, 4. See also Louis Fisher's review of this book, 56.

149. See previous footnote.

150. Hallaq, *Sharīʿa*, 209; but also see the sporadic abuses of the legal system by governors and rulers in ibid., 397; Hallaq, *Origins*, 187–189.

151. For *ḥadīth* subject matter bearing on this theme, see Muslim, *Ṣaḥīḥ*, III, 334–352.

152. Thus all accounts of the contestation between politics and knowledge in premodern Islamic contexts must be aware of the boundaries of such contestations, namely, that they remained at the outer layers of the legislative but squarely within the realm of the executive. Issues of legitimacy and ideology, as insightfully raised by Omid Safi (*Politics of Knowledge*) must always be understood to be about the *dawla* but not (until the nineteenth century) about the Sharīʿa.

153. For an illuminating discussion on these issues during the formative period, see Zaman, *Religion and Politics*.

154. Ibn Khaldūn, *Muqaddima*, Dawood's abridgment, 189.

155. Johansen, "Territorial Concepts," 452–453; Johansen, "ʿIṣma-Begriff im Hanafitischen Recht."

156. Both the mint and the inspector of the market, Ibn Khaldūn tells us, are religious functions that used to be performed by the (chief) *qāḍī* himself; however, by the twelfth century they have become separate offices, although still staffed by the ulama. Ibn Khaldūn, *Muqaddima*, 176–177.

157. Ibid.; Baghdādī, *Uṣūl al-Dīn*, 271–272; Ibn al-Ṭuqṭuqā, *al-Fakhrī*, 34–35.

158. This function came under the rubric of *maẓālim* courts. See Hallaq, *Origins*, 99–101; Hallaq, *Sharīʿa*, 208–213 and *passim*.

159. There is much in Al-Azmeh's *Muslim Kingship* to disagree with, but the following observation is not only unquestionable but also incisive: "It is clear . . . that Arabic, and more generally Muslim, writing on politics in the Middle Ages does not contain or constitute a theory of the state. Nor does it regard kingship as more than the sum total of royal activities, which are described and tabulated but not theorized. It is true that there are, in general, indications about the types of government, be they based on religion, on reason, or on caprice. But this is a typology of royal motivation, not a theory of state. . . . The state is here [i.e., in Ibn Khaldūn] abstract activity personified in the detailed actions of the king, while history is not the history of a state, but the history of a particular royal line. In this Ibn Khaldūn was in agreement with the historiographical tradition to which he was a faithful heir in his historical practice, regardless of his intention to subvert certain elements of this tradition. Writing on the state, moreover, even when restricted to the person of the king and certain classes of acts taking place during his reign, was formally not part of writing on politics, but of historical literature, in which the state is no more than the temporal extension of power" (113–114). This phenomenon may also be summed up simply by saying that there could not have been a theory of state because the state itself did not exist. This absence is all the more remarkable because Muslim jurists developed a theory for all important fields of praxis, but the *dawla* and its executive sultanism remained subsidiary to the Sharīʿa theories and an extension thereto.

160. Pierce, *Morality Tales*, 122; Hallaq, *Sharīʿa*, 214–216. Under the Ottomans, the longest-ruling dynasty in Islam, the *qāḍī* stood as the exclusive agent to enforce administrative regulations (*qānūns*). On the ground, he was the

ultimate administrator and final interpreter of the *qānūn*, which was unwavering in reiterating the decree that no punishment could be meted out without a trial by a *qāḍī*, and, indeed, evidence from court records overwhelmingly shows that the decision to punish was exclusively the *qāḍī*'s and that the meting out of penalties was normally the province of executive authority. The *qānūns*, which frequently restated and augmented earlier sultans' *qānūns*, in effect constituted a direct prohibition against conduct by government servants that might lead to injustice being inflicted upon the civilian population. The *qānūn* of Sulayman the Lawgiver (r. 1520–1566), for example, states that the "executive officials shall not imprison nor injure any person without the cognizance of the [Sharīʿa] judge. And they shall collect a fine according to [the nature of] a person's offense and they shall take no more [than is due]. If they do, the judge shall rule on the amount of the excess and restore it [to the victim]." The *qānūn* therefore upheld the Sharīʿa by enhancing and supplementing its position and provisions, while the Sharīʿa, on the other hand, required the intervention of sultanic justice. This complementary duality was endlessly expressed in various decrees and letters in the judicial discourse of the Ottoman authorities, be they sultans, Shaykh al-Islāms, viziers, or *qāḍīs*: justice had always to be carried out "according to the Sharʿia and *qānūn*." Jennings, "Limitations of the Judicial Powers of the Kadi," 166, 168; Peirce, *Morality Tales*, 119.

161. Johansen, "Territorial Concepts," 452.

162. *Ḥudūd* are Qurʾānically defined offenses and generally include *zinā* (fornication/adultery), slanderous accusation of sexual misconduct (*qadhf*), drinking alcohol (*shurb al-khamr*), theft (*sariqa*), highway robbery (*qaṭʿ al-ṭarīq*), rebellion (*baghī*), and apostasy (*ridda*). See Hallaq, *Sharīʿa*, 311–320.

163. This assumption is grounded in the "five universals" of the law, discussed in chapter 6, section 2.

164. Ibn Qutayba, *Kitāb al-Sulṭān*, 120–125; Ibn ʿAbd Rabbih, *Al-Luʾluʾa fī al-Sulṭān*, 160–163, 174–180.

165. Cited in Strawson, "Islamic Law and English Texts," 35.

166. Kelsen, *General Theory*, 282. See longer citation in main text, at n. 70.

167. Dunn, "Political Obligation," 24.

168. On this point, see chapter 6, section 2.

169. Dahl, "On Removing Certain Impediments," 235 (emphasis mine).

170. Rawls, *Political Liberalism*, 35 (emphasis mine).

4. The Legal, the Political, and the Moral

1. "Before anything else, the political is a relative sphere—for accommodations—and thus it cannot be treated with the same absolute logic of the religious field. . . . The recognition that sidestepping the logic of the political is an impossibility constitutes for contemporary political Islam an inescapable corridor." Ḥamza et al., "*Al-Ikhwān al-Muslimūn Muḥāṣarūn.*"

2. The words of Kenneth Stikkers. See his introduction to Scheler, *Problems*, 28. See also Gray's analysis in *Enlightenment's Wake*, 160–163.

3. Stark, *Sociology*, 33; Scheler, *Problems*, 129–130; Staude, *Max Scheler*, 197. In *Problems*, Scheler writes: "The voluntarist philosophies in the modern West, from Duns Scotus, Occam, Luther, Calvin, and Descartes to Kant to Fichte are not merely new 'theories' [but rather] *new sociologically conditioned forms of experience*. . . . They formulate the new idea of control and the new absolute value of control belonging to the new type of man, the Faustian man . . . [who] neither recognizes logical ideas and their interconnections nor an objective order of values and purposes that precede and limit his sovereign will" (127).

4. "An Answer to the Question: What Is Enlightenment?" in Gregor, *Immanuel Kant*, 17–22.

5. Guyer, *Kant on Freedom*, 2–7; see also Larmore, *Autonomy*, 105.

6. Scheler, *Problems*, 77.

7. For further on Weber (and Adorno) in this context, see chapter 5, section 1.

8. It must be noted, as does Frings (one of the most important Scheler scholars), that Scheler's theory of innate drive(s) "sets him apart from virtually all modern European philosophers." See Frings, *The Mind of Max Scheler*, 176, 244–247.

9. Stark, *Sociology*, 114.

10. Scheler, *Problems*, 98. On the Judeo-Hellenic conceptual roots of the Western domination of nature, see Singer, *Practical Ethics*, 265–269.

11. Scheler, *Problems*, 118 (emphasis mine).

12. Staude, *Max Scheler*, 191; Stark, *Sociology*, 19–21.

13. See, in particular, Horkheimer and Adorno, *Dialectic of Enlightenment*; and Adorno, *Negative Dialectics*. For a résumé of their work on the issues raised here, see Peukert, "Philosophical Critique of Modernity."

14. Scheler's theory is also of a wider compass than that of Foucault, who admittedly did not claim to speak about the non-European world. See Hallaq, *Sharīʿa*, 8.

15. Scheler, *Problems*, 119 (his emphasis), 78.

16. On "brute" and "inert" matter, see further below.

17. On this theme in the context of decimating the Amerindian populations, see Drinnon, *Facing West*, xxvii and *passim*. On natural resources and slavery, see Ferro, *Colonization*, 125–127.

18. What Foucault called "the technologies of the Self." Foucault, "Technologies of the Self," 223–251.

19. Cited in Stark, *Sociology*, 118; also Scheler, *Problems*, 129–130. For a critique of positivism, see Sprangens, *Irony of Liberal Reason*, 196–310.

20. Pérez-Ramos, "Bacon's Forms," 110–113; for Nietzsche's will to power and his influence on more recent European philosophers, including Foucault, see chapters 9 and 10 of *The Cambridge Companion to Nietzsche*.

21. Pérez-Ramos, "Bacon's Forms"; Rossi, "Bacon's Idea of Science," 37–42.

22. For an effective summary and incisive analysis of these views, see Bilgrami, “Gandhi, Newton,” 15–29.

23. Jacob, *Radical Enlightenment*, 6, as well as xi, 3–4, 64–67, and *passim.*

24. It is also in this sense, and not only in terms of paradigmatic rational morality (see main text, at n. 35, chapter 1), that such an argument as that of G. Stewart (“Scottish Enlightenment”) is rendered untenable. See also our discussion of paradigm in chapter 1.

25. Bilgrami, “Gandhi, Newton,” 25 and *passim.*

26. For further on this, see chapter 5, section 1.

27. On weltanschauung as an object of enquiry, see Mannheim, *Essays on the Sociology of Knowledge*, 33–83.

28. One can no more dominate a nature that is infused with value than subordinate and transform the Other whose human and cultural worth and moral constitution create a similar demand. More importantly, however, and as some social scientists (neo-Marxists and nonmainstream sociologists) have argued, the separation that denudes intellectual/scientific enquiry of value “*is ethically untenable*,” for it “disengages the observer from the social responsibility that should accompany his accounts, and it results in the status quo being presented as somehow natural and real, rather than as constructed and partisan.” This ethical dimension, indeed moral accountability, can hardly be overemphasized. Pressler and Dasilva, *Sociology*, 102–103 (emphasis mine).

29. Austin, *Province of Jurisprudence Determined.*

30. On the relevance of Hobbes to the nineteenth century and his epistemic anticipation of it, see Arendt, *Origins of Totalitarianism*, 139–157, esp. 146, 156.

31. Friedrich, *Philosophy of Law*, 84, 89–90.

32. On this theme in the context of ethics, see MacIntyre, *Short History*, 127–135. For a brilliant analysis of the relationship between and among violence, (im)morality, and the sovereign’s power in Hobbes’s thought, see Arendt, *Origins*, 139–147. On 144, Arendt perceptively remarks: “Hobbes’s deep distrust of the whole Western tradition of political thought will not surprise us if we remember that he wanted nothing more nor less than the justification of Tyranny which, though it has occurred many times in Western history, has never been honored with a philosophical foundation.”

33. On the latter two, see Friedrich, *Philosophy of Law*, 93–100. See also Bentham, *Introduction to the Principles of Morals*, 4, 309–330.

34. Austin, *Province of Jurisprudence Determined*, 157.

35. Ibid., 158; italics after “*ought*” are mine.

36. Ibid.

37. Unwin, “Morality, Law, and the Evaluation,” 538–549, at 538; Donoso, “Jurisprudence Today, 55–79, at 57.

38. See W. Rumble’s introduction to Austin’s *Province of Jurisprudence Determined*, xviii; Sprangens, *Irony of Liberal Reason*, 196–310.

39. Taylor, “Justice After Virtue,” 18.

40. See Kant’s manifesto, “An Answer to the Question: What Is Enlightenment?” 17–22.

41. For further on this theme, see chapter 7.

42. Kant, *Moral Law*, 14–15 (translator's epitome), 63–78, and *passim*. For an excellent overview of Kant's categorical imperative, see Schneewind, "Autonomy, Obligation, and Virtue," 309–333.

43. Arendt, *Origins of Totalitarianism*, 290–291.

44. On Protagoras, see Kerferd, *Sophistic Movement*, 84–93, 139–148; Taylor, *Good and Evil*, 56–67; Margolis, *Truth About Relativism*.

45. For criticism of Kant's categorical imperative, see Schneewind, "Autonomy, Obligation, and Virtue," 314–325; Field, "A Criticism of Kant," 487–491; Cartwright, "Schopenhauer's Narrower Sense of Morality," 254–263; Smith, *Viable Values*, 38ff.; Allison, "Kant," 437. For a pro-Kantian approach, see Gewirth, *Reason and Morality*. For further on this theme, see chapter 7.

46. Anscombe, "Modern Moral Philosophy," 1–2, 5; see also MacIntyre, *After Virtue*, 55.

47. See next section and *passim*.

48. Geuss, *Morality, Culture, and History*, 170.

49. Guyer rightly argues that Kant's concept of freedom was most central, underlying his notions of reason and morality and in effect overshadowing them. See his *Kant on Freedom*, 5, 8, 39–42, 51–59, 129–138.

50. Taylor, "Justice After Virtue," 20; MacIntyre, *After Virtue*, 56–61, 79–87; MacIntyre, *Short History*, 130–131, 166–171, 189–191.

51. Taylor, "Justice After Virtue," 20.

52. Ibid., 20–21.

53. Donoso, "Jurisprudence Today," 55, 66.

54. See, for instance, his discussion in the *Treatise of Human Nature*, in Smith and Greene, eds., 247f.

55. Nietzsche, *Will to Power*, 326: "The deeper one looks, the more our valuations disappear. . . . We have *created* the world that possesses values! Knowing this, we know, too, that reverence for truth is already the consequence of an illusion—and that one should value more than truth the force that forms, simplifies, shapes, invents. 'Everything is false! Everything is permitted' "; also see his *Twilight of the Idols*, 46.

56. Geuss, *Morality, Culture, and History*, 189. See also Gray, *Enlightenment's Wake*, 150–152.

57. For Hart, see his *Concept of Law*. For the exchange between Hart and Lon Fuller, see Olafson, *Society, Law, and Morality*, 439–470 (for Hart) and 471–506 (for Fuller). See also Fuller, *Morality of Law*, esp. 187–242. In the context of the fact/value split, Fiss's views in "Objectivity and Interpretation" still belong to this "internal moralistic interventions" in the law. So do, more generally, the ideas of such thinkers as Ronald Dworkin and Bruce Ackerman, among many others.

58. MacIntyre, *After Virtue*, 38.

59. Which I label, for lack of a better expression, the *Makārim al-Akhlāq* genre. See, for example, Raḍī Ṭabarsī, *Makārim al-Akhlāq*; Ibn Abī al-Dunyā, *Makārim al-Akhlāq*; Ḥasanī, *Tahdhīb al-Akhlāq*.

60. See, by way of background, Bloor, "The Question of Linguistic Idealism Revisited."

61. Lexically, the premodern concept *akhlāq* was associated with innate qualities having more to do with *ṭab*ʿ (nature, but not second nature) and *sajiyya* (disposition, character) than with ethics and morality, especially as the latter two have come to acquire modern meanings. See Ibn Manẓūr, *Lisān al-ʿArab*, X, 104–105. In the premodern Islamic conception, *akhlāq* was nonetheless susceptible to acculturation and refinement. See sources listed in n. 59; also Miskawayh, *Tahdhīb al-Akhlāq*; Ghazālī, *Iḥyā*ʾ *ʿUlūm al-Dīn*; and chapter 5, section 2. Yet these processes by which *akhlāq* are cultivated and refined revolve precisely around the absence of distinction between law and morality, injecting in them a heavy "legal" (not to mention theological) ingredient that modern notions of morality lack. For an illustration of the contrast—both substantive and semantic—between premodern and modern concepts of *akhlāq*, compare Ḥasanī's (d. 1341/1922) *Tahdhīb al-Akhlāq* with the work of the distinguished contemporary Muslim moral philosopher Ṭāha ʿAbd al-Raḥmān, *Rūḥ al-Ḥadātha*; and, in particular, the same author's *Suʾāl al-Akhlāq*.

62. Hallaq, *Sharīʿa*, 1–3.

63. The problem, however, is insoluble, as I have argued, on the basis of Nietzsche, in "What Is Sharīʿa?" 151–152. The nature of this problem should therefore explain why I continue to use such terms as "law" and "morality," since, as Nietzsche convincingly argued, they have become "legislated." See Nietzsche, "On Truth and Lies in a Nonmoral Sense," 81, 83.

64. The subject of our discussion in chapter 5, section 2.

65. A *locus classicus* of this weltanschauung is Ghazālī's expansive project, evidenced in his numerous works. See, e.g., *Iḥyā*ʾ *ʿUlūm al-Dīn*; *al-Munqidh min al-Ḍalāl*; *Mishkāt al-Anwār*, etc., and our discussion in chapter 5, section 2.

66. As used here, "deep" bears the moral sense given to it in the movement of Deep Ecology, championed by Arne Naess, Pierre-Félix Guattari, and others. See, e.g., Naess, *Selected Works*, 13–55.

67. The theme of inducing life from death and death from life is a common one in the Qurʾān. See 2:164, 259; 6:95; 26:81; 30:19, 24, 50; 35:9; in the context of moral conduct, see 67:2.

68. Qurʾān 30:8: "Have they not pondered upon themselves? God created not the Heavens and the earth, and that which is between them, save with the truth and for a destined end." More specifically, 53.31: "And to God belongs whatever is in the heavens and whatever is in the earth, that He may reward those who do evil with that which they have done, and reward those who do good with goodness." Observe the total effect of the foregoing verses as combined with 6:13, 59, 63, 65, 95, 96, 102; 13:1–43; 18:7; 22:5–6, 18; 23:1–16; 30:11, 12, 15, 19, 27; 31:29–34; 52:9; 53:31, 42–62; 81:1–29; 82:1–19; 89:1–30; and more systematically and extensively, Sūrahs 30 and 67.

69. Qurʾān 18:47; 19:90; 20:105; 27:88; 52:10.

70. Qurʾān 2:50; 20:77.

71. Qurʾān 41:13–17; 51:41; 89:6.

72. Qurʾān 21:33; 31:29; 35:13; 71:16.

73. Qurʾān 2:60; 6:141; 16:11; 45:5; 50:6–11; 54:12.

74. Qur'ān 2:155; 16:112.

75. Qur'ān 7:78, 91; 16:26; 17:37; 29:37; 69:5; 99:1–2.

76. Qur'ān 17:69; 33:9; 41:16; 51:41; 69:6.

77. Qur'ān 13:2; 30:8; 31:29.

78. Qur'ān 99:7–8.

79. Qur'ān 67:1–2: "*Tabāraka al-ladhī bi-yadihi al-mulku wa-huwa ʿalā kulli shayʾin qadīr. Al-ladhī khalaqa al-mawta wal-ḥayāta li-yabluwakum ayyukum aḥsanu ʿamalā, wa-huwa al-ʿazīz al-ghafūr.*" Most Qur'ān translations render "*al-ladhī bi-yadihi al-mulku*" as "in whose hands is the Sovereignty." While this manner of translation is eminently reasonable, it is equally plausible to attach to *yad* the more emphatic meaning of possession, a common connotation in old and middle Arabic.

80. See also Izutsu, *Ethico-Religious Concepts*, 106.

81. Pickthall, *Meanings of the Glorious Koran*, 289–290.

82. Qur'ān 11:7: "He it is Who created the heavens and the earth in six days . . . that He might try you: Which of you is best in conduct" (*li-yabluwakum ayyukum aḥsanu ʿamalā*); 18:7: "Lo, We have placed all that is in the earth as an ornament thereof that we may try them: Which of them is best in conduct."

83. Qur'ān 5:39; 6:54; 25:70.

84. See Izutsu, *Ethico-Religious Concepts*, 108, who asserts that the structure of the present world in the Qur'ān "is most profoundly determined by the ultimate (eschatological) end to which the present world (*al-dunyā*) is destined."

85. Qur'ān 3:104, 110; 9:67, 71, 112; 22:41.

86. Qur'ān 2:158; 4:147; 35:30; 76:22.

87. See next note.

88. Qur'ān 17:70. Also see 2:57, 172; 5:88; 6:142; 7:50, 160; 8:26; 16:72, 114; 40:64.

89. Qur'ān 55:3–13; 96:6.

90. Izutsu, *Ethico-Religious Concepts*, 120, 124–125.

91. On *mujrimūn* and other derivatives of *J.R.M.*, see Qur'ān 6:124; 10:13; 11:35; 20:74; 30:47. On *ẓālimūn* and other derivatives of *Ẓ.L.M.*, see Qur'ān 2:59, 272; 3:135; 8:60; 39:51; 46:12.

92. Qur'ān 2:126; 4:10, 97, 115; 8:16; 22:72; 57:15; 64:10; 87:12; 111:3.

93. See, e.g., Qur'ān 2:25, 62, 82, 277; 3:57; 4:57, 122, 173; 5:9, 69, 93; 7:42; 10:4, 9; 11:11, 23; 13:29; 16:97; 18:30, 88, 107; 19:60; 20:75, 82; 25:70, 71; 28:67, 80; 30:44; 45:15. For all relevant entries, see ʿAbd al-Bāqī, *al-Muʿjam al-Mufahris*, 410–412. It will be noted that the form *aṣlaḥa* has an added meaning of "to become good," in the sense of reforming oneself from a state of *ẓulm* (transgression) and *fasād* (doing ill) to one of *taqwā* (piety) and *īmān*. In this sense, the Qur'ān contains at least a dozen references, e.g., 6:54; 7:35.

94. Qur'ān 2:184; 3:30, 115.

95. Qur'ān 16:97; 18:30–31, 107, 110; 35:7, 29; 41:8.

96. Izutsu, *Ethico-Religious Concepts*, 204. See, for example, Qur'ān 2:112; 16:97; 18:2, 30, 107, 110; 30:44–45; 32:19–20; 34:4; 41:7–8; 95:6.

97. Izutsu, *Ethico-Religious Concepts*, 106.

98. Kelsen, *General Theory*, 189.

99. None of my arguments here should be construed to mean that Islamic governance is doomed, for if it must face this destiny, it would simply share the fate of modernity itself. And as the last chapter of this book indicates, the modern condition is unsustainable and must be made to pass. The question that remains open is whether the next phase of world history (the so-called future) can accommodate Islamic governance with the realization that this system is attentive to the spiritual-moral self, to family and community, to economic equitability, and, as importantly, to the environment. For to transcend the problems of the modern project in a true sense, this list of considerations must achieve priority for *all societies in our world, not just the Islamic*. In one important sense, the paradigmatic problems and seeming impasses facing Islamic governance are virtually identical to those facing non-Muslim societies nearly everywhere. Islam and its promise of Islamic governance do not have a monopoly over crisis. (Hence, the word "impossible" in the title of this book would be as much a statement about the sustainability of the current state of the modern project as it is one about the Islamic state.)

100. Scheuerman, "Carl Schmitt and the Road to Abu Ghraib," 108; also Schwab's introduction to Schmitt's *Concept of the Political*, 5.

101. Ulmen, "Sociology of the State," 38.

102. Bolsinger, *Autonomy*, 29.

103. Ibid., 38, 180.

104. Meier, *Greek Discovery of Politics*, 17.

105. See Strong's forward to Schmitt's *Concept of the Political*, xvi.

106. This includes the ability of the political to harness the legal in its service. Even the laws of war, presumably intended to "humanize" bellicosity, in effect does the opposite. Despite "noble rhetoric . . . , the laws of war have been formulated deliberately to privilege military necessity at the cost of humanitarian values. As a result, the laws of war have facilitated rather than restrained wartime violence. Through law, violence has been legitimated." See Jochnick and Normand, "Legitimation of Violence," 50. See also our account of paradigms in chapter 1.

107. Bolsinger, *Autonomy*, 178–179.

108. Ibid., 182.

109. Geuss, *Morality, Culture, and History*, 189.

110. See chapters 1 and 7.

111. Schmitt, *Concept*, 29.

112. Ibid., 28.

113. The reason for this qualification is the impact the Bolshevik Revolution had on Schmitt's thinking, where a political party could, like the state, define, in the field of politics, the lines of separation between an enemy and a friend.

114. Schwab's introduction to Schmitt's *Concept*, 6–7.

115. Finlayson, "Psychology, Psychoanalysis, and Theories of Nationalism," 159.

116. Breuilly, *Nationalism and the State*, 366–401; Gray, *Enlightenment's Wake*, 13.

117. On territoriality and Islam, see Grosby, "Nationality and Religion," 110.

118. Kahn, *Putting Liberalism*, 230–231, 240.

119. Cited, from Schmitt's *Glossarium* (320), in Strong's forward to his *Concept of the Political*, xxxi.

120. Kahn, *Putting Liberalism*, 238–239.

121. Nelson, *Making of the Modern State*, 107–108.

122. Gill, *Nature and Development*, 5.

123. Murdoch, *Metaphysics as a Guide to Morals*, 350.

124. Bolsinger, *Autonomy*, 38–39, in the context of discussing Schmitt.

125. Nietzsche, *Thus Spoke Zarathustra*, 75; see also Nozick, *Anarchy, State, and Utopia*, 169–174.

126. It must be asserted, however, that in the discourse of the jurists (i.e., in *fiqh* literature), the general status of *jihād* is always a *farḍ kifāya* (generally stated as "*al-jihād huwa min furūḍ al-kifāya*"). See Māwardī, *al-Ḥāwī al-Kabīr*, XIV, 149–150; Rāfiʿī, *ʿAzīz*, XI, 345; Ramlī, *Nihāyat al-Muḥtāj*, VIII, 42–43; Khurashī, *Ḥāshiya*, IV, 5–9; Ibn Māza, *Muḥīṭ*, VII, 90; Nawawī, *Rawḍat al-Ṭālibīn*, VII, 411; Ibn al-Sāʿātī, *Majmaʿ al-Baḥrayn*, 792; *al-Mawsūʿa al-Fiqhiyya*, XVI, 129.

127. See sources cited in the previous note.

128. Nawawī, *Rawḍat al-Ṭālibīn*, VII, 412, where he states that those who cannot afford to buy their own weapons and pay for travel to and from the battle zone are not obliged (morally or legally) to participate in *jihād*.

129. Ibn Māza, *Muḥīṭ*, VII, 89–91.

130. See sources quoted in n. 126. Even then, only after the so-called *nafīr* takes place does *jihād* become incumbent upon every legally competent Muslim. *Nafīr* is the public announcement of an imminent attack on an inhabited Muslim territory. Ibn Māza, *Muḥīṭ*, VII, 90.

131. Ibn Māza, *Muḥīṭ*, VII, 91.

132. See, for example, Maqrīzī's *Sulūk*, vol. 1.

133. Nawawī, *Rawḍat al-Ṭālibīn*, VII, 413, 415.

134. Ibn Māza, *Muḥīṭ*, 110, 133–134; Ibn Juzay, *Qawānīn*, 108; Maghribī, *al-Badr al-Tamām*, IV, 486–488.

135. Ibn Māza, *Muḥīṭ*, 110; Kāsānī, *Badāʾiʿ al-Ṣanāʾiʿ*, IX, 382; Maghribī, *al-Badr al-Tamām*, IV:486–488.

136. Ibn Māza, *Muḥīṭ*, 133.

137. Ibid., 134; Māwardī, *al-Ḥāwī al-Kabīr*, XIV, 123; Rāfiʿī, *ʿAzīz*, XI, 362.

138. Ibn Māza, *Muḥīṭ*, VII, 90. Ibn Māza died in A.D. 1220, having lived and written his magnum opus during the Crusades.

139. Ibid., 93. For a definition of "consensus," see glossary.

140. Nawawī, *Rawḍat al-Ṭālibīn*, VII, 411.

141. Generally, flight from battle was deemed permissible "if there are more than two infidels to each Muslim fighter"; see *Baḥr al-Favāʾid*, 29; Nawawī, *Rawḍat al-Ṭālibīn*, VII, 448–449; Ibn ʿĀbidīn, *Ḥāshiya*, IV, 127; Ibn Juzay, *Qawānīn*, 109.

142. See chapters 1 and 7.

143. Gamble, *Politics and Fate*, esp. 6–8.

144. Kelsen, *General Theory*, 186.

145. On the relationship between war and the formation of the modern state, see Tallett, *War and Society in Early Modern Europe*; Tilly, *Coercion, Capital, and European States*; Mann, *States, War, and Capitalism*; Black, *European Warfare: 1494–1660*; Black, *European Warfare: 1660–1815*.

5. The Political Subject and Moral Technologies of the Self

1. Marx, "Manifesto," 9: "The Executive of the modern state is but a committee for managing the common affairs of the whole bourgeoisie."

2. van Creveld, *Rise and Decline*, 168–169, 417–418. On the further growth of prisons more recently, see Teeple, *Globalization*, 122–126.

3. This paragraph essentially summarizes van Creveld, *Rise and Decline*, 205–224. See also Lasch, *Culture of Narcissism*, 125–153.

4. This last reference is intended to evoke Foucault's analysis in *The Order of Things*.

5. Tallett, *War and Society*, 39–44.

6. Foucault, *Discipline and Punish*, 138.

7. See Foucault's exordium to this chapter; see also ibid., 137.

8. Hall and Ikenberry, *State*, 14; originally, this is in good measure Weber's argument. See Scaff, "Weber on the Cultural Situation," 106, although Weber had a good deal of appreciation for the aporia this argument raised.

9. See chapter 4, section 1.

10. But this is not to underrate or deny the complexity, in academic and modern thought, of the tension between the real as the rational and the real as illusion. As Herbert Marcuse observed, this tension constitutes the boundaries of a single concept, namely, "the antagonistic structure of reality, and of thought trying to understand this reality." See his *One-Dimensional Man*, 123. Yet it must be added that this "understanding" encompasses conscious engagement, participation, and acceptance, hence its virulent positivist nature. It is not a detached understanding, nor is it, in any way, a resisting strategy that persistently and systematically invokes the moral against the real. For this general context, and for academic Orientalism in particular (a prototype of academia in general), see Hallaq, "Orientalism, Self-Consciousness, and History."

11. Further on this matter in the context of Orientalism (a form of knowledge supported and sustained by the humanities and social sciences at large), see Hallaq, "Orientalism, Self-Consciousness, and History."

12. See, for example, Bourdieu, *Algerians*; Hallaq, *Sharīʿa*, 357–370, 443–499.

13. Illustrative of the points raised here is Donzelot, *Policing of Families*; Polanyi, *Great Transformation*, 81–107 and *passim*; Hallaq, *Sharīʿa*, 337–370, 443–499.

14. This form-property is both implied by and subsumed under the form-properties discussed in chapter 2.

15. For a specific case of accommodation, see Stiglitz, *Globalization and its Discontents*, x.

16. Rose and Miller, "Political Power," 182.

17. The mild qualification is occasioned by the recognition that the citizen must be, in certain restricted and narrow spheres, distinguished from the moral individual. But this is not a paradigmatic distinction, since the moral individual as an archetype—whose province neither enters the political nor counts in the legal—pales in significance when compared with his role as citizen. It is in this light that one should interpret Murdoch on this point. See her *Metaphysics as a Guide to Morals*, 357.

18. Bourdieu, *Practical Reason*, 71: "It is indeed clear that in modern societies the main agent of the *construction of the official categories* through which both populations and minds are structured is the state, which, through a whole labor of codification, accompanied by economic and social effects (family allowances, for example), aims to favor a certain kind of family organization, to strengthen those who are in a position to conform to this form of organization, and to encourage, through all material and symbolic means, 'logical conformism' and 'moral conformism' as an agreement on a system of forms of apprehension and construction of the world, of which this form of organization, this category, is without doubt the cornerstone."

19. See Glendon, "Power and Authority," 15–24. On the marginalization of the father in the modern family, see Lasch, *Culture of Narcissism*, 172–176. Although this trend has not yet gained serious momentum in the Muslim world, it is likely to do so in the not-so-distant future, especially if liberal economic and political models continue to be adopted.

20. Glendon, "Power and Authority."

21. Donzelot, *Policing of Families*, 103–104.

22. See also Giddens, *Modernity and Self-Identity*, 169–179: "The self in modern society is frail, brittle, fractured, fragmented—such a conception is probably the pre-eminent outlook in current discussions of the self and modernity" (169).

23. Donzelot, *Policing of Families*, 217–219, 227.

24. See his forward to ibid., xi.

25. From another perspective, that of Adorno's culture industry, see Johnson, "Social Philosophy," 121 and *passim*.

26. A masterly account of public rituals in the service of state power is Corrigan and Sayer, *Great Arch*.

27. Finlayson, "Psychology, Psychoanalysis, and Theories of Nationalism," 148.

28. Generally on this, see Breuilly, *Nationalism and the State*; Reicher and Hopkins, *Self and Nation*.

29. Breuilly, *Nationalism and the State*, 369.

30. DeGré, *Social Compulsions*, 66–112.

31. Staude, *Max Scheler*, 172; Scheler, *Problems*, 67.

32. Scheler, *Problems*, 67. Emphasis is Scheler's.

33. Mannheim, *Essays*, 33–83; Pressler and Dasilva, *Sociology*, 53.

34. Bailey, *Critical Theory*, 45.

35. Pressler and Dasilva, *Sociology*, 58–59.

36. Staude, *Max Scheler*, 165. Scheler, *Problems*, 72; K. W. Stikkers's introduction to Scheler, *Problems*, 26, 23; DeGré, *Social Compulsions*, 66ff. On Gadamer in this context, see Pressler and Dasilva, *Sociology*, 108–109.

37. Weber, *Protestant Ethic*, 13, 121.

38. Foucault, "Technologies of the Self," 228: "How then can respect for the self be the basis of morality? We are inheritors of a social morality that seeks the rules for acceptable behavior *in relation to others*. Since the sixteenth century, criticism of established morality has been undertaken in the name of the importance of recognizing and knowing the self. Therefore, it is difficult to see the self as compatible with morality. . . . In the modern world, knowledge of oneself constitutes the fundamental principle" (emphasis mine).

39. A distinction teased out nicely in Baracchi, *Aristotle's Ethics as First Philosophy*.

40. Foucault, "Technologies of the Self," 228.

41. Gerth and Mills, *From Max Weber*, 73, 63–66.

42. Ibid., 73. On this in general context, and on the culture industry in particular, see the work of Horkheimer and Adorno, *Dialectic of Enlightenment*; Adorno, *Culture Industry*; and Touraine, *Critique of Modernity*, 130–133. See also Lasch, *Culture of Narcissism*, 125–141.

43. Marcuse, *One-Dimensional Man*, 1.

44. Further on this, see Wood, *Origins of Capitalism*, 3 and *passim*.

45. See chapter 2, subsection 2, on sovereignty.

46. Scaff, "Weber on the Cultural Situation," 103.

47. Giddens, *Modernity and Self-Identity*, 169.

48. Adorno, *Culture Industry*, 132–157; Finlayson, "Psychology, Psychoanalysis, and Theories of Nationalism," 151.

49. Lasch, *Culture of Narcissism*, 232.

50. See in this context Bauman, *Modernity and the Holocaust*.

51. Finlayson, "Psychology, Psychoanalysis, and Theories of Nationalism," 153 (emphasis mine).

52. From a different but highly useful perspective on the construction and meaning of religion in Europe and Islam, see Asad, *Genealogies of Religion*.

53. On the nonformality (though not informality) of premodern Muslim education, see Berkey, *Transmission of Knowledge*.

54. Hallaq, *Sharīʿa*, 135–152. On this and on premodern Islamic education in general, see Tibawi, "Origin and Character of *Al-Madrasa*"; Makdisi, *Rise of the Colleges*; Berkey, *Transmission of Knowledge*.

55. See section 2 of chapters 3 and 4.

56. Prichard, "Does Moral Philosophy Rest on a Mistake?"; Rand, "Objectivist Ethics," 13–35; Rand, "Causality Versus Duty," 114–122; Smith, *Viable Values*; Hospers, "Why Be Moral?"

57. Questions asked by premodern philosophers were to a different purpose. See, for instance, S. MacDonald, "Ultimate Ends in Practical Reasoning."

58. Larmore, *Autonomy of Morality*, 87, unduly universalizes the question and its motives, claiming it to have received its first systematic expression in Plato's *Republic*. This claim, however, violates his own controlling and solid principle *that all thinking is situational*, tied to a place and time, a principle that he properly calls "contextualist epistemology" (1, 4). See also chapter 7, which in part argues that while the relationship of reason and reasons was a hotly debated issue during the first four centuries of Islam, the question of "why be moral?" did not occur, in the way it has been cast by modernity, to any of the parties to that debate.

59. For a critique of the conflation of Sharīʿa with "law," see Hallaq, *Sharīʿa*, 1–6.

60. I have dealt with this theme in my "Groundwork of the Moral Law."

61. This fusion can be said to have become problematic even in the First Amendment to the U.S. Constitution, where law was intended to be instrumental neither in establishing religion nor in prohibiting its practice.

62. An excellent example of such a project is Peirce, *Morality Tales*.

63. On these functionaries and audiences of the court, see, for a schematic exposition, Tyan, "Judicial Organization"; for historical evolution, Hallaq, *Origins*; for their moral role, Peirce, *Morality Tales*.

64. As expressed, for instance, by the jurists in the context of *shuhūd* and *bayyināt*. See Ibn Māza, *Muḥīṭ*, XII, 280.

65. El-Nahal, *Judicial Administration*.

66. See, in this regard, the citation from John Rawls, at chap. 3, n. 170.

67. On these claims, see Hallaq, "Model Shurūṭ Works," 109–112.

68. Further on this construction, see Hallaq, *Sharīʿa*, 1–6.

69. If it is true that the distinction *ʿibādāt/muʿāmalāt* is premodern, then it is self-evident that its structure and therefore *functions* served a premodern order. To claim that this—or many such distinctions—fulfill the same *functions* in modern law and legal system is to engage in both apologetics and classic forms of anachronism. For an example of such conflations, see Mohammad Fadel, "Tragedy of Politics"; and n. 9 of the introduction to this book.

70. To the exception of such matters as alms-tax (*zakāt*), which extended over to the nonritualistic realm.

71. See, e.g., Katz, *Body of Text*.

72. Ibid., 13–18.

73. In this discursive and conceptual act of segregation, a crucial point has been missed in the study of Sharīʿa and its history. For, on the whole, the Sharīʿa as a law and legal system has been viewed as having failed to match up to any version of European law. The Sharīʿa is seen as ineffective, inefficient, even incompetent; as having mostly applied to parts of the "private" sphere of the family; and having early on "divorced" itself from "state and society." Its penal law continues to be seen as little more than burlesque; it "never had much practical importance" and was in fact downright "deficient," in the words of one of the foremost scholars on the penal law of Islam. Heyd, *Studies*, 1. While generally shying away from such a flat condemnation, modernist Islamic legal thought has also subscribed to the premises of this transformation, adopting in

the process a qualitative distinction between *ʿibādāt* and *muʿāmalāt*. The overall effect was a concerted effort to separate state from religion and the private from the public (or rather to remanufacture the landscape of the private/public spheres). Such a view of the Sharīʿa could come about only on the basis of the assumption that the technologies of the self were absent. Yet a full appreciation of their effects demonstrably warrants a reversal of this evaluation, making these technologies the substrate and props of the *muʿāmalāt*. Without these technologies, the moral individual and the moral community, always assumed by the Sharīʿa and its practices to be preexistent, could not come about. Indeed, no law under the purview of *muʿāmalāt* can be properly understood (especially as functioning within a social site) without the *ʿibādāt* and the technologies of the self they had produced, which is to say that no "law proper" could be complete or deemed *proper* without the underlying substrate of the *ʿibādāt*. In both doctrine and practice, the *ʿibādāt partook in constituting the muʿāmalāt*. And it is for this reason that they were aptly labeled the "pillars of religion," the moral foundations upon which the Sharīʿa is supposed to rest. These claims (summarized in Hallaq, "Model Shurūt Works," 109–112) remain tenacious even in recent scholarship. See, for example, the descriptions of Collins, "Islamization of Pakistani Law," 511–522.

74. Infrequently, non-Sunnite *fiqh* books might begin with a chapter on *ʿilm* (virtues of learning and knowledge) or on *ijtihād* and *taqlīd*. See, e.g., the Zaydite jurist Ibn Muftāḥ, *Sharḥ al-Azhār*, I, 115ff. However, such prefaces (usually referred to as *khuṭbat al-kitāb*) are not regarded as integral to the main subject of the book, which substantively remains one of *fiqh*.

75. Ṣanʿānī, *Muṣannaf*, III, 42; Māwardī, *al-Ḥāwī al-Kabīr*, IV, 4; Miṣrī, *ʿUmda*, 278.

76. Goitein, *Studies*, 73–89; Beeston, "Religions of Pre-Islamic Yemen," 264.

77. However, the Mālikites add to these five a chapter on *jihād*, discussed by the other schools usually toward the end of their books. For the Mālikites, see Ibn al-Ḥājib, *Jāmiʿ al-Ummahāt*, 243ff. On the arrangement of subject matter in Islamic juristic works and the place of the chapter of *jihād* in them, see Hallaq, *Introduction*, 29–30.

78. Hallaq, *Sharīʿa*, 159–196.

79. Ibid., 377–378.

80. Ghazālī, *Mukhtaṣar*, 360–362 (henceforth cited as *Mukhtaṣar al-Iḥyāʾ*).

81. Ibid., 43.

82. Ghazālī, *Iḥyāʾ*, III, 57.

83. Qurʾān, 4:110, 34:37, 40:40, 18:30, 29:7, 39:35.

84. Qurʾān, 57:25.

85. That is, *niyya*, to be discussed in due course.

86. Buhūtī, *Rawḍ*, 15.

87. For example, in Maqdisī's *ʿUdda* and Ḥalabī's *Multaqā*, the chapter on purification occupies about one-fifth of subject matter devoted to the pillars.

88. Ḥalabī, *Multaqā*, I, 11–12; Shaʿrānī, *al-Mīzān al-Kubrā*, I, 147–156; Ibn al-Ḥājib, *Jāmiʿ al-Ummahāt*, 44–51.

89. Māwardī, *al-Ḥāwī al-Kabīr*, I, 57; Miṣrī, *ʿUmda*, 95–97.

90. Insisted upon by the great majority of jurists. See Māwardī, *al-Ḥāwī al-Kabīr*, I, 87–92.

91. Shaʿrānī, *al-Mīzān al-Kubrā*, I, 148–149.

92. Powers, *Intent*, 32–33, 49–50; see also Messick, "Indexing the Self."

93. Ibn Qayyim, *Iʿlām*, III, 122.

94. Ibid., III, 123; IV, 199. Similarly, see Ibn Mufliḥ, *Ādāb*, I, 31. For numerous *ḥadīths* on *niyya* in this context, see al-Ḥurr al-ʿĀmilī, *Wasāʾil al-Shīʿa*, I, 41–47.

95. al-Ḥurr al-ʿĀmilī, *Wasāʾil al-Shīʿa*, I, 56.

96. Miṣrī, *ʿUmda*, 138.

97. On the same point in fasting, see further below.

98. This is why I have insisted, earlier in this chapter, that the Sharīʿa takes for granted the formation of the moral subject prior to the juridical event, prior, that is, to the unfolding of the "law" in the realia of life and living.

99. See Singer, *Charity in Islamic Societies,* 30–65, 157–165; Sabra, *Poverty and Charity*, 32–58, 69–100.

100. Qurʾān 3:180. *Zakāt* is due on property that is (a) in full ownership, precluding freely grazing wild animals as well as property that is not in the possession (*yad*) of the owner (e.g., an unlawfully appropriated herd, *maghṣūb*). Derivative of this requirement is the ability to make payment at the time it is due, since property could perish between the end of the "fiscal" year and the time payment becomes due. "Ability" (*imkān*) is a condition obtaining in the law and applicable to all the "pillars"; (b) capable of growth, such as cattle, agricultural lands, and commercial goods. Goods for personal consumption, e.g., animals intended for food, personal clothing, and furniture, are exempt. On the other hand, precious metals, such as gold and silver, are taxable since they are commonly used in profit-based enterprises; (c) in excess of subsistence (e.g., food, shelter, household furniture, etc.); or (d) productive for a minimum of one full lunar year, with the exception of agricultural crops and minerals extracted from underground (in which case, *zakāt* is due upon "harvesting" since this in itself constitutes "growth"). Finally, it is due on property that is (e) free of impediments, such as a debt that is owed.

101. Saḥnūn, *Mudawwana*, I, 308; Mawāq, *Tāj*, II, 292; Nawawī, *Rawḍa*, II, 3; Ḥalabī, *Multaqā*, I, 169. Ṭūsī, *Khilāf*, I, 316, requires *zakāt* on minors' productive property.

102. Ṭūsī, *Khilāf*, I, 321.

103. The *niṣāb* of cattle is thirty, of goats forty, of gold is twenty *mithqāl*, of silver a hundred *dirhams*, and so forth. The Shāfiʿites and Ḥanbalites require that the *niṣāb* be maintained throughout the year without interruption. Should a cattle owner have, say, thirty heads, one of whom died during the eleventh month of the taxation year, and a few hours later a calf was born, she would owe no *zakāt* on her herd for that year. By the same principle, she would owe *zakāt* on this *niṣāb* a year after the birth of that calf, provided there is no diminution in the number for any duration. The *zakāt* levy on gold and silver is generally 2.5 percent, and so is the production of all types of mines (Maqdisī, *ʿUdda*, 132; Ḥalabī, *Multaqā*, I, 183–185). The rate on agricultural produce is

10 percent if the crops are irrigated by natural resources but 5 percent if they are irrigated artificially, whether the water is purchased or carried through paid labor. In *muḍāraba* (*commenda*) partnerships, the sleeping partner pays *zakāt* on the principal, but the jurists disagreed as to who must pay on the profits. The Shāfiʿites assigned responsibility entirely to the sleeping partner, whereas the Ḥanafites required the worker to pay for his own share of gains. In commonly owned, joined, and commingled property (*māl mushtarak*), the majority of jurists held *zakāt* to be due not on the *niṣāb* of the total property owned but rather on each partner's share (Ṭūsī, *Khilāf*, I, 314). The Shāfiʿites, however, took the position that the *niṣāb* must be based on the total aggregate of property (Nawawī, *Rawḍa*, II, 27ff.).

104. See, in a comparative context, Bynum's magisterial work, *Holy Feast and Holy Fast*.

105. Ghazālī, *Iḥyāʾ*, III, 86.

106. Ḥalabī, *Multaqā*, I, 196; Nawawī, *Rawḍa*, II, 230–231.

107. Nawawī, *Rawḍa*, I, 214–215; Miṣrī, *ʿUmda*, 282.

108. See Sabra, *Poverty and Charity*, 32–58, 69–100; Singer, *Charity in Islamic Societies*, 30–65, 157–65; Çizakça, *History of Philanthropic Foundations*.

109. Hallaq, *Sharīʿa*, 271–272.

110. Miṣrī, *ʿUmda*, 286.

111. Buhūtī, *Kashshāf*, II, 456–457.

112. For an encyclopedic treatment of *istiṭāʿa*, see Māwardī, *al-Ḥāwī al-Kabīr*, IV, 7–15.

113. Ḥalabī, *Multaqā*, I, 208–209.

114. Nawawī, *Rawḍa*, II, 282–284.

115. Buhūtī, *Kashshāf*, II, 469; Nawawī, *Rawḍa*, II, 307; Ṭūsī, *Khilāf*, I, 417.

116. Ḥalabī, *Multaqā*, I, 212–213.

117. Miṣrī, *ʿUmda*, 340.

118. To the liberal mind, submission to some suprahuman agency seems an anathema. In the moral technologies of the self, however, submission acquires a different meaning. Lenn Goodman perceptively put the matter thus: "Islam may be interpreted to mean resignation to the will of God; but if that will remains no longer other, but is accepted by the consciousness as self, then the I can expect of itself the ability to move mountains. . . . This was the meaning of Islam: the progressive assimilation of self to God (so far as lies in human power). This entails acceptance of the divine will, *but not as something alien*. The transmuting of selfish purpose to the will of God need not imply a surrender of will because the assimilation of self to God does not imply a surrender to self. On the contrary . . . this assimilation is the meaning of man's fulfillment *qua* man, the substance of Plato's answer to the cryptic challenge of the oracle, "Know thyself!" To know oneself was to see in oneself affinities to the divine and to accept the obligation implied by such recognition to develop these affinities—to become, in as much as was in human power, like God." Goodman, *Ibn Tufayl's Hayy Ibn Yaqzān*, 17–18 (emphasis mine).

119. We must be careful here to distinguish in Foucault between two strands of technologies: one based on the premodern "European" religious sub-

ject (a technology "now obscure and faded"), the other based on the modern and "free" subject whose self-conducted technology is integral to, if not the product of, the Enlightenment concept of freedom. It is obviously in the analysis of the former type of subject, where a metaphysical cord must be struck, that Foucault may be relevant for us to illustrate a transition from the first to the second type of subject.

120. This exemplarity is most evident in his *Munqidh min al-Ḍalāl*, a work that transcends the limits of conventional autobiography.

121. The *Iḥyā*ʾ (henceforth cited in this form) became the subject of numerous commentaries by both Sunnite and Shīʿite authors. See, for example, Zabīdī, *Itḥāf al-Sāda* and Kāshānī's *al-Maḥajja al-Bayḍā*ʾ. See also Moosa, *Ghazālī and the Poetics of Imagination*; Meisami's introduction to *Sea of Precious Virtues* (*Baḥr al-Favāʾid*), xiv–xv; and Buchman's introduction to Ghazālī's *Mishkāt al-Anwār*, xxvi.

122. *Iḥyā*ʾ, III, 12–13. These three potentialities possess similar expansive powers but only by implication. Ghazālī obviously privileges the divine potentiality with proactive characteristics.

123. Ibid., III, 10: "*wal-ʿilm huwa maqṣūdu al-insāni wa-khāṣṣiyyatuhu al-latī li-ajlihi khuliqa.*"

124. Ibid., III, 13.

125. Ibid., III, 5; *Mukhtaṣar al-Iḥyā*ʾ, 182.

126. *Iḥyā*ʾ, I, 217; III, 111; *Mukhtaṣar al-Iḥyā*ʾ, 109.

127. *Iḥyā*ʾ, I, 216–217; III, 92, 93.

128. Ibid., III, 9.

129. Ibid., III, 65, 70; see also Miskawayh, *Tahdhīb*, 32ff. For an excellent anthropological analysis of this training in a modern context, see Mahmood, *Politics of Piety*, esp. 118–152.

130. *Iḥyā*ʾ, III, 88, 98–99.

131. Foucault, "Technologies of the Self," 226ff.

132. *Iḥyā*ʾ, III, 100.

133. Ibid., III, 70. Although Ghazālī makes no obvious connection between this technology of the self and the *uṣūl* theory of *tawātur*, the epistemic foundation for both processes is a shared one. Repeated performance of an act engenders certitude: in *uṣūl*, the effect of corroborative transmission is a theoretical acquisition of information that engenders certainty, whereas in the technologies of the self, it is a practical acquisition of ethical conduct that engraves itself onto the soul with an equal measure of such knowledge (hence the resultant *ṭab*ʿ). Hallaq, "Inductive Corroboration," 3–31. Ibn Khaldūn writes: "An action done once adds an attribute (*ṣifa*) to the essence of the soul. With repetition it becomes a 'condition' (*ḥāl*), which is an attribute that is not firmly established. After more repetition it becomes a habit (*malaka*), that is, a firmly established attribute." Quoted in Lapidus, "Knowledge," 53–54.

134. *Iḥyā*ʾ, III, 70. See also Mahmood, *Politics of Piety*, 135–139, where she elaborates on the "ethical pedagogy . . . in which external performative acts (like prayer) are understood to create corresponding inward dispositions" (135).

135. *Iḥyā*ʾ, I, 209–211.

136. Ibid., I, 212.

137. *Mukhtaṣar al-Iḥyāʾ*, 311, 324–325.

138. Note here that Ghazālī's meaning of love as pertains to the Self is to be sharply distinguished from the relationship of love/Self in other Ṣūfī doctrines. Cf., e.g., Attar, *Conference of the Birds*. It is such mystical doctrines—going far beyond the paradigmatic and mainstream Ṣūfism as expounded by Ghazālī—that gave rise to Ibn Taymiyya's virulent attacks against mystical pantheism. See Hallaq, *Ibn Taymiyya Against the Greek Logicians*.

139. *Iḥyāʾ*, I, 276. It is instructive to compare Ghazālī's views here with the modern narrative offered by Charles Taylor, *Sources of the Self*, esp. 93–94.

140. Prichard, "Does Moral Philosophy Rest on a Mistake?" 31–32.

141. On the "mild" and "moderate" asceticism that characterized Sunnite Islam, see Hurvitz, "Biographies and Mild Asceticism." But it must be noted that non-Sunnite Muslims also shared much of this mildly mystical ethic.

142. E.g., Miskaway, *Tahdhīb*; Zabīdī, *Itḥāf al-Sāda*; Kāshānī's *al-Maḥajja al-Bayḍāʾ*.

143. Ibn Mufliḥ, *Ādāb*, III, 464–465.

144. Giddens, *Modernity and Self-Identity*, 170: "Narcissism presumes a constant search for self-identity, but this is a search which remains frustrated, because the restless pursuit of 'who I am' is an expression of narcissistic absorption rather than a realistic quest."

145. See chapter 4, section 1.

146. See chapter 3, section 2; Hallaq, *Sharīʿa*, 159–196.

147. See chapter 3.

148. It is no exaggeration to say that in premodern Islam nine out of ten jurists, small and great, belonged to one brand of mysticism or another. This, one might fear, is still a severely understated estimation.

149. Leading figures in this strand are Charles Taylor and, especially, Alasdair MacIntyre. For the former, see *Sources of the Self* and the *Malaise of Modernity*; for the latter, see *After Virtue* and *Whose Justice?* Further on this, see chapters 1 and 7 of this book.

6. Beleaguering Globalization and Moral Economy

1. Breuilly, *Nationalism*, 369.

2. On the differences between modern and premodern forms of globalization, see Held et al., *Global Transformations*, 340–341, 363–369.

3. Guibernau, "Globalization and the Nation State," 246; Sørensen, *Transformation of the State*, 33.

4. "If globalization has not succeeded in reducing poverty, neither has it succeeded in ensuring stability. . . . The critics of globalization accuse Western countries of hypocrisy, and the critics are right. The Western countries have pushed poor countries to eliminate trade barriers, but kept up their own bar-

riers, preventing developing countries from exporting their agricultural products and so depriving them of desperately needed export income. The United States was, of course, one of the prime culprits." Stiglitz, *Globalization and Its Discontents*, 6.

5. Teeple, *Globalization*.

6. Kahn, *Putting Liberalism*, 235–236; Teeple, *Globalization*, 1–5. For an effective summary of liberal and neoliberal market philosophy, see Jessop, *Future of the Capitalist State*, 218–220.

7. Let us recall that, in chapter 2, we did not count capitalism (or any other economic model) as an essential form-property of the state, rejecting the notion that for a state to be state it must necessarily adopt a particular economic orientation. We adduced as an example the former Soviet Union, with Cuba furnishing yet another (and, until recently, China and the Socialist Republic of Vietnam). This is why we insist on the word "comport," since the capitalist ideology of globalization could have just as easily been socialist (for instance) had the great economic, military, and political powers in the world been socialist with a vested interest in spreading socialism and socialist economic models across the world.

8. Typologies of "theses" or "schools" abound. For a quintile classification, see Marsh et al., "Globalization and the State," 172–189.

9. Representative of this thesis are Strange, *Retreat of the State*; Spruyt, *Sovereign State*; Albrow, *Global Age*; Wriston, *Twilight of Sovereignty*; and Ohmae, *End of the Nation State*.

10. Bauman, *Globalization*, 55–76.

11. Representative of this thesis are Hirst and Thompson, *Globalization in Question*; Jessop, *Future of the Capitalist State*; and Sørensen, *Transformation of the State*.

12. Hirst and Thompson, *Globalization in Question*, 98.

13. Marinetto, *Social Theory*, 125, quoting Henri Lefebvre's *De l'État: l'État dans le monde moderne*, vol. 1.

14. On the role of globalization in increasing poverty worldwide, see Stiglitz, *Globalization and Its Discontents*.

15. This statement should be mitigated by a relative neglect by the state of the poor. On this subject, see Ashford, "Constitution of Poverty," 149–167. Furthermore, it should be mitigated by the evincive argument that the state's social reforms have declined in the so-called age of globalization. See Teeple, *Globalization*, 51–80.

16. Sørensen, "Transformation of the State," 190–208.

17. Shaw, "State of Globalization," 497–513; Held et al., *Global Transformations*.

18. A nuanced assessment crossing over the two theses is Mann, "Has Globalization Ended?"

19. Held et al., *Global Transformations*, 327–363.

20. Ibid., 87–148.

21. Shaw, "State of Globalization," 497.

22. Ibid., 502.

23. On the IMF and World Bank as significant actors in globalization, see Stiglitz, *Globalization and Its Discontents*. See also Held et al., *Global Transformations*, 149–188.

24. Shaw, "State of Globalization."

25. Sørensen, *Transformation of the State*, 30.

26. Kahn, *Putting Liberalism*, 235–236; Teeple, *Globalization*, 1–5.

27. Strange, *Retreat of the State*, 198. Strange also argues that the so-called global governance will continue to lack any systemic structure as long as its "powers" are not pitted or balanced against each other in the way the separation of powers operates in the state.

28. Hirst and Thompson, *Globalization in Question*, 98; Sørensen, *Transformation of the State*, 23–45.

29. Held et al., *Global Transformations*, 242–259.

30. Schmitter, "Still the Century of Corporatism?" 111–113, 119–120.

31. Bakan, *Corporation*, 5–8, 12: In both Europe and America, the corporation was initially opposed on moral grounds because "it allowed investors to escape unscathed from their companies' failures . . . the critics believed it would undermine personal moral responsibility, a value that had governed the commercial world for centuries." See also Korten, *When Corporations Rule the World*.

32. Buchanan, *Ethics*, 27–28.

33. See, for example, Ghazanfar, *Medieval Islamic Economic Thought*.

34. See Hallaq, *Sharīʿa*, 371–442.

35. For an introduction, see Opwis, "Islamic Law and Legal Change," 66–71; Hallaq, *History of Islamic legal Theories*, 168–174, 180–187. These universals, together with allied concepts, were refashioned during the twentieth century, in the process obliterating the very system from which they themselves derived. In an earlier article ("Can the Shariʿa Be Restored?" 46), I argued that these modern reformulations were lodged in an "incurable subjectivity." By contrast, in the premodern period they constituted the foundations of the law and were made integral to the theory of *uṣūl*.

36. Hallaq, "*Maqāṣid and the Challenges of Modernity*," 1–10.

37. See chapter 5, section 2.

38. On *jihād* and apostasy, see Hallaq, *Sharīʿa*, 318–320, 324–341; and our discussion in chapter 5, section 2.

39. Shāṭibī, *Muwāfaqāt*, vol. 2; Shawkānī, *Irshād*, 214–218; Ibn ʿĀshūr, *Maqāṣid*, 430–449.

40. Shāṭibī, *Muwāfaqāt*, II, 3: "*al-Sharīʿa wuḍiʿat li-maṣāliḥ al-ʿibād*."

41. Hallaq, *History of Islamic Legal Theories*, 162–206.

42. It is because of all these characteristics that the theory of universals (as both *kulliyyāt* and *maqāṣid*) has emerged in the last decade or so as the subject of intense discussion. See, for example, the conference proceedings *al-Nadwa al-ʿĀlamiyya ʿan al-Fiqh al-Islāmī*, 3 vols.

43. These interdependent relationships continue to be well understood by some modern authors. See, for example, Bāqir al-Ṣadr, *Iqtiṣādunā*, 290–298 and

passim (for a useful discussion of this theme in al-Ṣadr, see Mallat, *Renewal of Islamic Law*, 115–119); Qutb, *Social Justice*, 127 and *passim*. However, the majority of modern Muslim writers on the subject do not exhibit such complex understanding, even when they oppose capitalism and its effects. For the latter, see Tripp, *Islam and the Moral Economy.*

44. Al-Ḥurr al-ʿĀmilī, *Wasāʾil al-Shīʿa*, XII, 323–325, 329–331, where the virtues of highly commended commerce include "sharpening the wit and intelligence."

45. Qurʾān 62:10; Sarakhsī, *Mabsūṭ*, XXX, 245.

46. See percentage allocation to each of these subjects in Hallaq, *Introduction*, 29–30.

47. See chapter 5, section 2.

48. Shawkānī, *al-Sayl al-Jarrār*, II, 575ff., 586ff., 641–642, 744ff.; Nawawī, *Rawḍa*, III, 5; Māwardī, *al-Ḥāwī al-Kabīr*, V, 13.

49. A Prophetic tradition. See Bukhārī, *Ṣaḥīḥ*, II, 617.

50. A Prophetic tradition. See Tirmidhī, *Sunan*, III, 335.

51. Also the theme of other Prophetic traditions. See ibid. Likewise, see the aggregate signification of the Qurʾānic verses 2:83, 177, 188, 198, 200, 215, 275–279; 4:2, 6, 10, 29, 36, 161; 5:89; 9:35, 60, 103; 17:26; 24:22; 30:39; 58:13; 62:10.

52. Al-Ḥurr al-ʿĀmilī, *Wasāʾil al-Shīʿa*, XII, 349–350, 352–353. On the prohibition on *ribā* and risk (*gharar*), see Hallaq, *Sharīʿa*, 243–244; Vogel and Heyes, *Islamic Law and Finance.*

53. On *zakāt* in modern debates, see Tripp, *Islam and the Moral Economy*, 56–57, 124–126.

54. Ibn Qudāma, *Mughnī*, II, 702. For a vivid account of institutions and established practices supporting wayfarers throughout the Muslim world, see Ibn Baṭṭūṭa, *Travels.*

55. This conception of wealth remains as powerful today as it was a millennium ago. See, for example, Bahī, *al-Dīn wal-Dawla*, 121–130.

56. See, e.g., Ghazali, *Ghazali's Path to Sufism*, 35.

57. *Al-Fatāwā al-Hindiyya*, V, 348–349; Ibn Mufliḥ, *Ādāb*, III, 423–424, 428; Sarakhsī, *Mabsūṭ*, XXX, 250–251.

58. The Sharīʿa recognizes five legal norms under which all human acts must fall. These are the permissible, forbidden, obligatory, disapproved/reprehensible, and recommended.

59. *Al-Fatāwā al-Hindiyya*, V, 349; Ibn Mufliḥ, *Ādāb*, III, 424.

60. See previous note.

61. Ibn Mufliḥ, *Ādāb*, III, 424–426. Only a minority of jurists restricts rights of *nafaqa* to a narrow circle of relatives, a limitation that social custom and cultural practice often informally defy.

62. Cf. Ashford, "Constitution of Poverty," 166.

63. Qurʾān, 51:19, 70:22–25: The latter verse reads as follows: "the worshipers who are constant at their worship and in whose wealth there is a fixed right (*ḥaqq maʿlūm*) in favor of the beggar and the destitute." In the same vein, it is as forbidden to turn away the beggar as it is to mistreat the orphan. See Qurʾān, 93:9–10.

64. See chapter 5, section 2.

65. Al-Ḥurr al-ʿĀmilī, *Wasāʾil al-Shīʿa*, XII, 340.

66. Ibid., XII, 69–208, where dozens of virtues acquired by *jihād al-nafs* are discussed.

67. Ibn Mufliḥ, *Ādāb*, III, 426–442; *Al-Mawsūʿa al-Fiqhiyya*, XXXIV, 235.

68. On the dilemmas of "Islamic finance" and reflecting these dilemmas, see the writings of El-Gamal, especially his *Islamic Finance*.

69. Thus, such explanations as provided by Kuran, "Why the Islamic Middle East Did Not Generate an Indigenous Corporate Law," are not only misguided in their intellectual quest (i.e., asking the wrong questions) but also deeply flawed as historical and analytical projects.

70. Hanneman and Hollingsworth, "Refocusing the Debate," 50.

7. The Central Domain of the Moral

1. A strong claim for state neutrality is made in An-Na'im, *Islam and the Secular State*, 1 and *passim*. If this claim—central and essential to An-Na'im's overall thesis—cannot be sustained, then that thesis must be reconsidered. Similarly, see Turabi's views (remaining no more than bare outlines) of an "Islamic state" that must not be wholly sovereign or even nationalistic. Euben and Zaman, *Princeton Readings*, 213–215.

2. For the metaphysical implications of syllogism and the theory of universals on which it rests, see Hallaq, *Ibn Taymiyya Against the Greek Logicians*. For a classic critique of Aristotelian metaphysics, see Ghazālī, *Tahāfut al-Falāsifa*.

3. Kahn, *Putting Liberalism*, 277 (obviously by now, Kahn's use of the term "state"—in a context in which the "state" is subordinated to a higher will—must be taken in a metaphorical sense). See also Scanlon, "Rights, Goals, and Fairness," 93.

4. Abou El Fadl, "Islam and the Challenge of Democratic Commitment," 69: "Effectively, a religious State law is a contradiction in terms. Either the law belongs to the State or it belongs to God, and as long as the law relies on the subjective agency of the State for its articulation and enforcement, any law enforced by the State is necessarily not God's law. Otherwise, we must be willing to admit that the failure of the law of the State is, in fact, the failure of God's law and, ultimately, God Himself. In Islamic theology, this possibility cannot be entertained." However, Abou El Fadl does not tease out the full implications of this penetrating insight, largely taking the modern state for granted.

5. Magill, "Beyond Powers and Branches," 605. See also Marshall, *Constitutional Theory*, 97, 124; Hansen, "Mixed Constitution," 509, and our discussion in chapter 2, section 1.

6. For the norms that must apply to any act, including one that is "neutral" (i.e., allowing for what we nowadays call personal/private choice), see Hallaq, *History of Islamic Legal Theories*, 40–42. It should be noted here that the private sphere in the modern state is left "unregulated" by a deliberate

choice (or *decision*) of the state and not by virtue of the inherent autonomy of that sphere, for when the state decides that a matter in this domain must henceforth belong to the public sphere, there can be no criteria by which this decision is judged other than that by the state's will, which, after all, is said to express popular sovereignty. Further on this latter point, see Asad, *Genealogies of Religion*, 200–208.

7. Murdoch, *Metaphysics as a Guide to Morals*, 350 (her emphasis); see also Strauss, "On the Spirit," 13.

8. See chapter 1.

9. Giddens, *Capitalism*, 99–100; Miller, *Durkheim, Morals, and Modernity*; Nisbet, *Sociology of Emile Durkheim*, 187–208.

10. See chap. 4, n. 99.

11. See chapter 4, section 1.

12. Prichard, "Does Moral Philosophy Rest on a Mistake?"; Larmore, *Autonomy of Morality*; Larmore, *Morals of Modernity*.

13. Discussed in chapter 4, section 1.

14. Larmore, *Autonomy of Morality*, 10–11, 56–60, 64–65: "Reasons have their own authority. . . . Reasons for belief and action depend on the physical and psychological facts being as they are. There is a reason to take an umbrella only if it is indeed raining, or a reason to get a drink of water only if I happen to be thirsty. . . . A reason is a reason for someone, and for someone able to take up the possibility the reason endorses. In short, reasons are rational in character: they consist in certain features of the natural world *counting in favor* of possibilities of thought and action belonging to intelligent beings" (10–11). The "idea of a responsiveness to reasons makes no sense if reasons are denied a causal influence. Where there is no action, there cannot be a response. . . . There is only confusion, it can seem, if we imagine that the space of reasons consists ultimately in anything other than the law-governed processes of the natural world, explicable in the terms of modern science. To many, reasons will look 'spooky' . . . if they are assumed to be . . . both sui generis and causally active in the world. The sensible approach, one easily concludes, is to regard reasons for belief and action as simply the expression of our own commitments, and not as something 'there anyway,' awaiting our discovery: the reasons there are simply the reasons we take there to be. For our commitments themselves are psychological phenomena, and their place in the causal order of the world poses no similar problem of intelligibility" (64–65). On the "contents" of reason, see Smith's critique in *Viable Values*, 38–53.

15. As I have argued in "Groundwork of the Moral Law," 253; see also chapter 4, section 1. Further to sources cited in this and the previous paragraph, see Schneewind, "Autonomy, Obligation, and Virtue"; Field, "A Criticism of Kant"; Cartwright, "Schopenhauer's Narrower Sense of Morality," 254–263; Smith, *Viable Values*, 38ff.; Anscombe, "Modern Moral Philosophy"; Gray, *Enlightenment's Wake*.

16. Larmore, *Autonomy of Morality*, 111–112.

17. Spengler, *Decline of the West*, 120.

18. Taylor, "Justice After Virtue."

19. See chapter 4, section 1; and Guyer, *Kant on Freedom*; Larmore, *Autonomy of Morality*, 105.

20. Prichard, "Does Moral Philosophy Rest on a Mistake?" 36.

21. Korsgaard, *Sources of Normativity*, 5, as cited (and critiqued) by Larmore, *Autonomy of Morality*, 112.

22. Larmore, *Autonomy of Morality*, 109 (added parenthetical mine). See also Smith, *Viable Values*, 40–53.

23. Larmore, *Autonomy of Morality*, 109, 112.

24. Ibid., 112.

25. Ibid., 122 (his emphases).

26. Ibid., 123–129, esp. 129.

27. Twenty-first, because Larmore (2008) here locks horns with his contemporary, the neo-Kantian Korsgaard.

28. For a detailed account of this synthesis, see Hallaq, *Origins* (Index therein, under "Great Synthesis"); Hallaq, *Sharīʿa*, 55–60, 72.

29. This is often defined in the field of Islamic studies in terms of conflict or opposition between "reason and revelation," a rudimentary conception that preempts asking hard questions. Once reasons are reduced to "revelation," then it would be a short step to assigning them to irrational religion, rendering the "contest" between reason and reasons winnable by the *noblesse de raison*.

30. In this regard, see Hallaq, *Sharīʿa*, 72–124.

31. See chapter 4, section 1.

32. The juristic manifestations of this maxim are explored in detail in Hallaq, *Authority, Continuity, and Change*.

33. See Hallaq, "Can the Shariʿa Be Restored?"

34. Of course, much can be said in the way of proposing solutions to the challenges and problems this book raises, but an elaborate outline of such solutions would require writing another and much longer book.

35. A similar call, in a different contest, was issued in Massad's important work *Desiring Arabs*.

36. Although it is very likely that a paradigmatic shift in the Western liberal order will, almost automatically, weaken the Muslim and Arab liberal movement, perhaps to the point of collapse, for Islamic and Arab liberalism is a current that suffers from more profound contradictions and incoherence than even the Euro-American liberal order. For a general critique of the liberal order, see Nicolacopoulos, *Radical Critique of Liberalism*; Schmitt, *Crisis of Parliamentary Democracy*; MacIntyre, *After Virtue*; MacIntyre, *Whose Justice?*; Sandel, *Liberalism and Its Critics*; Gray, *Enlightenment's Wake*; Gray, *Straw Dogs*; Gray, *Liberalism*; Amin, *Liberal Virus*; Bell, "Communitarian Critique"; MacLean and Mills, *Liberalism Reconsidered*; Kahn, *Putting Liberalism*; Sprangens, *Irony of Liberal Reason*; and (from the Islamic reformist perspective) Haj, *Reconfiguring Islamic Tradition*, among countless others.

37. As already evident in the remarkable work of Ṭāha ʿAbd al-Raḥmān, for instance. See the list of his works in the bibliography.

38. See chap. 4, n. 99.

39. Gray, *Enlightenment's Wake*, 153–155 (emphasis mine).

Glossary of Key Terms

In classifying terms, no account is taken of the letters ʿayn and hamza.

AUTHOR-JURIST: an accomplished jurist who exercised certain faculties of *ijtihād* (q.v.) in writing legal manuals and/or longer treatises on law.

CALIPH: the political and religious head of Islamic government; a deputy of the Prophet, also known as the Commander of the Faithful and Imam (q.v.). After the ninth century, and with the ascendancy of tribal dynasties hailing mainly from Central Asia, the caliph gradually lost his political and military powers, and was progressively reduced to a religious symbol. The ruler became the sultan, the effective political and military authority.

CHARITABLE ENDOWMENT: *see waqf.*

CONSENSUS: the third source of Islamic law; the agreement of *mujtahids* (q.v.) belonging to an age on a particular point of law, said to be determined in a back-projected manner, namely, when jurists looked back at earlier generations and observed that there was no disagreement among them on a particular point of law. Cases or questions subject to consensus are deemed to be certain and therefore irrevocable, though they are relatively few in number.

DĀR AL-ḤARB: land or dominion in which the Sharīʿa does not reign supreme or does not exist at all. Such territories are theoretically subject to conquest through *jihād* (q.v.).

DĀR AL-ISLĀM: dominion of Islam where the Sharīʿa reigns supreme and where more than one Islamic sultanate can simultaneously rule.

DAWLA: dynastic rule; executive sultanic power; a ruling dynasty whose role is to enforce the Sharīʿa in a region of Dār al-Islām (q.v.). In modern Arabic, the term has come to denote the entire state, including legislative, judicial, and executive branches of government.

FAQĪH: an expert in the law, an *ʿālim* (pl. *ʿulamāʾ*, q.v.).

FARḌ ʿAYN: an act whose performance is incumbent upon each and every Muslim individual with full legal capacity.

FARḌ KIFĀYA: an obligatory act that, once performed by any number of legally competent Muslims, is deemed discharged and ceases to be a duty for the rest.

FIQH: discourse of substantive and procedural law (q.v.) as found in legal works and *fatwā* collections (q.v.).

FATWĀ: an authoritative legal opinion issued by a *muftī* (q.v.) on a particular point of law; judges sought and adhered to *fatwās* routinely, although *fatwās* are not formally binding.

FOUR SOURCES: the main sources of the law, i.e., the Qurʾān, the Prophetic Sunna (q.v.), consensus (q.v.), and *qiyās* (methods of legal reasoning).

ḤADĪTH: Prophetic traditions or reports of what the Prophet is assumed to have said, done, or tacitly approved with regard to a particular event or case; *see* Sunna.

ḤUDŪD: punishments for certain offenses specified in the Qurʾān.

ʿIBĀDĀT: religious works or performative acts of worship described and prescribed in the first chapters of substantive legal works (*fiqh*; q.v.). Mildly ascetic, they include ablution (*ṭahāra*), prayer (*ṣalāt*), fasting (*ṣawm*), pilgrimage (*ḥajj*), and alms-tax (*zakāt*; q.v.). Together with the *shahāda* (*see shahādatayn*), the last four constitute the pillars (q.v.) of Islam. Formally, no one can claim or be claimed to be a Muslim, nor can Islam itself claim to be what it is, without belief in, and practice of, *ʿibādāt*.

IJTIHĀD: legal methods of interpretation and reasoning by which a qualified jurist derives or rationalizes law on the basis of the Qurʾān, the Sunna, and/or consensus (q.v.); also, a court judge's evaluation of customary practices as they bear on a case brought before him.

IMAM: leader of Friday prayer; a caliph (q.v.) in Sunnite Islam; the infallible head of the Shīʿite Muslim community who is a descendant of Imam ʿAlī and who is in hiding (occultation).

ISTIṢLĀḤ: literally, to find something good or serving a certain public interest; technically, a method of inference that does not resort directly to a revealed text as the basis of reasoning but rather draws on rational arguments grounded in the five universals of the law, i.e., protection of life, mind, religion, family/community, and property (*see kulliyyāt*).

JIHĀD: disciplining the inner self; certain disciplinary operations exercised on the body, thought, and conduct; such operations that aim to fashion a moral subject or a moral way of living; the law regulating conduct of war and peace.

JUDGE: *see under qāḍī* and jurist.

JURIST: a legist (q.v.) who achieved a remarkably high level of legal knowledge, usually as a *muftī* (q.v.) and/or author-jurist (q.v.). Until the nineteenth century, all jurists in Islam were trained exclusively in Sharīʿa sciences.

KULLIYYĀT (AL-KHAMS): the five universals that capture the overarching principles governing the rights to life, religion, integrity of mind, family/community, and property. These universals are said to have been deduced from the entirety of the Sharīʿa values, regulations, and practices over the first five or six Islamic centuries, providing jurisprudential guidelines of legal thinking and legal reasoning for jurists of later centuries.

LEGAL NORM: any of five legal values under which each case or legal act must fall; the five norms/values are: permissible, forbidden, obligatory, disapproved/reprehensible, and recommended.

LEGAL SCHOOLS: an association of jurists who share loyalty to a particular set of legal precepts, a particular methodology of interpretation and of implementing law; in Sunnite Islam, the legal schools that have survived after the eleventh century are four, the Ḥanafite, Mālikite, Shāfiʿite and Ḥanbalite, each named after a master jurist to whom a particular way of doing law is attributed.

LEGIST: someone learned in the law, whether a *muftī* (q.v.), author-jurist (q.v.), judge, or law student.

MADRASA: college of law that is usually part of an endowment (q.v. *waqf*) where teaching was offered in language, *ḥadīth* (q.v.), and Qurʾānic studies and where circles of study in mathematics, astronomy, logic, and medicine were often found.

MAṢLAḤA: *see istiṣlāḥ*.

MUʿĀMALĀT: legal subjects expounded in works of *fiqh* (q.v.), works that include contracts, sales, family law, pledge, guaranty, transfer, etc. but exclude *ʿibādāt*; such laws and transactions as practiced among and between people in the social order.

MUFTĪ: a jurisconsult; a learned jurist who issues *fatwās* (q.v.); a jurist capable of one degree of *ijtihād* (q.v.) or another.

MUJTAHID: a highly learned jurist who is capable of reasoning about the law through applying complex methods and principles of interpretation; *mujtahids* are of various ranks, the highest of which is reserved for the one who is said to have fashioned the very methods and principles that he and others in his school apply, while those who are loyal to, and capable of applying, these principles belong to lower ranks (q.v. *ijtihād*).

NIYYA: intention; an internal psychological state geared toward giving each legal act its identity, separating that act from other identical acts that do not belong to the category of acts in question; e.g., forming the intent to wash one's face as an act of religious ablution rather than as everyday hygiene.

OTTOMAN: referring to the Ottoman Empire that ruled between 1389 and 1922, first in Anatolia, but later extending its domains to southeastern Europe, North Africa, and the Hejaz.

PILLARS: see *ʿibādāt*.

QĀḌĪ: the magistrate of the Sharīʿa court who also held extrajudicial functions, such as mediation, guardianship over orphans and minors and supervision and auditing of public works. *See also* jurist.

QĀḌĪSHIP: office or function of the *qāḍī* (q.v.).

RIBĀ: *see* usury.

ṢADAQĀT (SING. *ṢADAQA*): a mandatory or optional religious tax for the benefit of the poor.

ṢĀLIḤĀT: good works; charitable acts; morally and ethically motivated acts.

ṢĀLIḤŪN: those who perform *ṣāliḥāt* (q.v.).

SHAHĀDATAYN (SING. *SHAHĀDA*): the double-testimony of faith, the first part of which is the declaration that there is no god but God and the second that Muhammad is the messenger of God. To be valid, the *shahādatayn* must be uttered with *niyya* (q.v.).

SHARʿĪ: (*adj.*) that which is of the Sharīʿa or Sharīʿa based.

SIYĀSA SHARʿIYYA: a set of rules and regulations formulated by the jurists to guide the caliphal/sultanic executive in the administration of justice; the ruler's governance according to juristic political theory; discretionary legal powers of the ruler to enforce Sharīʿa court judgments and to supplement the religious law with administrative regulations; the ruler's extrajudicial powers to prosecute government officials on charges of misconduct.

SUBSTANTIVE LAW: the body of rules and general principles of which the law manuals of Sharīʿa consist. As there is no conceptual distinction in the Sharīʿa between procedural and other laws, substantive law may be used to cover adjectival/procedural law as well.

SUNNA: the second source of Islamic law; the exemplary biography of the Prophet, of which the *ḥadīth* (q.v.) is its literary expression and context-specific account.

TECHNOLOGIES OF THE SELF: in Islam, techniques of subjecting the self to consistent and systematic practice of the *ʿibādāt* (q.v.) with a view to producing and nurturing a moral subject.

ULAMA: a word of later predominance, referring to the learned class, especially the legists (q.v.).

UṢŪL AL-FIQH: a discipline or a field of study specializing in methods of interpretation and legal reasoning (q.v. *ijtihād*) and incorporating theories of language, hermeneutics, dialectic, law, theology, and logic. This discipline produced many important treatises dealing with the subject, referred to as *uṣūl al-fiqh* works.

USURY (*RIBĀ*): literally meaning excess, it refers to the prohibited practice of receiving or giving a thing having monetary value in excess of that for which the thing was exchanged, interest charged on a debt being a prime example.

WAQF: a charitable endowment; usually, immovable property alienated and endowed to serve the interest of certain beneficiaries, such as members of a family, the poor, the wayfarers, scholars, mystics, the general public, etc. Constituting more than half of real property in many parts of the Muslim world, endowments sustained the legal system and its institutions and supported public life and a flourishing civil society.

ZAKĀT: an annual alms-tax and one of the five pillars of Islam (*see ʿibādāt*); it also functions as a substantive legal sphere, constituting itself as a tax law. It is imposed on growth in property with a view to "purify" that property;

the recipients are the poor, the wayfarers, slaves seeking to pay for their manumission, insolvent debtors, *jihād* campaigns, and *zakāt* collectors. Some jurists allowed spending part of the *zakāt* on the annual pilgrimage to Mecca.

ZAKĀT AL-FIṬR: a religious tax imposed not on property but on every financially capable person upon breaking the Ramadan fast. The recipients are the poor who do not have the means to provide for themselves during the *fiṭr* holiday.

Bibliography

In classifying entries, no account is taken of the letter ʿayn, the hamza, and the Arabic definite article al-.

Sources in Arabic

ʿAbd al-Bāqī, Fuʾād. *al-Muʿjam al-Mufahris li-Alfāẓ al-Qurʾān al-Karīm*. Cairo: Dār al-Kutub al-Miṣriyya, 1945.

ʿAbd al-Raḥmān, Ṭāha. *Al-ʿAmal al-Dīnī wa-Tajdīd al-ʿAql*. Casablanca: al-Markaz al-Thaqāfī al-ʿArabī, 2006.

———. *Fiqh al-Falsafa*. 2 vols. Casablanca: al-Markaz al-Thaqāfī al-ʿArabī, 1999.

———. *Al-Ḥaqq al-Islāmī fī al-Ikhtilāf al-Fikrī*. Casablanca: al-Markaz al-Thaqāfī al-ʿArabī, 2005.

———. *Rūḥ al-Ḥadātha: al-Madkhal ilā Taʾsīs al-Ḥadātha al-Islāmiyya*. Casablanca: al-Markaz al-Thaqāfī al-ʿArabī, 2006.

———. *Suʾāl al-Akhlāq: Musāhama fī al-Naqd al-Akhlāqī lil-Ḥadātha al-Gharbiyya*. Casablanca: al-Markaz al-Thaqāfī al-ʿArabī, 2000.

ʿAbd al-Rāziq, ʿAlī. *al-Islām wa-Uṣūl al-Ḥukm*. Ed. Mamdūḥ Ḥiqqī. Beirut: Dār Maktabat al-Ḥayāt, 1966.

ʿĀmilī, Muḥammad b. Ḥasan al-Ḥurr. *Wasāʾil al-Shīʿa ilā Taḥṣīl Masāʾil al-Sharīʿa*. 20 vols. Beirut: Muʾassasat al-Aʿlamī lil-Maṭbūʿāt, 1427/2007.

ʿAṭṭār, Farīd al-Dīn. *Manṭiq al-Ṭayr*. *See under* Attar.

ʿAynī, Abū Muḥammad Maḥmūd b. Aḥmad. *al-Bināya fī Sharḥ al-Hidāya*. Ed. Muḥammad ʿUmar. 12 vols. Beirut: Dār al-Fikr, 1990.

Baghdādī, Abū Manṣūr ʿAbd al-Qāhir b. Tamīm. *Uṣūl al-Dīn*. Repr.; Beirut: Dār al-Kutub al-ʿIlmiyya, 1981.

Bahī, Muḥammad. *al-Dīn wal-Dawla*. Cairo: Maktabat Wahba, 1980.

Baḥr al-Favāʾid. See under Meisami, section II, below.

Bannā, Jamāl. *Mā Baʿd al-Ikhwān al-Muslimīn?* Cairo: Dār al-Fikr al-Islāmī, 1996.

Bāqir al-Ṣadr, al-Sayyid Muḥammad. *Iqtiṣādunā*. Beirut: Dār al-Taʿāruf lil-Maṭbūʿāt, n.d.

Buhūtī, Manṣūr b. Yūnus b. Idrīs. *Kashshāf al-Qināʿ ʿan Matn al-Iqnāʿ*. Ed. Muḥammad ʿAdnān Darwīsh. 6 vols. Beirut: Dār Iḥyāʾ al-Turāth al-ʿArabī, 1999–2000.

———. *al-Rawḍ al-Murbiʿ bi-Sharḥ Zād al-Mustaqniʿ*. Beirut: Dār al-Jīl, 1997.

Bukhārī, Abū ʿAbd Allāh Muḥammad b. Ismāʿīl. *Ṣaḥīḥ Bukhārī*. 5 vols. Beirut: al-Maktaba al-ʿAṣriyya, 1999.

Faḍlallāh, Muḥammad Ḥusayn. *al-Ḥaraka al-Islāmiyya: Humūm wa-Qaḍāyā*. Beirut: Dār al-Malak, 2001.

Al-Fatāwā al-Hindiyya. Compiled by al-Shaykh al-Niẓām et al. 6 vols. Repr.; Beirut: Dār Iḥyāʾ al-Turāth al-ʿArabī, 1980.

Ghazālī, Abū Ḥāmid Muḥammad b. Muḥammad. *Iḥyāʾ ʿUlūm al-Dīn*. 5 vols. Aleppo: Dār al-Waʿy, 2004.

———. *Mishkāt al-Anwār*. A parallel English-Arabic text, trans. David Buchman. Provo, Utah: Brigham Young University, 1998.

———. *Mukhtaṣar Iḥyāʾ ʿUlūm al-Dīn, al-Musammā Lubāb al-Iḥyāʾ*. Ed. Maḥmūd Bayrūtī. Damascus: Dār al-Bayrūtī, 2007.

———. *al-Munqidh min al-Ḍalāl wal-Mūṣil ilā dhī al-ʿIzza wal-Jalāl*. Ed. Aḥmad Shams al-Dīn. Beirut: Dār al-Kutub al-ʿIlmiyya, 1988; trans. R. J. McCarthy, *Al-Ghazali's Path to Sufism*. Louisville, Ky.: Fons Vitae, 2006.

———. *Tahāfut al-Falāsifa*. A parallel English-Arabic text translated, introduced, and annotated by Michael Marmura, *The Incoherence of the Philosophers*. Provo, Utah: Brigham Young University Press, 2000.

———. *al-Wajīz fī Fiqh Madhhab al-Imām al-Shāfiʿī*. Ed. Ṭāriq al-Sayyid. Beirut: Dār al-Kutub al-ʿIlmiyya, 2004.

Ḥalabī, Ibrāhīm b. Muḥammad. *Multaqā al-Abḥūr*. Ed. Wahbī al-Albānī. 2 vols. Beirut: Muʾassasat al-Risāla, 1989.

Ḥamza, Khālid et al. *"Al-Ikhwān al-Muslimūn Muḥāṣarūn ʿan Yasārihim wa-ʿan Yamīnihim . . . wa-hum Nitāj al-Dawla al-Qawmiyya," Dār al-Ḥayāt* (November 13, 2011). http://daralhayat.com/portalarticlendah/328023.

Ḥasanī, ʿAbd al-Ḥayy. *Tahdhīb al-Akhlāq*. Ed. ʿAbd al-Mājid al-Ghawrī. Damascus: Dār al-Fārābī, 2002.

Ḥasanī, ʿAlī. *al-Dawlah al-Sulṭāniyya: Ishkāliyyāt al-Qānūn al-ʿĀmm fī al-Sharīʿa al-Islāmiyya*. Casablanca: Maṭbaʿat al-Najāḥ al-Jadīda, 2005.

Ḥiṣnī, Taqī al-Dīn Muḥammad. *Kifāyat al-Akhyār fī Ḥall Ghāyat al-Ikhtiṣār*. 2 vols. Surabaya: Maṭbaʿat al-Hidāya, n.d.

Al-Ḥurr, al-ʿĀmilī. *See under* ʿĀmilī.

Ibn ʿAbd al-Barr, Abū ʿUmar Yūsuf. *Jāmiʿ Bayān al-ʿIlm wa-Faḍlihi*. Beirut: Dār al-Kutub al-ʿIlmiyya, n.d.

Ibn ʿAbd Rabbih, Aḥmad b. Muḥammad. *Kitāb al-Luʾluʾa fī al-Sulṭān*. In *al-Salṭana fī al-Fikr al-Siyāsī al-Islāmī: Nuṣūṣ Mukhtāra wa-Qirāʾāt ʿalā Imtidād Alf ʿĀm*, ed. Yūsuf Ībish and Yasūshī Kūsūjī, 127–205. Beirut: Dār al-Ḥamrāʾ lil-Ṭibāʿa, 1994.

Ibn Abī al-Dunyā, ʿAbd Allāh. *Makārim al-Akhlāq*. Ed. Bashīr ʿUyūn. Damascus: Maktabat Dār al-Bayān, 2002.

Ibn ʿĀbidīn, Muḥammad Amīn. *Ḥāshiyat Radd al-Muḥtār ʿalā al-Durr al-Mukhtār Sharḥ Tanwīr al-Abṣār*. 8 vols. Beirut: Dār al-Fikr, 1979.

Ibn ʿĀshūr, Muḥammad Ṭāhir. *Maqāṣid al-Sharīʿa al-Islāmiyya*. Ed. Muḥammad Ṭāhir al-Mīsāwī. Amman: Dār al-Nafāʾis, 2001.

Ibn al-Athīr, ʿAlī b. Abī al-Karam Muḥammad. *al-Kāmil fī al-Tārīkh*. Ed. C. J. Tornberg. 13 vols. Leiden: E. J. Brill, 1851.

Ibn Baṭṭūṭa. *Riḥlat Ibn Baṭṭūṭa*. *See under* Gibb, H. A. R.

Ibn al-Ḥājib, Jamāl al-Dīn b. ʿUmar. *Jāmiʿ al-Ummahāt*. Ed. Abū ʿAbd al-Raḥmān al-Akhḍarī. Damascus: al-Yamāma lil-Ṭibāʿa wal-Nashr, 2000.

Ibn al-Humām, Kamāl al-Dīn. *Sharḥ Fatḥ al-Qadīr*. 10 vols. Repr.; Beirut: Dār al-Fikr, 1990.

Ibn Jamāʿa, Muḥammad b. Ibrāhīm. *Taḥrīr al-Aḥkām fī Tadbīr Ahl al-Islām*. In *al-Salṭana fī al-Fikr al-Siyāsī al-Islāmī: Nuṣūṣ Mukhtāra wa-Qirāʾāt ʿalā Imtidād Alf ʿĀm*, ed. Yūsuf Ībish and Yasūshī Kūsūjī, 385–392. Beirut: Dār al-Ḥamrāʾ lil-Ṭibāʿa, 1994.

Ibn Juzay, Muḥammad b. Aḥmad al-Kalbī. *al-Qawānīn al-Fiqhiyya*. Ed. Muḥammad Amīn al-Ḍannāwī. Beirut: Dār al-Kutub al-ʿIlmiyya, 2006.

Ibn Khaldūn, ʿAbd al-Raḥmān. *al-Muqaddima: Kitāb al-ʿIbar wa-Dīwān al-Mubtadaʾ wal-Khabar fī Ayyām al-ʿArab wal-ʿAjam wal-Barbar wa-man ʿĀṣarahum min dhawī al-Sulṭān al-Akbar*. Beirut: Dār al-Kutub al-ʿIlmiyya, n.d.; trans. Franz Rosenthal, *The Muqaddimah: An Introduction to History*, 3 vols. London: Routledge and K. Paul, 1958; abridged, under the same title, by N. J. Dawood. Princeton, N.J.: Princeton University Press, 2005.

Ibn Manẓūr, Jamāl al-Dīn Muḥammad. *Lisān al-ʿArab*. Ed. ʿĀmir Aḥmad Ḥaydar and ʿAbd al-Munʿim Ibrāhīm. 15 vols. Beirut: Dār al-Kutub al-ʿIlmiyya, 2009.

Ibn Māza, Burhān al-Dīn Ṣadr al-Sharīʿa al-Bukhārī. *al-Muḥīṭ al-Burhānī li-Masāʾil al-Mabsūṭ wal-Jāmiʿayn wal-Siyar wal-Ziyādāt wal-Nawādir wal-Fatāwā wal-Wāqiʿāt, Mudallala bi-Dalāʾil al-Mutaqaddimīn*. Ed. Naʿīm Aḥmad. 25 vols. Karachi: Idārat al-Qurʾān wal-ʿUlūm al-Islāmiyya, 2004.

Ibn Mufliḥ, Shams al-Dīn Muḥammad. *al-Ādāb al-Sharʿiyya*. Ed. Shuʿayb al-Arnaʾūṭ and ʿUmar al-Qayyām. 4 vols. Beirut: Muʾassasat al-Risāla, 1977.

Ibn Muftāḥ, ʿAbd Allāh. *al-Muntazaʿ al-Mukhtār min al-Ghayth al-Midrār, al-Maʿrūf bi-Sharḥ al-Azhār*. 10 vols. Ṣaʿda, Yemen: Maktabat al-Turāth al-Islāmī, 2003.

Ibn Qayyim al-Jawziyya, Shams al-Dīn Muḥammad. *Iʿlām al-Muwaqqiʿīn ʿan Rabb al-ʿĀlamīn*. Ed. Muḥammad ʿAbd al-Ḥamīd. 4 vols. Beirut: al-Maṭbaʿa al-ʿAṣriyya, 1987.

Ibn Qudāma, Muwaffaq al-Dīn. *al-Mughnī*. 14 vols. Beirut: Dār al-Kutub al-ʿIlmiyya, n.d.

Ibn Qutayba, Muḥammad ʿAbd Allāh b. Muslim. *Kitāb al-Sulṭān*. In *al-Salṭana fī al-Fikr al-Siyāsī al-Islāmī: Nuṣūṣ Mukhtāra wa-Qirāʾāt ʿalā Imtidād Alf ʿĀm*, ed. Yūsuf Ībish and Yasūshī Kūsūjī, 49–126. Beirut: Dār al-Ḥamrāʾ lil-Ṭibāʿa, 1994.

Ibn al-Sāʿātī, Aḥmad b. ʿAlī b. Thaʿlab. *Majmaʿ al-Baḥrayn*. Ed. Ilyās Qablān. Beirut: Dār al-Kutub al-ʿIlmiyya, 2005.

Ibn al-Ṣalāḥ, Abū ʿAmr ʿUthmān b. ʿAbd al-Raḥmān. *Adab al-Muftī wal-Mustaftī*. Ed. Muwaffaq b. ʿAbd al-Qādir. Beirut: ʿĀlam al-Kutub, 1986.

Ibn Taymiyya, Taqī al-Dīn. *al-Siyāsa Sharʿiyya fī Iṣlāḥ al-Rāʿī wal-Raʿiyya*. In *al-Salṭana fī al-Fikr al-Siyāsī al-Islāmī: Nuṣūṣ Mukhtāra wa-Qirāʾāt ʿalā Imtidād Alf ʿĀm*, ed. Yūsuf Ībish and Yasūshī Kūsūjī, 395–416. Beirut: Dār al-Ḥamrāʾ lil-Ṭibāʿa, 1994.

Ibn Ṭufayl. *See under* Goodman, section II, below.

Ibn al-Ṭuqṭuqā, Muḥammad b. ʿAlī. *al-Fakhrī fī al-Ādāb al-Sulṭāniyya wal-Duwal al-Islāmiyya*. Beirut: Dār Ṣādir, n.d.

ʿĪd, Sulaymān b. Qāsim. *al-Niẓām al-Siyāsī fī al-Islām*. Riyadh: Dār al-Waṭan lil-Nashr, 2002.

Al-Ikhwān al-Muslimūn. "Al-Sharīʿa wal-Dawla fī al-Mafhūm al-Islāmī." http://www.ikhwan.net/wiki/index.php?title.

Kāsānī, ʿAlāʾ al-Dīn b. Masʿūd. *Badāʾiʿ al-Ṣanāʾiʿ fī Tartīb al-Sharāʾiʿ*. Ed. ʿAlī ʿĀdil and Muʿawwaḍ ʿAbd al-Mawjūd. 9 vols. Beirut: Dār al-Kutub al-ʿIlmiyya, 1997.

Kāshānī, Muḥammad b. al-Murtaḍā Muḥsin. *al-Maḥajja al-Bayḍāʾ fī Tahdhīb al-Iḥyāʾ*. 7 vols. Tehran: Maktabat al-Ṣadūq, 1920.

Kawtharānī, Wajīh. *al-Sulṭa wal-Mujtamaʿ wal-ʿamal al-Siyāsī min Tārīkh al-Wilāya al-ʿUthmāniyya fī Bilād al-Shām*. Beirut: Markaz Dirāsāt al-Waḥda al-ʿArabiyya, 1988.

Khurashī, Muḥammad b. ʿAbd Allāh. *Ḥāshiyat al-Khurashī ʿalā Mukhtaṣar Sīdī Khalīl*. 8 vols. Beirut: Dār al-Kutub al-ʿIlmiyya, 1997.

Maghribī, Ḥusayn Muḥammad. *al-Badr al-Tamām Sharḥ Bulūgh al-Marām min Adillat al-Aḥkām*. Ed. Muḥammad Khurfān. 5 vols. Manṣūra: Dār al-Wafāʾ, 2005.

Maḥmūd, Jamāl al-Dīn. *al-Dawla al-Islāmiyya al-Muʿāṣira: al-Fikra wal-Taṭbīq*. Cairo: Dār al-Kitāb al-Miṣrī, 1992.

Maqdisī, ʿAbd al-Raḥmān b. Ibrāhīm. *al-ʿUdda: Sharḥ al-ʿUmda fī Fiqh Imām al-Sunna Aḥmad Ibn Ḥanbal al-Shaybānī*. Ed. Khālid Muḥammad Muḥarram. Beirut: al-Maktaba al-ʿAṣriyya, 1995.

Maqrīzī, Taqī al-Dīn Aḥmad b. ʿAlī. *al-Sulūk li-Maʿrifat Duwal al-Mulūk*. Ed. Muḥammad ʿAṭā. 8 vols. Beirut: Dār al-Kutub al-ʿIlmiyya, 1997.

Mawāq, Muḥammad b. Yūsuf. *al-Tāj wal-Iklīl fī Sharḥ Mukhtaṣar Khalīl*. Printed on the margins of Ḥaṭṭāb, *Mawāhib al-Jalīl*, 6 vols. Repr.; Beirut?: Dār al-Fikr, 1992.

Māwardī, ʿAlī Muḥammad b. Ḥabīb. *Adab al-Dunyā wal-Dīn*. Beirut: Dār al-Kutub al-ʿIlmiyya, 2005.

———. *al-Aḥkām al-Sulṭāniyya wal-Wilāyāt al-Dīniyya*. Cairo: Dār al-Fikr, 1983.

———. *al-Ḥāwī al-Kabīr*. Ed. ʿAlī Muʿawwaḍ and ʿĀdil ʿAbd al-Mawjūd. 18 vols. Beirut: Dār al-Kutub al-ʿIlmiyya, 1994.
Al-Mawsūʿa al-Fiqhiyya. 48 vols. Kuwait: Dār al-Ṣafwa lil-Ṭibāʿa wal-Nashr, 1990.
Miskawayh, Aḥmad b. Muḥammad b. Yaʿqūb al-Rāzī. *Tahdhīb al-Akhlāq wa-Taṭhīr al-Aʿrāq*. Ed. Nawwāf al-Jarrāḥ. Beirut: Dār Ṣādir, 2006.
Miṣrī, Ibn Naqīb. *ʿUmdat al-Sālik*. Ed. and trans. N. H. M. Keller, *The Reliance of the Traveller*. Evanston: Sunna Books, 1991.
Muslim, Ibn al-Ḥajjāj Abū Ḥusayn. *Ṣaḥīḥ Muslim*. Ed. Ayman al-Zāmilī and Muḥammad Mahdī al-Sayyid. 5 vols. Beirut: ʿĀlam al-Kutub, 1998.
Al-Nadwa al-ʿĀlamiyya ʿan al-Fiqh al-Islāmī wa-Uṣūlihi wa-Taḥaddiyāt al-Qarn al-Ḥādī wal-ʿIshrīn: Maqāṣid al-Sharīʿa wa-Subul Taḥqīqihā fī al-Mujtamaʿāt al-Muʿāṣira. 3 vols. Kuala Lumpur: The International University of Malaysia, 2006.
Nawawī, Muḥyī al-Dīn Sharaf al-Dīn b. Yaḥyā. *al-Majmūʿ: Sharḥ al-Muhadhdhab*. 23 vols. Jadda: Maktabat al-Irshād, 1980.
———. *Rawḍat al-Ṭālibīn*. Ed. ʿĀdil ʿAbd al-Mawjūd and ʿAlī Muʿawwaḍ. 8 vols. Beirut: Dār al-Kutub al-ʿIlmiyya, n.d.
"'Al-Nūr' Awwal Ḥizb Salafī Yutamm Taʾsīsuh fī Miṣr Yaḍummu Masīḥiyyīn." *al-Sharq al-Awsaṭ* (June 13, 2011). http://aawsat.com/details.asp?section=4&issueno=11885&article= 626328&feature=.
Qalqashandī, Aḥmad b. ʿAlī. *Ṣubḥ al-Aʿshā fī Ṣināʿat al-Inshā*. Ed. Muḥammad Ḥusayn Shams al-Dīn. 15 vols. Beirut: Dār al-Kutub al-ʿIlmiyya, n.d.
Qurashī, Bāqir Sharīf. *al-Niẓām al-Siyāsī fī al-Islām*. Beirut: Dār al-Taʿāruf, 1982.
Quṭb, Sayyid. *al-ʿAdāla al-Ijtimāʿiyya fī al-Islām*. *See under* Qutb, section II, below.
Rāfiʿī, Abū al-Qāsim ʿAbd al-Karīm b. Muḥammad. *al-ʿAzīz: Sharḥ al-Wajīz al-Maʿrūf bil-Sharḥ al-Kabīr*. Ed. ʿAlī Muḥammad Muʿawwaḍ and ʿĀdil Aḥmad ʿAbd al-Mawjūd. 13 vols. Beirut: Dār al-Kutub al-ʿIlmiyya, 1997.
Ramlī, Muḥammad Shams al-Dīn b. Shihāb al-Dīn. *Nihāyat al-Muḥtāj ilā Sharḥ al-Minhāj*. 8 vols. Repr.; Beirut: Dār Iḥyāʾ al-Turāth al-ʿArabī, 1939.
Saḥnūn b. Saʿīd al-Tanūkhī. *al-Mudawwana al-Kubrā*. Ed. Aḥmad ʿAbd al-Salām. 5 vols. Beirut: Dār al-Kutub al-ʿIlmiyya, 1994.
Ṣanʿānī, Abū Bakr ʿAbd al-Razzāq. *al-Muṣannaf*. Ed. Ayman Azharī. 12 vols. Beirut: Dār al-Kutub al-ʿIlmiyya, 2000.
Sarakhsī, Muḥammad b. Aḥmad Shams al-Dīn. *al-Mabsūṭ*. 31 vols. Beirut: Dār al-Kutub al-ʿIlmiyya, 1993–1994.
Shaʿrānī, ʿAbd al-Wahhāb b. Aḥmad b. ʿAlī. *al-Mīzān al-Kubrā al-Shaʿrāniyya*. Ed. ʿAbd al-Wārith ʿAlī. 2 vols. Beirut: Dār al-Kutub al-ʿIlmiyya, 1998.
Shāṭibī, Abū Isḥāq Ibrāhīm. *al-Muwāfaqāt fī Uṣūl al-Aḥkām*. Ed. Muḥyī al-Dīn ʿAbd al-Ḥamīd. 4 vols. Cairo: Maṭbaʿat ʿAlī Ṣubayḥ, 1970.
Shawkānī, Muḥammad b. ʿAlī. *Irshād al-Fuḥūl ilā Taḥqīq al-Ḥaqq min ʿIlm al-Uṣūl*. Surabaya: Sharikat Maktabat Aḥmad b. Saʿīd b. Nabhān, n.d.
———. *al-Sayl al-Jarrār al-Mutadaffiq ʿalā Ḥadāʾiq al-Azhār*. Ed. Maḥmūd Ibrāhīm Zāyid. 3 vols. Damascus: Dār Ibn Kathīr, 2000.

Ṭabarsī, Raḍī al-Dīn b. Ḥasan. *Makārim al-Akhlāq*. Beirut: Muʾassasat al-Kharasān [al-Khursān?] lil-Maṭbūʿat, 1427/2006.
Ṭarsūsī, Najm al-Dīn Ibrāhīm b. ʿAlī. *Tuḥfat al-Turk fīmā Yajib an Yakūn fī al-Mulk*. Ed. Muḥammad Ḥasan Ismāʾīl. Beirut: Dār al-Kutub al-ʿIlmiyya, 1995.
Ṭurṭūshī, Muḥammad b. al-Walīd. *Sirāj al-Mulūk*. In *al-Salṭana fī al-Fikr al-Siyāsī al-Islāmī: Nuṣūṣ Mukhtāra wa-Qirāʾāt ʿalā Imtidād Alf ʿĀm*, ed. Yūsuf Ībsh and Yasūshī Kūsūjī, 290–325. Beirut: Dār al-Ḥamrāʾ lil-Ṭibāʿa, 1994.
Tirmidhī, Abū ʿĪsā Muḥammad. *Sunan*. 6 vols. Cairo: Dār al-Ḥadīth, 1999.
Ṭūsī, Muḥammad b. al-Ḥasan Shaykh al-Ṭāʾifa. *al-Khilāf fī al-Fiqh*. 2 vols. Tehran: Maṭbaʿat Rangīn, 1957.
Zabīdī, Muḥammad b. Muḥammad al-Ḥusaynī. *Itḥāf al-Sāda al-Muttaqīn bi-Sharḥ Iḥyāʾ ʿUlūm al-Dīn*. 11 vols. Beirut: Dār al-Kutub al-ʿIlmiyya, 1989.

Sources in Other Languages

Abou El Fadl, Khaled. "Islam and the Challenge of Democratic Commitment." *Fordham International Law Journal* 27 (December 2003): 4–71.
Abrams, Philip. "Notes on the Difficulty of Studying the State." *Journal of Historical Sociology* 1, no. 1 (1988): 58–89.
Abu El-Haj, Tabatha. "Changing the People: Legal Regulation and American Democracy." *New York University Law Review* 86, no. 1 (2011): 1–68.
Ackerman, Bruce. *The Decline and Fall of the American Republic*. Cambridge, Mass.: Belknap Press, 2010.
Adorno, Theodor. *The Culture Industry: Selected Essays on Mass Culture*. Ed. J. M. Bernstein. London: Routledge, 2001.
———. *History and Freedom*. Ed. R. Tiedemann. Malden, Mass.: Polity Press, 2006.
Agamben, Giorgio. *The Signature of All Things*. New York: Zone Books, 2009.
Albrow, Martin. *The Global Age: State and Society Beyond Modernity*. Cambridge: Polity Press, 1996.
Allison, Henry E. "Kant." In *The Oxford Companion to Philosophy*, ed. Ted Honderich, 466–470. Oxford: Oxford University Press, 1995.
Amin, Samir. *The Liberal Virus*. New York: Monthly Review Press, 2004.
Anderson, Benedict. *Imagined Communities: Reflections on the Origin and Spread of Nationalism*. 2nd ed. London: Verso, 2006.
An-Na'im, Abdullahi Ahmed. *Islam and the Secular State: Negotiating the Future of Shariʿa*. Cambridge, Mass.: Harvard University Press, 2008.
Anscombe, G. E. M. "Modern Moral Philosophy." *Philosophy* 33, no. 124 (1958): 1–19.
Antoun, Richard T. "The Islamic Court, the Islamic Judge, and the Accommodation of Traditions: A Jordanian Case Study." *International Journal of Middle East Studies* 12 (1980): 455–467.
Arendt, Hannah. *The Origins of Totalitarianism*. San Diego, Calif.: Harcourt, 1976.

Arjomand, S. Amir. "The Constitution of Medina: A Sociological Interpretation of Muhammad's Acts of Foundation of the *Umma*." *International Journal of Middle East Studies* 41 (2009): 555–575.
Asad, Talal. *Formations of the Secular: Christianity, Islam, Modernity*. Stanford, Calif.: Stanford University Press, 2003.
———. *Genealogies of Religion: Discipline and Reasons of Power in Christianity and Islam*. Baltimore, Md.: Johns Hopkins University Press, 1993.
Ashford, Douglas E. "Constitution of Poverty." In *State Theory and State History*, ed. Rolf Torstendahl, 149–167. London: Sage, 1992.
Attar, Farid Ud-Din. *The Conference of the Birds*. Trans., Afkham Darbandi and Dick Davis. London: Penguin, 1984.
Austin, John. *The Province of Jurisprudence Determined*. Ed. Wilfred E. Rumble. Cambridge: Cambridge University Press, 1995.
Austin, J. L. *How to Do Things with Words*. Cambridge: Cambridge University Press, 1962.
———. "Performative Utterances." In *Philosophical Papers*, 221–239. Oxford: Clarendon Press, 1961.
Ayer, Alfred Jules. *Language, Truth, and Logic*. New York: Dover, 1952.
Al-Azmeh, Aziz. *Muslim Kingship: Power and the Sacred in Muslim, Christian, and Pagan Polities*. London: I. B. Tauris, 1997.
Bailey, Leon. *Critical Theory and the Sociology of Knowledge*. New York: Peter Lang, 1994.
Bakan, Joel. *The Corporation: The Pathological Pursuit of Profit and Power*. New York: Free Press, 2004.
Baker, Keith M. "On Condorcet's '*Sketch*.'" *Daedalus* (Summer 2004): 56–64.
Balibar, Étienne. "Subjection and Subjectivation." In *Supposing the Subject*, ed. Joan Copjec, 1–15. London: Verso, 1994.
Barkey, Karen, and S. Parikh. "Comparative Perspectives on the State." *Annual Review of Sociology* 17, no. 1 (1991): 523–549.
Baracchi, Claudia. *Aristotle's Ethics as First Philosophy*. Cambridge: Cambridge University Press, 2007.
Bauman, Zygmunt. *Globalization: The Human Consequences*. New York: Columbia University Press, 1998.
———. *Intimations of Postmodernity*. London: Routledge, 1992.
———. *Modernity and the Holocaust*. Ithaca, N.Y.: Cornell University Press, 1989.
Beeston, A. F. L. "The Religions of Pre-Islamic Yemen." *L'Arabie du sud* 1:259–269. Paris: Éditions G.-P. Maisonneuve et Larose, 1984.
Behler, E., and A. Schrift, eds. *The Cambridge Companion to Nietzsche*. Cambridge: Cambridge University Press, 1996.
Bell, Daniel A. "A Communitarian Critique of Liberalism." *Analyse & Kritik* 27 (2005): 215–238.
Benjamin, Walter. "On Language as Such and on the Language of Man." In *Reflections*, trans. E. Jephcott, 314–332. New York: Schocken, 1978.
———. "Theses on the Philosophy of History." In *Illuminations*, ed. Hannah Arendt, 253–264. New York: Schocken, 1968.

Bentham, Jeremy. *An Introduction to the Principles of Morals and Legislation.* New York: Dover, 2007.

Berkey, Jonathan. *Transmission of Knowledge in Medieval Cairo: A Social History of Islamic Education.* Princeton, N.J.: Princeton University Press, 1992.

Berlin, Isaiah. *Vico and Herder: Two Studies in the History of Ideas.* New York: Viking, 1976.

Bilgrami, Akeel. "Gandhi, Newton, and the Enlightenment." In *Values and Violence*, ed. I. A. Karawan et al., 15–29. New York: Springer, 2008.

Black, Jeremy. *European Warfare: 1494–1660.* New Haven, Conn.: Yale University Press, 1994.

———. *European Warfare: 1660–1815.* London: Routledge, 2002.

Bloor, David. "The Question of Linguistic Idealism Revisited." In *The Cambridge Companion to Wittgenstein*, ed. H. Sluga and D. G. Stern, 354–382. Cambridge: Cambridge University Press, 1996.

Bolsinger, Eckard. *The Autonomy of the Political: Carl Schmitt's and Lenin's Political Realism.* Westport, Conn.: Greenwood Press, 2001.

Bonner, Michael, et al., eds. *Poverty and Charity in Middle Eastern Contexts.* Albany: State University of New York Press, 2003.

Bookchin, Murray, and D. Foreman. *Defending the Earth.* New York: Black Rose Books, 1991.

Bourdieu, Pierre. *The Algerians.* Trans. Alan Ross. Boston: Beacon Press, 1962.

———. *Practical Reason: On the Theory of Action.* Cambridge: Polity Press, 1998.

———. "Rethinking the State: Genesis and Structure of the Bureaucratic Field." In *State/Culture: State Formation After the Cultural Turn*, ed. George Steinmetz, 53–75. Ithaca, N.Y.: Cornell University Press, 1999.

Breuilly, John. *Nationalism and the State.* Manchester: Manchester University Press, 1993.

Bruff, Harold H. "On the Constitutional Status of the Administrative Agencies." *American University Law Review* 36 (Winter 1987): 491–517.

Buchanan, Allen. *Ethics, Efficiency, and the Market.* Totowa, N.J.: Rowman and Allanheld, 1985.

Buchman, David, trans. *Al-Ghazālī: The Niche of Lights.* Provo, Utah: Brigham Young University, 1998.

Bury, J. B. *The Idea of Progress.* Westport, Conn.: Greenwood Press, 1982.

Butler, Judith. *Excitable Speech: A Politics of the Performative.* New York: Routledge, 1997.

Bynum, Caroline Walker. *Holy Feast and Holy Fast: The Religious Significance of Food to Medieval Women.* Berkeley: University of California Press, 1987.

Calabresi, Steven G., and Saikrishna B. Prakash. "President's Power to Execute the Law." *Yale Law Journal* 104 (December 1994): 541–565.

Carey, George W. "Separation of Powers and the Madisonian Model: A Reply to the Critics." *American Political Science Review* 72, no. 1 (March 1978): 151–164.

Cartwright, David E. "Schopenhauer's Narrower Sense of Morality." In *The Cambridge Companion to Schopenhauer*, ed. Christopher Janaway, 252–292. Cambridge: Cambridge University Press, 1999.

Çizakça, Murat. *History of Philanthropic Foundations*. Istanbul: Bogaziçi University Press, 2000.

Cohen H. J. "The Economic Background and Secular Occupations of Muslim Jurisprudents and Traditionists in the Classical Period of Islam (Until the Middle of the Eleventh Century)." *Journal of the Economic and Social History of the Orient* (January 1970): 16–61.

Cohn, Bernard. *Colonialism and Its Forms of Knowledge: The British in India*. Princeton, N.J.: Princeton University Press, 1996.

Collins, Daniel. "Islamization of Pakistani Law: A Historical Perspective." *Stanford Journal of International Law* 24 (1987–1988): 511–584.

Comte, August. *August Comte on Positivism: The Essential Writings*. Ed. G. Lenzer. New Brunswick, N.J.: Transaction, 1998.

Condorcet, Marquis de. *Sketch for a Historical Picture of the Progress of the Human Mind*. London: Weidenfeld and Nicolson, 1955.

Corrigan, Philip, and Derek Sayer. *The Great Arch: English State Formation as Cultural Revolution*. Oxford: Basil Blackwell, 1985.

Dahl, Robert A. "On Removing Certain Impediments to Democracy in the United States." In *The Moral Foundations of the American Republic*, ed. Robert H. Horwitz, 3rd ed., 230–252. Charlottesville: University Press of Virginia, 1986.

Dawson, Christopher. *The Making of Europe*. New York: Meridian Books, 1956.

DeGré, Gerard. *The Social Compulsions of Ideas*. New Brunswick, N.J.: Transaction, 1985.

Dirks, Nicholas B. *The Scandal of Empire: India and the Creation of Imperial Britain*. Cambridge, Mass.: Belknap Press, 2006.

Donoso, Anton. "Jurisprudence Today: Naturalism vs. Positivism." In *The Predicament of Modern Politics*, ed. Harold J. Spaeth, 55–79. Detroit, Mich.: University of Detroit Press, 1969.

Donzelot, Jacques. *The Policing of Families*. New York: Pantheon, 1979.

Drinnon, Richard. *Facing West: The Metaphysics of Indian-Hating and Empire-Building*. New York: Schocken, 1990.

Dry, Murray. "The Separation of Powers and Representative Government." *Political Science Reviewer* 3 (Fall 1973): 43–83.

Dunn, John. "Political Obligation." In *Political Theory Today*, ed. David Held, 23–27. Cambridge: Polity Press, 1991.

El-Gamal, Mahmoud A. *Islamic Finance: Law, Economics, and Practice*. Cambridge: Cambridge University Press, 2006.

El-Nahal, Galal H. *The Judicial Administration of Ottoman Egypt in the Seventeenth Century*. Chicago: Bibliotheca Islamica, 1979.

Encyclopaedia of the Qurʾān. Ed. Jane D. McAuliffe. 5 vols. Leiden: Brill, 2001–2006.

Euben, Roxanne. *Enemy in the Mirror: Islamic Fundamentalism and the Limits of Modern Rationalism*. Princeton, N.J.: Princeton University Press, 1999.

Euben, Roxanne L., and Muhammad Qasim Zaman, eds. *Princeton Readings in Islamist Thought: Texts and Contexts from Banna to Bin Laden*. Princeton, N.J.: Princeton University Press, 2009.

Fadel, M. "A Tragedy of Politics or an Apolitical Tragedy?" *Journal of the American Oriental Society* 131, no. 1 (2011): 109–127.

Fay, Mary Ann. "Women and Waqf: Toward a Reconsideration of Women's Place in the Mamluk Household." *International Journal of Middle East Studies* 29, no. 1 (1997): 33–51.

Feldman, Noah. *The Fall and Rise of the Islamic State*. Princeton, N.J.: Princeton University Press, 2008.

Ferro, Marc. *Colonization: A Global History*. London: Routledge, 1997.

Field, G. C. "A Criticism of Kant." In *Readings in Ethical Theory*, ed. W. Sellars and J. Hospers, 487–491. New York: Appleton, Century, Crofts, 1952.

Finlayson, Alan. "Psychology, Psychoanalysis, and Theories of Nationalism." *Nations and Nationalism* 4, no. 2 (1998): 145–162.

Finlayson, Alan, and J. Martin. "Poststructuralism." In *The State: Theories and Issues*, ed. C. Hay et al, 155–171. New York: Palgrave, 2006.

Fisher, Louis. "Review of Bruce Ackermen, *The Decline and Fall of the American Republic*." *Federal Lawyer* 58 (June 2011): 56–58.

Fiss, Owen. "Objectivity and Interpretation." *Stanford Law Review* 34 (1982): 739–763.

Foucault, Michel. *The Archaeology of Knowledge*. Trans. A. M. Sheridan Smith. London: Routledge, 1969.

———. *Discipline and Punish: The Birth of the Prison*. Trans. Alan Sheridan. 2nd ed. New York: Vintage, 1995.

———. *Ethics, Subjectivity, and Truth*. Ed. P. Rabinow. New York: The New Press, 1994.

———. *The Foucault Reader*. Ed. Paul Rabinow. New York: Pantheon, 1984.

———. "Governmentality." In *Power: Essential Works of Foucault, 1954–1984*, ed. James Faubion, 201–222. New York: The New Press, 1973.

———. *The History of Sexuality*. Vol. 1: *An Introduction*. Trans. Robert Hurley. London: Pantheon, 1978.

———. *Les mots et les choses*. Paris: Gallimard, 1966. Cited in English as *The Order of Things: An Archeology of the Human Sciences*. Trans. R. D. Lang. New York: Pantheon, 1970.

———. *Power: Essential Works of Foucault, 1954–1984*, ed. James Faubion. New York: The New Press, 1973.

———. *Power/Knowledge: Selected Interviews and Other Writings, 1972–1977*. Ed. Colin Gordon. New York: Pantheon, 1980.

———. *"Society Must Be Defended."* New York: Picador, 1997.

———. "Technologies of the Self." In *Ethics, Subjectivity, and Truth*, ed. P. Rabinow, 223–251. New York: The New Press, 1994.

———. "Truth and Juridical Forms." in *Power: Essential Works of Foucault, 1954–1984*, ed. James Faubion, 1–89. New York: The New Press, 1973.

Frank, Andre. *ReOrient*. Berkeley: University of California Press, 1998.

Friedrich, Carl J. *The Philosophy of Law in Historical Perspective*. Chicago: University of Chicago Press, 1963.

Frings, Manfred S. *The Mind of Max Scheler*. Milwaukee, Wis.: Marquette University Press, 2001.

Fuchs, Barbara. *Mimesis and Empire: The New World, Islam, and European Identities*. Cambridge: Cambridge University Press, 2001.
Fuller, Lon. *The Morality of Law*. New Haven, Conn.: Yale University Press, 1969.
Gamble, Andrew. *Politics and Fate*. Malden: Polity, 2000.
Gerber, Haim. "Social and Economic Position of Women in an Ottoman City, Bursa, 1600–1700." *International Journal of Middle East Studies* 12 (1980): 231–244.
Geuss, Raymond. *Morality, Culture, and History*. Cambridge: Cambridge University Press, 1999.
Gewirth, Alan. *Reason and Morality*. Chicago: University of Chicago Press, 1978.
Ghazanfar, S. M. *Medieval Islamic Economic Thought: Filling the "Great Gap" in European Economics*. London: Routledge, 2003.
Gibb, H. A. R. "Constitutional Organization." In *Law in the Middle East*, ed. M. Khadduri and H. J. Liebesny, 3–27. Washington: Middle East Institute, 1955.
———. trans. *The Travels of Ibn Baṭṭūṭa*. Repr.; New Delhi: Goodword Books, 2003.
Giddens, Anthony. *Capitalism and Modern Social Theory: An Analysis of the Writings of Marx, Durkheim, and Max Weber*. Cambridge: Cambridge University Press, 1971.
———. *Modernity and Self-Identity: Self and Society in the Late Modern Age*. Stanford, Calif.: Stanford University Press, 1991.
Gill, G. *The Nature and Development of the Modern State*. New York: Palgrave, 2003.
Glendon, Mary Ann. "Power and Authority in the Family: New Legal Patterns as Reflections of Changing Ideologies." *American Journal of Comparative Law* 23, no. 1 (1975): 1–33.
Goitein, S. D. *Studies in Islamic History and Institutions*. Leiden: E. J. Brill, 1966.
Goodman, Lenn Evan, trans. *Ibn Tufayl's Hayy Ibn Yaqzān: A Philosophical Tale*. Chicago: University of Chicago Press, 2003.
Goody, Jack. *Capitalism and Modernity: The Great Debate*. Cambridge: Polity, 2004.
———. *The Theft of History*. Cambridge: Cambridge University Press, 2006.
Gorke, Martin. *Death of Our Planet's Species: A Challenge to Ecology and Ethics*. Washington, D.C.: Island Press, 2003.
Gray, John. *Enlightenment's Wake: Politics and Culture at the Close of the Modern Age*. London: Routledge, 1995.
———. *Liberalism*. Minneapolis: University of Minnesota Press, 1986.
———. *Straw Dogs: Thoughts on Humans and Other Animals*. New York: Farrar, Straus and Giroux, 2002.
Grosby, Steven. "Nationality and Religion." In *Understanding Nationalism*, ed. Montserrat Guibernau and J. Hutchinson, 97–119. Cambridge: Polity Press, 2001.
Guibernau, Montserrat. "Globalization and the Nation-State." In *Understanding Nationalism*, ed. Montserrat Guibernau and J. Hutchinson, 242–268. Cambridge: Polity Press, 2001.
Guyer, Paul. *Kant on Freedom, Law, and Happiness*. Cambridge: Cambridge University Press, 2000.

———, ed. *The Cambridge Companion to Kant*. Cambridge: Cambridge University Press, 1992.

Haj, Samira. *Reconfiguring Islamic Tradition: Reform, Rationality, and Modernity*. Stanford, Calif.: Stanford University Press, 2009.

Hall, John, and G. Ikenberry. *The State*. Minneapolis: University of Minnesota Press, 1989.

Hallaq, Wael. *Authority, Continuity, and Change in Islamic Law*. Cambridge: Cambridge University Press, 2001.

———. "Can the Shariʿa Be Restored?" In *Islamic Law and the Challenges of Modernity*, ed. Yvonne Y. Haddad and Barbara F. Stowasser, 21–53. Walnut Creek, Calif.: Altamira Press, 2004.

———. "From *Fatwās* to *Furūʿ*: Growth and Change in Islamic Substantive Law." *Islamic Law and Society* 1, no. 1 (1994): 29–65.

———. "From Regional to Personal Schools of Law? A Reevaluation." *Islamic Law and Society* 8, no. 1 (2001): 1–26.

———. "Groundwork of the Moral Law: A New Look at the Qurʾān and the Genesis of Sharīʿa." *Islamic Law and Society* 16, no. 3–4 (2009): 239–279.

———. *A History of Islamic Legal Theories*. Cambridge: Cambridge University Press, 1997.

———, trans., intro., and notes. *Ibn Taymiyya Against the Greek Logicians*. Oxford: Oxford University Press, 1993.

———. "*Iftaʾ* and *Ijtihad* in Sunni Legal Theory: A Developmental Account." in *Islamic Legal Interpretation: Muftis and Their Fatwas*, ed. Muhammad Khalid Masud et al., 33–43. Cambridge, Mass.: Harvard University Press, 1996.

———. *An Introduction to Islamic Law*. Cambridge: Cambridge University Press, 2009.

———. "Islamic Law: History and Transformation." In *The New Cambridge History of Islam*, ed. Robert Erwin, 4:142–183. Cambridge: Cambridge University Press, 2010.

———. "Maqāṣid and the Challenges of Modernity." *Al-Jāmiʿa* 49, no. 1 (2011): 1–31.

———. "Model *Shurūṭ* Works and the Dialectic of Doctrine and Practice." *Islamic Law and Society* 2, no. 2 (1995): 109–134.

———. "On Inductive Corroboration, Probability, and Certainty in Sunnī Legal Thought." In *Islamic Law and Jurisprudence*, ed. N. Heer, 3–31. Seattle: University of Washington Press, 1990).

———. "On Orientalism, Self-Consciousness, and History." *Islamic Law and Society* 18, no. 3–4 (2011): 387–439.

———. *The Origins and Evolution of Islamic Law*. Cambridge: Cambridge University Press, 2005.

———. "The *Qāḍī's Dīwān (Sijill)* Before the Ottomans." *Bulletin of the School of Oriental and African Studies* 61, no. 3 (1998): 415–436.

———. "Qāḍīs Communicating: Legal Change and the Law of Documentary Evidence." *al-Qanṭara* 20 (1999): 437–466.

———. *Sharīʿa: Theory, Practice, Transformations*. Cambridge: Cambridge University Press, 2009.

———. "*Uṣūl al-Fiqh*: Beyond Tradition." *Journal of Islamic Studies* 3 (1992): 172–202.

———. "What Is Sharīʿa?" In *Yearbook of Islamic and Middle Eastern Law, 2005–2006*, 12:151–180. Leiden: Brill, 2007.

Hanna, Nelly. "The Administration of Courts in Ottoman Cairo." In *The State and Its Servants: Administration of Egypt from Ottoman Times to the Present*, ed. Nelly Hanna, 44–59. Cairo: The American University in Cairo Press, 1995.

Hanneman, R., and J. R. Hollingsworth. "Refocusing the Debate on the Role of the State in Capitalist Societies." In *State Theory and State History*, ed. R. Torstendahl. London: Sage, 1992.

Hansen, Mogens H. "The Mixed Constitution Versus the Separation of Powers: Monarchial and Aristocratic Aspects of Modern Democracy." *History of Political Thought* 31, no. 3 (2010): 509–531.

Hardin, Charles M. *Constitutional Reform in America: Essays on the Separation of Powers*. Ames: Iowa State University Press, 1989.

Hart, H. L. A. *The Concept of Law*. 2nd ed. Oxford: Clarendon Press, 1994.

Hay, Colin, et al., eds. *The State: Theories and Issues*. New York: Palgrave, 2006.

Hayek, F. A. *Law, Legislation, and Liberty: A New Statement of the Liberal Principles of Justice and Political Economy*. 3 vols. London: Routledge, 1982.

Hayes, Carlton J. H. *The Historical Evolution of Modern Nationalism*. New York: Russell & Russell, 1968.

Held, David. *Political Theory and the Modern State: Essays on State, Power, and Democracy*. Cambridge: Polity Press, 1989.

Held, David, et al. *Global Transformations: Politics, Economics, and Culture*. Stanford, Calif.: Stanford University Press, 1999.

Hélie-Lucas, Marie-Aimée. "The Preferential Symbol for Islamic Identity: Women in Muslim Personal Laws." In *Identity Politics and Women: Cultural Reassertions and Feminisms in International Perspective*, ed. Valentine M. Moghadam, 188–196. Boulder, Colo.: Westview, 1994.

Heyd, U. *Studies in Old Ottoman Criminal Law*. Ed. V. L. Ménage. Oxford: Clarendon Press, 1973.

Hirst, Paul, and Grahame Thompson. *Globalization in Question: The International Economy and the Possibilities of Governance*. Cambridge: Polity Press, 1996.

Hobson, John M. *The Eastern Origins of Western Civilization*. Cambridge: Cambridge University Press, 2004.

Horkheimer, Max, and Theodor W. Adorno. *Dialectic of Enlightenment: Philosophical Fragments*. Ed. G. Schmid Noerr. Trans. E. Jophcott. Stanford, Calif.: Stanford University Press, 1987.

Horwitz, Morton. *Transformation of American Law 1870–1960: The Crisis of Legal Orthodoxy*. Oxford: Oxford University Press, 1992.

Hospers, John. "Why Be Moral?" In *Readings in Ethical Theory*, ed. W. Sellars and J. Hospers, 730–746. Englewood Cliffs, N.J.: Prentice-Hall, 1970.

Hurvitz, Nimrod. "Biographies and Mild Asceticism: A Study of Islamic Moral Imagination." *Studia Islamica* 85 (1997): 41–65.

Hutchinson, Allan, and P. Monahan. “Politics and the Critical Legal Scholars: The Unfolding Drama of American Legal Thought.” *Stanford Law Review* 36, no. 1–2 (1984): 199–245.
Izutsu, Toshihiko. *Ethico-Religious Concepts in the Qurʾān*. Montreal: McGill University Press, 1966.
Jackson, Sherman A. *Islamic Law and the State: The Constitutional Jurisprudence of Shihāb al-Dīn al-Qarāfī*. Leiden: Brill, 1996.
Jacob, Margaret C. *Radical Enlightenment: Pantheists, Freemasons, and Republicans*. Lafayette, La.: Cornerstone, 2006.
James, Susan. “Internal and External in the Work of Descartes.” In *Philosophy in an Age of Pluralism: The Philosophy of Charles Taylor in Question*, ed. James Tully et al., 7–19. Cambridge: Cambridge University Press, 1994.
Jennings, R. C. *Christians and Muslims in Ottoman Cyprus and the Mediterranean World, 1571–1640*. New York: New York University Press, 1993.
———. “Limitations of the Judicial Powers of the Kadi in 17th C. Ottoman Kayseri.” *Studia Islamica* 50 (1979): 151–184.
———. *Studies on Ottoman Social History in the Sixteenth and Seventeenth Centuries: Women, Zimmis, and Sharia Courts in Kayseri, Cyprus, and Trabzon*. Istanbul: Isis Press, 1999.
———. “Women in Early Seventeenth-Century Ottoman Judicial Records: The *Sharia* Court of Anatolian Kayseri.” *Journal of the Economic and Social History of the Orient* 18 (1975): 53–114.
Jessop, Bob. *The Future of the Capitalist State*. Cambridge: Polity, 2002.
Jochnick, Chris, and R. Normand. “The Legitimation of Violence: A Critical History of the Laws of War.” *Harvard International Law Journal* 35, no. 1 (1994): 49–95.
Johansen, Baber. *The Islamic Law on Land Tax and Rent: The Peasants’ Loss of Property Rights as Interpreted in the Hanafite Legal Literature of the Mamluk and Ottoman Periods*. London: Croom Helm, 1988.
———. “Der ʿIṣma-Begriff im Hanafitischen Recht.” In *Contingency in a Sacred Law: Legal and Ethical Norms in the Muslim* Fiqh, 238–262. Leiden: Brill, 1999.
———. “Legal Literature and the Problem of Change: The Case of the Land Rent.” In *Islam and Public Law: Classical and Contemporary Studies*, ed. Chibli Mallat, 29–47. London: Graham and Trotman, 1993.
———. “Territorial Concepts in Islamic Law.” In *The Oxford International Encyclopedia of Legal History*, ed. Stanley N. Katz, 5:451–454. Oxford: Oxford University Press, 2009.
Johnson, Pauline. “Social Philosophy.” In *Theodor Adorno: Key Concepts*, ed. Deborah Cook, 115–129. Stocksfield: Acumen, 2008.
Kahn, Paul W. *Putting Liberalism in Its Place*. Princeton, N.J.: Princeton University Press, 2005.
Kant, I. “An Answer to the Question: What Is Enlightenment?” In *Immanuel Kant*, ed. Mary J. Grego, 17–22. Cambridge: Cambridge University Press, 1996.
———. *The Moral Law: Groundwork of the Metaphysic of Morals*. Trans. H. J. Paton. London: Routledge, 2005.

Katz, M. *Body of Text: The Emergence of the Sunnī Law of Ritual Purity*. Albany: State University of New York Press, 2002.

Kaviraj, Sudipta. "On the Enchantment of the State: Indian Thought on the Role of the State in the Narrative of Modernity." *Archives of European Sociology* 46, no. 2 (2005): 263–296.

Kelsen, Hans. *General Theory of Law and State*. Trans. A. Wedberg. New York: Russell and Russell, 1961.

Kerferd, G. B. *The Sophistic Movement*. Cambridge: Cambridge University Press, 1999.

Khoury, Dina Rizk. *State and Provincial Society in the Ottoman Empire: Mosul, 1540–1834*. Cambridge: Cambridge University Press, 1997.

Korsgaard, Christine. *The Sources of Normativity*. Cambridge: Cambridge University Press, 1996.

Korten, David C. *When Corporations Rule the World*. West Hartford, Ct.: Kumarian Press, 1995.

Kourlis, Rebecca, and Dirk Olin. *Rebuilding Justice*. Denver, Colo.: Fulcrum, 2011.

Kuhn, Thomas S. *The Structure of Scientific Revolutions*. Chicago: University of Chicago Press, 1970.

Kuran, Timur. "Why the Islamic Middle East Did not Generate an Indigenous Corporate Law." *University of Southern California Law School: Law and Economics Working Paper Series* 16 (2004): 1–33.

Kurdi, Abdulrahman. *The Islamic State*. London: Mansell, 1984.

Lapidus, Ira. "Knowledge, Virtue, and Action: The Classical Muslim Conception of *Adab* and the Nature of Religious Fulfillment in Islam." In *Moral Conduct and Authority: The Place of* Adab *in South Asian Islam*, ed. Barbara Metcalf, 38–61. Berkeley: University of California Press, 1984.

Larmore, Charles. *The Autonomy of Morality*. Cambridge: Cambridge University Press, 2008.

———. *The Morals of Modernity*. Cambridge: Cambridge University Press, 1996.

Lasch, Christopher. *The Culture of Narcissism: American Life in an Age of Diminishing Expectations*. New York: Norton, 1978.

———. *The Minimal Self: Psychic Survival in Troubled Times*. New York: Norton, 1984.

Lawson, Gary. "Rise and Rise of the Administrative State." *Harvard Law Review* 107 (April 1994): 1231–1254.

Levinson, Daryl J. "Separation of Parties, Not Powers." *Harvard Law Review* 119 (June 2006): 2311–2386.

Lyons, Jonathan. *The House of Wisdom: How the Arabs Transformed Western Civilization*. New York: Bloomsbury, 2009.

MacDonald, S. "Ultimate Ends in Practical Reasoning: Aquinas' Aristotelian Moral Psychology and Anscombe's Fallacy." *Philosophical Review* 100 (1991): 31–66.

MacIntyre, Alasdair. *After Virtue: A Study in Moral Theory*. 3rd ed. Notre Dame, Ind.: University of Notre Dame Press, 2007.

———. *A Short History of Ethics*. London: Routledge, 1998.

———. *Whose Justice? Which Rationality?* Notre Dame, Ind.: University of Notre Dame Press, 1988.

MacLean, Douglas, and Claudia Mills, eds. *Liberalism Reconsidered.* Totowa, N.J.: Rowman and Allenheld, 1983.

Magill, M. Elizabeth. "Beyond Powers and Branches in Separation of Powers Law." *University of Pennsylvania Law Review* 150, no. 2 (December 2001): 603–660.

———. "The Real Separation in Separation of Powers Law." *Virginia Law Review* 86 (September 2000): 1127–1198.

Mahmood, Saba. *Politics of Piety: Islamic Revival and the Feminist Subject.* Princeton, N.J.: Princeton University Press, 2005.

Makdisi, George. *The Rise of the Colleges: Institutions of Learning in Islam and the West.* Edinburgh: Edinburgh University Press, 1981.

Mallat, Chibli. *The Renewal of Islamic Law: Muhammad Baqer as-Sadr, Najaf, and the Shiʿi International.* Cambridge: Cambridge University Press, 1993.

Mann, Michael. "Has Globalization Ended the Rise and Rise of the Nation-State?" *Review of International Political Economy* 4, no. 3 (1997): 472–496.

———. *States, War, and Capitalism.* Oxford: Basil Blackwell, 1988.

Mannheim, Karl. *Essays on the Sociology of Knowledge.* London: Routledge & Kegan Paul, 1968.

Mansfield, Harvey C. "Separation of Powers in the American Constitution." In *Separation of Powers and Good Government,* ed. Bradford P. Wilson and Peter Schramm, 3–15. London: Rowman and Littlefield, 1994.

Marcus, Abraham. "Men, Women, and Property: Dealers in Real Estate in Eighteenth-Century Aleppo." *Journal of the Economic and Social History of the Orient* 26 (1983): 137–163.

Marcuse, Herbert. *One-Dimensional Man.* Boston: Beacon Press, 1964.

Margolis, J. *The Truth About Relativism.* Oxford: Blackwell, 1991.

Marinetto, Michael. *Social Theory, the State, and Modern Society.* Buckingham: Open University Press, 2006.

Marrow, John. *History of Western Political Thought.* London: Palgrave Macmillan, 2005.

Marsh, David, et al. "Globalization and the State." In *The State: Theories and Issues,* ed. Colin Hay et al., 172–189. New York: Palgrave, 2006.

Marshall, Geoffrey. *Constitutional Theory.* Oxford: Clarendon Press, 1971.

Marx, Karl. "Manifesto of the Communist Party." In *Marx and Engels: Basic Writings on Politics and Philosophy,* ed. Lewis S. Feuer, 1–41. New York: Anchor, 1959.

Massad, Joseph A. *Colonial Effects: The Making of National Identity in Jordan.* New York: Columbia University Press, 2001.

———. *Desiring Arabs.* Chicago: University of Chicago Press, 2007.

Masud, M. Khaled, et al., eds. *Islamic Legal Interpretation: Muftis and Their Fatwas.* Cambridge, Mass.: Harvard University Press, 1996.

McCarthy, R. J., trans. *Al-Ghazali's Path to Sufism: His Deliverance from Error, al-Munqidh min al-Dalal.* Louisville, Ky.: Fons Vitae, 2006.

McClellan, James. *Liberty, Order, and Justice: An Introduction to the Constitutional Principles of American Government*. Indianapolis, Ind.: Liberty Fund, 2000.

Meier, Christian. *The Greek Discovery of Politics*. Cambridge, Mass.: Harvard University Press, 1990.

Meisami, Julie S., trans. *The Sea of Precious Virtues (Baḥr al-Favāʾid)*. Salt Lake City: University of Utah Press, 1991.

Meriwether, Margaret L. "The Rights of Children and the Responsibilities of Women: Women as *Wasis* in Ottoman Aleppo, 1770–1840." In *Women, the Family, and Divorce Laws in Islamic History*, ed. A. Sonbol, 219–235. Syracuse, N.Y.: Syracuse University Press, 1996.

———. "Women and Waqf Revisited: The Case of Aleppo, 1770–1840." In *Women in the Ottoman Empire: Middle Eastern Women*, ed. Madeline C. Zilfi, 128–152. Leiden: Brill, 1997.

Messick, Brinkley. *The Calligraphic State: Textual Domination and History in a Muslim Society*. Berkeley: University of California Press, 1993.

———. "Indexing the Self: Intent and Expression in Islamic Legal Acts." *Islamic Law and Society* 8, no. 2 (2001): 151–178.

Miliband, Ralph. *The State in Capitalist Society*. London: Weidenfeld and Nicolson, 1969.

Mill, J. S. *On Liberty*. Ed. David Bromwich and George Kateb. New Haven, Conn.: Yale University Press, 2003.

Miller, W. Watts. *Durkheim, Morals, and Modernity*. Montreal: McGill-Queens University Press, 1996.

Mitchell, Timothy. "Limits of the State: Beyond Statist Approaches and their Critics." *American Political Science Review* 85, no. 1 (1991): 77–96.

———. "Society, Economy, and the State Effect." In *State/Culture: State-Formation After the Cultural Turn*, ed. George Steinmetz, 76–96. Ithaca, N.Y.: Cornell University Press, 1999.

Moors, Annelies. "Debating Islamic Family Law: Legal Texts and Social Practices." In *Social History of Women and Gender in the Modern Middle East*, ed. M. L. Meriwether and Judith E. Tucker, 141–175. Oxford: Westview, 1999.

———. "Gender Relations and Inheritance: Person, Power, and Property in Palestine." In *Gendering the Middle East*, ed. Deniz Kandiyoti, 69–84. New York: Syracuse University Press, 1996.

Moosa, Ebrahim. *Ghazālī and the Poetics of Imagination*. Chapel Hill: University of North Carolina Press, 2005.

Murdoch, Iris. *Metaphysics as a Guide to Morals*. London: Random House, 2003.

Naess, Arne. *The Selected Works of Arne Naess*. Vol. 10. Dordrecht: Springer, 2005.

Nagel, Thomas. "Ruthlessness in Public Life." In *Public and Private Morality*, ed. Stuart Hampshire, 75–91. Cambridge: Cambridge University Press, 1978.

Naqvi, Nauman. "The Nostalgic Subject: A Genealogy of the 'Critique of Nostalgia.'" In *Centro Interuniversitario per le ricerche sulla Sociologia del*

Diritto e delle Instituzioni Giuridiche, Working Paper no. 23 (September 2007): 4–51.
Nelson, Brian. *The Making of the Modern State: A Theoretical Evolution*. New York: Palgrave, 2006.
Nicolacopoulos, Toula. *The Radical Critique of Liberalism: In Memory of a Vision*. Melbourne: Re-Press, 2008.
Nietzsche, Friedrich. *Human, All Too Human*. Trans. R. J. Hollingdale. Cambridge: Cambridge University Press, 1996.
———. "On Truth and Lies in a Nonmoral Sense." In *Philosophy and Truth: Selections from Nietzsche's Notebooks of the Early 1870s*, ed. and trans. Daniel Breazeale, 80–86. New Brunswick, N.J.: Humanities Press, 1979.
———. *Thus Spoke Zarathustra*. Trans. R. J. Hollingdale. Baltimore, Md.: Penguin, 1975.
———. *Twilight of the Idols*. Trans. R. J. Hollingdale. New York: Penguin, 1977.
———. *The Will to Power*. Trans. W. Kaufmann and R. J. Hollingdale. New York: Vintage, 1967.
Nisbet, Robert. *History of the Idea of Progress*. New York: Basic Books, 1980.
———. *The Sociology of Emile Durkheim*. New York: Oxford University Press, 1974.
Nozick, Robert. *Anarchy, State, and Utopia*. New York: Basic Books, 1974.
O'Connor, Brian. "Philosophy of History." In *Theodor Adorno: Key Concepts*, ed. Deborah Cook, 179–195. Stocksfield: Acumen, 2008.
Ohmae, Kenichi. *The End of the Nation State: The Rise of Regional Economies*. New York: Free Press, 1996.
Olafson H. A., ed. *Society, Law, and Morality*. Englewood Cliffs, N.J.: Prentice-Hall, 1961.
Opwis, Felicitas. "Islamic Law and Legal Change: The Concept of *Maṣlaḥa* in Classical and Contemporary Islamic Legal Theory." In *Shariʿa: Islamic Law in the Contemporary Context*, ed. Abbas Amanat and Frank Griffel, 62–82. Stanford, Calif.: Stanford University Press, 2007.
Parekh, Bhikhu. "Superior People: The Narrowness of Liberalism from Mill to Rawls." *Times Literary Supplement*, no. 4743 (February 25, 1994).
Peffer, R. G. *Marxism, Morality, and Social Justice*. Princeton, N.J.: Princeton University Press, 1990.
Peirce, Leslie. *Morality Tales: Law and Gender in the Ottoman Court of Aintab*. Berkeley: University of California Press, 2003.
Peukert, Helmut. "The Philosophical Critique of Modernity." In *The Debate on Modernity*, ed. Claude Geffré and Pierre Jossua, 17–26. London: SCM, 1992.
Pérez-Ramos, Antonio. "Bacon's Forms and the Maker's Knowledge." In *Cambridge Companion to Bacon*, ed. Markku Peltonen, 99–120. Cambridge: Cambridge University Press, 1996.
Pickthall, M. *The Meanings of the Glorious Koran*. New York: Mentor Classics, n.d.
Poggi, Gianfranco. *The Development of the Modern State: A Sociological Introduction*. Stanford, Calif.: Stanford University Press, 1978.

Polanyi, Karl. *The Great Transformation: The Political and Economic Origins of Our Time*. Boston: Beacon Press, 2001.
Powers, Paul. *Intent in Islamic Law: Motive and Meaning in Medieval* Sunnī Fiqh. Leiden: Brill, 2006.
Pressler, Charles, and Fabio B. Dasilva. *Sociology and Interpretation: From Weber to Habermas*. Albany: State University of New York Press, 1996.
Prichard, H. A. "Does Moral Philosophy Rest on a Mistake?" *Mind* 21, no. 81 (1912): 21–37.
Al-Qattan, Najwa. "Dhimmis in the Muslim Court: Documenting Justice in Ottoman Damascus, 1775–1860." Ph.D. diss., Harvard University, 1996.
———. "*Dhimmīs* in the Muslim Court: Legal Autonomy and Religious Discrimination." *International Journal of Middle East Studies* 31, no. 3 (1999): 429–444.
———. "Litigants and Neighbors: The Communal Topography of Ottoman Damascus." *Comparative Study in Society and History* 44, no. 3 (2002): 511–533.
Qutb, Sayyid. *Social Justice in Islam*. Trans. John Hardie. Oneonta, N.Y.: Islamic Publications International, 2000.
Rabb, Intisar. "We the Jurists: Islamic Constitutionalism in Iraq." *Journal of Constitutional Law* 10, no. 3 (March 2008): 527–579.
Rand, Ayn. "Causality Versus Duty." In *Philosophy: Who Needs It*, 114–122. New York: Bobbs-Merril, 1982.
———. "The Objectivist Ethics." In *The Virtue of Selfishness*, 13–35. New York: New American Library, 1964.
Rawls, John. *Political Liberalism*. New York: Columbia University Press, 2005.
Reicher, Steve, and Nick Hopkins. *Self and Nation: Categorization, Contestation, and Mobilization*. London: Sage, 2001.
Rose, N., and P. Miller. "Political Power Beyond the State: Problematic of Government." *British Journal of Sociology* 43, no. 2 (1992): 173–205.
Rosen, Lawrence. *The Anthropology of Justice: Law as Culture in Islamic Society*. Cambridge: Cambridge University Press, 1989.
———. "Justice in Islamic Culture and Law." In *Perspectives on Islamic Law, Justice, and Society*, ed. R. S. Khare, 33–52. Lanham, Md.: Rowman & Littlefield, 1999.
———. *The Justice of Islam: Comparative Perspectives on Islamic Law and Society*. Oxford: Oxford University Press, 2000.
Rossi, Paolo. "Bacon's Idea of Science." In *The Cambridge Companion to Bacon*, ed. Markku Peltonen, 37–42. Cambridge: Cambridge University Press, 1996.
Roy, Oliver. *The Failure of Political Islam*. Trans. Carol Volk. Cambridge, Mass.: Harvard University Press, 1994.
Sabra, Adam. *Poverty and Charity in Medieval Islam: Mamluk Egypt, 1250–1517*. Cambridge: Cambridge University Press, 2000.
Safi, Omid. *The Politics of Knowledge in Premodern Islam: Negotiating Ideology and Religious Inquiry*. Chapel Hill: University of North Carolina Press, 2006.

Saliba, George. *Islamic Science and the Making of the European Renaissance*. Cambridge, Mass.: The MIT Press, 2007.

Sandel, Michael, ed. *Liberalism and Its Critics*. New York: New York University Press, 1984.

Saunders, Cheryl. "Separation of Powers and the Judicial Branch." *Judicial Review* 11 (2006): 337–347.

Scaff, Lawrence A. "Weber on the Cultural Situation of the Modern Age." In *The Cambridge Companion to Weber*, ed. Stephen Turner, 99–116. Cambridge: Cambridge University Press, 2000.

Scanlon, T. M. "Rights, Goals, and Fairness." In *Public and Private Morality*, ed. Stuart Hampshire, 93–111. Cambridge: Cambridge University Press, 1978.

Scheler, Max. *Problems of a Sociology of Knowledge*. Trans. Manfred Frings. London: Routledge & Kegan Paul, 1980.

Scheuerman, William E. "Carl Schmitt and the Road to Abu Ghraib." *Constellations* 13, no. 1 (2006): 108–124.

Schirazi, Asghar. *The Constitution of Iran: Politics and the State in the Islamic Republic*. Trans. John O'Kane. London: I. B. Tauris, 1997.

Schmitt, Carl. "The Age of Naturalizations and Depoliticizations." In *The Concept of the Political*, trans. G. Schwab, 80–96. Chicago: University of Chicago Press, 2007.

———. *The Concept of the Political*. Trans. G. Schwab. Chicago: University of Chicago Press, 2007.

———. *The Crisis of Parliamentary Democracy*. Trans. Ellen Kennedy. Cambridge, Mass.: The MIT Press, 1988.

———. *Political Romanticism*. Trans. Guy Oakes. New Brunswick, N.J.: Transaction, 2011.

———. *Political Theology: Four Chapters on the Concept of Sovereignty*. Trans. George Schwab. Chicago: University of Chicago Press, 1985.

Schmitter, Philippe C. "Still the Century of Corporatism?" *Review of Politics* 36, no. 1 (January 1974): 85–131.

Schneewind, J. B. "Autonomy, Obligation, and Virtue: An Overview of Kant's Moral Philosophy." In *The Cambridge Companion to Kant*, ed. Paul Guyer, 309–333. Cambridge: Cambridge University Press, 1992.

Schultz, Peter L. "Congress and the Separation of Powers Today: Practice in Search of a Theory." In *Separation of Powers and Good Government*, ed. B. P. Wilson and P. W. Schramm, 185–200. Lanham, Md.: Rowman and Littlefield, 1994.

Semerdjian, Elyse. *"Off the Straight Path": Illicit Sex, Law, and Community in Ottoman Aleppo*. Syracuse, N.Y.: Syracuse University Press, 2008.

Seng, Yvonne J. "Standing at the Gates of Justice: Women in the Law Courts of Early Sixteenth-Century Isküdar, Istanbul." In *Contested States: Law, Hegemony, and Resistance*, ed. Susan Hirsch and M. Lazarus-Black, 184–206. New York: Routledge, 1994.

———. "Invisible Women: Residents of Early Sixteenth-Century Istanbul." In *Women in the Medieval Islamic World: Power, Patronage, and Piety*, ed. Gavin Hambly, 241–268. New York: St. Martin's Press, 1998.

Serjeant, R. B. "'Sunnah Jāmiʿah,' Pacts with the Yathrib Jews, and the Taḥrīm of Yathrib: Analysis and Translation of the Documents Comprised in the So-Called 'Constitution of Medina.'" *Bulletin of the School of Oriental and African Studies* 41, no. 1 (1978): 1–42.

Shaw, Martin. "The State of Globalization: Toward a Theory of State Transformation." *Review of International Political Economy* 4, no. 3 (2001): 497–513.

Simon, Thomas W. "The Theoretical Marginalization of the Disadvantaged: A Liberal/Commumitarian Failing." In *The Liberalism-Communitarianism Debate: Liberty and Community Values*, ed. C. F. Delaney, 103–135. Lanham, Md.: Rowman and Littlefield, 1994.

Simmel, Georg. *The Philosophy of Money*. London: Routledge, 1990.

Singer, Amy. *Charity in Islamic Society*. Cambridge: Cambridge University Press, 2008.

Singer, Peter. *Practical Ethics*. Cambridge: Cambridge University Press, 1993.

Skinner, Quentin. "Modernity and Disenchantment: Some Historical Reflections." In *Philosophy in an Age of Pluralism*, ed. James Tully, 37–48. Cambridge: Cambridge University Press, 1994.

Smith, Tara. *Viable Values*. Lanham, Md.: Rowan and Littlefield Publishers, 2000.

Smith, T. V., and M. Greene, eds. *Berkeley, Hume, and Kant*. Chicago: University of Chicago Press, 1957.

Sorel, George. *Illusions of Progress*. Berkeley: University of California Press, 1969.

Sørensen, George. *The Transformation of the State: Beyond the Myth of Retreat*. New York: Palgrave and Macmillan, 2004.

———. "The Transformation of the State." In *The State: Theories and Issues*, ed. Colin Hay et al., 190–209. New York: Palgrave, 2006.

Spengler, Oswald. *The Decline of the West: Form and Actuality*. Trans. Charles F. Atkinson. New York: Knopf, 1926.

Sprangens, Thomas A. Jr. *The Irony of Liberal Reason*. Chicago: University of Chicago Press, 1981.

Spruyt, Hendrik. *The Sovereign State and Its Competitors: An Analysis of Systems Change*. Princeton, N.J.: Princeton University Press, 1994.

Stanley, John. "Introduction." In *The Illusions of Progress*, by George Sorel. Berkeley: University of California Press, 1969.

Stark, W. *The Sociology of Knowledge: An Essay in Aid of a Deeper Understanding of the History of Ideas*. London: Routledge & Kegan Paul, 1960.

Staude, J. R. *Max Scheler*. New York: The Free Press, 1967.

Steinmetz, George, ed. *State/Culture: State-Formation After the Cultural Turn*. Ithaca, N.Y.: Cornell University Press, 1999.

Stewart, Gordon T. "The Scottish Enlightenment Meets the Tibetan Enlightenment." *Journal of World History* 22, no. 3 (2011): 455–492.

Stewart, Iain. "From 'Rule of Law' to 'Legal State': A Time of Reincarnation?" *Macquarie Law* (November 2007): 1–11.

Stiglitz, Joseph E. *Globalization and Its Discontents*. New York: W. W. Norton, 2002.

Strange, Susan. *The Retreat of the State: The Diffusion of Power in the World Economy*. Cambridge: Cambridge University Press, 1996.

Strauss, Leo. "On the Spirit of Hobbes's Political Philosophy." In *Hobbes Studies*, ed. K. C. Brown, 1–29. Cambridge, Mass.: Harvard University Press, 1965.

Strawson, John. "Islamic Law and English Texts." *Law and Critique* 6, no. 1 (1995): 21–38.

Tallett, Frank. *War and Society in Early Modern Europe, 1495–1715*. London: Routledge, 1992.

Taylor, Charles. "Justice After Virtue." In *After MacIntyre: Critical Perspectives on the Work of Alasdair MacIntyre*, ed. John Horton and Susan Mendus, 16–43. Cambridge: Polity Press, 1994.

———. *Malaise of Modernity*. Concord, Ont.: Anansi, 1991.

———. *Sources of the Self: The Making of the Modern Identity*. Cambridge, Mass.: Harvard University Press, 1989.

Taylor, Richard. *Good and Evil*. Amherst, N.Y.: Prometheus, 2000.

Teeple, Gary. *Globalization and the Decline of Social Reform*. Aurora, Ont.: Garamond, 2000.

Tibawi, A. L. "Origin and Character of Al-Madrasa." *Bulletin of the School of Oriental and African Studies* 25 (1962): 225–238.

Tilly, Charles. *Coercion, Capital, and European States: A.D. 990–1990*. Cambridge: Blackwell, 1990.

Touraine, Alain. *Critique of Modernity*. Trans. David Macey. Oxford: Blackwell, 1995.

Tripp, Charles. *Islam and the Moral Economy: The Challenge of Capitalism*. Cambridge: Cambridge University Press, 2006.

Tucker, Judith E. *In the House of the Law: Gender and Islamic Law in Ottoman Syria and Palestine*. Berkeley: University of California Press, 1998.

———. "Marriage and Family in Nablus, 1720–1856: Toward a History of Arab Marriage." *Journal of Family History* 13, no. 1 (1988): 165–179.

———. "Revisiting Reform: Women and the Ottoman Law of Family Rights, 1917." *Arab Studies Journal* 4, no. 2 (1996): 4–17.

Tyan, E. "Judicial Organization." In *Law in the Middle East*, ed. M. Khadduri and H. Liebesny, 236–278. Washington, D.C.: The Middle East Institute, 1955.

Ulmen, G. L. "The Sociology of the State: Carl Schmitt and Max Weber." *State, Culture, and Society* 1, no. 2 (1985): 3–57.

Unwin, Nicholas. "Morality, Law, and the Evaluation of Values." *Mind* 94, no. 376 (October 1985): 538–549.

van Creveld, Martin L. *The Rise and Decline of the State*. Cambridge: Cambridge University Press, 1999.

Van der Veer, Peter. *Imperial Encounters: Religion and Modernity in India and Britain*. Princeton, N.J.: Princeton University Press, 2001.

Vanderbilt, Arthur. *The Doctrine of the Separation of Powers and Its Present-Day Significance*. Lincoln: University of Nebraska Press, 1953.

van Leeuwen, Richard. *Waqfs and Urban Structures: The Case of Ottoman Damascus*. Leiden: Brill, 1999.

Vikør, Knut S. "The Sharīʿa and the Nation State: Who Can Codify the Divine Law?" In *The Middle East in a Globalized World*, ed. B. O. Utvik and K. Vikør, 220–250. Bergen: Nordic Society for Middle Eastern Studies, 2000.
Vile, M. J. C. *Constitutionalism and the Separation of Powers*. 2nd ed. Indianapolis, Ind.: Liberty Fund, 1998.
Vincent, Andrew. *Theories of the State*. Oxford: Blackwell, 1987.
Vogel, Frank, and Samuel Heyes. *Islamic Law and Finance: Religion, Risk, and Return*. Boston: Kluwer Law International, 1998.
Weber, Max. *Economy and Society: An Outline of Interpretive Sociology*. Vol. 1. Berkeley: University of California Press, 1978.
———. *From Max Weber: Essays in Sociology*. Ed. H. Gerth and C. W. Mills. New York: Oxford University Press, 1958.
———. *The Protestant Ethic and the "Spirit" of Capitalism, and Other Writings*. New York: Penguin, 2002.
Weiss, Bernard. "Interpretation in Islamic Law: The Theory of *Ijtihād*." *American Journal of Comparative Law* 26 (1978): 199–212.
Wilson, Charles H. "Separation of Powers Under Democracy and Fascism." *Political Science Quarterly* 52, no. 4 (1937): 481–504.
Wood, Ellen M. *The Origins of Capitalism: A Longer View*. London: Verso, 2002.
Wriston, Walter. *The Twilight of Sovereignty: How the Information Revolution Is Transforming Our World*. New York: Maxwell MacMillan International, 1992.
Zaman, Qasim M. *Religion and Politics Under the Early ʿAbbāsids*. Leiden: Brill, 1997.
———. *The Ulama in Contemporary Islam: Custodians of Change*. Princeton, N.J.: Princeton University Press, 2002.
Zamboni, Mauro. *Law and Politics: A Dilemma for Contemporary Legal Theory*. Heidelberg: Springer, 2008.
Zarinebaf (-Shahr), Fariba. "Women, Law, and Imperial Justice in Ottoman Istanbul in the Late Seventeenth Century." In *Women, the Family, and Divorce Laws in Islamic History*, ed. Amira el-Azhary Sonbol, 81–96. Syracuse, N.Y.: Syracuse University Press, 1996.
———. *Crime and Punishment in Istanbul, 1700–1800*. Berkeley: University of California Press, 2010.
Zilfi, Madeline C. "'We Don't Get Along': Women and *Hul* Divorce in the Eighteenth Century." in *Women in the Ottoman Empire: Middle Eastern Modern Women in the Early Modern Era*, ed. M. C. Zilfi, 264–296. Leiden: Brill, 1997.
Zubaida, Sami. "Islam and Secularization." *Asian Journal of Social Science* 33, no. 3 (2005): 438–448.
———. *Law and Power in the Islamic World*. London: I. B. Tauris, 2003.

Index

central domain: force relations and, 9; moral desideratum as, 12, 162–67, 175nn49–50; paradigm and, 7; peripheral domains and, 8–9; of Schmitt, 7–9, 12; Sharīʿa as, 10, 175nn40–41
centralization, 32
charitable endowment. *See waqf*
citizens, x, xi, 2, 21, 26–28, 39, 45, 73, 104, 106, 142, 160, 178n45; democratic unfreedom for, 108; identity of, 96–97; iron cage for, 107–8; in Islamic governance, 96–97, 111, 140, 158; in modern Islamic state, 93; of modern states, 96–97, 158; moral individual compared to, 201n17; narcissism of, 108–10; nationalism and, 106; in political, 91–92; production of, 99–110. *See also* community
citizens' subjectivity: family and, 104–5, 201nn18–19; father in, 105, 201n19; frailty from, 105, 201n22
colonialism, 1–2; over Islamic governance, 2, 63, 65, 147, 167–68
community, 4, 52, 53, 65, 66, 96, 148, 160, 203n73; definition of, 49–50, 184n77; without Enlightenment, 170; executive power and Sharīʿa compared to, 50, 57, 63–64, 67, 188n131; government servants compared to, 68; *ʿibādāt* for, 159–60; ideal, 6, 173n21; individuals as, 106–7, 114; in Islamic governance paradigm, 49–50, 184n77; legislation, law, and violence and, 29–30, 178n47, 179n48; Middle, 166; as *nasl*, 147–48; for nationalism, 106–8; nation-state compared to, 49
Condorcet, Marquis de, 17, 176n65
conscription: Islamic governance without, 93–95, 199n126, 199n128, 199n130; in political, 74, 92–96, 199n126, 199n128, 199n130
consensus, 49, 95, 215
Constitution, xii, 26, 27, 37, 39, 40, 74; democracy and, 45, 73, 184n70; on executive, 42, 43, 64, 182nn2; of Medina, x, 155; multilayered social, 113–14; nation-state separation of powers and, 41, 42–43, 181nn30–31, 182nn42–43, 183n46; on religion, 203n61; Sharīʿa and, 51–52, 60–62, 64, 66, 158, 185n88
contextual epistemology, 203n58
control, 193n14; class and, 99, 200n1; knowledge of, 75–76, 193n3; law and, 82–83, 89; of nature, 76–78, 194n28; of Self, 76, 193n18
corporations: globalization and, 145, 153–54, 210n31, 212n69; morality of, 145, 153–54, 210n31; for wealth, 145
cultural hegemony: cooperation in, 35, 179n68; education in, 35, 179n70; for modern states, 33–36, 179n68, 179n70; necessity of, 34, 179n64, 179n66
culture, 35–36; globalization related to, 143–44, 153; Islamic governance and, 153; of West, 143–44
Culture of Narcissism, The (Lasch), 1

Dahl, Robert, 72, 183n49
Dār al-Ḥarb, 49, 215
Dār al-Islām, 49, 215
dawla, 190nn145; definition of, 62–63, 190n144, 215–16; sultan compared to, 190n146
Dawson, Christopher, 175n57
Declaration of the Rights of Man and the Citizen, 39
Deleuze, Gilles, 105
democracy, 26, 37, 48, 71, 73, 102, 182n43; civilization compared to, 183n59; Constitution and, 184n70; critique of practice of, 40, 43, 180n10, 182n43; democratic unfreedom, 108; Islam's compatibility with, 52, 72, 185n88; legislative and, 71–72; as representation in Islamic governance, 53, 61, 63–64, 70, 71–72; rule of law for, 39, 72–74
desires, x, 131
dīn (religion), 147

discipline: of European state, 99–101, 200n1; internal, 98, 101; of modern states, 99–100; of traditional societies, 98–99
divine grace, 130
Donzelot, Jacques, 105
double-*shahāda*, 118–20, 204n85
Durkheim, E., 163

economics: of globalization, 144–46; Islamic governance related to, 153–54; in modern states, 22; Sharīʿa paradigm and, 10–11; social justice related to, 154; socioeconomics, 45–46, 184n70; state and, 21–22. *See also* Islam's moral economy
education: academia in, 35, 102–4, 200n10; in cultural hegemony, 23, 35, 45, 76, 146, 160, 179n70; for ethical conduct, 132; for European state, 100, 102; *ʿibādāt* for, 132–33; iron cage as, 107–8; in Islamic governance, 110–11, 140; power and, 104; in Sharīʿa, 10, 13, 51, 52, 110–11
Enlightenment, 3, 5–6, 13, 16–17, 75, 77, 80, 83, 99, 163, 173n21; community without, 170; core project of, 8, 174n35; history and, 16, 24; modern Muslims compared to, 166; modern states and, 24; for paradigm, 7–8, 170, 174n35
Enlightenment's Wake (Gray), 19
environment, physical, 4, 131
ethical conduct, 132
ethics of autonomy, 165
Euro-America, 3, 22, 70, 72, 156, 162
Europe, 23–24, 177n13
European state, 110; discipline of, 99–100, 200n1; education for, 100; institutions in, 102; ordering of, 99–101; policing for, 100; poverty of, 100; submission in, 101
executive: Constitution on, 42, 182nn2; despotism of, 44, 183n49; in Islamic governance paradigm, 52; judiciary and, 43–44, 46; legislative and, 44–45, 183n49, 183n59; without nation-state separation of powers, 41–43, 46–47, 181n30, 183n49. *See also* caliph; *dawla*; rulers' appointments; sultan
executive power and Sharīʿa, 56–57; administrative regulations in, 67–68, 191nn158–59; communication in, 70; community compared to, 63–64; community in, 63–64, 66; *dawla* in, 62–63, 190nn144–46, 215–16; education and, 111; executive duties in, 62, 66–67, 189n140, 191n156; *ḥudūd* in, 68, 192nn162–63, 216; moral accountability in, 69–70; Oriental despotism and, 65; *siyāsa Sharʿiyya* for, 64–67, 69; sovereign will in, 66; standards in, 68–69; sultanic code in, 68–69; sultans and, 65–66, 69, 191n152; Western executive compared to, 64

fāḍil, 175n43
Fall and Rise of the Islamic State (Feldman), 180n9
family: citizens' subjectivity and, 104–5, 201nn18–19; community disintegration and, 4
faqīh, 216
farḍ ʿayn, 94–95, 151, 216
farḍ kifāya, 94–95, 216
fasting (*ṣawm*), 116–17; almsgiving related to, 126; invalidation of, 126–27; *niyya* for, 125; options for, 125–26; during Ramaḍān, 125; rationales for, 126; technologies of self and, 136–37
fatwā: collections of, 54; definition of, 53–54, 216; practicality of, 54–55
Feldman, Noah, 180n9
Finlayson, Alan, 178n36
fiqh: definition of, 216; morality and, 115; *uṣūl al-fiqh*, 58, 218
Fiss, Owen, 195n57
form-properties, xii; capitalism and, 209n7; enumeration of, 23; under globalization, 145–46; for modern states, 22–25, 36

Foucault, Michel, 6–7, 20, 174n23, 177n13, 193n18; on dominance, 76, 101, 179n49, 193n14; al-Ghazālī related to, 129, 132, 206n119, 207n133; Kelsen and, 33–34, 38; technologies of self from, 98, 107, 129, 137, 193n18, 206n119
four sources, 216
freedom, 7, 17, 80, 81, 108, 206n119; to control, 75–76; Is/Ought and, 80; Kant on, 164, 195n49
Frings, Manfred S., 193n8
Fuchs, B., 177n12

Geuss, Raymond, 81
al-Ghazālī, Abū Ḥāmid, 133; autobiography of, 129, 207n120; commentaries on, 207n121; Foucault related to, 129, 132, 206n119, 207n133; on love, 134–36, 208n138; Mahmood and, 207n134; on potentialities, 129–30, 207n122; technologies of self related to, 132, 135–36, 207n133; theory of human nature from, 129–31, 207n122
globalization: change and, 142–43; corporations and, 145, 153–54, 210n31, 212n69; criticism of, 141, 208n4; culture related to, 143–44, 153; description of, 140–41; economics of, 144–46; first thesis on, 141–42; form-properties under, 145–46; Islamic governance and, 143; liberalism related to, 141, 144, 209n7; second thesis on, 142, 209n15; separation of powers and, 210n27; states in, 140–42, 209n8; tradition related to, 143–44; transformationalism and, 142; U.S. and, 208n4; wealth and, 144–45. *See also* Islam's moral economy
God: assimilation to, 128–29, 206n118; attributes of, 118–19; believers in, 87–88, 197n93; contract with, 87–88; human relationship to, 86–88, 197n93; Islamic governance and, 158–59; in Islamic governance paradigm, 49–51, 71, 184n77; matter and, 84, 196n68; property from, 151; punishment by, 30, 119, 124, 134, 159; rewards from, 119; as sovereign will, 50–51; wealth related to, 124–25, 131, 135, 139, 161
Goodman, Lenn, 206n118
grace, divine, 130
Gramsci, Antonio, 20
Gray, John, 1, 8, 14, 173n21; on modernity, 19
Guyer, Paul, 75, 195n49

ḥadīth, 121, 175nn40–41, 216
ḥajj. *See* pilgrimage
Hall, John, 35, 179n68
Hanna, Nelly, 187n105
Hansen, Mogens, 37
Hart, H. L. A., 82
Hayek, F. A., 37, 180n12, 183n47, 183n59
Hegel, G. W. F., 17, 20
Held, David, 22
Herder, Johann Gottfried, 98
history, xiv, 147, 174n22; Enlightenment and, 16, 24; immaturity of, 17; Is/Ought and, 81; modern states from, 23–25, 156, 177nn11–13, 177n20; morality from, 6; nostalgia related to, 14–15; progress and, 16, 175n57; for Sharīʿa paradigm, 12–13, 175n51; state and, 21; of West, 3–4
ḥiyal, 175n42
Hobbes, T., 78–79, 194n32; Schmitt and, 89, 91, 198n113
Horwitz, Morton, 42
ḥudūd, 68, 192nn162–63, 216
humanism, 1, 170
hunger, 132

ʿibādāt (five pillars), 13; for community, 159–60; definition of, 216; for education, 132–33; morality and, 118; purification related to, 116, 120, 123–24, 204n87, 205n100; religious works of, 116–17. *See also*

almsgiving; fasting; intention; pilgrimage; prayer
ʿibādāt /muʿāmalāt, 115–16, 118, 203nn69–70, 203n73
Iḥyāʾ ʿUlūm al-Dīn. *See* al-Ghazālī, Abū Ḥāmid
ijtihād, 167, 215, 218; definition of, 58, 216; interpretation of, 58–59
Ikenberry, G., 35, 179n68
ʿilm. *See* knowledge
imam, 216
India, 179n66
intellect, 130–31
intention (*niyya*): definition of, 217; for fasting, 125; love and, 134; for prayer, 120–22, 133–34
Introduction to Islamic Law (Hallaq), xiv, 174n22
Irony of Liberal Reason, The (Sprangens), 74
Is/Ought, 10, 74–75, 89–90, 158, 163, 186n90; Christianity and, 80–81; freedom and, 80; history and, 81; law and, 79–82, 195n55; paradigm of, 160–61; in Qurʾān, 82–83; reasons related to, 163
Islam, 3, 185n88; asceticism in, 136; legal works of, 116, 204n74, 204n77; as Middle Community, 166; prostration in, 121–22; puberty and, 122–23; taxation in, 62, 123–25, 189n140, 190n141. *See also* *ʿibādāt*; *specific pillars*
Islam and the Secular State (An-Naʿim), 212n1
Islamic governance: antiuniversalism for, 168–69, 214n36; citizen identity in, 96–97; citizens in, 96–97, 111, 158; colonialism over, 2, 63, 65, 147, 167–68; without conscription, 93–95, 199n126, 199n128, 199n130; culture and, 153; economics related to, 153–54; education in, 110–11; globalization and, 143; God and, 158–59; language for, 169, 214n36; militarism related to, 144, 152–53; modern states compared to, 49, 51–52, 89, 110–11, 158, 160–62, 168–70, 185n88, 198n99; nascent institutions for, 168–69; nonconformist thought for, 168–69; practice of, 6, 174n22; premodern states compared to, 3; rule of law in, 158; sovereign will for, 157–58, 212nn3–4; without unity, 38
Islamic governance paradigm, 6, 48, 89; community in, 49–50, 184n77; conditions for, 139–40; executive in, 52; God in, 49–51, 71, 184n77; legislative in, 71–72, 110; metaphysics in, 51; Muslim identity in, 70–71; poverty in, 50, 158–59, 161, 185n81; as well-ordered, 72–73. *See also* executive power and Sharīʿa; globalization; law and society relationship; Sharīʿa
Islamic law, 174n22, 205n98; double-*shahāda* in, 118–20, 204n85; *ʿibādāt* in, 13, 116–18, 120, 159–60, 204n87, 216; *ʿibādāt/muʿāmalāt* in, 115–16, 118, 203n73, 203nn69–70; multilayered social constitution for, 113–14; *niṣāb* in, 124–25, 205n103; perceived failure of, 112–13, 203n61, 203n73; religion within, 113, 203n61; schematic perspective of, 114–15, 203n64; sociomoral force for, 113–14, 203n64
Islamic Republic of Iran, 2
Islam's moral economy: modern liberal economics compared to, 146; in premodern history, 147; from Sharīʿa, 147. *See also* universals
istiṣlāḥ, 216
istiṭāʿa, 127–28
Izutsu, Toshihiko, 87–88

Jackson, Justice, 43
Jackson, Sherman, 50, 185n79
jihād, 93, 117, 127, 132, 147, 148, 151, 215, 219; definition of, 216; as duty, 94–95, 199n130; as moral obligation, 95, 199n141; private obligations over, 94–95; in Sharīʿa paradigm, 11–12; types of, 94, 199n126

Johansen, Baber, 66
judge. *See* jurists; *qāḍī*
judiciary: executive and, 43–44, 46; legislative and, 44–45; nation-state separation of powers and, 41, 43–46; oppression and, 46; socioeconomics and, 45–46
jurists: definition of, 216; mysticism of, 137–38, 208n148; in Sharīʿa, 52–53, 186nn90–91. *See also* author-jurist

Kahn, Paul, 27, 74, 92, 177n11; on state, 157, 212n3
Kant, I., 16, 19, 195n49; autonomy from, 75, 80, 165; on freedom, 164; reason related to, 80–81, 164–66
Kāsānī, 188n131
Kelsen, Hans, 20, 29–30, 177n3, 178n47; Foucault compared to, 33–34, 38; for legislative, 71; on nation-state separation of powers, 41, 48, 52, 186n103
Khomeini, Ayatullah, 179n55
knowledge, xiv; of control, 75–76, 193n3; as *ʿilm*, 129–30; from modern states, 155–56; as power, 76–77
Kuhn, Thomas S., 6–7
kulliyyāt (al-khams), 217. *See also* universals
Kuran, Timur, 212n69

language, 15, 17, 112; Arabic, 82, 195n59, 196n61; for Islamic governance, 169, 214n36; of prayer, 133–34; for Sharīʿa, 10, 56, 58, 94, 111, 112, 134
Larmore, Charles, 5–6, 155, 163, 173n20, 203n58; for Kant, 164; on reasons, 164–66, 213n14, 214n27
Lasch, Christopher, 1
law, 174n22, 187n108; of consequences, 84–85, 197n79, 197n82; control and, 82–83, 89; Is/Ought and, 79–82, 195n55; morality and, 79–80, 83, 196n63; *muʿāmalāt* as, 115–16, 203n69; sovereign will and, 37–38, 78; state or, 158, 212n4; substantive, 13, 59, 71, 115, 218; term use of, 82–83. *See also* legislation, law, and violence
Law, Legislation, and Liberty (Hayek), 37
law and society relationship: litigants and, 55–56, 187n105; lived and living tradition in, 55–56; pluralistic legal doctrine in, 58–59, 188n125; ruler in, 59–60; state in, 186n103. *See also muftī*; *qāḍī*
Lawson, Gary, 37
legal: moral compared to, 82–83, 112–14, 203n61; morality and, 75–89
legal norms: definition of, 217; moral norms compared to, 10, 167, 174n38
legal schools, 217
legal works, 116, 204n74, 204n77
legislation, law, and violence: community and, 29–30, 178n47, 179n48; in modern states, 29–30, 178n47, 179n48–49; sovereignty for, 29–30, 179n49
legislative: democracy and, 71–72; executive and, 44–45, 183n49, 183n59; in Islamic governance paradigm, 71–72, 110; judiciary and, 44–45; without nation-state separation of powers, 41–42, 46–47, 181n30; Sharīʿa and, 57, 187nn107–8
legist, 217. *See also muftī*; *qāḍī*
Levinson, Daryl J., 37, 42–43, 183n46
liberalism, 74, 146; globalization related to, 141, 144, 209n7
love, 136; intention and, 134; as morality, 155; prayer and, 134–35, 208n138; self related to, 134–35, 208n138

MacIntyre, Alasdair, 5–6, 82, 169, 173nn20–21, 208n149
madrasa, 110–11, 217
Magill, M. Elizabeth, 37
Mahmood, Saba, 207n134

Mālikites, 124, 187n105, 204n77
Mann, Michael, 35, 144
Mannheim, Karl, 106
Marcuse, Herbert, 108, 200n10
Marshall, Geoffrey, 26
Martin, J., 178n36
Marx, Karl, 20, 31, 99, 200n1
maṣlaḥa. See istiṣlāḥ
materialism, 107–8; for modern states, 161
matter: God and, 84, 196n68; inertia of, 77–78
Meinecke, Friedrich, 17
Miliband, Ralph, 45
militarism, 144, 152–53
mind, protection of, 147
Mistretta v. United States, 41, 182n35
"Mixed Constitution Versus the Separation of Powers, The" (Hansen), 37
modern Islamic state, ix; citizen in, 93; Feldman on, 180n9; implausibility of, xiii, 48–49; inconceivability of, 1, 51; postcolonial nationalism and, 1–2; without separation of powers, 40; tradition for, 39–40
modernity, xii, xiii, 4–5, 10, 14, 15, 17, 19, 77, 78, 90, 96, 108, 109, 112, 162, 163, 170, 172n15, 176n71, 198n99; moral accountability and, 4, 5, 89, 162–63, 194n28. *See also* capitalism; citizens; education; Is/Ought; narcissism; progress
modern Muslims, 12, 168–70; Enlightenment compared to, 166
modern states, 19; academia in, 102–3, 200n10; Aristotle and, 155; change for, 156; citizen identity in, 96–97; citizens of, 96–97, 158; cultural hegemony for, 33–36, 179n68, 179n70; discipline of, 99–100; duty of, 160; economics in, 22; Enlightenment and, 24; essential features of, 22–36; failure of, 93; form-properties for, 22–25, 36; from history, 23–25, 156, 177nn11–13, 177n20; institutions of, 102; Islamic governance compared to, 49, 51–52, 110–11, 158, 160–62, 168–70, 185n88, 198n99; knowledge from, 155–56; legislation, law, and violence in, 29–30, 178n47, 179n48–49; materialism for, 161; metaphysic of, 157; morality and, 138, 160–61, 208n149; private sphere in, 212n6; problems in, 102–3; Qurʾān and, x; relative heterogeneity of, 38; rule of law in, 158; science and, 24; sovereignty and its metaphysics in, 25–28, 177n26, 178n32, 178n36, 178n40, 178nn44–45; traditional societies compared to, 102–3; unity of, 38; weak, 156. *See also* modern Islamic state; rational bureaucratic machine
moral, 95, 199n141, 201n17; *akhlāq* as, 82, 196n61; legal compared to, 82–83, 112–14, 203n61; reason for, 111–12, 202n57, 203n58; term of, 82. *See also* universals
moral accountability, 4–5; in executive power and Sharīʿa, 69–70, 154; modernity and, 162–63; Qurʾān cosmology and, 83–84, 196n66
moral desideratum, 12, 175nn49–50
moral economy, 146–47
morality, xii, 169–70, 173n18; autonomy of, 157, 165; of corporations, 145, 153–54, 210n31; *fiqh* and, 115; from history, 6; *ʿibādāt* and, 118; law and, 79–80, 83, 196n63; legal and, 75–89; love as, 155; modern states and, 138, 160–61, 208n149; nature and, 84–86, 163, 196n68; the political without, 93; property related to, 149–50, 211n51, 211n55, 211n58, 211n61, 211n63; rationality compared to, 107–8, 164–66; reasons and, 78–80, 163–65, 194n32, 213n14; rise of legal and, 75–89; self and, 202n38; sovereignty related to, 84–85, 158–59, 197n79, 197n82; state and, 5, 24, 145, 210n31; virtue related to, 135

moral norms: legal norms compared to, 10, 167, 174n38; Sharīʿa as, 10–11, 175n43
muʿāmalāt ("law proper"), 115–16, 203n69
muftī: definition of, 217; as law professors, 187n108; *qāḍī* compared to, 55; responsibility of, 53–54, 186n95
Muhammad (the Prophet), 119–20, 149
mujtahid, 58–59, 217
Muslim Brothers, xi, 172n14
Muslim identity, 70–71
Muslim Kingship (Al-Azmeh), 191n159
Muslims, 3; modern, 12, 166, 168–70
mysticism: of jurists, 137–38, 208n148; Sharīʿa related to, 135, 137–38, 208n141, 208n148

El-Nahal, Galal H., 189n139
narcissism, 1, 208n144; hubris and, 14; of national citizens, 108–10, 153; technologies of self and, 136
nasl, as community, 147–48
nationalism, x; autonomy from, 109–10; citizens and, 106; community for, 106–8; narcissism and, 108–10; postcolonial, 1–2; state and, 107, 109–10
nation-states: community compared to, 49; Sharīʿa and, x–xi, 167–70, 171n9, 184n77, 214n34, 214n36; subjectivity formation and, xiii
nation-state separation of powers: administration in, 42, 46; agencies in, 181n31; Constitution and, 42–43, 182nn42–43, 183n46; danger of, 40, 181n22; degree of, 40–41, 72; distribution instead of, 41; duality of, 43, 183nn46–47; executive without, 41–43, 46–47, 181n30, 183n49; judiciary and, 41, 43–47; Kelsen on, 41, 48, 52, 186n103; legislative without, 41–42, 46–47, 181n30; mutual independence of, 39; in nation-states, 39–48; party politics and, 42–43, 182n43, 183nn46–47; practice without, 41–42, 181nn30–31, 182n32; rule of law without, 47–48; scholarship on, 40; socioeconomics and, 184n70; sovereign will and, 47; United Kingdom without, 182n32
natural resources, 77–78, 194n24
nature: control of, 76–78, 194n28; human, 129–31, 207n122; mechanics of, 77; morality and, 84–86, 163, 196n68; physical environment as, 4, 131; reasons related to, 165
Nelson, Brian, 19, 177n3
Nietzsche, Friedrich, 19, 74, 81–82, 93
niṣāb (subsistence exemption), 124–25, 205n103
niyya, 217. *See also* intention
nostalgia, 1, 14–15

Ottoman, 217; Egypt, 187n105, 189n139

paradigm, xii, 1; central domain and, 7; concept of, 7, 174n27; definition of, 7–8; diversity within, 9–10; driving forces of, 6–7; Enlightenment for, 7–8, 170, 174n35; force relations and, 9; ideal community, 6, 173n21; of Is/Ought, 160–61; of living, 6, 174n22; progress as, 18, 176n72; self-authentification of, 15–16; shift of, 9–10; of state, 23, 177n11; theory of, 173n22. *See also* Islamic governance paradigm; Sharīʿa paradigm
Paxton, Tom, 98
Philosophy of Money, The (Simmel), 139
physical body, 132, 207n134; power related to, 137; technologies of self and, 136–37; *zakāt al-fiṭr* for, 125–26
Pickthall, M., 85
pilgrimage (*ḥajj*): components of, 128; exceptions for, 127–28; obligation of, 127; rationale of, 128–29, 206n118
pillars. *See ʿibādāt*
Plato, 5, 173nn17–18

rationality, 6, 200n10; morality compared to, 107–8, 164–66; of reason, 213n14
Rawls, John, ix, 72–73
"Real Separation in Separation of Powers" (Magill), 37
reasons: autonomy related to, 164–65; Is/Ought related to, 163; Kant related to, 80–81, 164–65; Larmore on, 164–66, 213n14, 214n27; for moral, 111–12, 202n57, 203n58; morality and, 78–80, 163–65, 194n32, 213n14; nature related to, 165; rationality of, 213n14; revelation compared to, 166, 214n29
religion, 170; Christianity, 80–81; Constitution on, 203n61; *dīn* as, 147; within Islamic law, 113, 203n61; technical progress compared to, 7. *See also* *ʿibādāt*; Islam
ribā. *See* usury
"Rise and Rise of the Administrative State" (Lawson), 37
rule of law, xii; for democracy, 39, 74; in Islamic governance, 158; in modern states, 158; without nation-state separation of powers, 47–48
rulers' appointments, 189n133; death and, 61, 188n131; of *qāḍī*, 59–62, 188n131, 189n137

ṣadaqāt, 151, 218
Safi, Omid, 191n152
ṣāliḥāt, 87–88, 218
Saunders, Cheryl, 182n32
ṣawm. *See* fasting
Scheler, Max, 17; on control, 75–76, 193n14
Schmitt, Carl, 19, 25, 89; central domain of, 7–9, 12; Hobbes and, 89, 91, 198n113; Islamists related to, 12; theology and, 28, 178n40, 178n44
self: care of, 132, 207n133, 207nn133–34; love related to, 134–35, 208n138; morality and, 202n38
"Separation of Parties, Not Powers" (Levinson), 37
separation of powers, 210n27. *See also* nation-state separation of powers
shahādatayn (*sing. shahāda*), 218
sharʿī, 218
Sharīʿa: as central domain, 10, 175nn40–41; Constitution and, 51–52, 185n88; current use of, x, 13; definition of, 51; desires regarding, x; education in, 111; *ʿibādāt/muʿāmalāt*, 115–16, 118, 203n73, 203nn69–70; interaction of, 114–15; Islam's moral economy from, 147; jurists in, 52–53, 186nn90–91; language for, 112; as legal norm, 10; legislative and, 57, 187nn107–8; limitation of, ix; Message in, 119–20, 204n85; modern Muslims and, 12; as moral norm, 10–11, 175n43; mysticism related to, 135, 137–38, 208n141, 208n148; nation-state and, x–xi, 167–70, 171n9, 184n77, 214n34, 214n36; property regulations of, 149; punishments of, x, 66, 68, 95, 171n4; Qurʾān related to, 88–89; separation of powers in, 60–62, 71–72, 188n129, 189nn137–39; taxation and, 62, 189n140; women and, 184n77. *See also* executive power and Sharīʿa; *muftī*; *qāḍī*
Sharīʿa: History, Theory, and Practice (Hallaq), xiv, 174n22
Sharīʿa and modern state, x, 171n9; contradictions of, xi–xii, 172n14; failure of, 2; reconstitution of, xi–xii, 172n15
Sharīʿa paradigm, ix; economics and, 10–11; history for, 12–13, 175n51; *jihād* in, 11–12; premodern paradigm, 2–3, 173n5; violations of, 11, 175nn42–43
Shaw, Martin, 144
Signature of All Things, The (Agamben), 1
Simmel, George, 139
societies, traditional. *See* law and society relationship; traditional societies

socioeconomics: judiciary and, 45–46; nation-state separation of powers and, 184n70
sociomoral force, 113–14, 203n64
Sorel, George, 179n70
soul, 130–31
sovereignty, 177n26; for legislation, law, and violence, 29–30, 179n49; morality related to, 84–85, 158–59, 197n79, 197n82
sovereignty and its metaphysics: abstractness of, 25, 177n26; domesticity in, 26–27; internationality in, 26; in modern states, 25–28, 177n26, 178n32, 178n36, 178n40, 178nn44–45; monotheism compared to, 27; nation for, 27, 178n36; subject in, 26–28, 178n45; theology and, 27–28, 178n40, 178n44; violence and, 26–27, 30, 178n32, 179n49; will in, 25, 27–28
sovereign will, xii, 25, 27–30, 34–35; in executive power and Sharīʿa, 66; God as, 50–51; for Islamic governance, 157–58, 212nn3–4; law and, 37–38, 78; nation-state separation of powers and, 47; state or, 157–58, 212nn3–4
Spengler, Oswald, 164
Sprangens, Thomas A., Jr., 74
states: change and, 142–43; content of, 21; definitions of, 19–20, 29–30; economics and, 21–22; form of, 21–22, 24–25, 177n20; in globalization, 140–42, 209n8; history and, 21; Kahn on, 157, 212n3; in law and society relationship, 186n103; law or, 158, 212n4; morality and, 5, 24, 145, 210n31; nationalism and, 107, 109–10; paradigm of, 23, 177n11; perspectivism on, 20; popular sovereignty as, 177n26; poverty related to, 141–42, 209n15; receding power of, 141–42; sovereign will or, 157–58, 212nn3–4; theory of, 67, 191n159; timelessness of, 24; West for, 24–25. *See also* European state; modern states; nation-state separation of powers
Stewart, Gordon, 174n35, 194n24
Strange, Susan, 210n27
Straw Dogs (Gray), 1
subject. *See* citizens
subjectivities, 135–38
subsistence exemption (*niṣāb*), 124–25, 205n103
substantive law, 13, 59, 71, 115, 218
sultans, 60, 188n128; *dawla* compared to, 190n146; executive power and Sharīʿa and, 65–66, 69, 191n152
sultanic code, 68–69
Sunna, 132, 216, 218

ṭahāra. *See* purification
taxation: almsgiving related to, 123–25, 190n141; Sharīʿa and, 62, 189n140
Taylor, Charles, 5–6, 80–81, 169, 173nn20–21, 176n71, 208n149
technical progress, 7
technical science, 15
technologies of self, x, xiii, 12, 13, 83, 127, 135–36, 147, 148, 149, 151, 152, 160, 203n73, 206n118; definition of, 218; fasting and, 136–37; from Foucault, 98, 107, 129, 137, 193n18, 202n38, 206n119; al-Ghazālī related to, 132, 135–36, 207n133; narcissism and, 136; physical body and, 136–37
theory: of human nature, 129–31, 207n122; of paradigm, 173n22; of progress, 16–18, 176nn71–72; of states, 67, 191n159
Thus Spoke Zarathustra (Nietzsche), 19, 74
tradition: globalization related to, 143–44; lived and living, 55–56; for modern Islamic state, 39–40
traditional societies: discipline of, 98–99; modern states compared to, 102–3
training, 107, 132–33, 207n133
transformationalism, 142
Turgot, 179n70
Ṭurṭūshī, Muḥammad b. Al-Walīd, 185n79
Tyan, Émile, 60, 62, 188n29, 189n139